About the Author

Jan Zimmerman has found marketing to be the most creative challenge of owning a business for the nearly 30 years she has spent as an entrepreneur. Since 1994, she has owned Sandia Consulting Group and Watermelon Mountain Web Marketing in Albuquerque, New Mexico. (*Sandia* is Spanish for *watermelon.*) Her previous companies provided a range of services including video production, grant writing, and linguistic engineering R&D.

Jan's web marketing clients at Watermelon Mountain are a living laboratory for experimenting with the best techniques for web success in site design, content development, social media, word-of-web marketing, search engine optimization, and offline integration.

Ranging from hospitality and tourism to retail stores, B2B suppliers, trade associations, and service companies, her clients have unique marketing needs but share similar business concerns and online challenges. Jan's consulting practice keeps her aware of the real-world issues facing small-business owners and provides the basis for her pragmatic marketing advice.

Throughout her business career, Jan has been a prolific writer. In addition to writing two earlier editions of *Web Marketing For Dummies,* she co-authored *Social Media Marketing All-in-One For Dummies* (John Wiley & Sons), wrote four editions of another book about marketing on the Internet, wrote *Doing Business with Government Using EDI* (John Wiley & Sons), and co-authored *Mainstreaming Sustainable Architecture.* Her concern about the impact of technological development on women's needs led to her book *Once Upon the Future* and the anthology *The Technological Woman.*

The writer of numerous articles and a frequent speaker on web marketing topics, Jan has long been fascinated by the intersection of business, technology, and human beings. In her spare time, she crews for the hot air balloon named *Levity* to get her feet off the ground and her head in the clouds. Jan can be reached at books@watermelonweb.com or www.watermelonweb.com.

Web Marketing

FOR

DUMMIES®

3RD EDITION

by Jan Zimmerman

Web Marketing For Dummies®, 3rd Edition

Published by
John Wiley & Sons, Inc.
111 River Street
Hoboken, NJ 07030-5774

www.wiley.com

Copyright © 2012 by John Wiley & Sons, Inc., Hoboken

Published by John Wiley & Sons, Inc., Hoboken, New

Published simultaneously in Canada

No part of this publication may be reproduced, stored in a retrieval system or transmitted in any form or by any means, electronic, mechanical, photocopying, recording, scanning or otherwise, except as permitted under Sections 107 or 108 of the 1976 United States Copyright Act, without either the prior written permission of the Publisher, or authorization through payment of the appropriate per-copy fee to the Copyright Clearance Center, 222 Rosewood Drive, Danvers, MA 01923, (978) 750-8400, fax (978) 646-8600. Requests to the Publisher for permission should be addressed to the Permissions Department, John Wiley & Sons, Inc., 111 River Street, Hoboken, NJ 07030, (201) 748-6011, fax (201) 748-6008, or online at http://www.wiley.com/go/permissions.

Trademarks: Wiley, the Wiley logo, For Dummies, the Dummies Man logo, A Reference for the Rest of Us!, The Dummies Way, Dummies Daily, The Fun and Easy Way, Dummies.com, Making Everything Easier, and related trade dress are trademarks or registered trademarks of John Wiley & Sons, Inc. and/or its affiliates in the United States and other countries, and may not be used without written permission. All other trademarks are the property of their respective owners. John Wiley & Sons, Inc. is not associated with any product or vendor mentioned in this book.

LIMIT OF LIABILITY/DISCLAIMER OF WARRANTY: THE PUBLISHER AND THE AUTHOR MAKE NO REPRESENTATIONS OR WARRANTIES WITH RESPECT TO THE ACCURACY OR COMPLETENESS OF THE CONTENTS OF THIS WORK AND SPECIFICALLY DISCLAIM ALL WARRANTIES, INCLUDING WITHOUT LIMITATION WARRANTIES OF FITNESS FOR A PARTICULAR PURPOSE. NO WARRANTY MAY BE CREATED OR EXTENDED BY SALES OR PROMOTIONAL MATERIALS. THE ADVICE AND STRATEGIES CONTAINED HEREIN MAY NOT BE SUITABLE FOR EVERY SITUATION. THIS WORK IS SOLD WITH THE UNDERSTANDING THAT THE PUBLISHER IS NOT ENGAGED IN RENDERING LEGAL, ACCOUNTING, OR OTHER PROFESSIONAL SERVICES. IF PROFESSIONAL ASSISTANCE IS REQUIRED, THE SERVICES OF A COMPETENT PROFESSIONAL PERSON SHOULD BE SOUGHT. NEITHER THE PUBLISHER NOR THE AUTHOR SHALL BE LIABLE FOR DAMAGES ARISING HEREFROM. THE FACT THAT AN ORGANIZATION OR WEBSITE IS REFERRED TO IN THIS WORK AS A CITATION AND/OR A POTENTIAL SOURCE OF FURTHER INFORMATION DOES NOT MEAN THAT THE AUTHOR OR THE PUBLISHER ENDORSES THE INFORMATION THE ORGANIZATION OR WEBSITE MAY PROVIDE OR RECOMMENDATIONS IT MAY MAKE. FURTHER, READERS SHOULD BE AWARE THAT INTERNET WEBSITES LISTED IN THIS WORK MAY HAVE CHANGED OR DISAPPEARED BETWEEN WHEN THIS WORK WAS WRITTEN AND WHEN IT IS READ.

For general information on our other products and services, please contact our Customer Care Department within the U.S. at 877-762-2974, outside the U.S. at 317-572-3993, or fax 317-572-4002.

For technical support, please visit www.wiley.com/techsupport.

Wiley also publishes its books in a variety of electronic formats and by print-on-demand. Not all content that is available in standard print versions of this book may appear or be packaged in all book formats. If you have purchased a version of this book that did not include media that is referenced by or accompanies a standard print version, you may request this media by visiting http://booksupport.wiley.com. For more information about Wiley products, visit us at www.wiley.com.

Library of Congress Control Number is available from the publisher.

ISBN: 978-1-118-06516-7 (pbk); 978-1-118-05096-5 (ebk); 978-1-118-19939-8 (ebk); 978-1-118-19940-4 (ebk)

Manufactured in the United States of America

10 9 8 7 6 5 4 3 2 1

WILEY

Dedication

For Barbara and Donald and Susan and Marylyn, whose voices no longer sound in my ears but will always resound in my heart

Author's Acknowledgments

The idea of a writer, locked in a cell alone with her computer and literary agony, is a myth — at least for nonfiction. This book could not have been written without the assistance of dedicated researchers who dug out the meaning of seemingly contradictory statistics, identified inspiring examples of businesses to cite as case studies, and found hundreds of online screen shots to illustrate exactly the points I want to make. I am truly grateful to the efforts of Diane Duncan Martin, Kira Luna, and Esmeralda Sanchez. Working on my truly crazy schedule, they checked thousands of links, reviewed sites for screen shots, unearthed intriguing facts, examined trends, and cleared copyrights. Their level of organization, attention to detail, and willingness to track down answers to my sometimes odd or vague questions made this book possible. Shawna Araiza, senior marketing associate at Watermelon Mountain Web Marketing, supplemented their efforts, drawing on her extensive knowledge of the Internet to suggest sites or ways to locate information and helping with Photoshop. I am particularly indebted to her for taking on client responsibilities and giving me the time to write — not to mention her patience and computer assistance. As always, my family, friends, and cats earn extra hugs for their constant support and encouragement. I'm lucky to have friends who accept that I cannot always be there for them. The garden and the cats, alas, are not so forgiving.

Special thanks to all my clients, who have taught me so much and have given me the opportunity to put into practice what I preach.

I'd also like to thank project editors Kim Darosett and Susan Pink for their flexibility, skills, and patience, and copy editor Rebecca Whitney. Together, they have made this book much better than it started out. My thanks also to technical editor Dr. Debra Zahay, Professor of Interactive Marketing, at Northern Illinois University College of Business, for her encyclopedic knowledge of Internet marketing, and to all the other staff at Wiley — from the graphics department to marketing — who have provided support. If errors remain, I am certain they are all mine.

My appreciation goes to senior acquisitions editor Steve Hayes, for making this project possible, and to my agent, Margot Hutchison of Waterside. Margot and her extraordinary family teach us all a lesson about what's important in life. If you enjoy this book, please join me in donating to The Magic Water Project in honor of Sam Hutchison at www.magicwater.org/donate. Thank you in advance, dear readers.

Publisher's Acknowledgments

We're proud of this book; please send us your comments at http://dummies.custhelp.com. For other comments, please contact our Customer Care Department within the U.S. at 877-762-2974, outside the U.S. at 317-572-3993, or fax 317-572-4002.

Some of the people who helped bring this book to market include the following:

Acquisitions and Editorial

Project Editors: Kim Darosett, Susan Pink

Acquisitions Editor: Steve Hayes

Copy Editors: Barry Childs-Helton, Rebecca Whitney

Technical Editor: Debra Zahay

Editorial Manager: Kevin Kirschner

Editorial Assistant: Amanda Foxworth

Sr. Editorial Assistant: Cherie Case

Cover Photo: © iStockphoto.com/ Henrik Jonsson

Cartoons: Rich Tennant (www.the5thwave.com)

Composition Services

Project Coordinator: Patrick Redmond

Layout and Graphics: Melanee Habig

Proofreaders: Laura Bowman, Melanie Hoffman

Indexer: Glassman Indexing Services

Publishing and Editorial for Technology Dummies

    Richard Swadley, Vice President and Executive Group Publisher

    Andy Cummings, Vice President and Publisher

    Mary Bednarek, Executive Acquisitions Director

    Mary C. Corder, Editorial Director

Publishing for Consumer Dummies

    Kathleen Nebenhaus, Vice President and Executive Publisher

Composition Services

    Debbie Stailey, Director of Composition Services

Contents at a Glance

Table of Contents

Part II: Building Websites for Marketing Success.......... 45

Chapter 3: Producing a Successful Business Website............47

Chapter 4: Creating a Profitable Online Store.....................75

Introduction

. . . .

*I*t looks so simple on TV: Launch website, count money. If only real life were that easy! Alas, with billions of web pages competing for attention, it's not simple at all.

On the other hand, marketing online isn't rocket science. This book charts a practical course of action to put your business website and social media to work, adding profits to your bottom line. Whether you're just beginning to develop an online presence or you've been online for years and are eager to build traffic, this book helps you drive prospects to various components of your web presence and convert them into customers.

Web Marketing For Dummies, 3rd Edition, leverages your offline knowledge of marketing into mastery of the web. Because I've written this book for owners of small businesses, where cash is king, I suggest dozens of free to low-cost guerrilla marketing ideas that you can try online.

No simple formula says that shoe companies should use this web marketing method and architects should use that one. I urge you to keep in mind a picture of your customers or clients as you read this book. If you always ask yourself whether a particular method would appeal to your target market, you'll make the right decisions. Answer your customers' question, "What's in it for me?" and your web marketing plan will work magic for you.

About This Book

This book is a reference guide to web marketing, a concise overview to help you make confident business decisions about your online presence. It's written like good web copy: short sentences, short paragraphs, short chapters, with lots of bullets and tables so that you can find information quickly.

Please look at the pretty pictures in this book. Not only can they save you 1,000 words of reading, but they're also good examples of what you're trying to accomplish.

Dip into a chapter when you confront a particular problem with web marketing to find the information you need right then and there. The rest will wait. Use the supplemental, linkable resources tables on the companion website (at `www.dummies.com/go/webmarketingfd3e`) to explore specific options.

This book is intended for businesspeople, not for techies. Wherever I present technical information, I suggest that you share the tip with your web developer. Let that person worry about Apache Mod Rewrites for search-engine-friendly URLs. You worry about your business.

Conventions Used in This Book

Doing something the same way over and over again can be boring, but consistency makes stuff easier to understand. In this book, these consistent elements are *conventions,* and I use only a few:

- ✔ When URLs (web addresses) appear within paragraphs, captions, or tables, they look like this: `www.dummies.com`.

- ✔ New terms appear in *italics* the first time they're used, courtesy of this book's copy editor.

- ✔ All trademarks and service marks, whether designated or not, are the property of their registered owners. Usually these marks are capitalized, but considering the way companies spell their names and products these days, there's no guarantee.

- ✔ Anything you have to type is in **bold**, but frankly, I don't think you have to type a single thing in this book. Mostly, you just have to think.

Fortunately, web marketing is independent of platform and operating system. It doesn't matter whether you're on a Mac or a PC, though I recommend a high-speed Internet connection. You can no longer realistically monitor your website, upload content, review statistics, or research your market at turtle speeds (dialup).

What You Don't Have to Read

You don't have to read anything that seems irrelevant to your business! You can scoot past the text in a paragraph labeled with a Technical Stuff icon, for example, because that information is intended for your developer. You can bypass the stories in sidebars, though you might enjoy reading about the experiences of actual business owners who tried the marketing techniques under discussion. Sometimes, a sidebar divulges a helpful insider secret or two.

Chapter 4, which discusses building and merchandising an online store, applies only if you plan to sell online. If that description doesn't apply to you, skip that chapter. If you're just getting started or have a limited budget, you might want to postpone reading Part IV. Instead, stick with the affordable, basic techniques described in Part III and the social media techniques described in Part V until your site generates revenue or produces solid leads.

Foolish Assumptions

In my head, I've constructed a picture of you, the reader. I assume that you (or your designated staff member) already

- Have a computer with high-speed Internet access.
- Are (or soon will be) an owner or a department manager in a small-to-midsize business.
- Have or plan to write a business plan.
- Frequently use standard applications such as Word and Excel, e-mail, and browsers.
- Are comfortable searching the web by using keywords and search engines.
- Can write and do basic arithmetic, especially when dollar signs are involved.
- Know your business and target markets.
- Prefer a pragmatic approach that focuses on profitable results, not on technique.
- Have a passion for your business and a commitment to providing excellent customer service.

If my assumptions are incorrect, you'll probably find this book either too easy or too difficult to read. On the other hand, if my description is accurate, this book is just right for you.

How This Book Is Organized

I've divided this book into parts that follow a chronological development process, from business planning and market research through the design of a marketing-effective website and online store to online promotion that pushes qualified traffic.

For information on a specific topic, check the headings in the table of contents or look at the index.

By design, this book enables you to get as much (or as little) information as you need at any particular moment. If you're starting from scratch, you might want to start with Part I. If you already have a successful website and want to increase its traffic, start with Part III.

Part I: Getting Going with Online Marketing

Unless you have endless wealth and infinite time, you need some idea of what you're trying to accomplish online before you start. This section stresses the importance of planning your web presence as it intersects with other aspects of your business, including the financial ones. Stocked with useful planning forms and checklists, Part I shows how to plan for success from the beginning.

Part II: Building Websites for Marketing Success

Profitable business websites don't happen by accident. From a marketing perspective, a successful site attracts visitors, keeps them on the site, and brings them back for repeat visits. Part II addresses building a marketing-effective website and online store as well as implementing marketing ideas right on your site. Onsite marketing methods, including viral techniques, are usually either free or inexpensive, making them especially attractive for businesses getting started online.

Part III: Maximizing Your Online Success

The core of this book, Part III covers the absolutely essential components of online marketing: natural search engine optimization, word-of-web techniques, and link campaigns. It also addresses paid methods such as e-mail marketing, webinars, and marketing on mobile devices (smartphones and tablets). Though some methods in this part are time consuming, most don't require extremely deep pockets.

Part IV: Spending Online Marketing Dollars

Use with caution: The advertising and marketing techniques in this part cost real moolah. Both pay per click and banner advertising can escalate to expensive media buys. Marketing techniques that use advanced technology and multimedia are expensive to produce. However, paid advertising may play a role in a strategic marketing plan.

Part V: Making the Most of Social Media Channels

Free social media channels are all the rage, but they can be difficult to use effectively for online marketing. Part V helps you identify which social media channels (such as Facebook, Twitter, LinkedIn, content-sharing sites, or others) would best reach your market and helps you manage the process.

Part VI: The Part of Tens

Like all *For Dummies* books, this one has The Part of Tens. These two chapters list ten free ways to kick off your web marketing campaign and ten tips to rejuvenate a tired site.

Icons Used in This Book

To make your experience easier, I use various icons in the margins to indicate particular points of interest.

Whenever I provide a hint that makes an aspect of web marketing easier, I mark it with the Tip icon. It's my way of sharing what I've figured out the hard way — so that you don't have to. Of course, if you prefer to get your education through the school of hard knocks, be my guest.

This icon is simply a friendly reminder. This book holds more details than any normal person can remember. Use this icon to help you remember basic principles of web marketing. Look up all the rest when you need it!

Ouch! This icon is the equivalent of an exclamation point. Heed these warnings to avoid potential pitfalls.

Sometimes I feel obligated to give developers technical information; they don't always know as much as they think they do. I mark that stuff with this geeky guy so that you know it's information to share, not necessarily to understand.

This icon is your cue to go to the companion website for this book at `www.dummies.com/go/webmarketingfd3e`, where you can find supplemental material on the Downloads tab. Look for copies of the planning forms and checklists that appear throughout this book — and a few extra ones. Use them to develop your own web marketing plans or to track and analyze what you've done.

On the same tab is a Bonus Chapter for every part of this book. Some Bonus Chapters have additional text content, but all have multiple, linkable resource lists. For convenience, use the live links to investigate specific alternatives, stay up to date, subscribe to blogs or newsletters, or simply find out more than fits between any two book covers.

Please note that software and sites listed in the resource tables are simply examples, not recommendations; the listings don't imply endorsement of any product. Your developer needs to select the right software application or third-party resource link based on your budget, requested features, ease of implementation and maintenance, and the technical structure of your site.

Where to Go from Here

If you find errors in the book, or have suggestions for future editions, please e-mail me at `books@watermelonweb.com`.

Now go have some fun with web marketing. If you enjoy what you're doing, you're already on the path to success.

Part I
Getting Going with Online Marketing

The 5th Wave   By Rich Tennant

In this part . . .

*U*nless you're Mr. or Ms. Moneybags, you need to know what you're doing before you start spending money and time on online marketing. Part I stresses the importance of web planning as it intersects with all aspects of your business, including financial ones.

Chapter 1 puts web marketing and social media in the context of overall marketing. You discover that what you already know about marketing is true, such as the importance of return on investment (ROI). At the same time, web marketing confronts you with new techniques and terms, such as the *conversion funnel,* which measures the percentage of site browsers who convert to buyers.

Before you create — or redesign — your website for success, come to terms with your own limitations. Except for genius-types who work 48-hour days, everyone needs help. In Chapter 1, you also can see when and how to select good professional help and identify some online tools to help you get going online.

You can easily become so enthralled by web technology that you lose site of your business goals. Take advantage of basic planning tools in Chapter 2 to maintain a focus on your bottom line, even as your marketing world grows more complex. A quick review of basic business and marketing principles demystifies web marketing and positions you at the starting line.

Chapter 1

Taking Your Marketing to the Web

In This Chapter

▶ Absorbing the web into your overall business plans

▶ Adjusting your marketing for the web and social media

▶ Understanding what your web presence must accomplish

▶ Finding someone to design your site

*1*s it hypnosis? Seduction? Simple amnesia? Don't let dot-com technobabble dazzle you into forgetting every business lesson you learned the hard way. You know there are no magic marketing bullets offline; there aren't any online either. You know that you build a customer list slowly, experimenting with a variety of techniques until word-of-mouth marketing kicks in. You want to be successful online? Then approach the web the same way you approach your offline business — with an awareness of business fundamentals, a combination of marketing techniques, and an indelible focus on your customers:

✔ **You must have the business fundamentals right before you can have a truly successful web presence.** Many sites flounder on straightforward business issues of cost, merchandising, back-office support, or customer service. Too many confuse revenues with profits, only to discover in quarterly financials that their sites are sinking into the Red Sea.

✔ **Successful web marketing requires a combination of methods.** Nowhere in this book do you read that the solution to all your web woes lies in content, search engine optimization, link campaigns, pay per click ads, e-newsletters, Facebook, or any one online or offline marketing technique. Many are necessary, but none alone is sufficient to bring in all the traffic you need. Instead, you must select judiciously from an extensive marketing menu: a little appetizer, a nice side dish, maybe an entree that takes the most of your web marketing dollars and efforts. Oh, don't forget social media for dessert.

✔ **The customer is the measure of all things web, from site design to marketing.** Don't let technology or personal inclination distract you from a focus on what the customer wants. And don't get carried away with what web technology can do.

From those principles, you can see that web marketing fits within the definition of marketing you're already familiar with. When they're well implemented, online techniques might offer a more cost-effective marketing mix, greater flexibility, or easier expansion to new markets than offline techniques. With this book as your reference guide, you can master these new tools, adding a sense of adventure, as well as profits, to your bottom line.

If it doesn't make dollars, it doesn't make sense.

Rearranging Your Marketing Mix

If you're already in business, you know you have to spend money to make money. You may need to redistribute your marketing budget to free up funds for marketing online. Here's a method to elevate your marketing analysis from guesswork to grand plan. First, make a four-column list organized as follows:

- ✔ The first column lists all the marketing techniques you currently use.
- ✔ The second column lists the target market you reach with that technique.
- ✔ The third column lists how many new customers that technique brings in.
- ✔ The fourth column lists how much you spend per year on that technique.

If you've been in business for a while, you might have forgotten some of your recurring marketing investments. Here are a few examples to spark your memory: a Yellow Pages listing, signage, business cards and letterhead, logo design, a listing in a local business club directory, T-shirts for the girls' soccer team, newspapers or other print ads, direct mail, local fliers, word of mouth, radio spots, or billboards. If you're not sure where new customers come from, ask them! You might be surprised where word has spread.

If you don't have extra money to invest in developing and promoting a web presence, decide which existing methods you can cut in favor of more cost-effective online marketing. If you duplicate your reach at a lower cost online, you can put the difference into your website.

What you already know about marketing is true. Profit from your own success. Unless you're starting a new business online, your new customers are going to look similar to your old ones. You already know how to sell to them, what they need, what appeals to their emotions, and what satisfies their inner cravings. Your website and web marketing need to do the same. Take advantage of what you know in your head and in your gut.

Reaching your current audience online

If you haven't done so in a while, write a paragraph describing your current customers: age, gender, income level, education, geographical region, or job title (if you sell business-to-business). What else do they buy? What do they like to read? It's easy to research your markets online.

If you need to, segment your customers into different groups that share the same characteristics. Try to figure out which segment of customers spends time online. Do they still use e-mail? Do they research purchases online before buying? What other websites do they visit often? Which forms of social media, if any, do they like to use? Are they attached to their smartphones? (I discuss researching your online market in more detail in Chapter 2.) When you design your site and implement your web marketing campaign, use these profiles to decide what to do and where to spend.

Incorporating social media

Social media — online services that encourage interaction between you and your customers, or among your customers — presents both opportunities and challenges. On the one hand, services like Facebook (networking) and Twitter (short messaging service) open up potentially huge numbers of new prospects. On the other hand, it's difficult for your target audience to find your social media page among all the clutter. In Part V, I discuss many social media options so you can select the best ones for you.

Here are a few key points to keep in mind about social media:

- ✔ **Contrary to popular opinion, social media are *not* free.** While many social media services don't carry an up-front charge, they can eat up your time faster than the Cookie Monster consumes Oreos. Time is money!

- ✔ **You can't use social media *instead of* having a website or blog** with your own domain name. Research shows that people still go back to your website as the first source of information for your company; in spite of the popularity of social media, the website is king.

Finding new customers

If you intend to use the web to find new customers, decide which of the following goals you're aiming for:

- ✔ Expand your geographical reach.

- ✔ Go after a new consumer demographic or vertical industry segment for existing products.

- ✔ Sell new products and services to completely new audiences.

All the guerrilla marketing aphorisms apply online. Rifles, not shotguns! Target one narrow market at a time, make money, and reinvest it by going after another market. Don't spread your marketing money around the way bees spread pollen — a little here, a little there. That will dilute your marketing dollars and reduce the likelihood of gaining new customers.

Write up the same type of profile for your new target audience(s) that you wrote up for your existing ones. As you read through this book, match the profiles of your target markets to a given technique to find a good fit.

Plan your work, and work your plan. Every marketing problem has an infinite number of solutions. You don't have to find the perfect one, just one that works for you.

Understanding Web Marketing Essentials

While this book is full of the endless details that make up a successful web marketing campaign, you need to keep only three overarching points in mind:

- ✔ Do your plans fit with the needs and interests of your target audience?

- ✔ Do your plans make financial sense?

- ✔ Are your plans within your capabilities to execute?

If you measure everything you do against these criteria, you'll come out fine.

Right this very minute, create two new folders in your browser's bookmarks, one for sites you love and another for sites you hate. Better yet, set up an account at StumbleUpon (www.stumbleupon.com) or another bookmarking site. These services gather all your bookmarks in one, convenient, online account, accessible anywhere. With one click, you can bookmark any site you see for future reference.

Whatever your online activities, make a habit of tagging or bookmarking the sites that appeal to you and the ones you can't stand. Don't worry if you don't yet have the vocabulary to explain your reactions. By the time you're ready to talk to a developer about designing a new site or upgrading an existing one, your library of saved sites can supply essential design information.

Understanding What Your Web Presence Must Accomplish

A business site has to succeed on multiple levels to pull a prospect or visitor into your marketing orbit. Without initial curb appeal, your site doesn't have a chance to establish itself in visitors' minds. If your site lacks strong content, visitors don't have a reason to stay long enough to find out what you have to offer and how wonderful you are. And without a reason to return, visitors might never establish enough confidence to purchase your goods or services. Chapter 3 covers design in greater detail, but the following introduction helps.

Catching the visitor's attention

You have only four seconds (that's right — *four* seconds) to make a first impression. That isn't enough time for a visitor to read your content. It's time enough only for our emotion-based lizard brains to react to color, layout, design, navigation (maybe), and perhaps a headline. If you haven't caught people in your cybernet by then, they're gone, probably never to return. In Figure 1-1, Encountour (www.encountour.com) uses an attention-grabbing marketing tag, "Naked Travel, Fully Clothed" (located in the upper-left corner below the logo), along with great visuals, to engage viewers.

Fonts, images, activities — everything on the site must appeal to the target audience you're trying to reach. You wouldn't put bright colors on a site selling urns for pet ashes, or pastels on a site aimed at teenagers. A high-tech site in silver and black has a very different look and feel than one selling country decor with gingham and duckies. A site selling high-priced goods needs lots of white (empty) space to look rich; a discount site does well with crowded images. That's why I recommend finding a designer who knows about marketing communications.

Marketing tag

Figure 1-1:
The marketing tag is one of several attention-grabbers on Encountour.

Getting visitors to stick around

Stickiness is the technical term for keeping people on a website. If your average viewers visit fewer than two pages of your site or stay fewer than 30 seconds, most of them see only your home page and flee! (See Chapter 6 for more on site statistics.) You need more cyber-glue. Ideally, you want the average visitor to stick with the site for a minimum of three pages and at least a few minutes. Otherwise they haven't spent enough time to figure out what you have to offer.

Lay down a sticky trail with content, calls to action, things to do, media to download, and interaction with site elements. Every action users take, every click they make, binds them kinesthetically to your site. For example, gURL.com (shown in Figure 1-2) is notable for its stickiness, which makes it especially appealing to advertisers. Its community features for teenage girls keep visitors on the site for multiple page views and an extended period of time.

For an example of an integrated marketing strategy that addresses all the issues in this chapter, see the sidebar, titled "Digital marketing strategy strengthens Hope," about the Hope Institute for Children and Families. Their home page and Facebook page are shown in Figure 1-3.

Bringing 'em back for more

Research shows that many people don't buy on the first visit to a site. Some use the web simply for research before making a purchase in a bricks-and-mortar store. Others research multiple sites for comparison shopping, but return only if they have a reason.

Figure 1-2: gURL.com is a very sticky site.

Courtesy of ALLOY MEDIA+ MARKETING

Figure 1-3: The Hope Institute's website (top) and Facebook page (bottom) are part of a complex, integrated digital media strategy.

Digital marketing strategy strengthens Hope

The Hope Institute for Children and Families (www.thehopeinstitute.us) is a nonprofit organization providing educational, residential, and health services to children in Illinois with multiple developmental disabilities, including autism spectrum disorders. Founded in 1957, Hope has grown from a small schoolhouse to an organization with more than $40 million in revenue and more than 600 employees, affecting more than 29,000 children and families.

When Jarid Brown was hired as the Manager of Online Interactions in October 2009, Hope Institute had a fledging social media presence but no overall strategic marketing plans. Hope had no e-mail newsletter, and the website was a passive online brochure with limited interactivity, few graphics, and too little information — and it was unable to accept donations.

Working with Lynn Storey, Hope's Manager of Direct Response, Brown plotted a strategy to initially address the marketing needs of the umbrella organization — improve promotion, services, awareness, advocacy, engagement, and donations — and then to apply the strategy at the program level. "The digital platform was designed . . . to enhance and integrate our successful traditional marketing tools, at the heart of [which] is our direct mail program."

While the digital marketing plan was under development (a three- to four-month proposition), the pair undertook some basic steps:

- Storey conducted a multichannel marketing program audit and wrote the proposal to renovate and grow the digital program.

- They consolidated the e-mail address lists and established an e-mail marketing strategy to increase the subscriber base (run through *Constant Contact*) by soliciting e-mail opt-ins at events, within direct mail, and by referrals. Their efforts have increased open rates, click-through rates, and subscriber numbers.

- Brown began redesigning Hope's primary website into a marketing tool geared primarily toward the general public and donors. He supplemented this with resource pages to meet the information needs of parents and professionals. In six months, page views rose from 4,000 to 35,000 per month.

- He implemented search engine optimization (SEO) and search engine marketing (SEM) best practices throughout all components of Hope's web presence. Brown constantly rotates and writes fresh content, blogs, metadata, press releases, and other material to improve search engine placement.

- By focusing initially only on Hope's two largest Facebook accounts, he increased the fan base, identified key influencers, and developed an approach for content. Now the Institute runs a full-blown, complex social media campaign with more than 4,700 Facebook fans across multiple pages and 8,000 followers on several Twitter accounts.

The Pepsi Refresh Challenge ran a contest to give charitable awards to nonprofits based on the number of "votes" they received. Hope not only won two grants worth a total of $75,000 but also used the Challenge to increase its number of e-mail subscribers and social media followers. Hope has since won other charitable giving contests.

In late 2010, Hope officially launched its digital marketing strategy. A core messaging matrix serves as a planning calendar for the entire fiscal year. The matrix outlines upcoming events, campus activities, and the direct mail schedule, allowing planning for online campaigns.

(continued)

(continued)

The core message is built around one child's story each month. "Ultimately, the website becomes the focal point of all our marketing activities. I know that the more time I can get the public to spend on my website, the greater the opportunity to build a relationship," says Brown. "While we can certainly start the conversation on Facebook, we can't tell the story there."

Brown continuously monitors social media traffic, link sharing, and comments to identify core constituencies so he can gear content to their interests. He uses HootSuite and TweetDeck to manage social media activity, and Twitterfeed to cross-post feeds. Occasionally, he uses programs such as Socialoomph to schedule tweets, but he prefers to write personalized messages. For alert services, he relies on a combination of Google Reader and Google Alerts.

Brown gathers analytics from every available source and has developed his own spreadsheet to track results. For the website, he combines Google Analytics with analytics from their domain host and another third party. In addition, he tracks social media analytics with ShareThis and AddThis services as well as multiple other services. He relies on Constant Contact's in-depth reporting for each e-mail. He doesn't look at data just for its own sake. "Using these tools allows us to better focus our postings," Brown notes.

"I am driven by metrics and a belief that if you cannot measure effectiveness and results, then you cannot successfully market an organization," Brown admits. "Even our online donation processing is built upon this principle. We track the origin of every dollar flowing into the system by coding each donation link. Over the next six months, we plan to integrate *QR* (Quick Response) codes into each direct mail and print marketing piece to further drill-down user analytics and better target our audience."

The Hope Institute also takes advantage of a Google Grant that provides the organization with up to $10,000 per month of free PPC (pay per click) advertising. To effectively use that amount, Brown creates specific content to fit a broader range of keywords and attract audiences that he would not normally reach.

Each page of the site, blogs, and printed material promote Hope's social media presence. The website and blogs also include bookmarking options. In addition, every e-mail sent from anyone in the organization includes a link to Hope's Facebook page. Brown particularly likes Facebook's new Send Now button, which encourages users to message their friends or family directly.

"The biggest mistake I see organizations make . . . is to treat social media differently from other forms of marketing," he says. He recommends using the same best practices as in traditional marketing campaigns: "Develop, test, measure, refine." His parting advice to others: "Don't follow the herd, lead. . . . Planning is key, patience is a necessity, and endurance leads to victory."

Check out these URLs for the Hope Institute: `www.thehopeinstitute.us`, `www.thehopeinstitute.us/social media`, `http://twitter.com/advancinghope`, and `www.linkedin.com/in/jaridbrown`.

For example, TravBuddy, shown in Figure 1-4, offers viewers many reasons to come back (`www.travbuddy.com/travel-widgets`). Personalized travel maps, travel reviews, users' shared photographs, forums, and a page to find travel partners, all visible in the main navigation, encourage viewers to return many times.

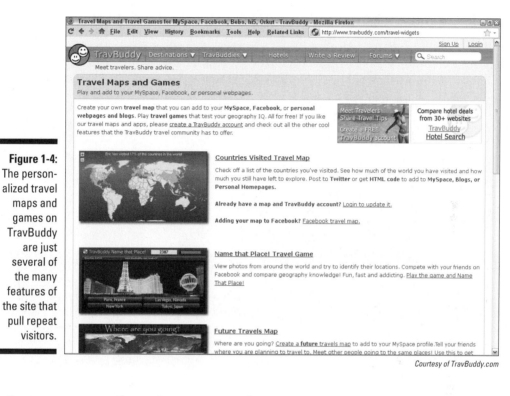

Courtesy of TravBuddy.com

Figure 1-4: The personalized travel maps and games on TravBuddy are just several of the many features of the site that pull repeat visitors.

Gearing the Site to Your Visitors' Interests

Sorry to be the bearer of bad tidings, but customers and clients don't really care about *you*. They care about themselves. In terms of gaining business, your website has to make clear what you can do for the visitor, not why you got into business in the first place or your favorite products, places to visit, or movies (save that for your blog).

Throughout this book, you can find techniques to ensure that your website answers the question "What's on this site for me?" immediately and repetitively. As long as visitors are having a good time, finding useful information, or locating products and services that appeal to them, they will stay on your site. As soon as you lose their interest, you lose their business.

You sell benefits to visitors via graphics, content, interactive opportunities — and appealing text. In Figure 1-5, TheResumator (www.theresumator.com) uses benefits statements (such as "Make Great Hiring Decisions Faster") and calls to action (with imperative verbs such as "Get Started") to tell visitors the advantages of its services rather than focus on features.

What's in it for me? Answer this question at every step, and your website will work magic for you.

Benefits statements

Figure 1-5:
The calls to action and benefits statements on The Resumator resonate with site visitors.

Calls to action

Deciding Who Will Design Your Site

The Oracle at Delphi was famous for the saying, "Know thyself." Web design reinforces the importance of self-knowledge. Be honest about your skills. Are you a programming geek? A gifted photographer? A colorful writer? Do you dream in web-safe colors, JavaScript, or Flash animation? No? Then designing your own website is probably not your forté. Don't be hard on yourself. With the possible exception of Leonardo da Vinci, should he be reincarnated in the 21st century, everyone needs help of some sort with website development.

As the owner of a business with a passion for excellence, or the person delegated to oversee the company website, your job is that of *producer,* not creative director or technical manager. There's wisdom, not weakness, in playing to your strengths as a business owner and leaving the implementation to someone else. As producer, you select the team and coordinate their efforts, cheer them on when the inevitable problems arise, answer their marketing questions, resolve conflicts based on your business acumen, and arrange the celebration when the site goes live.

Understanding why it isn't practical to do it all yourself

Besides overseeing the content, managing the money, and handling the marketing, are you going to educate yourself in HTML, PHP, JavaScript, database programming, Dreamweaver, social media, marketing communications, copywriting, photography, and graphic design in the next six weeks? Are you also fantasizing about winning the Tour de France, or are you just a victim of some misbegotten belief that this will save you money? Forget about it!

Unless you're already a professional web designer, don't do it all yourself; this is the biggest mistake you can make. Playing with your personal website is one thing, but creating a successful business website is a job for the pros. You wouldn't let someone without experience design your ads, dress your store window, serve customers, buy goods from vendors, or negotiate contracts. So why would you trust your website to a novice?

Novices include friends, neighbors, children, or siblings, unless they have experience creating business sites for a living. Even then, treat people you know as you would any professional — write an agreement so expectations are clear. An agreement won't only save you aggravation and disappointment; it might save your relationship.

A nonprofessional who does websites on the side and takes three or four times as long as a pro will end up costing you marketing opportunities and sales as well as money.

Deciding who will design your site is a strategic marketing decision. Your site won't measure up if it's obviously homemade, with links that don't work, when your competitors' sites look professional and run smoothly. If your competitors' sites are equally sad, your poor website wastes an obvious opportunity to get an edge.

Using a professionally designed template to create your site

Do you remember when desktop publishing software first came out? Unskilled users distributed newsletters that looked like font catalogs, using every imaginable typeface and style. The resulting newsletters were almost unreadable. You can avoid the website equivalent of desperado design by using a professionally designed template.

Templates are not as flexible as a custom site, but they can save you significant money while maintaining graphic integrity. You can launch a template site very quickly and be confident that navigation will work. With a template to take care of design and programming, you can focus on content.

Think of templates as the equivalent of buying business stationery from an office supply store. You can hire a graphic designer for custom work or order letterhead and business cards from a store catalog, customizing ink colors and paper stock. In terms of the web, you select a template with navigation and customize it with your color selection, logo, text, and photographs. (I discuss selecting templates for online stores in Chapter 4.)

If you can't afford a custom design right now, use a template as a placeholder. Put your money into marketing until you build a web presence and set aside the revenues. Later, you can redesign the site with your profits.

You can choose templates based on three factors: cost, customizability, and skills required. Here are some options to consider:

- ✔ **Select a package solution that includes your choice of template design, hosting, and a variety of other options, based on your needs.** This is the simplest and usually the least expensive option, but also the least flexible. If you want, you can hire a designer to advise you on color choice or to tweak the template a bit to make it look terrific. Figure 1-6 shows the Gusto Pizza site (www.gustopizza.com) created with a template from Virb (www.virb.com). The site combines sophisticated graphic sensibility with straightforward navigation.

- ✔ **Buy a template design that is specific to your industry and upload it to a host that you've selected separately.** This requires more knowledge and skill.

- ✔ **Hire a company that specializes in a particular industry, with a selection of templates that they customize for you.** This is more expensive than the other two solutions but still less costly and less time-consuming than a fully custom design.

Courtesy of Gusto Pizza Co.

Figure 1-6:
The Gusto Pizza site is an excellent example of a template-based design.

Using blog templates to create your site

As long as you own your own domain name (see Chapter 2), you can quickly and inexpensively create a website that will serve as your core web presence by using a blog platform instead. A *blog* (short for web log) is a type of website that permits you to enter content, often in reverse chronological order, with the option of allowing readers to comment on your entry. Because blog content is easy to change without assistance from a programmer or developer, a blog-based website is great for these types of sites:

- Simple business card or informational sites
- Sites with information that changes often, like news or events
- Sites that don't require catalogs or complicated on-site transactions
- Sites that require the option of two-way communication with customers or site visitors

Blogs have many functions besides serving as free-standing websites. I discuss how to use blogs as part of an existing site in Chapter 5 and how to use other people's blogs for marketing purposes in Chapter 9.

In Bonus Chapter 1 on the Downloads tab at `www.dummies.com/go/ webmarketingfd3e`, you'll find a table titled "Some Template Sites," which lists just a few of the many template offerings available from blogging sites, from sites that supply multiple industries, and from sites addressing specific vertical sectors.

You can always do an Internet search for *web templates for [your industry]* (such as restaurants, authors, and so on) to find more alternatives.

Dreamweaver and other web design programs also offer templates that are already designed to work in those programs as part of the basic library that comes with their offerings.

Opting for professional web design services

If you've decided to invest in professional web design services, you need to find the right designer for your objectives.

Deciding what expertise you need

For most business sites, it helps to select designers who come from a marketing communications background, not a pure programming or art background. Your developer must have the ability to design with an eye toward your target market, be knowledgeable about achieving business objectives, and be skilled enough to do the programming tasks required. Not every designer is right for every type of business or has staff with the experience to meet the specific requirements your site may need.

The designer is only one of several professionals you might need, as you can see from the following list:

✔ Web developer/designer

✔ Graphic designer

✔ Illustrator

- ✔ Photographer
- ✔ Copywriter
- ✔ Merchandising expert
- ✔ Videographer
- ✔ Audio engineer
- ✔ Animator (Flash, virtual reality)
- ✔ Ad agency
- ✔ Online marketing specialist

Developers with enough staff might be able to help with all the tasks in the preceding list, or they might subcontract these services, saving you the trouble of finding providers yourself. At the very least, they probably have a list of people they recommend.

Most small businesses can't afford all these professionals. Decide which aspect of the site is most important to its marketing success. For instance, online stores and tourist sites depend on high-quality photography. A content-rich site inherently demands good writing, while a multimedia site might need an animator, videographer, or audio engineer. Prioritize by outsourcing the most critical element. Do the best you can with the rest.

For some help with this process, check out the Web Developer Capability Questionnaire and Web Developer Reference Questionnaire on the Downloads tab of the companion website.

Finding good providers in your area

Locating qualified professionals is like finding any good service provider. A recommendation can't be beat. Take the time to review designers' and other providers' portfolios online to ensure that you like their style and to assess their talents. Match their description of skills and experience against your needs. Always check references — not only those that providers give you, but also several others randomly selected from the developers' portfolios.

Try one of these techniques or sort through one of the directories of web providers listed in Bonus Chapter 1 on the Downloads tab at www.dummies. com/go/webmarketing3e. Professionals generally self-submit or pay to be in those directories, so a listing might not say anything about the quality of their work or their suitability for your needs.

Here are a few other ways to find good web professionals:

- ✔ If you've been bookmarking and creating a list of sites you love, start by approaching those designers.
- ✔ See who designed those sites or your competitors' sites by looking at the footer or the resource page or by calling the company.
- ✔ Ask others in a local trade association to recommend providers.
- ✔ Research regional or statewide associations of web professionals.

Generally, you get what you pay for! You can pay a lot for someone who isn't capable, but you can't pay a little for someone who's really good.

Chapter 2

Planning for Web Marketing

. . . .

In This Chapter

▶ Establishing goals and objectives for your web presence

▶ Finding out about target markets

▶ Applying the four Ps of marketing

▶ Putting it all together in an online marketing plan

. . . .

*Y*ou can easily get so involved with the web or social media that you lose sight of your business goals. In this chapter, I show you how a few, simple, planning tools can help you track the big picture while maximizing the contribution of your web presence to your bottom line.

If you mastered marketing principles in business school long ago, this chapter connects cybermarketing to your memories of business plans, the four Ps of marketing (product, price, placement, and promotion), and Maslow's Triangle. If your marketing knowledge comes from the school of hard knocks or if you're new to business, these conceptual marketing tools enable you to allocate marketing dollars in a new environment.

As you go through the planning process, I suggest that you summarize your decisions on the forms shown in this chapter. Refer to them whenever you're uncertain about a web marketing decision. These forms also make it easier to convey your site goals and objectives consistently to developers, graphic designers, other service providers, and employees. For your convenience, you can download full-page versions of these forms from the Downloads tab of the book's companion website at www.dummies.com/go/webmarketingfd3e.

Planning to Fit Your Business Goals

Before you state the goals for your website, you must be clear about the goals for your business. Your answers to a few basic questions establish the marketing framework for your site. Answer the questions in the Business Profile section of the Web Site Planning Form in Figure 2-1. (This form is available on the Downloads tab of the book's companion website at `www.dummies.com/go/webmarketingfd3e`.) These questions apply equally to businesses of any size and to not-for-profit organizations, educational institutions, and governments.

Here are a few examples of business profile questions:

- ✔ Are you a new company or an existing one with an established customer/client base?
- ✔ Do you have an existing bricks-and-mortar store or office?
- ✔ Do you have an existing website or other web presence?
- ✔ Do you sell goods or services?
- ✔ Do you market to individuals (which is called *B2C* for *business-to-consumer*) or to other businesses (which is called *B2B* for *business-to-business*)?
- ✔ Who are your customers or clients (generally referred to as your *target markets*)?
- ✔ Do you sell — or want to sell — locally, regionally, nationally, or internationally?

Answer the other questions of the Business Profile section of the form to get an overall idea of what your business looks like.

Your website is the tail, and your business is the dog. Let business needs drive your web plans, not the other way around.

Setting Goals for Your Online Presence

After you've outlined your business goals, you need to decide what your website must accomplish from a marketing perspective. The goals you set for your site plus the definition of your target market should drive both your web design and marketing campaigns.

Business websites generally have a primary goal, although large, sophisticated sites now address several goal categories. The following sections discuss these goals in more detail.

Unless you have a large enough budget and staff to handle the demands of marketing to multiple audiences, select only one or two of these goals. You can add others later after benefits from your site start flowing to your bottom line.

Website Planning Form

For website (URL): _____

Prepared by: _____ **Date:** _____

Web Producer/coordinator: _____

Webmaster/developer: _____

Business Profile

Is the website for a new or established company?

    ○ New company   ○ Existing company, in business_____ years

Does the company have an existing bricks-and-mortar operation?

    ○ Yes   ○ No

Does the company have an existing website or web presence?

    ○ Yes   ○ No

Does the company have an existing blog or social media presence?

    ○ Yes   ○ No

    If yes, list all current URLs for social media.

Will your site serve:

    ○ Business   ○ Consumers

Does the company have an existing logo?

    ○ Yes   ○ No

What type of business is the website for?

    ○ Manufacturer   ○ Service provider   ○ Retailer

    ○ Distributor   ○ Professional

What type of products does the company sell?

    ○ Goods   ○ Services

Describe your goods or services:

What geographical range does the web presence address?

    ○ Local (specify)   ○ Regional (specify)

    ○ National (specify)   ○ International (specify)

Website Goals

Rank the applicable purposes of your site, with 1 being the most important.

_____ Information

_____ Branding

_____ Lead generation and qualifying prospects

_____ Generating online sales revenue

_____ Generating on-site ad revenue

_____ Achieving internal needs and building relationships

_____ Improving business process (e.g., customer service, tech support)

Figure 2-1:
Web Site Planning Form.

Financial Profile

Break-even point: $ _____ Within: _____

Return on investment: _____% Within: _____

Website Budget for First Year

Outside development: $ _____

Special elements (such as video): $ _____

Marketing: $ _____

Inhouse labor: $ _____

Other costs, e.g., tools, equipment, software: $ _____

TOTAL: $ _____

Sample Objectives

Repeat for each goal within time fram specified (for instance, 1 year).

Traffic objective (viewers / month): _____ Within: _____

Conversion objective: _____ % Within: _____

Sales objectives (sales / month): _____ Within: _____

Average $ per sale: _____ Within: _____

$ revenue per month: _____ Within: _____

Other objectives specific to your site, e.g., branding, relationships, search ranking, saving money on paid advertising Within: _____

Marketing Profile

Describe your target markets. Give specific demographic or segment information. For B2B, segment industry or job title or both.

What is your marketing tag?

Value proposition: Why should someone buy from your company rather than another?

Name at least six competitors and their websites.

_____

_____

_____

_____

_____

_____

Providing customer service through information

Brochureware or business card sites are an inexpensive solution. These sites, which contain no more than the minimal information included in a small trifold brochure, might provide a small business with an adequate web presence. For example, the two-page "business card" site at www. sistersnailsalon.com links to a second page listing available services. Other information-based sites are much more extensive. Medical, technical support, or news sites may contain hundreds or thousands of pages in a searchable, linkable, *static* format (standard HTML pages containing only text and photos). Businesses save money by hiring fewer staff to provide the information live while taking advantage of the Internet to offer support online 24/7 to accommodate customers worldwide.

Branding your company or product

Sites such as www.coca-cola.com serve primarily a branding function. Branding sites may include games, coupons, entertainment, feedback sections, interactive functions, and corporate information, but they generally don't sell the product online. They generate leads or sales only indirectly. For instance, consumers can buy a keychain or other branded paraphernalia on the Coca-Cola site but can't buy a bottle of Diet Coke.

Branding can be tricky when the name of a site is not the same as the existing business or when the URL and logo don't match. For example, the domain name for the State of Maryland's stop-smoking site is www.smokingstops here.com, but its logotype reads "1-800 Quit Now." This two-pronged approach dissipates marketing efforts because it isn't clear which of the two the visitor should remember; goodness knows, it's difficult enough to get a visitor to remember even one.

Generating leads or qualifying prospects

Some sites, especially those for services and expensive products such as cars and homes, allow potential customers to research offerings, but customers must call, e-mail, or visit the bricks-and-mortar establishment to close a sale. Interactive techniques, such as the Live Help feature used by www.candy direct.com, may improve service, in this case making it so convenient to order bulk candy that prospects are less tempted to visit competing websites. (Chapters 3 and 5 describe many interactive techniques you can use on your site for this purpose.)

If you're clever, you can qualify your leads online. For instance, House of Bamboo, a supplier of bamboo building materials, requires visitors to categorize their Contact Us inquiry as a general request, request for quote, or request for consultation at www.houseofbamboo.com.au/contact.html.

Generating revenue through sales

Transaction sites, which are, perhaps, the most familiar type of site, are used to sell goods or services online. Travel reservations, magazine subscriptions, organizational memberships, B2B (business-to-business) sales, and even donations fall into this category, as do retail sites from Amazon to the smallest, home-based micro-store. Good transaction sites take advantage of the web to gather information about customer demographics, needs, and preferences and to test response to special offers.

Generating revenue through advertising

A business model that calls for generating revenue by selling ads operates in a fundamentally different marketing mode than one that generates revenue by selling products or services. When you sell advertising, the primary product is the audience you deliver — either the number of eyeballs that view an ad or the number of click-throughs to an advertiser's site.

Achieving internal needs or building relationships

Sites in this category attract investors, identify strategic business partners, locate suppliers, recruit dealers, or solicit franchisees. The audience for these sites is quite different from the audience for a site targeted at customers or clients. This distinction is critical because elements of your marketing plan are derived from the definition of your target market. Sites with this goal may also seek to cement their relationship with existing customers by building loyalty through special offers, sending related information, and encouraging repeat visits.

Improving business processes

The goal of transforming business processes applies to more than giant corporations whose websites integrate just-in-time inventory, smooth supply chains, online sales, and accounting systems. Many innovative small businesses create online processes that fundamentally change the way they do business.

Surprisingly, innovation doesn't have to cost much. Pablo's Mechanical (www.pablosmechanical.com), a plumbing and heating contractor, captured the second-home market in the rural tourist area near Angel Fire, New Mexico. Pablo's Mechanical realized that owners of second homes are usually well off, are frequent Internet users, and often live out of state, perhaps in a different time zone. His simple, inexpensive site directs his customers to click links to large plumbing manufacturers' sites to select fixtures and then e-mail him their decisions.

Specifying Objectives for Your Online Marketing

What can convince you that your site is successful? After you establish online marketing goals, you need to specify the criteria that satisfy them. That means establishing measurable objectives. First, enter your calculations from Chapter 1 for break-even point, return on investment (ROI), and budget onto the Financial Profile section of the Web Site Planning Form (refer to Figure 2-1). Your budget and ROI expectations might constrain how much you can spend on marketing and, therefore, on how much traffic your site will receive. Take this into consideration as you specify numerical targets for your objectives and the dates you expect to accomplish them. There's no point in setting unrealistic objectives that doom your site to failure before you start.

Table 2-1 suggests some possible measurements for different website goals, but you have to determine the actual quantities and time frames for achievement. Define other objectives as appropriate. Enter the numbers and time frames for the criteria you'll use on the Sample Objectives section of the Web Site Planning Form. These numbers are specific to each business.

Table 2-1	Site Goals and Objectives
Site Goal	*Possible Objectives to Measure*
Managing customer service	Number of phone calls and e-mails, amount of traffic to various pages, hours of site use, cost savings, time savings
Branding	Onsite traffic, time onsite, activities performed, coupons downloaded, gross revenues

(continued)

Table 2-1 *(continued)*

Generating qualified leads	Number of phone calls and e-mails, conversion rate of visits to leads, conversion rate of leads to sales as compared to other lead sources, traffic to various pages, number of e-mail addresses acquired, cost of customer acquisition
Generating online sales	Conversion rate of visitors to buyers, sales revenue, average dollar value of sale, number of repeat buyers, profit from online sales, cost of customer acquisition, promo code use, sales closed offline that are generated from the web, if possible (that is, enter phone orders into the system)
Generating ad revenue	Ad revenue, click-through rate, page views per ad, traffic to various pages, visitor demographics
Measuring internal goals	Conversion rates for various actions, site traffic, other measurements (depending on specific goals)
Improving business process	Site revenues, costs, profit, time savings, costs savings, repeat visits, other measurements (depending on specific goals)

If you don't have objectives, you won't know when you've reached or exceeded them. Setting objectives ahead of time also ensures that you establish a method for measurement.

For instance, you can obtain site traffic numbers from your web statistics, as I discuss in Chapter 6, but you can't count leads that come in over the phone that way. Your receptionist must ask how a caller heard about you and tally the results. Or you can display a separate number, e-mail address, person, or extension for web visitors to use, just as you would establish a separate department number for a direct mail campaign.

Try to track data for a 13-month period so you can compare same-date results. Almost all businesses experience some cyclical variation tied to the calendar.

Defining Your Target Market

In the Marketing Profile section of the Web Site Planning Form (refer to Figure 2-1), you need to define your target market(s). For each goal you select on your Planning Form, decide who your audience is. Phrases such as "everyone who eats chocolate" or "all airplane passengers" are way too broad. Unless you are Toyota or General Mills, you won't have the funds to reach everyone, so you need to segment and prioritize your markets.

Note: I discuss how to fill out the rest of the Marketing Profile section in the section "Writing Your Online Marketing Plan," later in this chapter.

Market segmentation (dividing your market into smaller sets of prospects who share certain characteristics) takes many different forms. You need to select the one that's the best fit for your business. For your online marketing plan, you need to locate the various sites on the web where your target audiences hang out, so you need to know who they are. Think about it for a moment. The sites that appeal to opera lovers might not appeal to teenagers, and vice versa.

One caveat: Your online target audience might differ slightly from your offline audience. It might be more geographically diverse, wealthier, older, younger, more educated, more motivated by price than features, or vice versa. You discover these variations only from experience.

Here are a few forms of market segmentation:

- ✔ **Demographic segmentation:** Sorts by age, gender, socioeconomic status, or education for B2C companies.

- ✔ **Life cycle segmentation:** Acknowledges that consumers need different products at different stages of life (teens, young singles, married couples, families with kids, empty nesters, active retirees, frail elderly).

- ✔ **Psychographic segmentation:** Profiles consumers by a combination of attitudes, values, beliefs, self-image, lifestyles, or opinions.

- ✔ **Geographic segmentation:** Targets areas as small as a neighborhood or zip code or as broad as a country or continent.

- ✔ **Vertical industry segmentation:** Targets all elements within a defined industry as a B2B strategy.

- ✔ **Job segmentation:** Identifies different decision makers (such as engineers, purchasing agents, and managers) at specific points of the B2B sales cycle.

- ✔ **Specialty segmentation:** Targets a narrowly defined market (such as 45- to 65-year olds, female caregivers of people with Alzheimer's, or 16- to 35-year-old male owners of classic Mustangs).

Follow classic guerrilla marketing principles: Focus on one market segment at a time, gain market share and profits, and then invest in the next market segment. Otherwise, your limited marketing time and advertising funds are spread too thinly to have a significant impact. For more information on market segmentation, try www.pablosmechanical.com or http://money.howstuffworks.com/marketing-plan12.htm.

If you aren't sure how to define your market segments, check the table of online market research sites in Bonus Chapter 1 on the Downloads tab. The websites in that table offer a wealth of statistical data about the demographics of online users, what types of products sell well, and the growth of Internet use by demographic segments.

Writing Your Online Marketing Plan

Your business might have a formal marketing plan, or perhaps you have been in business so long that your marketing basics are second nature. For the sake of completeness and easy communication with others, fill out the additional questions of the Marketing Profile section of Figure 2-1:

- ✔ **Marketing tag:** Enter your *marketing tag,* which is the five- to seven-word phrase that describes what your business offers or who you are. This phrase probably appears (or should) on almost all your stationery, business cards, advertising, and packaging. Like your logo, your marketing tag helps define your public image. Your marketing tag should appear on your website as well. Many companies include a tag in their header graphic to reinforce branding. You can see an example tag ("Live, Work, Play") on the city of SantaFe's website (www.santafe.com), shown in Figure 2-2 and described in the "Planning gives a new boost to an old site" sidebar in this chapter.

- ✔ **Value proposition:** Why should someone buy from your company rather than from a competitor?

- ✔ **Competitors:** Enter the names of at least six competitors and their web addresses.

After you go online, your universe of competitors expands phenomenally. If you've been selling locally but plan to expand your market size, you'll find lots of other competitors online. You'll find competitors for your type of business in search engines, online Yellow Pages, or online business directories. This effort can be a bit sobering, but it's better to be prepared than surprised.

Planning gives a new boost to an old site

Scott Hutton, owner and general manager of Hutton Broadcasting, was in the market for a city-branded website to match his recent acquisition of six local radio stations in Santa Fe, New Mexico. "I looked into buying open domains and researched existing sites like Santafe.biz, among others," Hutton said. "When I learned we might actually be able to purchase Santafe.com, I was elated."

In 2010, Santafe.com was a tourism-driven site with more than 10,000 active pages, great local writers and a decent business directory. The site had moderate traffic, with 30,000 unique visitors per month, but visitors didn't stay long and they didn't return. To make the site financially successful through advertising, Hutton and his investors realized that they needed to create a vibrant resource for the community with active social communication channels that would draw a loyal audience of repeat local visitors.

Hutton's goal was to shift the content to appeal to local residents, aiming now at a target market of active, highly educated 25-to-54-year-old residents of Santa Fe county and nearby areas. By contrast, the Santa Fe tourist audience tends to be somewhat older, childless, and less active.

He quickly realized the synergy with broadcasting. SantaFe.com would be a natural fit to stream the broadcasting company's six local radio stations, to create new niche Internet-only radio stations, and to make the site the "go-to" resource for bands, DJs, artists, authors. and poets, who could own their own pages.

"We had lots of plans, including giving them free radio time to promote their web pages," Hutton notes. "The only trick is that we had

to sell enough ad space and advertorial messages to provide an almost immediate revenue stream." His business plan showed he would quickly need to counter the large upfront cost in personnel required to re-design the website and create exciting new content.

At a minimum, Hutton initially calculated that he would need the equivalent of six full-time employees for eight months. That meant redesigning the web pages to handle far more ads than before, as well as re-structuring advertising rates to match the new business model. As SantaFe.com conformed to the profile of an online startup, Hutton realized that it was crucial for his financial projections to satisfy his investors.

Figure 2-2:
The relaunch of SantaFe.com as an advertising-supported website required a new business plan.

Courtesy of SantaFe.com, Hutton Broadcasting LLC

Given the experience of watching his business plan continually evolve along with SantaFe.com, Hutton advises other business owners to "Have a great marketing strategy and extra cash because it will take longer and cost more than you think." Before writing an online marketing plan, consider how other traditional marketing concepts apply in cyberspace: the classic four Ps of marketing (discussed in the next section) and the obvious, but often-forgotten, need to fish where the fish are. Use these tools as part of your planning process to resolve problems before they impede your online success.

Examining the four Ps of marketing

Marketers name product, price, placement (distribution), and promotion as the traditional elements of marketing. These terms apply to the web as well.

If you plan to update an existing site, it's particularly important to review the four Ps. For instance, you might think you need a site update because you receive too little traffic from search engines, but after a review of the four Ps, you find out that the real issue is pricing. Chapter 6 explains how to diagnose problems with the four Ps by using your web statistics.

Product

Your *product* is whatever good or service you sell, regardless of whether the transaction takes place online. Review your competition to see what features, benefits, or services they offer. (To find your competitors, look up your product in Google or another search engine.) Product also includes such elements as performance, warranties, support, variety, and size. If you have an online store, look at your entire product mix and merchandising, not just individual products. Ask yourself the following questions:

- ✔ Do you have enough products in your online catalog to compete successfully?
- ✔ Are you selling what people want to buy?
- ✔ Are you updating your product catalog regularly, quickly removing items that are out of stock and promoting new items?

Price

The expanding presence of discount stores online puts significant *price* pressure on small businesses. Price comparison sites such as Shopping.com, which cost-conscious shoppers check frequently, also compel lower prices. Use those sites to assess your prices against your online competition. Are you significantly higher, lower, or price-competitive? What about your shipping prices?

I talk more about shipping in Chapter 4, but for now, remember that more than half the shoppers who abandon their shopping carts cite the high cost of shipping as a reason. If necessary, bury some of the handling and shipping costs in the basic product price and reduce the visible price for shipping.

It's hard for your small business to compete in the market for standard manufactured goods like baby clothes or DVDs unless you have really good wholesale deals from manufacturers or distributors. But you can compete pricewise on customized goods or services or by offering unique benefits for buying from your company. If you must charge higher prices than your online competitors, review your value proposition so that people perceive an extra benefit. That could be a $5 promotional code for a discount on another purchase, a no-questions-asked return policy, exclusivity, or your reputation for quality service.

You don't need to compete with offline prices because people value the convenience of, and time saved by, shopping online. It's perfectly okay to price online products higher than identical items in your bricks-and-mortar store.

In a drive to compete, many dot-com businesses drive themselves into the ground by charging less for products than they cost. The more products they sell, the more money they lose. What a business model! While every business sometimes offers loss leaders, you have to cover the loss with profits from other products.

Placement

Placement refers to your distribution channels. Where and how are your products and services available? Inherently, the web gives you an advantage, with 24/7 hours of operation for research, support, and sales online. However, you might face distribution challenges, particularly if you're constrained by agreement to a particular territory or are a distributor or manufacturer who plans to sell online directly to consumers.

Avoid *channel cannibalization* (the use of multiple distribution channels that pull sales from each other). Don't compete on price with your retailers. Otherwise your direct sales might cost you sales from other outlets, in a destructive cycle of eating your own. Before competing with retailers, review the increased level of staffing and expenses that are required to meet expectations of consumer support. Are you really able to take this on? If so, you might want to open a completely separate retail site at a different URL from the one that your dealers and distributors see.

Promotion

Your web marketing plan is one of the four Ps. All the different ways you communicate with customers and prospects are part of *promotion*. Market your website as much as you market your company and products. Careful integration of online and offline advertising is critical. Are your methods reaching your target audience? Are you sending the right message to encourage customers to buy?

Fishing where the fish are

When you advertise offline, you put your ads where the target market is likely to see them. Ads for muscle cars run in the sports section of the paper or on billboards near gyms. The same thing applies online. You need to place your lures where your fish hang out.

Figure 2-3 lists the standard online marketing methods discussed in this book. (You can download the Web Marketing Methods Checklist shown in the figure from the Downloads tab at www.dummies.com/go/webmarketingfd3e.) In Chapter 13, I provide a more detailed checklist of social media marketing methods. As you read different chapters, check off methods you think are possibilities for your site. I also recommend that you compile a marketing notebook or desktop folder with ideas, articles, and websites, and create sub-folders to store online research.

Finding your fish in the social media pond

Social media has complicated the lives of web marketers because user demographics shift constantly. Currently, search engine results are still more important than social networking sites when it comes to driving traffic to websites, especially among older users. For younger Internet users, social media are much more popular.

However, some studies show rapid growth in the use of social media by older adults and an increasing number of women using Facebook. It's almost impossible to keep up with these trends, especially as new social channels evolve continuously.

Your best bet is to use Quantcast or Alexa to obtain current demographic data for any social media site that you plan to use.

To organize your findings, build a spreadsheet with rows for each of the marketing methods selected on your checklist. Then create columns for audience, *impressions* (the number of times an ad is seen), cost per month, venues, and delivery schedule. (In Chapter 10, I explain more about cost per thousand impressions, or CPM. You have to research costs for each technique.) You can incorporate offline marketing in this spreadsheet or duplicate this arrangement for offline expenses and then add the two together.

You'll find a sample spreadsheet on the Downloads tab of the book's companion website.

The combination of marketing methods you decide to implement is called your *marketing mix.* When completed, this spreadsheet encapsulates your marketing plan, showing how your marketing mix will achieve the objectives you've already established.

Web Marketing Methods Checklist

Check all possibilities.

Offline Promotion

- [ ] Community events
- [ ] Direct mail
- [ ] Marketing collateral (brochures, spec sheets)
- [ ] Offline advertising
- [ ] Offline public relations and press releases
- [ ] Packaging
- [ ] Product placement
- [ ] Promotional items (specify)
- [ ] Site launch activities
- [ ] Stationery

Free E-Mail Techniques

- [ ] Autoresponders
- [ ] FAQs and packaged blurbs
- [ ] Group or bulk e-mail
- [ ] Signature blocks

Onsite Promotion

- [ ] Affiliate program
- [ ] Automatic updates (specify type of content, such as date, quote)
- [ ] Blog on site
- [ ] Bookmark reminders
- [ ] Calls to action
- [ ] Content updates
- [ ] Contests, drawings, and games
- [ ] Coupons and discounts
- [ ] Downloads (e.g., BBBOnLine, TRUSTe, VeriSign)
- [ ] Favicons
- [ ] Forums (message boards) on site
- [ ] Free offers (giveaways)
- [ ] Guest books
- [ ] Make This Your Home Page tool
- [ ] Internal banners
- [ ] Live events onsite
- [ ] Logo
- [ ] Onsite auction

- [ ] Onsite newsletter registration
- [ ] Onsite search
- [ ] RSS (Real Simple Syndication) feeds
- [ ] Samples
- [ ] Social communitiess (onsite)
- [ ] Surveys and polls
- [ ] Tell a friend (send a link)
- [ ] Testimonials
- [ ] Viral marketing
- [ ] What's New page
- [ ] Wiki

Figure 2-3:
Web
Marketing
Methods
Checklist.

Online Promotion (Buzz Campaigns)

- [ ] Posting to review and opinion sites
- [ ] Reciprocal links
- [ ] Viral techniques
- [ ] Webinars or Webcasts

Opt-In E-Mail Newsletters

Specify audience, frequency, and method.

- [ ] **Own e-mail lists**
  - Audience: _____
  - Frequency: _____ Method: _____
- [ ] **Paid (subscription) newsletters or e-zines**
  - Audience: _____
  - Frequency: _____ Method: _____
- [ ] **Public mailing lists**
  - Audience: _____
  - Frequency: _____ Method: _____
- [ ] **Rental e-mail lists**
  - Audience: _____
  - Frequency: _____ Method: _____
- [ ] **Viral e-mail**
  - Audience: _____
  - Frequency: _____ Method: _____

Search Engine Submissions

- [ ] Directory submissions
- [ ] Industry engine submissions
- [ ] International search engines
- [ ] Local and map submissions
- [ ] Shopping search engines (free)
- [ ] Specialty search engines (for blogs, videos, images, and so on)
- [ ] Paid submission service
- [ ] Search engine optimization onsite
- [ ] XML feeds

Paid Online Advertising

- [ ] Banner advertising
- [ ] Banner exchange
- [ ] Classifieds online
- [ ] Google AdWords PPC and other options
- [ ] Newsleter sponsorships
- [ ] Nonprofit sponsorships
- [ ] Other PPC engines and directories
- [ ] Site sponsorships
- [ ] Social Media PPC
- [ ] Yahoo!/Bing Search Marketing PPC and other options

Social Media Services

- [ ] Blogs
- [ ] Video Sharing, e.g. YouTube
- [ ] Photosharing
- [ ] Podcasts
- [ ] Facebook
- [ ] Social Bookmarking
- [ ] Social Media Monitoring Tools
- [ ] Twitter
- [ ] LinkedIn and other Professional Networks
- [ ] Geolocation Services (e.g. Foursquare)
- [ ] Social Meetups
- [ ] Social News
- [ ] Social Media Management Tools
- [ ] Social Sharing Buttons

If you lose direction, you'll end up wasting money. After several months, discard the methods that don't work and put more money into the ones that are successful — or add another method or two. Over time, you'll develop an optimized, online marketing program that you can monitor and tweak as needed.

Marketing online is part of overall marketing

Exclusive online promotion of a website is rare. Your web address should appear on your stationery, packaging, and brochures, at the very least. As you build an online marketing plan, you might decide to redirect some of your existing advertising dollars, but don't abandon successful offline advertising. Will you still need a listing in the local bridal consultants brochure? Will you still hand out promotional items or exhibit at trade shows?

Put your *domain name* (that's just a techie word for *Internet address*) everywhere that you put your phone number and more. Put it on your shopping bags. Put it on your outdoor signs. Put it on your business truck. Heck, you can even hire someone to put it on his shaved head.

What you already know about your business is right — the web is a new medium, not a new universe. Don't let technology fool you into abandoning hard-won knowledge of your business, your target markets, and how to appeal to them. When in doubt, follow your instincts and let your bottom line guide your decisions.

Part II
Building Websites for Marketing Success

The 5th Wave   By Rich Tennant

Cleopatra Carpet Cleaners

"So far our web presence has been pretty good. We've gotten some orders, a few inquiries, and nine guys who want to date our logo."

In this part . . .

Marketing is only part of your website, but all of your website is marketing. Successful business websites don't happen by accident. This section addresses marketing that occurs directly on your site and how to use statistical information to analyze your success.

If you drive site design and features by target audience and business goals, you'll jump over half the web marketing hurdles. From the look and feel of your site to navigation, content, and features, Chapter 3 looks at how marketing affects the various components of web design.

Chapter 4 does the same for companies that sell online. Opening an online store is similar to opening a brick-and-mortar store in a new location. It takes just as much planning, time, money, maintenance, and care. Forget those commercials about money rolling in while you sit back and count it!

Chapter 5 lays out specific techniques you can use on your site to attract new visitors, keep them on your site, and bring them back for repeat visits. Onsite marketing is fairly inexpensive, requiring more labor and creativity than cash.

Chapter 6 discusses using basic web statistics about traffic and sales to understand user behavior and improve the performance of your site. Combined with financial statistics, you can use web analytics as part of a cycle of continuous, quality improvement to make sure your site (and your profits) spiral upward.

Chapter 3

Producing a Successful Business Website

Successful business websites don't happen by accident. Companies with sophisticated web marketing staffs deliberately place every item in a specific place on a page, think through each headline, and consider every graphic element and photograph for impact. They don't spend hundreds of thousands of dollars on the mere chance that a site will achieve its marketing and sales objectives.

If those companies can be organized, so can you. This kind of detailed care may take more time, but it doesn't have to cost any more money.

Your defined business goals and target audience drive site design. Those factors determine how a site looks on the screen and how visitors navigate it, which is often called the *look and feel* of a site. This chapter focuses on the marketing elements for any site. The next chapter considers, specifically, the marketing aspects for a successful online store.

Incorporate your business goals and objectives, your list of competitors, and your target audience as you search for web service providers. If you've already selected a developer, take your planning pages to your first meeting, along with a list of sites you like and sites you hate. A good developer should ask for all this information, regardless of whether you come prepared.

Finding the Right Domain Name for Your Site

Selecting or changing a domain name (sometimes called a *URL* for *uniform resource locator*) is a critical marketing decision. The problem is more than just a simple search for availability at Network Solutions, Register.com, BuyDomains.com, or another registration site. The following sections give you the lowdown on how to choose the right name for your site.

A good domain name is

- **Easy to say in person.** It's unwieldy to say *digit* before a number in a URL, or the word *dash* or *hyphen;* besides, people have a difficult time finding the dash (—) character on the keyboard. Although hyphens are allowed in domain names, try to avoid them.

- **Easy to understand over the radio or on the phone.** Words that include the *ess* and *eff* sounds are often confused when listening, as are certain consonant pairs like *b/p, c/z,* or *d/t.* If you're selling in other countries, confusion between English consonants is different, such as *b/v* in Spanish or *r/l* in Japanese.

- **Easy to spell.** Using homonyms might be a clever way to get around a competitor who already owns a name you'd like to have; however, you're just as apt to drive traffic to your competitor as you are to gain some for yourself. Also, try to avoid foreign words, words that are deliberately misspelled just because they are available (for example, *valu* rather than *value*), and words that are frequently misspelled.

- **Easy to type.** The longer the URL, the more likely a typo. Your domain name can be as long as 59 characters, but unskilled typists average an error every 7 keystrokes!

- **Easy to read in print and online ads.** You can insert capital letters or use a different color for compound domain names to make them easier to read in print. Be sure your domain name can also be read easily in black and white and in a logotype (a word-only logo in a custom font) if you design one.

✔ **Easy to read in the address toolbar.** You can't use colors or capitaliza-tion to distinguish parts of a compound name or acronym in address bars or search engine boxes. Depending on the browser fonts set by the user, the letters *m, n,* and *r* next to each other (mrnrnm) are very hard to read, as are the characters l/i (lilllil) and the similar digit/letter combi-nation of 1/l.

✔ **Easy to remember.** Words or phrases are easier to remember than a stream of letters in an acronym, unless your target audience already knows the acronym from extensive branding (for example, AARP). Your domain name may be, but doesn't need to be, your business name, unless you enjoy a preexisting brand identity.

Stick with original, *top-level domains* (TLDs — the primary categories into which Internet addresses are divided): `.com` for businesses, `.org` for non-profits, and `.net` for network providers. Except in specific marketing arenas (for example, `.tv` for television programs), avoid top-level domains such as `.info`, `.biz`, odd country TLDs unrelated to your business location, and generic TLDs (such as `.pro` for professional) just to get the name you want. It's too confusing for users. The one exception is .mobi, which you might want to (but don't have to) purchase for your mobile website.

In 2011, the Internet Corporation for Assigned Names and Numbers (ICANN) approved a controversial plan to start expanding in 2012 from the current 11 generic suffixes to an almost unlimited number with such endings as `.eco`, `.god`, `.sport`, `.ibm`, `.google`, `xerox`, `.jam` or any other custom name for which qualified registrars are willing to pay at least $185,000.

If you have an easily misspelled proper noun in your domain name, you might want to register common misspellings of your name with the same TLD and redirect them to your primary site.

Don't bother taking the same name with multiple, top-level domains unless you think your audience might be confused. You probably won't want to spend money branding your URL with both extensions; generally one site redirects to the other. The only exceptions are geographically limited or international selling. You might want to register the same domain in different countries with a large target market, such as members of the European com-munity or Japan, so you can get into search engines restricted by national registration.

With more than 210 million domain names registered, finding a name might seem impossible. Take comfort in knowing that fewer than half (about 93 million) are `.com` names and that many domain names are now expiring or abandoned.

If your first choice of domain name isn't available, try the suggestion tool available on many registration sites. Use those suggestions to brainstorm more names. Get reactions from friends, customers, clients, and strangers about your options. If you're really desperate to get a particular name, go to the WhoIs database at `www.networksolutions.com/whois/index.jsp` or other registrar sites to see who owns the domain name and bid to buy it. You can also reserve a name in case the current owner decides not to renew.

Thinking About the Structure of Your Website

The most important criterion for a successful business website is whether it accomplishes its goals. Your site doesn't have to be beautiful or cutting edge as long as it ultimately has a positive effect on your bottom line. The second most important criterion is how well the site works from the user's perspective. The easier you make it for users to achieve what they want — whether that's buying a product, obtaining information, or connecting with others — the more likely your site is to succeed.

A preliminary site index helps you gather your ideas in one place. Outlining — the way you learned in junior high — is one easy way to organize and track site content. As you can see on the site index for the fictional SillySox.com in Figure 3-1, the top-level navigation, which appears on your main menu, shows up as Roman numerals in the outline. Secondary pages under that topic appear as capital letters, and third-level pages appear as Arabic numerals.

Organize your site index strategically, with the most important information for each level at the top of its section. Then review the site index against the site objectives that you wrote in Chapter 2. (If you skipped ahead to this chapter, no worries! Just go back to Chapter 2 and come back to this one when you've established your objectives.) Keep rearranging the index until it reflects the marketing goals you want to accomplish. Be sure to include any special functions the user might need to access, such as a Contact Us page, newsletter signup, or blog. The site index might change after discussion with your developer and during the development process.

Sample Site Index for SillySox.com (fictional)

Top Navigation

(fom left to right, with the element at the top right being most important)

I. Home

II. About Us

    A. Links

    B. Advertise With Us

        1. Traffic and Demographics

        2. Media Kit

III. Sock It To Me

    A. Kid's Game 1 (Sock Design Coloring Contest)

    B. Kid's Game 2 (Follow the Footprints)

    C. Kid's Game 3 (Land of the Lost Socks)

IV. Sign Up for Sox Savings News

Left Navigation

(fom top to bottom, with the element at the top left being most important)

V. Onsite Search

VI. Shop Our Catalog

    A. Women's Socks

        1. Knee Socks

        2. Short Socks

        3. Patterned Tights

    B. Children's Socks

        1. Knee Socks

        2. Short Socks

        3. Baby Socks

    C. Shoelaces

    D. Accessories

        1. Hair Ornaments

        2. Scarves

VII. Customer Care

    A. Shipping & Wrapping

    B. Return Policy

    C. Payment Methods

    D. Privacy and Kids' Policies

VIII. Contact Us

© 2011 Watermelon Mountain Web Marketing www.watermelonweb.com

Figure 3-1:
Sample
site index
for (the
fictional)
SillySox site.

The order in which navigation items appear on the screen is crucial. The viewer's eye goes first to the upper-right corner. Place there the most important action you want your audience to take. The top-left corner of the navigation is the second most important spot. The less-important activities go in the middle of the list of activities on the left sidebar or in the middle of horizontal navigation across the top. Because acquiring e-mail addresses is considered the most important marketing activity for SillySox.com, that function appears in the upper-right area of the navigation, as shown in Figure 3-2.

Figure 3-2: The fictional SillySox site reflects the index shown in Figure 3-1.

© 2011 Watermelon Mountain Web Marketing www.watermelonweb.com

Your site index becomes an important planning tool for scheduling and budgeting. When you ask developers for a price quote, the index will have a direct impact on the bids you receive. You can later convert the site index into tables to track which pages need to be written, which pages need photographs, and which pages are complete.

You can find out more about organizing your website in *Web Design For Dummies,* 2nd Edition, by Lisa Lopuck (John Wiley & Sons, Inc.).

You can't count on a linear experience. Websites aren't like most books, read from front to back. Visitors might not arrive on your home page, and they might skip all around your site. Not every visitor wants the same thing, so you must juggle appeals to multiple subsegments of your target audience.

Assessing Your Website and Others

Most business owners say, "I don't know anything about web design, but I know what I like." Are you in that category? If so, a few simple terms can help organize your visceral reaction when it's time to evaluate other websites, plan your own, or communicate effectively with your web designer and staff. While many people use different wording, these five elements cover the ground of site design:

- ✔ **Concept:** The underlying design metaphor for your site, intimately connected to your brand and target audience

- ✔ **Content:** All the words, products, pictures, audio, interactive features, and any other material you put on your site

- ✔ **Navigation:** The way users move through a site by using menus, links, and sitemaps

- ✔ **Decoration:** All the supporting design elements, such as buttons, fonts, and graphics that your designer creates

- ✔ **Marketing efficacy:** Methods such as calls to action or signup forms that get users to do what you want them to do

The Website Assessment Form (shown in Figure 3-3) provides a detailed breakdown for assessing sites. Try it on your existing site, if you have one, or on any of the sites that appear in this book. See what happens when other people evaluate the same sites by using this form. You might be surprised! The higher the score, the better, but you may find that others rate a site quite differently from the way you do. If several people consistently score a site below 50, it is probably in real trouble. (If a question doesn't apply, just ignore it and reduce the possible total by 5 points.)

You can download the Website Assessment Form using the Downloads tab on the book's companion website at www.dummies.com/go/webmarketing fd3e.

The following sections of this chapter describe the design elements in the preceding list in more detail.

Website Assessment Form

Concept or Presence	Lowest				Best
How well is a coherent, visual metaphor carried through the site?	1	2	3	4	5
How well is that metaphor carried through on each screen?	1	2	3	4	5
How well does the metaphor fit the company image?	1	2	3	4	5
How well does the metaphor suit the purpose of the site?	1	2	3	4	5
How well does the metaphor suit the target audience?	1	2	3	4	5
CONCEPT SUBTOTAL:					

Content	Lowest				Best
How appropriate is the text-intensiveness of the site?	1	2	3	4	5
How well does the site answer any questions you might have?	1	2	3	4	5
How easy is it to ask questions via e-mail or phone or both?	1	2	3	4	5
How well does the content engage viewers and compel them to to continue (e.g., correct spelling and grammar, vivid words, short paragraphs, bullets, second person [you], active voice)?	1	2	3	4	5
How well does the content suit the target audience?	1	2	3	4	5
CONTENT SUBTOTAL:					

Navigation	Lowest				Best
How consistent is the navigation?	1	2	3	4	5
How obvious, simple, or intuitive is the navigation?	1	2	3	4	5
How easy is the access to the menu, site index, and home page from each screen?	1	2	3	4	5
How accessible are navigation tools (screen visibility and position)?	1	2	3	4	5
How effectively are internal links used to move through the site?	1	2	3	4	5
How well arranged is the content (number of clicks needed)?	1	2	3	4	5
NAVIGATION SUBTOTAL:					

Decoration	Lowest				Best
How attractive is the decoration?	1	2	3	4	5
How well does the decoration support the concept?	1	2	3	4	5
How well does the decoration support the content?	1	2	3	4	5
How well does the dectoration support the navigation?	1	2	3	4	5
How well does the decoration suit the purpose of the site?	1	2	3	4	5
How well does the decoration suit the target audience?	1	2	3	4	5
DECORATION SUBTOTAL:					

Marketing Efficacy	Lowest				Best
How well does the site convey its central value message?	1	2	3	4	5
How well does it meet the buying needs of its target market?	1	2	3	4	5
How effectively does it use calls to action and contact information?	1	2	3	4	5
How well does the site promote itself (encourage repeat visits)?	1	2	3	4	5
Does the site include "follow me" and social sharing buttons?	1	2	3	4	5
MARKETING EFFICACY SUBTOTAL:					
SITE TOTAL:					

Figure 3-3:
You can use this form to assess your own site or others.

Creating a Concept

Concept is the design metaphor that holds your site together. For example, look at how AcomaSkyCity (`http://acomaskycity.org`), an historical Indian pueblo and museum, uses the shape of a pot on its entry page to set the stage for this visually rich site. After entering the site, the spiral logo is repeated as a border detail above the navigation, maintaining visual continuity even as photos rotate in Flash below it.

A good designer integrates marketing communication principles, branding considerations, and your target audience into the concept for your website.

Marketing communications integrates marketing and sales principles with graphic design to achieve business objectives. It acknowledges that the presentation of information affects emotional response and thus influences buying decisions. Designers ask about your target audiences to be sure to select or create appropriate design.

While essential for any type of sales collateral or packaging, marketing communications is particularly critical because of the short window for grabbing attention on the web. Experienced web designers intuitively adjust the font style, graphic style, colors, images, and white space to have a positive impact on your marketing process while reinforcing your brand.

For example, without reading any text or looking at the navigation, compare `www.smarties.com` with `www.scottbowingsconstruction.com`. Can you work backwards to analyze the marketing communications success of these designs? How would you describe the demographics of the audiences for Smarties versus Scott B. Owings Construction? What about the economic status of the users? (Check your demographic assumptions at Quantcast.)

From color to animated cartoon graphics, Smarties is a sweet site for kids and parents with young children. The construction company, with its formal fonts, structured design, fleur-de-lis, and darker color palette, aims at an older, wealthy audience; it breathes respectability and responsibility. Can you identify any similarities between these sites?

Color meaning is culturally dependent. If you sell internationally, research the meaning of colors in your target country. For instance, in many Asian countries, white, not black, signifies death, and red, not green, symbolizes prosperity.

Developing Content

Content refers to everything you provide for the website, from written copy to photographs, from product information for a database to a calendar of events. As I discuss in Chapter 2, you might decide to outsource content production to a copywriter, designate one or more of your employees as *content expert(s),* or combine the two solutions. In any case, you or an employee should allow time to provide a rough draft or raw materials, offer guidance, and review content for accuracy and quality. No outsider knows your business the way you do.

Writing and photography for the web face different constraints than they do with print or film. However, they remain just as critical online as offline when it comes to moving your prospects along the AIDA (attention, interest, desire, and action) pathway. You still need headlines that grab attention, images that pique interest, copy that builds desire, and calls to action that move web visitors to buy.

Writing effective marketing copy

People don't read online; they scan to save time. That makes sense because it takes 25 percent longer to read the same material onscreen than it does to read it on paper. Because of the limitations of time and screen space, you need to adapt your writing style for the web. Try to follow these precepts:

- **Use the inverted pyramid.** Use the journalistic convention of the inverted pyramid, with the most important information at the beginning of each page. Readers might never reach the end of the first paragraph, let alone the end of the page.

- **Grab readers with headlines.** Good headlines grab readers by the lapels. Subheads help break up the text on a page, making it easier to read. If you use a different font size, style, or color for your headings and if your headlines or subheads include a search term, you might receive extra points in search engine rankings.

- **Write strong leads.** The first sentence on the page is called the *lede.* Hook readers with benefits, telling them what they'll find on your site, store, or page. It improves search engine ranking to include three to four search terms in the first paragraph.

- **Keep important information above the fold.** Users spend about 80 percent of their time reading what's *above the fold* — that is, on the part of a web page that's viewable without scrolling.

✔ **Be cautious with long, scrolling pages.** Although users will scroll, they don't bother unless they believe it will be worth their time and the invitation to keep going is obvious. To keep important information above the fold, consider using a Frequently Asked Question (FAQ) format. At the top of a page, create a list of links to *anchor paragraphs* (text, often below the fold, that viewers access from links at the top of the same page, without scrolling).

✔ **Limit the use of PDF files.** While designers like PDF files because PDFs preserve designs, this file format isn't great for users. Generally, restrict PDF files to distributing long documents or extensive forms intended for print, not for reading online.

✔ **Use active voice.** Shun passive voice in favor of active voice. That is, the subject performs the action rather than receives it. The active sentence, "Search engines skip Flash pages" is preferable to the passive version, "Flash pages aren't read by search engines." Hints that you are using passive voice: forms of the verb *to be,* including the constructions *there is, there are,* or *it is.*

✔ **Emphasize second person.** Use *your* or *you* explicitly as the subject, or implicitly with imperative verbs, such as *buy, review, call,* or *sign up.* Second person forces you to talk about benefits, not features, thus telling visitors what they'll get from your site. Even the *New York Times* notes the growing use of *you, yours, my,* and *ours* as Madison Avenue follows the trend toward customization and personalization. Possessives imply ownership, empowering consumers. Your marketing copy must establish a relationship that breaks through the boundary of the screen.

✔ **Use first and third person judiciously.** You can slide in some first person (*our* or *we,* especially in sentences like "We offer a money-back guarantee"). Just don't spend a lot of time talking about yourself and your business. Your readers don't care. On most sites, third-person descriptions of products (*it* or *they*) are fine, but don't put off your visitors with long pages written in third person. Those pages often become impersonal and distant.

✔ **Stay informal.** With a few exceptions, an informal, conversational tone works better than dissertation-style, proper English. That's no excuse, however, for obvious grammatical errors such as lapses in subject/verb agreement.

✔ **Keep it short.** People are busy and don't have time to read everything. Use short words, short sentences, short paragraphs, and short pages, always placing the most important words and information near the beginning.

✔ **Use bullet lists.** Sentence fragments are fine, especially in bulleted lists. Think PowerPoint style, not essay. Bullet points help readers scan text quickly.

✔ **Include text links.** Link liberally to other parts of your site within the text. These contextual, internal links help users find in-depth information quickly and move people to multiple pages of your site. If the linked text happens to be one of your search terms, you might earn extra points toward improved ranking in search engine results, too.

Of course, the basic principles of good writing still apply. Especially, keep these points in mind:

✔ **Write vividly.** Use specific nouns and verbs rather than strings of gratuitous adjectives and adverbs.

✔ **Skip the jargon.** Use your readers' ordinary language.

✔ **Be yourself.** In spite of all these directions, let your personality shine through. When appropriate, include an emotional jolt of humor or wit as a payoff to the reader.

✔ **Check spelling and grammar.** If you don't have a content management system (see the "Choosing how to update your content" section, later in this chapter) that checks spelling and grammar, write the text first in a word processing application. Save your checked and corrected content as a `.txt` file or in Notepad to remove formatting.

✔ **Have others read what you write.** It's easy to get too close to your writing. Have someone else read it for clarity, accuracy, and omissions.

✔ **Proofread your text.** Read your text out loud. It's the fastest, easiest way to find mistakes. A site full of errors gives visitors the impression that you're sloppy. If you don't care about your own site, how do visitors know you'll care about them as customers?

Not On Tobacco, the American Lung Association's site to help teens stop or reduce smoking, follows these guidelines. Visit the site, at `www.noton tobacco.com`, to see its use of the second person *you,* multiple calls to action, short sentences, and bulleted lists.

You'll find excellent resources for web writing at

✔ W3C Style Guide for Online Hypertext at `www.w3.org/Provider/ Style`

✔ Web Style Guide, 3rd edition, at `www.webstyleguide.com/index. html?/index.html`

✔ Writing for the Web (Jakob Nielsen) at `www.useit.com/papers/ webwriting`

Telling stories with pictures

Photography is a powerful method of reaching your audience with immediacy and impact. While it's absolutely critical to show pictures — including close-ups — of any products that you sell, that isn't the only reason to use photography. Well-selected and appropriately positioned images can tell a story about your business, your processes, your tourist destination, and most importantly, your people. Good photos are good sales tools!

Sometimes, the web seems to exist in a strangely depopulated part of the universe. Many sites omit photographs, perhaps because of a legacy of concern about download time. Others have photographs only of buildings, machines, products, landscapes, nature, or artwork.

That's fine, but the most powerful images in the world have faces; our human brains are designed to react to them. When viewers see a picture with people, they can imagine themselves visiting that place, doing that activity, or using that product. They move themselves one step further along the buying process.

While faster access has made it easier to use photos, a page that takes more than eight seconds to download will lose much of its audience.

To reduce download time, be sure to save each photo in the correct format for the web: JPGs with a file size of no more than 85K; less if you have multiple photos on a page. Use smaller images of 10–20K, called *thumbnails,* that people click to view an enlargement in a pop-up window. This process is especially common on pages with multiple images, such as catalog pages for an online store. Here are a few other tips for using photos on your website:

- ✔ **Photos that work in print don't always work online, especially as thumbnails.** Long-distance shots or images with multiple points of interest might look fine when expanded, but not as small images.

- ✔ **Crop photos to remove extraneous background information that detracts from the message you're trying to send.**

- ✔ **It's worth the cost of digital doctoring if the picture helps tell your story.** Some photos might need additional processing in Photoshop to improve their color, contrast, brightness, or hue, or to erase something that you don't want seen. Of course, ethical and professional constraints limit manipulation of images for reasons other than quality.

- ✔ **Start with a high-resolution photo resized and saved for the web as a JPG.** You cannot make a low-resolution photo better, but you can easily make a high-resolution photo smaller while maintaining image quality.

- ✔ **If you expect users to print pages with photos, make sure the photos are "readable" in black and white.**

If photographs are an integral part to the story you're telling or the appeal you're making, they need to be good ones. A photo that is too small, out of focus, too busy, or poorly framed makes your company and your products look as bad as the photo. Hire a pro, buy stock photos from a source like www. istockphoto.com, look for images in the public domain (meaning not subject to copyright) at images.google.com, or search for items on photo-sharing sites like Flickr or PhotoBucket that carry a Creative Commons license for "all rights granted," which places work in the public domain. Go to http://CreativeCommons.org/licenses for a description of various licensing options.

For an example of the role played by well-edited photos, check out WineToWater.org, a charity fundraising site shown in Figure 3-4.

Figure 3-4: Photos involve the viewer in the site's efforts to bring safe water to third-world communities.

Courtesy of Wine to Water™

Using rich media

Multimedia, sometimes called *rich media,* has increased in popularity as broadband use has exploded. Audio clips, music, video, virtual reality, and Flash animation all fall into this category. If using rich media appeals to you, here are a few reasons why it might be worthwhile for your site:

✔ **Use of rich media adds marketing value.** It might extend your brand, help sell a product — as a virtual-reality tour of real estate or a complex product might — or explain a process or service, as a video could. It might also demonstrate your capabilities, such as music downloads for a composer selling songs online or animation for a web designer. See Chapter 13 for more about using rich media-sharing services like YouTube, Flickr, or Podcast Alley as effective marketing tools.

✔ **It makes the site easier to use or otherwise enhances the user's experience.** For instance, a live webcam at a daycare center offers clients security and reassurance — assuming access is password-protected so only parents can view it.

✔ **The goal for your website demands it.** A site that earns its keep by advertising might use rich media techniques to keep visitors on the site longer, encourage more page views, or attract repeat visits.

✔ **Your target audience wants or expects it.** Younger audiences are much more attracted to rich media than older audiences; a consumer audience with time for entertainment is more susceptible to rich media than a busy, B2B audience of engineers — unless there's a reason for the rich media, such as a product demo.

✔ **You need rich media to stay even with, or ahead of, your competitors.**

If you're now convinced that rich media is right for your site, here are a few other important considerations before you take the final plunge:

✔ **Will your target audience have the plug-ins, know-how, and access speed to take advantage of rich media?**

✔ **Can you afford the cost of doing it right?** Good multimedia is rarely cheap. If you can't afford to do it right, don't do it at all. Visitors won't know what they're missing, but they will know if something doesn't work properly or looks terrible.

✔ **Can you locate professionals to create the rich media, whether a good audio recording studio, a videographer, or an animator?** Very few web designers can do everything, but they might know subcontractors who can help. As always, review portfolios, get several bids, and check references.

✔ **Can you launch your website without rich media and add it later, or is it intrinsic to the purpose and design of your site?** Adding features later lets you test site operation and assess the value of your baseline site first. Later, you can announce new features in e-mail, newsletters, and press releases and on the site itself. Implementing rich media can delay the launch of your site, as it might be the most complex and time-consuming element of your site.

✔ **Can you display your Flash, video, or other rich media on a page other than a splash page?** (A *splash page* is an introductory web page used as a lead-in to the home page. Splash pages are usually graphically intensive or use rich media, but lack navigation other than a link to enter the site. A splash page with navigation is called an entry page.) Search engines can't read Flash pages.

✔ **Can you give your visitors a choice of viewing a Flash versus non-Flash version of your site?** Many Macintosh computers will not play Flash.

✔ **Can you give your viewers control of turning on both video and audio?** Don't automatically play something that the user doesn't want; let them choose to turn on sound.

✔ **How much use would justify the expense?** Will your statistics (see Chapter 6) display the number of visits or downloads for your rich media? Can you track an association from rich media access to business outcome?

Do not use rich media just because you can. Establish a reason, an objective measure of value, and a way to measure impact on something other than your ego. For a creative use of Flash, take a look at the site developed by interior design firm Wonderwall at `www.wonderwall.msn.com`.

If you're uncertain about rich media, apply the KISS principle. (Keep it simple, stupid.) Be sure that sophisticated rich media will be worth the investment of money, time, and effort that it will take. It's nice to have bragging rights but even nicer to make a profit.

Choosing how to update your content

Chapter 5 discusses the importance of updating content regularly and the type of information that should be updated. To make changes cost-effectively, you need a method of changing content that doesn't require knowing HTML or paying your web designer every time you need to make a small change.

Updates are critical to your customers' perceptions of your company, as well as to search engine ranking. Decide how you will update your site before you start developing it. You have several choices, none of which require technical knowledge beyond word processing:

✔ **Have your developer handle the updates.** On a small, HTML-only site, updates are fairly easy. Ask your developer to quote a price for development and/or hosting that includes an hour of support per month.

✔ **Do the updates yourself.** Template- or blog-based sites allow you to update content at any time, without any special knowledge.

✔ **Use content update software.** Adobe Contribute (`www.adobe.com/products/contribute`) and Easy WebContent (`www.easyweb content.com/products/website_editor/complete`) are two of many affordable software solutions. Contribute can be purchased for $199; Easy WebContent has a $23 monthly fee. Both solutions allow you and/or other content experts to update an HTML site without knowing any HTML. Let your developer know in advance if you plan to use software like this so the site is designed to be compatible.

✔ **Use your developer's CMS.** Many developers have written their own password-protected, in-house content management systems (CMSs). They might call this capability their *admin pages* or *backroom*. Some customize CMS software that they purchase to offer all their clients. The complexity and flexibility of a proprietary CMS depends totally on the developer, but it rarely requires technical knowledge. However, a proprietary CMS is generally tied to a particular developer or host. If the company goes out of business or you switch to another provider or host, you might lose this access.

✔ **Use an open-source CMS.** *Open source* refers to source code that is available to developers to use, modify, and redistribute without charge. Open-source CMS software such as Drupal (`http://drupal.org`), Joomla (`www.joomla.org`), and Mambo (`http://mambo-foundation.org`) have many customizable options. They're generally designed for fairly large sites with many pages, a product database, or a structured approval process. Of the dozens of alternatives, your developer will select one based on the type of website you have, the language it's written in, the features you need, the skills of your staff, and what your developer is familiar with. Most online store packages (see Chapter 4) already incorporate the ability for ordinary staff members to manage the product catalog and store; you need a separate CMS for nonstore pages.

✔ **Buy a commercial CMS.** CMS solutions are available at all prices and levels of sophistication. They're often built into high-end, enterprise-level, web development systems. In large, corporate environments, many content experts need different levels of access to specific pages. Some such web development packages are designed for certain environments, such as colleges or publications.

Figure 3-5 (top) shows an editing page from an in-house content management system from 1uffakind (`http://1uffakind.com`) that supports easy changes for Google maps, as well as for the text block shown toward the bottom of the page. The results appear in Figure 3-5 (bottom). As you can imagine, CMS was a powerful tool for the New Mexico Humanities Council, which created the Atlas of Historic New Mexico at `http://atlas.nmhum.org`.

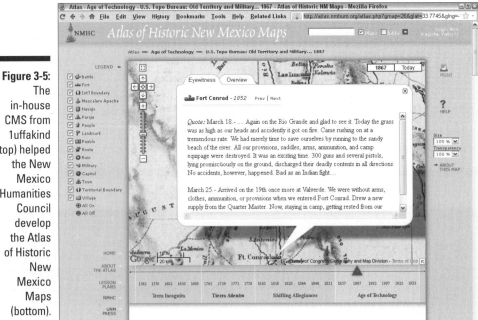

Text block

Figure 3-5:
The
in-house
CMS from
1uffakind
(top) helped
the New
Mexico
Humanities
Council
develop
the Atlas
of Historic
New
Mexico
Maps
(bottom).

Courtesy of 1uffakind Design (top) and the New Mexico Humanities Council (bottom)

For additional informational about CMS options, check out the reviews at
`www.infoworld.com/t/data-management/open-source-cmses-prove-well-worth-price-915` or `www.adobe.com/newsletters/edge/april2008/articles/article4/index.html`.

Ensuring Easy Navigation: A Human-Friendly Site

You have marketing goals and objectives for your site, but if visitors can't find the information they want or can't execute an action, you don't have a chance of meeting those objectives. Most good marketing websites follow a few essential principles of navigation:

- The main menu of options appears consistently on every page in the same place.

- The footer of each page includes links to the main pages so users don't have to scroll back to the top of a page to navigate elsewhere. (This is also helpful for search engine optimization.)

- Secondary menus cue users with a glimpse of what they will find within a section.

- A linkable sitemap or index offers the overall layout of a site at a glance. (This, too, is helpful for search engine ranking.)

- The appearance of contextual and navigation links changes to let users know where they are and where they've been.

- An onsite search engine is available for large, information- and product-loaded sites so visitors can quickly find what they're looking for. Onsite search has a high marketing value. Be sure your developer makes results of failed searches available to you. This immediate consumer feedback tells you what your site is missing.

- The navigation has words, not nameless icons that visitors have to remember. It's even better if those words are also search terms. Search engines can't read icons.

- All contextual and navigation links are verified to be sure they work, open correctly, and go to the right content page.

Mountain Springs Lake resort (`www.mslresort.com`) deploys flyouts to the side of second-tier drop-down navigation to help users find their way around. (See Figure 3-6.) The most important call to action *(Book online)* appears in the upper-right corner above the header graphic and again to the far right of the navigation as Reserve Now.

Figure 3-6: Mountain Springs Lake resort displays drop-down and flyout navigation.

Mastering usability issues

Navigation is just one of several usability factors that might dramatically affect the success of your website. A site that is obvious and easy to use gives viewers a positive impression of your company. A site that doesn't run on their browsers does just the opposite!

Generally, you don't know how any specific users have set their browser options — whether they block all pop-up windows, which plug-ins they've installed, how accurately their monitors display colors, what screen resolution they use, or how fast their Internet connections are. Some high-end application developers purchase software like BrowserHawk (www.cyscape.com/products/bhawk) to detect users' browser settings.

The rest of us need a feel for the numbers. For instance, according to a Pew Internet research report (http://pewinternet.org/Reports/2010/Home-Broadband-2010.aspx), only two-thirds of American adults in 2010 have a home broadband connection. Most of the others go online elsewhere; about 5 percent still use dial-up. This varies with age: The younger the users, the more likely they are to have broadband. While adults over 65 don't seem worried about a lack of broadband access, minority Americans see that lack as a major hindrance.

These statistics have a direct impact on whether you provide rich media and how you design your site.

You can garner some browser-use statistics for your site over time (see Chapter 6), and by all means, research configuration across a more narrowly defined group of users in your target market. Because that still doesn't tell you what will happen with a specific user, you might need to provide links to plug-ins with automated installation. If you're targeting a rural or low-income market, offer dial-up or non-Flash alternatives for those with slower connections.

Test your site on all popular, current browsers and versions for compatibility and download speed. In August 2011, slightly less than a quarter of all users run some version of Internet Explorer; about 40 percent use Firefox, 30 percent use Chrome, and the remainder use a variety of other browsers such as Safari or Opera.

Sites such as NetMechanic (www.netmechanic.com/products/browser-index.shtml) or BrowserCam (www.browsercam.com/Default2.aspx) sell software to developers for use with multiple clients or offer versions for one-time, limited use, often for $20 or less.

Taking human factors into consideration

Every website places a significant cognitive load on users, who basically learn to use a new piece of application software for each site they visit. The more your site conforms to web conventions and to the reality of the human mind, the easier it is to use. Visitors reward your efforts by staying on the site.

You'll find more resources for web usability and design in Bonus Chapter 2 on the Downloads tab of the book's companion website. The table includes UseIt.com, the website created by Jakob Nielsen, one of the grandfathers of research on the computer/human interface.

Some human factors to consider as you design your site include:

- **The brain is built for recognition, not recall.** Don't make your users try to remember what icons mean or how to find information.
- **The brain likes the number seven.** Seven seconds is the limit for short-term memory. It is also the number of things that most people can remember at once (so don't overwhelm them with choices) and the number of times they need to see a name or ad to remember it.
- **Contrast helps the mind organize information.** Contrast in design might occur in type, color, empty space, or size.
- **Brains like patterns.** Group objects by function or appearance and use consistent page design and site operation to give your viewers a boost.

✔ **Users need reassurance.** Provide feedback within a reasonable time, such as thanking a visitor for submitting a form.

✔ **The kinesthetic experience of click actions reinforces a message.** Ask visitors to click to request something, download an item, or submit information. The act of checking a box on an order form puts shoppers in the mindset to buy.

✔ **Provide on-site search so users can find information quickly.** See Chapter 4 for additional discussion.

✔ **Provide easily accessible help to use the site.**

Decorating Your Site

When people think about websites, more often than not they think about surface decoration. *Decoration* encompasses colors, buttons, backgrounds, textures, rules, fonts, graphics, illustrations, photos, sounds, and any other elements that support the overall concept. Often, developers will add small applications called apps or widgets to attract repeat visitors or keep viewers on a site longer.

Incorporating decorative graphics, fonts, and icons

Ask your designer to establish a stylebook specifying colors, fonts, and other elements that should be followed as the site expands. Otherwise the site can lose its visual coherence over time as people move around and memories fade. A stylebook might specify design elements such as these:

✔ Icons

✔ Typography

✔ Photography

✔ Windows

✔ Sounds

✔ File formats

The site for All Star Lanes (http://allstarlanes.co.uk) is an excellent example of using decoration to support a concept. This company, which is a bowling alley with a restaurant and bar, uses 1950s retro imagery to set the tone for its site.

Using gadgets, widgets, and apps

Here an app, there an app, everywhere an app, app. *App* is simply an abbreviation for application — a single function, pre-packaged bit of code that requires only a single click to activate. Apps provide information and add functionality without additional programming on your part, and they can be used for many tasks: to calculate interest, convert currency, track stock prices, check the weather, display headlines, play games, or view a calendar.

Generically speaking, apps can run on the Internet, on a computer, or on a smartphone, tablet, or other electronic device, but apps are not interchangeable. Because of the proliferation of incompatible platforms, programmers must write multiple, platform-specific versions for each app.

You can install *web widgets* (also called *gadgets*) on your website, blog, or social networking profile to add value and pull repeat visitors. Web widgets can be used for such tasks as personalizing an online music playlist, playing a YouTube video on another site, or translating text. The actual applications run from multiple other servers, not from your web host. Because they must run from a web page, an open browser is required.

When you look at lists of widgets to add to your site, select the web versions, not the desktop versions. A *desktop widget* is a mini-application that runs from your computer, even though it may access the Internet in the background to acquire information.

Be careful to get widgets from reputable sources. A widget created by a third party may contain malicious code that exploits your pages once it's installed. Practice safe computing: Don't install any "inline" gadgets that access user account information.

You'll find a table of web design resource sites in Bonus Chapter 2 on the Downloads tab of the book's companion website.

Improving Marketing Efficacy

Marketing efficacy refers to other onsite techniques that encourage users to do what you want them to do. Chapter 5 covers many onsite features that pull visitors to your site, keep them there long enough to establish a positive memory, and bring them back for repeat visits. One technique deserves special attention here: the *call to action*. Calls to action are usually, but not always, imperative verbs (such as *buy, view, register,* and *get*). They move visitors from one page of the site to another, building interest and desire until visitors take the desired action.

On average, sites lose about half their visitors with every additional click. If visitors wander around your site without finding what they want, they're likely to be goners.

The conversion funnel

Conversion rate is one of the most important statistics you track for your site. It is the number of people who take a desired action divided by the number of people who visit. Across the board, the average conversion rate is only 2–4 percent, as shown in Figure 3-7. That's a sobering number. While conversion rate varies widely — from 0.1 percent to over 35 percent — from site to site, the 2 percent to 4 percent number is a useful yardstick for predicting and assessing success.

Figure 3-7: The conversion funnel illustrates why it's important to move your visitors through your site until they take a desired action.

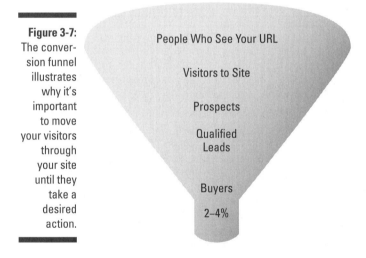

People Who See Your URL

Visitors to Site

Prospects

Qualified Leads

Buyers

2–4%

Of course, "average" conversion rate can be quite misleading. Not all industries or businesses are the same, and not all conversions are measured as sales. Assuage your ego with the results of an August 2010 Practical eCommerce survey of online purchase conversions. Three-quarters of respondents confessed to a conversion rate of less than 5 percent; 5.6 percent claimed 5 to 10 percent; and 11.1 percent boasted of more than 10 percent. The remaining 8.3 percent proclaimed ignorance. There was no explanation why those companies even bothered to have websites.

The moral of this conversion story: Be careful with your expectations, watch for trends, and focus on your own bottom line.

To achieve the standard conversion rate, you must bring 25–50 times as many visitors to your site as the number of conversions you're looking for. In turn, that number dictates elements of your strategic marketing plan. Again, on average, only 5 percent of people who see your URL somewhere end up visiting your site. Therefore you must generate between 500 and 1,000 URL impressions for every conversion you want to make.

Calls to action

A few simple rules for calls to action can help improve the conversion rate of your site:

✔ **Set up two clicks to action.** Enable users to take the action or action(s) you most want in two clicks or less. Keep your primary calls to action, such as Add to Cart or Sign Up to Save, on the main navigation or catalog pages at all times. A second click submits the request. Your site is off and running!

✔ **Generate leads.** In the world of web marketing, e-mail addresses are gold. If you don't have a newsletter, offer visitors a benefit to sign up or register, such as *Register to download our free white paper* or *Sign up for savings.* Of course, let people opt in to give you permission to contact them by e-mail in the future.

✔ **Use links as internal motivators.** A link is an implicit call to action, with *click here* understood at this point by most web users. With the right phrasing, a link call to action pulls the user to another page with an appeal to self-interest. For instance, a link might read *Live Longer* or *Warm Nights, Cool Drinks, Hot Dates.*

The four-letter word that starts with F

Free is marketing's other magic word. Especially on the Internet, with its legacy of free information, visitors expect to get something for nothing. It might be free shipping, a free gift with order, a free newsletter, a free five-year warranty, free gift wrapping, free maintenance tips, a free color chart, or free tech support. Offer anything, as long as it's free (*and* you can make good on the offer). *Free* works even when targeting wealthy retail customers or B2B prospects.

Free is one call to action that doesn't need a verb. By itself, the word *free* generates an impulse to act. Without a doubt, *free* is one of the most potent tools in your online marketing workshop.

OfficeVP (www.officevp.com) uses many different calls to action on its home page, even repeating the most important ones, as shown in Figure 3-8. Several of them include the magic "F" word.

The Zen of websites: intention and attention. Build your site with deliberate marketing intent and pay attention consistently to make sure that your site is working hard for you.

As you can tell from Figure 3-9 and the nearby sidebar ("Reaching a television audience with an online lens"), Norwood Community Television (www.nctonline.org) absorbed many of the lessons of this chapter as they worked on their site.

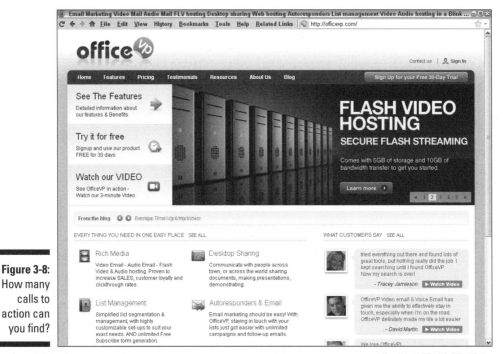

Figure 3-8: How many calls to action can you find?

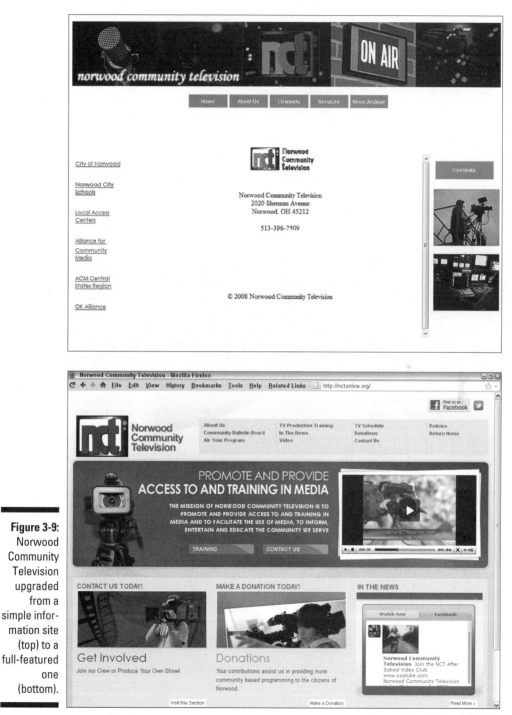

Figure 3-9:
Norwood
Community
Television
upgraded
from a
simple infor-
mation site
(top) to a
full-featured
one
(bottom).

Courtesy of Norwood Community Television

Reaching a television audience with an online lens

Norwood Community Television (NCT) is a 501(c)3 nonprofit organization that provides government, educational, and public access television programming to the residents of Norwood, Ohio. It also offers training and equipment for community members who want to produce their own programming.

For years NCT had only a basic information site with a phone number and mailing address and simple navigation (refer to Figure 3-9, top). In late 2009, it initiated a site redesign. "We wanted a site that people could actually inter-act with us on, and also a way to get our local programming out to a larger group of people . . . other than cable subscribers," explains Tyler Meyer, executive director of NCT. This time NCT opted for an actual web design company (www.webfeat.com), even though it would be more expensive than doing the site in-house or with one individual. "We really needed to get it right. And it was worth the money," Meyer notes.

The redesign (refer to Figure 3-9, bottom) has gone over very well with the people NCT serves. NCT has received good feedback from city officials and school board members about the video streaming it added. And for the first time since it began producing programs, NCT can tell how many people are watching videos and which shows are most popular. It's also receiving a lot more e-mail from the public. "You never know how effective something is going to be until you actually try it out," Meyer observed.

"Nothing surprised me about the process except the fact that it never ended," he added. NCT continues to look at the site to find ways to improve it. When its ideas are too expensive, NCT (facing the challenges of a nonprofit world) tries to find a cheaper, less high tech solution. For example, Meyer requested a news editor to post updates and press releases. When the cost estimate was too high, he opted instead to post a widget for the NCT Twitter account. This allows NCT to update its site with the most cur-rent information about activities and program-ming whenever it tweets.

Meyer advises that "It's very important to have a website that is both well designed and func-tional. Your website is the first impression [your customers] get of your company. If it isn't pro-fessional-looking and easy to use, they'll move on to another website. It'll cost money to have it done right, but it's money well spent."

Chapter 4

Creating a Profitable Online Store

• •

• •

*O*nline stores come in two forms: *pure-play* stores that exist only online and *bricks-and-clicks* stores that supplement a real-world storefront with a cyberstore. Both require the careful decision making that businesses routinely devote to opening a new location on Main Street. Online stores achieve maximum value when they're customercentric, anticipating users' needs and filling them.

According to a 2011 U.S. Department of Commerce report on retail e-commerce sales, 2010 was a banner year for B2C (business-to-consumer) online sales, with a 7 percent increase from 2010, almost twice the overall growth of retail during that time. The 2010 dollar value of $165.4 billion in online, nontravel sales represents 4.2 percent of all retail sales, up from 3.9 percent in 2009. (Add to that another 85.2 billion in online travel spending.)

When excluding sales in categories not commonly bought online — automobiles, fuel, grocery, and food service sales — *Internet Retailer* calculates that e-commerce accounted for 7.6 percent of total retail sales during 2010, up from 7.0 percent in 2009.

In spite of these numbers, don't get snookered by TV commercials that show money rolling in from online sales the minute you go live. Success requires a realistic estimate of how much time and money you need to invest. You must also apply what you already know about retail marketing to your cyberstore.

This chapter emphasizes the marketing characteristics of a successful online store rather than the technical details of implementing a storefront solution. I cover merchandising, simplifying the online sales process, enhancing revenue, and offering customer support.

If you're interested in finding out more about setting up an online store, check out *Starting an Online Business For Dummies,* 6th Edition, by Greg Holden (John Wiley & Sons, Inc.).

Examining the Key Components of an Online Store

When the tough go online, the tough go shopping. If you aren't already an online shopper, that's your first assignment. Look at other storefronts, particularly your competitors'. Buy products. Assess not only your competitors' products and prices but also the ease of using their sites and their customer support, return policies, product quality, order fulfillment, and shipping processes. Try buying from a mobile phone and from a recommendation you find on a social media service.

To get an idea of how a good store operates, study some online stores that are consistently ranked among the best, such as Amazon at www.amazon. com (pretty much everything), Schwans at www.schwans.com (food), Drs. Foster and Smith at www.drsfostersmith.com (pet supplies), or Land's End at www.landsend.com (catalog/clothing).

Only then are you ready to start building your store. It will share a few standard components with others, such as

- ✔ **Product catalog:** The catalog component organizes your inventory and presents products consistently. Unless you have only a few products, you generally enter your product list into a database or spreadsheet that includes at least the product name, category, description, price, and photo filename.

- ✔ **Shopping cart:** Users place their tentative purchases into a cart, which tracks the contents, allows shoppers to delete items or change quantities, and provides a subtotal of the amount due. If you have a small store with only a few items, you can use an online order form rather than a cart. Be sure that your developer programs the form to handle arithmetic automatically. Too many people can't double a price or add a column of numbers.

- ✔ **Check stand:** This portion of your online store computes shipping and taxes, totals the bill, and accepts shipping and billing information (including credit card numbers) in a secure manner. The check stand or other element of the storefront should issue an onscreen *Thank You* to confirm order submission and e-mail an order confirmation.

✔ **Reporting and order tracking:** Unless your store is very small, it helps to have easy-to-understand reports on sales, customers, and product popularity. The larger your store, the more store analytics you want. Order tracking allows you, and your customer, to know the status of an order in terms of fulfillment and shipping.

✔ **Other add-ons:** Large, sophisticated stores might interface with inventory, point-of-sale, and accounting systems. They might also integrate with live sales interaction capability, customer relationship management (CRM) systems that track a customer's experience with your business, or other enterprise-level solutions.

Online shoppers buy convenience and time, not just products.

The same four Ps of marketing that I discuss in Chapter 2 in the context of your overall business also apply to your online store:

✔ **Product:** The products that sell well online are not necessarily the same as the ones that sell well offline.

✔ **Price:** You don't have to price products the same in online and offline environments unless your online audience is likely to come into the store to purchase. Your competition, overhead, cost of sales, and cost of shipping might differ between online and offline stores, just as they might between stores in different physical locations. If you decide to keep prices the same, you might need to adjust the price in both channels to maintain your profit margin.

✔ **Placement:** The placement of items on a page determines how much attention they receive and, therefore, how well they sell. Think of your site as containing multiple internal distribution channels.

✔ **Promotion:** You can use onsite promotion, such as internal banners, discounts, upsales, and other techniques to move products and increase sales.

For more detailed information about each of these Ps, see the section "Merchandising Your Online Store," later in this chapter.

Selling B2B (Business-to-Business) with an Online Store

Given the retail sales numbers noted at the beginning of this chapter, you might be surprised to know that the vast majority of online transactions by dollar value in North America are consistently from B2B (business-to-business) sales, not from B2C (business-to-consumer).

Even if businesses are your primary customers, you can organize your online store in much the same way you would set up a retail store. Customer friendliness and ease of use remain as primary goals. Other than a different online promotional strategy, your main changes are pricing, merchandising (how you stock your store), and packaging — most businesses buy larger quantities than individuals.

If you're looking for resellers or franchisees, include a secure application form with spaces for a state resale number and credit references. At the very least, ask them to call or e-mail! You might also have an online form for them to apply for a trade account and pay by purchase order (PO). At www.lamalwholesale.com/application-forms/trade-application-form.html, shown in Figure 4-1, you can see how Findhorn Flower Essences, a manufacturer and retailer of healing floral extracts, handles applications for trade accounts. It might take a bit of work to accept trade applications and POs online and to integrate them with accounting software for proper billing.

If you're a wholesaler or manufacturer, consider implementing a password login so that only approved dealers can view your wholesale prices and place orders.

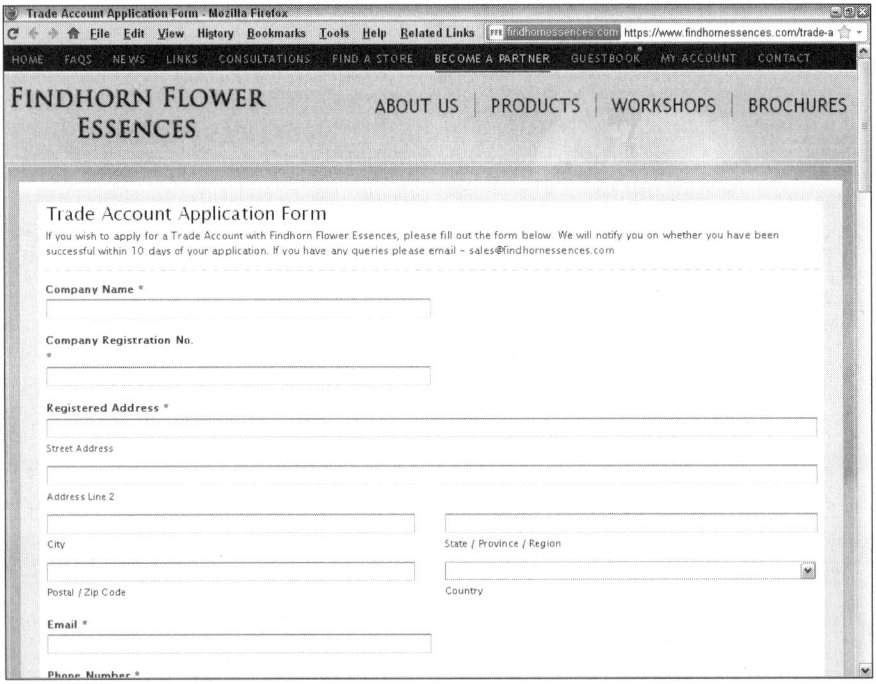

Figure 4-1:
Qualified companies can apply for a trade account at Findhorm Flower Essences.

© findhornessences.com

Don't undercut your retailers by competing with them directly on price. As I mention in Chapter 2, you can lose more revenue from channel cannibalization than you make from selling directly. Instead, link customers to your dealers' web sites to buy, and have dealers link back to your site for product details or tech support. Consider offering co-op support for dealers' online advertising — it pays off in additional business for your company.

If you must sell online B2C, perhaps because you're opening a new territory or your business plan calls for a second income stream, sell your products at the manufacturer's suggested retail price (MSRP) and let your dealers offer discounts.

Merchandising Your Online Store

Merchandising refers to the selection and display of products in your store. If you have a bricks-and-clicks operation, you're under no compulsion to sell *any* of the same products both online and offline, let alone *all* of them.

Selecting and pricing products

Your product selection and pricing levels are key elements to your online success. Some products sell better online than others, just as different products sell in different locations of the country. At the same time, price competition online is intense.

You need to make astute business decisions about what you sell and at what price. Don't be afraid to run financial projections or to ask your accountant for help.

First, decide what you'll sell, whether it's a subset of your inventory or all of it. If you're just starting a business, check out the criteria for choosing products suitable for online sales at www.powerhomebiz.com/vol148/ebay.htm. Items that sell well on the Internet change over time, as shown in Figure 4-2, which lists sales for selected categories in 2007 and 2012. Travel and home sales aren't included in this list.

Your second decision is how many items will be in your catalog to start with and how many items your catalog must eventually accommodate. Catalog size is a primary factor to consider when selecting a storefront solution. Some catalogs are intended for fewer than 100 items; a different solution is needed for 100,000 products. Given intense competition online and shoppers' desires for good selections, you need a critical mass of products and choices — unless you have a narrow niche with high demand.

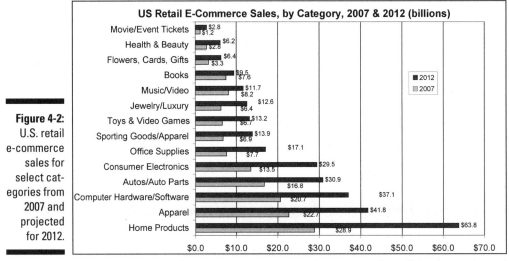

US Retail E-Commerce Sales, by Category, 2007 & 2012 (billions)

Category	2012	2007
Movie/Event Tickets	$2.8	$1.2
Health & Beauty	$6.2	$2.8
Flowers, Cards, Gifts	$6.4	$3.3
Books	$9.5	$7.6
Music/Video	$11.7	$8.2
Jewelry/Luxury	$12.6	$6.4
Toys & Video Games	$13.2	$6.7
Sporting Goods/Apparel	$13.9	$6.9
Office Supplies	$17.1	$7.7
Consumer Electronics	$29.5	$13.5
Autos/Auto Parts	$30.9	$16.8
Computer Hardware/Software	$37.1	$20.7
Apparel	$41.8	$22.7
Home Products	$63.8	$28.9

Figure 4-2:
U.S. retail e-commerce sales for select categories from 2007 and projected for 2012.

Source: eMarketer (www.emarketer.com)

If you have only one or two products to sell, review your business plan to determine whether an online store will be profitable. Also, consider whether you might do better selling "one-offs" through another outlet, such as

- eBay or another auction site
- Amazon Marketplace (`www.amazon.com/gp/help/customer/display.html?nodeId=1161232`)
- A distributor at another online store
- A classified ad on a site such as Craigslist.org

Finally, decide on pricing. Your planning guides from Chapter 2 come in handy as you set price points. (If you skipped ahead and didn't read Chapter 2, no problem. Just take a look at it when you get a chance.) Check competitors' prices on one of the many comparison sites, such as PriceGrabber, Shopzilla (`www.shopzilla.com`), MySimon (`www.mysimon.com`), or BizRate (`www.bizrate.com`).

If your prices will be substantially higher than those of your competitors, be sure to state your value proposition clearly (as I discuss in Chapter 2) so that shoppers perceive a benefit for paying more. Do you offer better support, a warranty, onsite service, a money-back guarantee, free shipping, a discount on the next purchase, free add-ons, or gift-wrapping?

Your online prices can differ from your bricks-and-mortar prices unless your site drives customers to your real-world store to make purchases or pick up orders. In those cases, your prices should match. This is particularly important when local shoppers compare prices on a smartphone before they come into your store. Also consider your shipping and handling costs before finalizing prices.

In most cases, think about setting a minimum online order of $10 if you intend to make money. (Music and similar downloads at $1 or $2 apiece are exceptions.) The costs of handling, customer acquisition, and marketing can eat up your profits. Let visitors know your minimum order immediately. Alternatively, package low-priced items together, such as three pairs of socks for $9.99.

Displaying products

Most online stores are arranged hierarchically. At the top level, a storefront page displays thumbnails representing every category (equivalent to a department). Depending on the nature and size of the inventory, categories are sometimes broken down with navigation into subcategories that make sense to shoppers. You might subdivide the category Shoes into Men's, Women's, and Children's, for instance. Clicking a category or subcategory takes the user to a thumbnail display of products within that category. Clicking a product thumbnail brings the user to a product detail page.

Make key merchandising decisions for each product category:

- **Choose which products to feature:** You might want to feature products within a category because they are bestsellers, have high profit margins, or are ready to be dumped. Place featured items at the top of a category display, and certainly *above the fold* (high enough on the page that users don't need to scroll to see them). Put the others in descending order of importance. That way, new customers can quickly find the products they're most likely looking for. Online always plays to strength!

- **Sort products:** Although it's appropriate to offer an option to sort by alphabet or price, don't rely on them as your only method. Sometimes you can insert an extra space before a product name to force an item to the top of the alphabetical display, much like putting the letter *A* before your company name so that it appears at the beginning of the yellow pages.

- **Provide product detail pages:** An individual page for every product makes displaying searchable text, color and size options, upsale items, and additional photos much easier. A product page also provides a specialized landing page for the desired product when a user conducts a search or clicks an ad.

✒ **Position special items on the page:** Think "grocery store." The upper-right corner of your home or catalog page acts like an endcap in a supermarket — that's where your specials go. You can use that space for sales, gifts, events, seasonal items, or an internal banner. Link from there directly to a specific product detail page where users can make a purchase.

The rows of products above the fold are like shelves at eye level, holding items that are heavily promoted, such as high-margin granola or fancy soups. The rows below the fold display items that people will search for on the bottom shelf, no matter how inconvenient, such as corn flakes or chicken soup. Viewers can scan more products at once if you display categories with three to four items in a row than if you have arranged category contents in a long, scrolling column only one product wide.

Informing users of product options

Product detail pages should offer shoppers choices of color, size, or other attributes, as does the product detail page from Sock Dreams (www.sockdreams.com/products/socks/over-the-knee/dreamy-knees) in Figure 4-3. Actual attributes vary according to what you're selling.

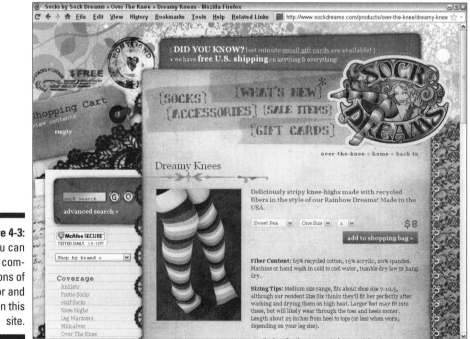

Figure 4-3: You can select combinations of color and size on this site.

Courtesy of Indigo Shadows Inc. DBA Sock Dreams

If your storefront doesn't allow attributes, each available combination requires a separate entry and stock keeping unit (SKU) number. Most storefront software doesn't let you assign the same SKU to two separate entries.

You or your staff members enter all this information into a product database. Although a minimum of technical training is generally required, try to select staff familiar with your stock to enter the data. Make sure that you designate all the possible categories in which a product should appear.

Be sure to spell-check your product names and descriptions before you open the store. Also check prices, SKUs, category assignments, product attributes, and photos. Data entry errors are common.

If a product is out of stock, either remove it immediately from your catalog or notify customers onscreen at the category or page level. Offer a substitute online, and let people know how long they must wait for back orders. If you wait until checkout to inform a shopper that a product is unavailable, you risk losing that customer forever.

Enhancing revenue with upsells, impulse buys, and more

Depending on the storefront software you use, you can implement revenue-enhancing features to increase the dollar value of an average purchase or to improve the likelihood that customers make repeat visits. You can find almost all these concepts on highly ranked selling sites, such as Amazon, which displays more than eight revenue-enhancing options, including a gift organizer, daily deals, and personalized recommendations. Even small companies such as Wanderlust, shown in Figure 4-4, can use revenue enhancement. In addition to categories labeled What's New, Free Shipping, and Gift Certificates, be sure to see the section labeled Customers Who Bought This Product Also Purchased.

Figure 4-4:
Wanderlust
Jewelry
includes
several
revenue-
enhancing
options.

Courtesy of Wanderlust Jewelry

Including product detail

In the real world, shoppers might use all five senses to evaluate a product and make a decision. Online shopping constrains the user to sight and sound at best. There's no way yet for users to sample your new chipotle dip, to enjoy the fragrance of freshly baked chocolate chip cookies or the scent of perfume, to run their fingers over soft-as-a-cloud leather or plush velvet. They have no way to hold a sparkling ring up to the light or to tell whether the black-on-black labels on the DVD player are readable.

To the greatest extent possible, you must overcome those constraints with text, photography, 3D, or virtual reality accessed on product detail pages. Product photography is critical to a sales site. Close-ups are essential, sometimes from multiple angles. Complex equipment or items, such as sculpture, that visitors need to see from more than one side, benefit from 3D, virtual reality, or video. If you can't hire a professional, at least

✔ Check out tips for tabletop photography at `www.tabletopstudio.com/TTS_Product_Photography_Tips.html` or `www.picturecorrect.com/tips/still-life-tabletop-photography`.

✔ Buy a decent digital camera.

✔ Set up a simple tabletop studio with two lights at a 45-degree angle from above the product and a solid-color background.

✔ Use a tripod.

✔ Crop and maximize the appearance of your photos by using Photoshop or similar software.

✔ If you're selling gift items, display how the wrapped package will look when received, complete with bow.

✔ Photograph packaged sets of goods priced as one basket or kit.

✔ When possible, picture people using or modeling your products. The added interest factor increases sales. Hats in the Belfry (`www.hatsin thebelfry.com`) incorporates people as models on its site, as shown in Figure 4-5, as well as multiple photographic views of products. Visit `www.hatsinthebelfry.com/product/flintstone-lodge-hat-7074.html` for an example. Hats in the Belfry sells serious hats, too, but this one is worth a laugh.

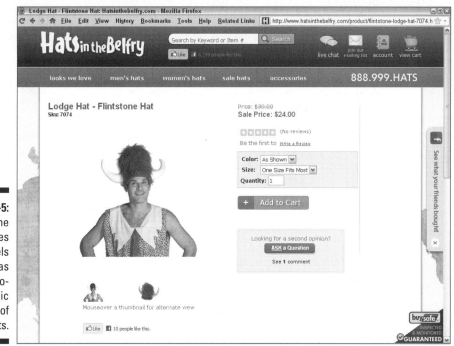

Figure 4-5: Hats in the Belfry uses live models as well as multiple photographic views of products.

Courtesy of Hats in the Belfry

You enter the filenames for photos in your product database, along with product descriptions. Write sparkling copy, as I describe in Chapter 3, offering benefits and distinguishing which products are best for which applications. In other words, anticipate answers to questions that customers might ask.

Include text information about warranties, service, technical support, and other specifications according to the product. If your products are available in different colors, display color swatches on the detail page. Color choice isn't a trivial matter. Different manufacturers have different color palettes — it isn't easy being green!

Making It Easy for Your Customers to Buy

From a marketing perspective, you need to convert shoppers to buyers. Make it easy. Studies show that many online shoppers give up early in the process, long before they open a shopping cart. Many shoppers' complaints are the same as those for any website: poor navigation, long download times, and inability to find what they want. The following sections detail some ways that you can enhance the shopping experience for your customers.

Providing a product search engine

The larger and more complex your store, the more you need an onsite product search engine. Besides the obvious category and subcategory choices, users might want to search by the following criteria, alone or in combination:

- ✔ Product name
- ✔ Product type
- ✔ Price
- ✔ Product attributes, such as size, color, or material
- ✔ Brand

Depending on your storefront solution and the nature of your site, you might want two search engines: one that searches the product database and another that searches content-rich HTML pages.

As always, the trade-off is between flexibility and complexity. Don't make the search function more complicated than most of your users can handle.

Search engines can locate items only if the entered keyword appears somewhere in the product record. Ask your developer which fields of a record are searched. High-quality search engines can respond by algorithm (rule) to misspellings and synonyms. Otherwise, you might want to include misspellings and synonyms in a nonprinting field of each record.

Try to use drop-down searches wherever there might be confusion about the data, such as whether to include dollar signs in a price or how to spell a brand name. Drop-down lists that work with the search engine allow visitors to choose from a list of search options rather than type keywords. (Or, you might want to presort products into some of these categories and put them in the storefront as navigational choices instead.)

Product search is an excellent source of market intelligence. Confirm that you can get reports on both successful and unsuccessful searches. Unsuccessful results tell you what your customers are looking for but can't find. That's market intelligence!

Some storefront solutions come with built-in search engines, which range from fully customizable to completely inflexible. Your developer can install a third-party alternative on some storefront solutions; others don't allow it.

Google's powerful search algorithm is available for as little as $100 per year for ad-free results on as many as 20,000 queries at www.google.com/site search/index.html.

Information on purchasing Google's more powerful, enterprise-level search engines is available at www.google.com/commercesearch for retail sites or www.google.com/enterprise/itstime/index.html for data-intensive sites. You can search for other free or advertising-supported, third-party search engines, such as Zoom, which is free for small sites, at www.wrensoft.com/zoom/index.html.

Implementing two clicks to buy

The same principle of "two clicks to action" that I discuss in Chapter 3 applies to your online store. To move clients toward purchase as quickly as possible, put a Buy Now (good) or Add to Cart (better because it doesn't remind shoppers that they're spending money) button at the level of category thumbnails, as well as on product detail pages. Don't force users to click any more than necessary.

The standard View Cart button usually opens a full-page window with shopping cart contents. Have the button instead open a small window or pop-up that shows users a summary of their cart contents. Or show the cart contents on every page of the website. (Web developers call this element a *minicart*.) A minicart saves users two clicks: one to view their cart and the other to return to shopping.

Duckloe Furniture, whose Shop Duckloe screen is shown in Figure 4-6, implemented many of these user-friendly suggestions in its new shopping cart at `http://duckloe.com/our_products.asp`. Details about Duckloe's experience in implementing a shopping cart appear in the nearby sidebar, "Furnishing an online store."

Figure 4-6:
Duckloe
Furniture
added an
online shop-
ping cart
when it
redesigned
its site.

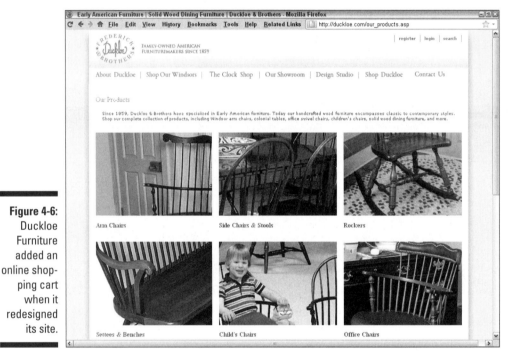

Courtesy of Frederick Duckloe & Brothers, Inc.

Offering multiple payment options

Making it easy for customers includes making it easy to pay. Even though online ordering has become more secure and commonplace, many customers still worry about providing credit card information online. A best practice is to offer options for calling in an order, printing and faxing the shopping cart and payment information, or mailing an order with a check. These multiple payment options increase your conversion rate.

Any significant online store must accept credit cards. Ask your developer or hosting company about options. Try the comparison shopping site for credit card processing from FeeFighters (`http://feefighters.com`), where top-tier processors bid for your business, to evaluate the cost of different plans.

Furnishing an online store

Frederick Duckloe & Brothers, Inc., a family-owned American furniture maker for more than 150 years, handcrafts Windsor chairs and other fine wood colonial and contemporary furniture.

When the company decided to redesign its website, it opted to replace its static product display with new navigation, a searchable product database, online transactions, and interactive options for finishes and upholstery.

The site supplements Duckloe's Pennsylvania showroom to reach a national market of individual buyers, colleges, restaurants, hotels, businesses, and museums seeking quality reproductions. Using e-newsletters, search engine optimization techniques, and pay per click campaigns, the site expands Duckloe's appeal well beyond its New England and mid-Atlantic roots.

Barbara Duckloe Townsend, secretary-treasurer of the company, says she was "surprised how much detail work and time was required to build a shopping cart" (see `http://duckloe.com/our_products.asp`), especially because Duckloe has had a website for more than 15 years. Its high-end artisan products require additional high-quality product photos, elegant design, and searchable text for product detail pages to appear to their full advantage.

Online sales, she notes, are complicated by the high cost of shipping furniture via UPS or common carrier. A shipping expert calculates common carrier (freight) costs, which are especially important for institutional sales, rather than tries to include them in the online transaction.

The entire process took much longer than anticipated. To control the process, Townsend recommends interviewing several professionals and having a deadline for completion.

If you already have a merchant account, you can process credit card transactions offline as long as you have a secure server (`https`) for this portion of your site. After you reach about ten sales per day, you might want to shift to *real-time card processing.* (Cards are verified online before the transaction enters your system, rather than offline, like phone orders.) At that point, the savings in labor costs offset the increased cost of real-time processing.

Real-time gateways (the software that manages real-time processing) also validate credit cards for billing address, card verification number, and spending limits, all of which reduce your risk as a merchant. Ask your developer or template host for pricing. Unless they're included in your storefront package, both the secure server and real-time gateway usually incur start-up and annual fees.

Other payment options, including the following, are available for special situations:

- ✔ **PayPal:** Now owned by eBay; allows you to accept credit card payments without having a merchant card account. Fees run 1.9 to 2.9 percent (standard rate) plus 30 cents per transaction. Find out more at `https://merchant.paypal.com`. By early 2011, 94.4 million people worldwide were using PayPal. Many e-commerce hosts aggregate their stores through similar services.

- ✔ **Google Checkout:** Provides one-stop checkout for stores with compatible check stands. A buyer enrolls on Google and enters profile information; the profile completes billing forms on other sites with one click. Google charges 1.9 to 2.9 percent, plus 30 cents per transaction. See `http://checkout.google.com/sell` for more information. Retailers using Google Checkout can also obtain a free Google store gadget for use on blogs, websites, and social media services at `https://storegadget wizard.appspot.com/storegadgetwizard/index.html`.

- ✔ **Prepaid deposits:** Debits for small purchases, such as downloading articles, music, or photos. This approach reduces the per-transaction cost that might otherwise make credit cards too expensive to accept for small purchases (unless you have the volume of iTunes) and establishes a minimum order amount.

- ✔ **Electronic bill presentation and payment (EBPP):** Works well for billing and payment on a monthly basis, or for B2B stores using purchase orders. Basically, EBPP allows you to invoice electronically and then receive payment by electronic funds transfer from the customer's bank account to yours. This service is available from multiple providers, such as Electronic Banking Systems EFT (`www.ebseft.com/dpage.php?idp=9&idt=1`) and Inovium Electronic Funds (`http://electronicfunds.com`).

Supporting customers

Keeping customers satisfied throughout the sales cycle might start online, but it finishes offline when customers are happy with the products they receive.

Always respond to e-mail and phone inquiries within one business day. Sadly, companies often violate this most basic rule offline as well as online. If problems occur with order fulfillment or shipping, let your customers know as soon as you recognize the problem, and offer a substitution. An honest effort retains customers; delay or denial loses them for eternity.

To offer customer support through the buying process, try these strategies:

- ✔ **Enable customers to communicate with a real person.** If you sell online, get a toll-free number. In a prominent spot on the site, display the hours when the phone is answered. If your customer base and geographic area become large enough, you might need to create or outsource a call center for sales and technical support. Alternatively, offer live chat, live calls online, or a click-to-call option that dials your office.

✔ **Build trust.** Publish your business hours and a street address, not a post office box, to establish basic business credibility. Post the logos of all organizations that validate your standing, preferably in the footer so that they appear on every page. At the least, post them on the About Us page. Include the logo of the following:

- *The company that supplies your secure certificate,* such as VeriSign (www.verisign.com) or Authorize.net (www.authorize.net)

- *Safe shopping services,* such as the electronic Better Business Bureau (www.bbbonline.org/online), ePublicEye (www.epubliceye.com), or TRUSTe (www.truste.com)

- *Business rating services,* such as the free Shopzilla Customer Certified Rating program (http://merchant.shopzilla.com/oa/registration)

- *Local memberships,* such as in a chamber of commerce or trade association

✔ **Spell out warranty, refund, and return policies.** Look at your competitors' sites to understand what's standard in your industry. Be sure to promote on your site any special offers, such as satisfaction guaranteed or free shipping on returns. Anything that reduces a customer's perceived risk encourages purchase. It's equally important to be clear about constraints; for example, *DVDs can be returned only if unopened, Exchanges Only,* or *No Refunds after 30 Days.* Some sites use Warranties and Return Policies as separate navigational items. Others group them together with Privacy and Security statements under a Customer Support or Customer Care tab.

✔ **Ensure privacy and security.** Reassure your customers that their personal information, including e-mail addresses, won't be used elsewhere, rented, or sold. Tell them about encrypting data — not just during transmission but when storing it on your computers. In these days of identity theft, never ask for anyone's Social Security number. Chapter 14 has more information about privacy policies.

✔ **Notify customers if you place cookies on their computers.** To reduce the amount of data entry on repeat purchases, many sites create password-protected customer accounts on their servers. Others place a *cookie* (a small data file with unique identification numbers) on the customer's hard drive that recognizes whenever a repeat customer visits the site. Cookies allow personalization, purchase history, records of open shopping carts, and convenient reordering. However, some customers worry about them. If cookies are required, you might need to tell people how to modify cookie settings on their browsers; most people don't know how.

Fulfilling orders

Customers don't separate your website from other aspects of your business. If they receive the wrong item or their package gets lost in shipping, they blame your business for a poor online shopping process, not for poor follow-up. You must ensure that the positive experience your customers have onsite carries through to completion.

In the best of all possible worlds, customers receive an e-mail confirmation when they complete their order as well as a reminder to print their order details. If your shipping process assigns a unique tracking number to the order, they can access a link directly to the carrier's site to keep an eye on the progress of their shipment, whether you use UPS, the U.S. Postal Service, FedEx, or other carriers.

Sophisticated, storefront packages offer additional automated features, including the following:

- ✔ **Packing slips and shipping labels:** Well-integrated systems print packing slips and shipping labels. This feature might require buying an additional module or third-party software.

- ✔ **Production tracking:** Some systems track an order through production, which is particularly useful if your products involve customization or have a long fulfillment cycle. Customers receive an e-mail when the products they ordered, such as checks or monogrammed towels, enter the production queue. Complex B2B sites integrated with manufacturing systems might allow buyers to track progress on their orders.

- ✔ **Shipping confirmation:** You can set up your sophisticated storefront to send another e-mail to the customer when a package has shipped. This tells buyers when to expect their order and how to reach you if there's a problem. It offers another opportunity to thank customers for their order, remind them about your return policies, and link them back to your site. It's also a window for a customer feedback survey, but keep it short!

A best practice is to charge a customer's card only when a product has shipped. Check to see whether your software or manual transaction process can accommodate this feature.

Very large stores might arrange for third-party companies to handle their order fulfillment and shipping. Amazon, which has perfected this element of online selling, contracts its fulfillment service to many of its large merchant partners.

Selling an additional product to a satisfied customer is much less expensive than acquiring a new customer.

Shipping Is a Marketing Issue

Nothing is likely to infuriate online buyers more than the price of shipping. Because shipping is expensive, especially as the price of gas increases, research alternatives upfront to decide which carrier and delivery choices you will offer. If possible, let customers select the shopping method they prefer. Of course, not everything can go by ground — baked goods and fresh flowers always need fast delivery!

According to the Direct Marketing Association, "more than 70 percent of consumers say they compare the total cost of a product, including shipping and handling charges, when they compare sellers. Those who shop online say excessive shipping charges is the number-one reason they abandon their shopping carts before buying." Positive consumer perception of your charges is critical to your success.

The overall rate of shopping cart abandonment is 71 percent as of June 2010, according to Forrester Research. That's right — more than 70 percent of all started shopping carts never result in a purchase, and that number is rising as shoppers become more sophisticated at comparing prices. Of that 70 percent, studies show 44 percent of shoppers abandon carts because of high shipping costs or hidden charges.

Deciding what to charge for shipping

Decide whether the shipping charge is a flat fee per order or item or varies by price or weight. If you decide on weight, you must enter the weight of every product in your product database. After you have an estimate of shipping volume, you might be able to schedule pickups and negotiate a discount rate with a carrier.

Handling isn't free either. You incur costs for packaging materials and wrapping, picking products out of inventory, packing cartons, and labeling.

If you're new to this business, test your packaging, shipping, and carrier selection, especially for fragile or perishable goods. Simply ship samples to yourself or friends.

Your store software should separately report revenues from product sales, taxes, and shipping charges. If you're careful with financial records, you can track shipping and handling costs against shipping revenues to ensure that you aren't losing money on shipping. If you incorporate a portion of shipping and handling costs in the product price, adjust this calculation accordingly.

In many cases, it's better to bury some of the cost of shipping and handling in the online product price and reduce the published shipping price. This strategy reduces customer resistance to shipping charges perceived as high relative to product price. People balk at paying $10 to ship a $30 item but are more willing to pay $5 shipping for the same item priced at $35.

Communicating your shipping policies

Create a separate page for shipping information that is quickly available on either main or secondary navigation. Let people know how long it takes for products to leave your facility or order fulfillment center — the same day for orders received by 1 p.m.? The next business day? A week for custom-made goods? Make sure your shipping page is covered by your onsite search function. Your policy should clearly inform buyers about shipping alternatives, from standard ground to overnight, and whether they face any limitations.

For instance, the U.S. Postal Service delivers to P.O. boxes, but FedEx and UPS don't. The Postal Service delivers on Saturday with no additional charge; FedEx charges extra; UPS delivers on Saturdays but only for an additional $15 per package. Some companies or products ship only to certain countries. Some companies don't ship products such as chocolate year-round unless the buyer pays for special refrigerated handling and overnight delivery.

Don't surprise users at the check stand with shipping prices or taxes. Let people estimate in advance their likely shipping charges, especially when shippers are adding fuel surcharges.

Shipping decisions might affect many elements of your online business plan, from manufacturing to merchandising and from pricing to revenue projections.

Specifying Storefront Requirements

Plan your marketing and sales process before you develop your online store. Your input from a marketing perspective is essential to selecting the right storefront package. For instance, you may want promotion codes for special offers, statistics that tabulate sales by category and subcategory, or the ability to sequence the appearance of products on a catalog page.

The Storefront Checklist on the Downloads tab at `www.dummies.com/go/webmarketingfd3e` may help you think through this process.

After you make the strategic business decisions and decide on your budget, you can prioritize the needs that the storefront must meet. If you ask developers to provide a quote, be sure to include your storefront requirements.

Because the ultimate selection might have technical consequences, let your selected developer determine the specific package to implement.

Assess prospective developers for their e-commerce experience and determine which solutions they're capable of implementing. Because of the complexity of some storefronts, developers often specialize in one product line. Your selections of software, host, and developer are interdependent.

Your choices for selling online start with the simplest — a listing on eBay — or an inexpensive template for starter stores with a small catalog. They range in complexity all the way to enterprise-level solutions for stores with thousands of products that integrate with inventory control, accounting, and retail point-of-sale (POS) software. As usual, the more flexible and complicated the store, the higher the price tag and the greater the technical skills required.

Selecting the right type of storefront

The easiest and least expensive storefront solutions offer the least flexibility and fewest features. If you're just starting your business, you can use one of these solutions to establish your store and then invest in a more complex, fully featured, e-commerce solution as you grow. The following sections explain storefront options, sequenced roughly from simple to complex.

No-storefront selling solutions

By far, the least expensive way to start selling online is to use the *no-storefront* selling solution. In other words, forego all the hassle of a website and storefront. Simply sell your products directly at Amazon Marketplace, eBay or other auction sites, or craigslist or other classified sites. You won't have your own domain name, but you can link from a separate, small, HTML website to your listings on most of these.

Social media selling solutions

Unfortunately, you can't sell directly from most social media outlets; they simply aren't set up to support e-commerce. However, you can add a storefront widget to your blog, your Facebook page, or another social networking site to provide your buyers a convenient window into your store. Alternatively, you can link directly to specific products or store pages from your profile or wall, or you can include a link in a post or tweet.

Widgets for selling from social media channels are listed in a table in Bonus Chapter 2 on the Downloads tab of this book's companion website. For more information about social media in general, see Part V of this book.

One-stop store builders

As the e-commerce variant of the template sites I discuss in Chapter 3, *one-stop store builders* (think Web Store in a Box) are generic, somewhat inflexible solutions, but they quickly solve most of your problems — except content. It's true that one-stop store builders help you buy a domain name, build template-based web pages, stock a product catalog, supply the shopping cart and check stand components, provide a payment system through PayPal or a merchant gateway, and host your site. Inexpensive and relatively easy to use, the entry-level versions work best for small stores. Many hosting companies offer these packaged solutions, but they're available also through eBay Stores (`http://pages.ebay.com/storefronts/start.html`), Yahoo! Stores (`http://smallbusiness.yahoo.com/ecommerce/?p=PASSPORT`), and elsewhere.

Specialty store builders

Sometimes called *malls,* specialty store builders have a mission. Usually, a hosting company decides to focus on a particular industry or geographical area and markets e-commerce templates tailored to the needs of that audience. The host then creates a directory of all its shops as a virtual mall and promotes the mall as an online destination. Some high-end malls, such as `www.shop.com`, allow buyers to use a universal shopping cart across all their stores, saving the user time and making purchasing easier.

Watch out for malls that are nothing more than a directory of links. Ask about traffic and promotion for the mall. Also, be cautious if a mall doesn't let you use your own domain name. When that happens, you can't promote the store in search engines; you still need your own website for promotion and branding.

Assembly storefronts

Many companies host storefront solutions on their third-party servers that you link to from your site, wherever it might be hosted. These assembly storefronts have all the essential components for e-commerce, but you might need technical assistance to smooth the link interface. In essence, you create and support two sites that share a similar look and feel. If you order a book at `www.dummies.com`, you see that the URL in the navigation bar changes several times, ending with `https://customer.wiley.com` (a secure server) after you add an item to your cart and request checkout.

Integrated storefronts

Developers integrate commercial, off-the-shelf, or open-source e-commerce components with your existing site to create a seamless online store solution. Depending on its size and other factors, your storefront might be hosted on a dedicated server, your shared server, or the developer's server. This approach is more complex but also more customizable and flexible than others. Translation: Integrated storefronts cost more money. Some developers license and resell the same storefront solution to all their e-commerce customers. This approach is fine, as long as the store does what you need. You have the advantage of working with someone who is expert in that particular package and secure about the future as well. If something happens to your developer, you can find someone else who knows this package.

Custom e-commerce solutions

For maximum flexibility and control, some developers prefer to write their own e-commerce packages. The upside: A custom shopping site that's industry-tailored might be cost-effective for your particular business. The downside: Depending on how many other stores use the software, it might not be fully debugged and might need a lot of testing. If you ever change developers, you're most likely to lose your storefront.

Enterprise e-commerce solutions

Usually expensive, integrated solutions for large, high-end stores interface with retail, point-of-sale (POS) bookkeeping, inventory, manufacturing, customer relationship management (CRM), enterprise resource planning (ERP), and other systems. Choosing a solution at this level generally means you have made a significant investment and are working with a team of technical, merchandising, and content developers. An enterprise solution from UniteU (www.uniteu.com) was assembled to build the storefront for RCC Western Stores (www.rccwesternstores.com), shown in Figure 4-7.

Figure 4-7: The site for RCC Western Stores is an enterprise store solution from UniteU.

Courtesy of RCC Western Stores, Inc. RCCWesternStores.com

Narrowing the options

Unfortunately, no simple way exists to find the best solution for your business from literally hundreds of options. Base your individual business decision on the type of products you sell, the size of your catalog, your budget and development timeframe, the items your competition offers, and the expectations of your target market.

You might also ask the owners of several online stores which solutions they implemented (if the answer isn't visible on the site) or ask your business colleagues. The Storefront Checklist (available for download on the Downloads tab of this book's companion website, at www.dummies.com/go/webmarketingfd3e), lets you compare your wish list of capabilities with the capabilities found in different storefront solutions.

To get started, read some of the reviews for storefront solutions and research other online retailing resources found in Bonus Chapter 2 on the Downloads tab of the book's companion website.

Chapter 5

Marketing with Features on Your Own Website

*H*ave you heard the phrase "Marketing is only part of a business, but all of a business is marketing"? If you look at an organizational chart, you might point to little boxes labeled Sales and Advertising and say, "That's our marketing department." But what about the way a receptionist answers the phone? The appearance of the repair technician who visits a customer's office? The cleanliness of your store? The freshness of your products?

Everything your company does affects customers in some way. Everything contributes to the impression those customers have of your business and affects their expectation of the quality of service they'll receive. That, in a nutshell, is marketing.

The same idea is true of your website: Marketing is only part of your website, but all your website is marketing. In Chapter 2, I identify the three goals your website needs to accomplish to be successful as a business tool:

✔ Attract new visitors.

✔ Keep them on your site.

✔ Bring them back as repeat visitors.

In this chapter, I describe some onsite marketing techniques to help you achieve these goals. I recommend ideas that can increase traffic and win customers. No website needs all of them. The challenge is to select the best ones for your business.

Onsite marketing has a great advantage over other forms of advertising: It's fairly inexpensive, requiring more labor and creativity than cash.

Deciding Which Onsite Marketing Techniques to Use

Alas, I know of no rule that says, "Create a blog or some interactive media only if you have a young audience," or "Women respond more to testimonials." You can implement many combinations of the onsite marketing features described in this chapter to create a site that grabs your audience and pulls them back for future visits.

As you read this chapter, mark the possibilities on your Web Marketing Methods Checklist from Chapter 2. (You can download this handy planning form from the Downloads tab of this book's companion website at `www. dummies.com/go/webmarketing3e`.)

By the time you complete your online marketing plan, you'll have a good feeling for several techniques to retain as the most appropriate for your site, staff, and budget. It's too expensive to do them all!

Always update your site to keep its content fresh. Next, incorporate these three cost-effective options: internal banners, testimonials, and a social sharing tool. Then select no more than one or two of the other techniques described in this chapter for your initial site launch or upgrade.

Follow the KISS maxim (Keep It Simple, Stupid) whenever you do anything on the web or with social media. You can always note options to implement downstream in Phase 2, 3, or 12 of your web development plan. When you're choosing these initial, onsite marketing techniques, consider these factors:

- ✔ What you're trying to accomplish with your site
- ✔ Your target market
- ✔ How much money you've budgeted for site development
- ✔ Your server configuration
- ✔ Your developer's abilities
- ✔ How much time you have before site launch

✔ How much time you have to maintain the activity

✔ The number of staff available to do maintenance

✔ Your interest in the technique

✔ The potential payoff to the bottom line

 Whichever techniques you select, be sure to discuss them with your web developer. This task is essential for accurately estimating the price and for scheduling work on your site. Even if you don't implement special features all at once, your developer needs to know what you're considering for the future. In some cases, a developer can make provisions so that it's easy to add a feature downstream. Otherwise, you might face major programming costs to integrate a feature that wasn't planned for.

Freshening Your Content

Adding fresh content is the single must-do task in this chapter. If you visit a website marked *Last Updated June 6, 2007,* you're likely to immediately take off for another site. Why waste your valuable time looking at old, irrelevant content when you can find dozens, if not hundreds, of other, more recent websites? Even if you're looking at a simple, information-only site whose URL you entered from a business card, you can't be sure that the hours of operation or location are still correct. If you think that you still need to call the company for confirmation, you're more likely to visit another website instead.

Updated content impresses customers and prospects. It demonstrates your commitment to your website, and even more so, your respect for customers' time. As such, an updated site helps attract new customers in those first crucial seconds and brings them back for repeat visits.

 Some search engines consider updated content when ranking your site in search results. The more often a site is updated, the more relevant search engines consider it to be. As you discover in Chapter 7, you need every advantage in the competitive world of search engine ranking.

Establishing an update schedule

Your content update schedule depends on the nature of your site, as shown in the Sample Update Schedule in Table 5-1. At the very least, review all site content at least once a year, and budget a complete site overhaul every few years. During that time, viewers' expectations of a contemporary site change as technology improves and graphics styles evolve.

Table 5-1	Sample Update Schedule
Frequency	*Task*
Every three to five years	Redesign site and add new content and features
Annually	Review and update all content and photos as needed
Monthly	Update at least one page of the site with news and seasonal content
Weekly	Offer new products and special promotions
Daily	Have the date change automatically
As needed	Maintain product inventory, especially price changes, deletions, and back orders

Updating some content at least once a month is much better for search engines and is achievable for most businesses. The more frequently you update your site with changing content, the more you need easy, inexpensive access to an onsite blog, a content management system, a storefront administration package, or software such as EasyWebContent or Adobe's Contribute, as I discuss in Chapter 3.

Paying a developer for updates can get expensive, although some developers sell a hosting package that includes monthly update services. As a last resort, someone in-house who is already familiar with HTML or various web publishing software tools can make changes to your site and upload them via File Transfer Protocol (FTP).

Whatever the frequency of updates, decide who is responsible for making them and who will confirm that they're complete. In other words, plan! I have yet to see a site that doesn't need updating.

Determining what content to update

You can use a simple rule to decide which parts of your site to update: anything and everything! There's no need to develop a case of writer's block. Even small changes can keep your site current — look at these elements, for example:

- ✔ The **home page** might need changes, perhaps because you've introduced a new product or want to promote a special offer.

- ✔ The **About Us page** might need to reflect changes in staffing. Perhaps you have updated summer hours, a new location, or new e-mail addresses for Contact Us.

- ✔ **Product pages** might need to be amended with price changes, additions, or deletions.

- ✔ Your **event calendar** may need updating with classes, trunk shows, trade shows, training schedules, or other events.

- ✔ If you have a **media page,** you might want to add new press releases, newsletters, or mentions in other media.

Remember that your viewers are interested in what affects them, not what's important to you. Although you might be quite proud of your latest contract, that news probably doesn't belong on your home page unless your target audience consists of investors or business press.

Some people create a What's New page specifically to collect all the changes between site updates. What's New pages are helpful when you have a constant stream of changing news, but you get more search engine mileage by changing multiple pages on your site. For example, PE Central, a site for health and physical education, posts new information weekly or monthly in multiple categories on different pages of its site. In Figure 5-1, it displays its new content in an easy-to-find format. A link labeled What's New on PEC appears on the home page.

Figure 5-1:
PE Central offers, in one location, links to multiple categories of newly updated content.

Courtesy of PE Central (pecentral.org)

Your developer can create a linkable, changing headline that is fast and easy for you to modify with your latest news or product promotion. Drawing a blank? Try some of these ideas:

- New products and services

- Seasonal specials or page appearance, especially for retail

- Sales and special offers

- Product modifications or deletions

- Price changes

- Trade shows where you're exhibiting, especially if you have entrance passes for the show floor

- Planned speeches, signings, performances, or other public appearances where you can meet customers

- New distributors or retail outlets where customers can shop

- A link to a schedule of classes or activities

- Changes in hours, phone numbers, addresses, location, maps

- Copies of press releases, newsletters, and mentions in other media

- Company news, such as new contracts or installations

- A link to a calendar of events that you can update easily, with such software as CalendarScript (`www.calendarscript.com`)

Using content that updates automatically

One way to update content quickly is to use an automated service that feeds your site such information as the date, the weather, or news and stock tickers. You can also find sites that provide daily word-of-the-day entries, jokes, or quotations!

Automated updates are a reasonable option for businesses with information-only sites that remain fairly static, as long as the content is relevant to the purpose of your site and appropriate for your audience. For instance, a stockbroker might want to include a stock ticker, but a joke of the day can be quite inappropriate. Be cautious about using religious or political quotation services unless you're sure your audience won't be offended. Automated updates might help with your search engine ranking, but they're no substitute for reviewing your own content regularly.

Some content services are free, some require that you advertise a link back to the source, and others charge a monthly rate for their services. Your developer can place a date, stock ticker, or weather script directly into a server-side include (SSI) or footer so that it appears on every page. Rather than use scripts, you can now use Real Simple Syndication (RSS) feeds to provide news or weather or another type of information to your site.

In Bonus Chapter 2 on the Downloads tab at the book's companion website, look for the table called "Sample Sources for Automated Content Updates." It lists a few of the many sources for scripts (code) that your developer can insert on your site. Sometimes these scripts are simple links to a third-party site; sometimes they require inserting a small piece of code. You can find many other scripts of this type by simply entering *scripts for* (fill in whatever type you're looking for) in your favorite search engine.

Don't use a visible, automated page counter on your website. Although a page counter may count as a content update for search engine purposes, it can provide negative information unintentionally. If viewers stumble across a counter that reads *58 visits since 2006,* for example, they might wonder why they should bother reading the page. The page counter becomes a "reverse testimonial," in effect bad-mouthing your site. In Chapter 6 you find out about "invisible" page counters and other options for web statistics to determine the number of visitors to your site.

Using Onsite Blogs and Wikis

Blogs (we*b logs*) have supplanted message boards as the preferred technique for discussions that allow people to read and comment at different times. A *blog* is a form of online journal that allows you to wax eloquently (or tongue-tied) about a subject in your field and solicit suggestions or comments from responsive readers. Unlike message boards, blogs look like web pages, complete with links, graphics, sound, and video.

Once seen as a quick-and-easy alternative for individuals to publish online without needing a domain name or an HTML education, blogs were quickly adopted for use as online diaries. Writers on media and political sites use blogs to comment (without encountering the limit of column inches of print media) and to engage in dialogue with their readers. Of course, on these advertising-supported sites, controversial blogs that generate page views also generate ad revenues from additional eyeballs.

On business, financial, retail, and professional service sites, a blog is something of a chameleon. In addition to the community-building function of a message board, a blog might take on characteristics of an online e-zine or newsletter. You can use yours as an opportunity to educate your prospects on different aspects of your business or product while learning about their questions and concerns. For example, the business blog from Heronswood Nursery (www.heronswoodvoice.com) links to its parent site at www.heronswood.com. By using this approach, the blog may help improve the search engine ranking for the main site.

Depending on your marketing strategy, you might prefer to host your blog elsewhere, such as `www.blogger.com`, with its own domain name, so that links to your primary site come from another source. Google, in particular, ranks inbound links from blogs highly. Alternatively, you can host your blog elsewhere, but give it a subdomain name (*yourblog.yoursite*.com) and maintain graphical consistency.

Business marketers have discovered that an onsite blog allows creative opportunities to

- ✔ Attract and retain traffic on a site
- ✔ Obtain positive and negative feedback from customers
- ✔ Generate links to other pages on the website
- ✔ Announce new products and test price points
- ✔ Build brand awareness
- ✔ Recruit beta testers
- ✔ Seed product promotions
- ✔ Identify opinion setters

Like other forms of community building, blogs take lots of time. You need to post at least once a week to keep a blog lively and to encourage feedback, so having a blog is easier if you like to write. Chapter 14 contains more about blogs, especially using other people's blogs as marketing tools.

Blogs can bite! Although blogs might be a great way to position yourself as an expert, they have a way of producing challenging feedback. You might want to monitor how people respond to your postings, but don't become defensive if your customers — perhaps your competitors — make negative comments online. Some companies, such as Comcast, now monitor not only their own blogs but also other blogs, message boards, and websites for customer complaints to try to defuse difficult situations and reduce bad publicity.

Wikis are related to blogs, but instead of one primary writer waiting for other people to respond, wikis make everyone a writer. They allow multiple users to add, delete, and edit each other's web content quickly without having much technical knowledge. Wikis are especially suited for collaborative writing. For example, see the SmallBusiness.com wiki, a free, editable sourcebook with articles on a variety of business-related topics, shown in Figure 5-2.

The Wikipedia free encyclopedia is a prime example of group content that reflects many views — even some that have turned out to be wrong or malicious.

To see some sources for blog and wiki software, go to Bonus Chapter 2 on the Downloads tab at the book's companion website.

Figure 5-2:
The Small
Business.
com wiki
is a free,
editable
resource
guide.

Building Communities

As human beings, we not only need but also want to communicate with one
another. The web offers a seemingly endless stream of techniques to do just
that — blogs, wikis, chat rooms, message boards, social networking, and
more. Any technique that allows users to interact with one another or to generate content is sometimes designated *social media.*

Virtual online communities establish a give-and-take exchange with and
among viewers who share a specific interest. Communities have sprung up
on almost every subject, from movie star fan sites to do-it-yourself advice
and from computer technical support to online investing. Health care information sites, among the most frequent targets of online searches, are also
some of the most likely places to find online communities.

Make a reality check before you start: Do you have the long-term interest to
keep the community ball rolling? Does the content of the community fit well
into the purpose of your site? Does the community feed into your business
goals, either directly or indirectly?

Online communities may occur *synchronously* (where many people at a time can be online) via chat rooms, wikis, or instant messaging, or *asynchronously* (where participants post messages at different times) via message boards, blogs, or guest books.

Traditional community building

Ideas for community building are limited only by your imagination. For example, people like to be asked their opinions and then return to see the results of a poll or survey. You can easily add a bit of code from a third-party provider to conduct a simple poll ("Who do you think will win the Oscars?") or a survey of attitudes toward any topic of interest to your audience.

Other, rather old-fashioned, techniques from early websites have been recycled for community-building uses. *Message boards* — sometimes, *bulletin boards, discussion boards,* or *forums* — allow asynchronous communication on your site. Bulletin boards, like the one shown in Figure 5-3 from Ancestry. com (`http://boards.ancestry.com/topics.software/mb.ashx`), were one of the earliest uses of the Internet, predating the development of the World Wide Web. The computer scientists working on the Internet created these boards to encourage the open discussion of technical issues.

Figure 5-3: Ancestry. com offers multiple message boards within the Genealogy Software category.

Board	Threads	Messages	Last Post
General	678	2458	1 Apr 2011 1:48PM GMT
Agest	1	1	27 Nov 2009
Ancestry Family Tree	236	919	27 Mar 2011
Brother's Keeper Software	60	165	1 Nov 2010
Cumberland Family Tree [CFT]	8	24	31 Jan 2011
Family Historian	2	4	28 Nov 2010

Courtesy of Ancestry.com

You can use message board software to host one discussion topic or many, allow limited or unlimited participation, and select whether the boards are *moderated* (someone reviews the posts to filter them for propriety) or *unmoderated* (a posting free-for-all).

Guest book software — a variant of an unmoderated message board — was previously used to register visitors to a website and perhaps to gather e-mail addresses. With these functions replaced by more advanced features, guest books are now used to share communal experiences, to solicit feedback from event participants, to collect congratulations on a wedding, or even to convey words of sympathy.

Chat room software operates in a similar manner, except that multiple participants can be online simultaneously. Managing real-time chats can be more challenging; often, an expert handles the content response, and a separate moderator manages and edits the question flow.

Creating your own social network onsite

Supporting a social network on your website is one of the most reliable ways for you to ensure that visitors return to your site again and again. These online communities may increase traffic, time onsite, sales, and return on investment (ROI). You might find that you need to promote the social networking feature itself online and off to generate traffic and recruit members until you reach a self-sustaining, critical mass of participants.

Keep in mind that any online community requires a commitment of time, people, and attention to keep it from degrading. Participants need skill and judgment to monitor messages, correct technical inaccuracies, remove offensive language before it posts, avoid liability, keep an eye out for online stalkers in a social network, write content for a blog, and recruit participants. Social networks are such a sponge for energy that some, such as YouTube (www.youtube.com), ask members of the community to monitor each other and notify the administrator of objectionable postings.

If you don't have time to oversee a social network, you're probably better off selecting other methods of onsite promotion. The size of the community, the number of participants, and the nature of the topic determine the amount of time required and the level of liability exposure you incur. On medical topics in particular, consult your attorney for disclaimer language to include on the site.

As always, the choice of software depends on your audience, how your audience will use the site, and your developer's technical assessment of the best software for your needs. Your developer can also explore the alternative of linking to a third-party site that provides these services.

Check out Bonus Chapter 2 on the Downloads tab of the book's companion website for some sources for building online communities on your website.

Tooting Your Own Horn

Your website is no place to be shy! Because you have only one chance to make a first impression, you have to make it a good one. Consider using tried-and-true techniques on your site for shameless self-promotion: advertising (internal banners), testimonials, reviews, and awards. These tools can help you increase the time that people spend on your site.

Displaying internal banners

You know those ubiquitous banner ads that litter the web? (I cover them in detail in Chapter 12.) You can take advantage of similar banners within your own site. Rather than have paid advertising that links to someone else's site, however, link your internal banners to pages within your own site. Driving viewers to additional pages increases the time they spend on your site and the likelihood that they'll remember your business or buy your product.

Although special features on your site should be easily accessible by way of navigation, the user's eye usually isn't attracted to the navigation. In addition, grab viewers' attention with an eye-catching banner that promotes a monthly special, opens the newsletter sign-up page, or accesses a community-building page. Internal banners are a no-brainer for onsite marketing, but plan them as part of the overall site layout and graphical design.

Collecting testimonials and validations

Offline testimonials reassure prospects about the quality of the product or service you offer. Testimonials can come from an objective press rating, a celebrity, experts in the field, or other customers. Collect testimonials from satisfied customers and media mentions at all times, not just while you're working on site content. (The testimonial from your mother doesn't count. Sorry.) These recommendations are more no-brainers. You spend some effort — but no cost — to collect them initially and to freshen them over time.

If you have a business-to-business (B2B) site, get permission from your customers before using their names, titles, and company names. Some firms don't permit their names or their employees' names to be used in endorsements; you don't want to risk losing their trade. Sometimes, you can create the same effect by using a job title and a description, such as *Director of Engineering,*

Fortune 500 Company. The same principle applies if you have a recognizable celebrity or expert whose name carries cachet with prospective customers: Get permission first. The National Mail Order Association has a sample permission form at `www.nmoa.org/articles/dmnews/usingtestimonials.htm`, or you can simply search for *permissions testimonial* at your favorite search engine.

Although the situation is less sensitive with "ordinary" customers, you're still better off requesting permission. If you can't locate the source, you can use a first name and last initial, or vice versa, and their city or state: *J Zimmerman, Albuquerque, NM,* or *Jan Z, Albuquerque, NM,* for example. If your customer comes from a small town where he might be recognized or has an unusual name, use only his name or only his state or country (for example, *P Tchaikovsky, Russia*). However, the less specific the attribution, the less potent the testimonial.

The person's location has value, especially if you want to communicate to prospects that your product has "reach," or that you've been able to satisfy customers from places like the one where they live.

There's no point in pasting a long list of testimonials on a single web page — no one will read them! Instead, try these suggestions for getting the most from this onsite marketing technique:

- ✔ **Scatter the testimonials on multiple pages throughout the site.**

- ✔ **Judiciously select short phrases or single sentences that are relevant to the content of a particular page.** In a case where web media differs from print, an online testimonial carries more punch when it's short and to the point.

- ✔ **Break a long testimonial into several endorsements on different pages of the site.**

- ✔ **Rotate testimonials as part of your content update.** You can rotate the text manually or ask your developer to set up a quote database that posts a different testimonial every day or every time your site is accessed. Testimonials can be effective on almost any site, as long as you don't overuse them.

Figure 5-4 shows how Paragon 360 (`www.paragon360.com`), a developer of professional performance venues and multimedia productions, features client testimonials in the header graphic on each page of its site, choosing a different quote and image for every section.

One other type of endorsement helps build trust in your site for online transactions. If you're a member of the Better Business Bureau (`www.bbbonline.org`), TRUSTe (`www.truste.com`) for privacy, or a well-established trade association that vouches for its members, display their seals prominently on your site. These memberships generally require a fee and a site analysis, but they might give you a competitive edge in the online world.

Figure 5-4:
The site for
Paragon
360 uses
a different
testimonial
for every
section of
its site.

Incorporating Freebies and Fun

The onsite marketing techniques in this section are designed primarily to increase time onsite, to encourage repeat visits, and to increase your ROI. To use these techniques effectively, you need to publicize their existence on web clearinghouses with master lists of links to coupons, free offers, games, and contests.

Go to Bonus Chapter 2 on the Downloads tab of the companion website to find a table with software sources and promotional sites for items in this category.

Coupons and discounts

Coupons and discounts work offline and online, particularly when your target audience has a bargain orientation — but even high-end audiences like to believe that they're getting a deal. Although most coupons are never even used, they improve branding and name recognition. The online execution of a discount occurs with a promotion code that users enter during the checkout process on your website, whereas a coupon may be printed for use at your own, or another, bricks-and-mortar store. You need to determine how the cost of these discounts will affect your gross revenue and the average dollar value of a sale.

Not all shopping carts can accept all forms of discounts. You must ask your developer what your software can handle before you establish your discount plan. For example, some sites can discount a total price by a percentage, but can't discount a specific product or by a flat dollar amount. Some can't tie together two purchases to execute a complex instruction, such as *Buy one at full price and get the second at half off.* Some carts can't handle promotion codes at all.

Free offers

Free is marketing's four-letter word. (I talk about the power of *free* in Chapter 3 as well.) You can tie a free offer to another purchase, such as a two-for-one deal, or to a product that's paired with a purchase, such as *Free socks when you buy shoes* or *Buy one shirt and get a second free.* Or, *free* can mean a separate promotional item shipped as a reward for taking an action, such as *Free bracelet when you sign up for our jewelry newsletter.*

Include in your marketing budget the cost of promotional goods and their differential shipping expenses.

Be careful! Dockers was burned by its ad for a free pair of pants during the 2010 Super Bowl. Within seconds, responses overwhelmed the website, which barred incoming traffic or produced server errors. Irritated visitors quickly tweeted their frustration or posted angry messages on Facebook. For want of adequate web infrastructure, an expensive advertisement was lost. You should also check with your shipping department to make sure that it can package and track the shipping of promotional items.

Games and contests

Online games and contests often carry an age or gender appeal (or both). The right game matched to the right audience can result in significant traffic to your site and many repeat visits. For this strategy to pay off beyond traffic, you might want to sell advertising on your site or provide another business rationale for the game. It also helps to tie the award, if any, to the audience. Many games don't include prizes, but most contests do. Some contests are games of skill (for example, trivia or interactive contests); others, such as sweepstakes or drawings, are simple matters of luck.

Whenever you include a contest or sweepstakes on your site, be sure to include a detailed page of rules and legal disclaimers. Consult your attorney if you have questions; some states have strict rules.

Letting Others Do the Talking

The best and cheapest form of advertising is word of mouth. A product — or a website — can have no stronger recommendation than the approval of a trusted friend. Fortunately, the web now offers such word-of-web opportunities as social sharing options and product review functions.

Providing share options

Old-fashioned "Tell a Friend" scripts allow site visitors to e-mail others a link to your site. The message arrives from the sender's e-mail address, not yours, making recipients more likely to open it. Best of all, Tell a Friend is another no-brainer for onsite marketing. It's cost-effective and generally low maintenance unless you're offering a reward. Depending on your site, you might want to rename the feature according to your target audience: Tell a Colleague, Tell a Bride, or Tell a Hiker, for example. Tell a Friend functionality has now mostly been replaced by social sharing functionality, of which e-mail is only one of many choices. A Share button, such as the one from New Mexico Creates shown in Figure 5-5, allows users to quickly recommend your site on their own accounts on multiple social networking sites, such as Facebook or Twitter, or submit it to shared bookmarking sites such as delicious (`www.delicious.com`) or StumbleUpon (`www.stumbleupon.com`). Most Share widgets allow you to select the options you want to offer; sometimes, you can include e-mail, print, or bookmark opportunities. In most cases, limit users to half a dozen visible choices to avoid overwhelming them; they can always click the button to view more.

Many web hosting and site template companies, as well as third-party providers and individual social networking sites, offer free Social Sharing buttons. Select your Share button from a provider that offers analytics.

For a list of a few sites that offer these buttons for free, go to Bonus Chapter 2 on the Downloads tab of the book's companion website.

Adding share functionality on almost every website is appropriate as a method of driving additional traffic with a recommendation from an extremely well-targeted audience of similar viewers. Share functionality is the simplest online equivalent of word-of-mouth. To improve the number of referrals, consider adding a minor incentive or a chance to win a drawing for every friend someone notifies. To do this, the script must include a thank-you or confirmation message following its use so that you can track the action.

Figure 5-5: New Mexico Creates invites visitors to share each of its web pages with an expandable Share button.

Share button

Courtesy of www.newmexicocreates.org

If you want something more elaborate, consider the Social Notes widget from `www.strongmail.com/products/social-media-marketing/social notes`, which facilitates the sharing of product referrals with a message, directly from your e-commerce site.

Soliciting product reviews

Some people prefer the illusion that they make rational purchasing decisions rather than emotional ones. For these buyers, product reviews from a third party offer a perceived objective rating. Sometimes, you can attract reviews by submitting your products or services to magazines, trade journals, or other press outlets. Or, you can include your site for a fee on comparison shopping engines such as Bizrate (`www.bizrate.com`) to solicit reviews. (See Chapter 7 for more information on shopping search engines.)

If you're confident in your products, open your site to ratings from customers with a *Review this product* link. Sites such as Hot Scripts offer free rating scripts for your site. Go to `www.hotscripts.com/php/scripts_and_programs/reviews_and_ratings/index.html` for more information. If you solicit ratings from customers, don't post only the good ones. When all reviews are uniformly excellent, viewers don't trust them. Many sites that offer product reviews are distributors, rather than creators, so they face no risk. For example, users rate movies on Netflix (www.netflix.com), and they can rate or review absolutely anything on Amazon. These large sites compile the results of reviews, as well as what other people buy, to recommend new purchases based on products a viewer has already bought.

A site that uses many of these techniques is shown in Figure 5-6 and described in the nearby sidebar, "Repeat traffic is always in style."

Schedule time to check third-party sites that include professional reviews or user ratings to see how your business ranks on sites such as CNET (www.cnet.com), Epinions (www.epinions.com), or Shopping.com (www.shopping.com).

Figure 5-6:
365 Days of Style incorporates many features designed to build repeat traffic.

Courtesy of 365DaysofStyle.com

Repeat traffic is always in style

Heather Claus, the self-described Grand High Poohbah of 365 Days of Style, feeds her passion with her website, `365daysofstyle.com`. The site takes to heart many of the concepts in this chapter to build repeat traffic. She launched the site in July 2010 as an online enterprise devoted to personal style. The site targets women experiencing a life change, new mothers, empty nesters, and menopausal women who feel that they may have lost their personal style, panache, or feeling of attractiveness.

Claus quickly built a loyal following with rapidly changing content, giveaways and contests, and plenty of opportunity for user participation.

The site already draws 13,000 unique visitors every month, with an average page view per visit of 6.8 and returns of 7.4 times per month. To build repeat traffic, 365 Days of Style features daily and weekly content updates, user ratings, contests, and more. The most popular section, Style Question of the Week, collects opinions from more than 180 style experts. That section of the site is now 52 percent more popular than the rest of the site averaged. "Everything I do is with an eye towards showing women that there are as many different ways to express style as

there are women. I not only encourage differing opinions — I focus on them, because it is the variety of our beauty and personalities that really drives style (as opposed to fashion)."

To gauge content popularity, Claus watches overall traffic, pages per view, percentage of repeat-to-new visitors, and number of responses. "I get quite a few direct e-mails about that section of the site [Style Question], asking questions and showing interest."

For marketing, Claus relies on Facebook, Twitter, networking with style experts, commenting on other style blogs, and generally trying to be as generous as possible with information.

"If you want people to come back, give them a reason!" Claus insists. "First, be awesome. Next, let them know your content changes. Use dynamic content in your sidebars (widget areas on WordPress sites), [and] post to Twitter and Facebook, or wherever your visitors hang out. Don't make them come to see you to decide if they should come to see you! And last, but not least, change the look and feel of the site every now and again."

Reaching out to your customers

Feedback from your customers and prospects keeps your site, and your business, on track. Feedback helps you identify problems that need to be fixed immediately and garner ideas for new products, features, and services. I guarantee that listening beats apologizing any day! Let your customers know about your thoughtful changes by way of e-mail newsletters or on your site. Some companies go even further than personalizing items, encouraging their customers to submit, and sometimes vote on, product designs for everything from shoes (`www.fluevog.com/files_2/os-1.html`) to soda labels (`www.myjones.com`) and T-shirts (`http://threadless.com/submissions`).

Your customers and prospects are the best experts at closing the marketing circle! You have lots of ways, online and off, to let your customers do the talking:

- ✔ Add a survey to your website.
- ✔ Ask viewers what they think on every page with a Feedback tab like the one at Get Satisfaction (`http://getsatisfaction.com`). Clicking the Feedback tab opens a dialog box that can contain comments, ideas, or complaints. A slightly different approach, from HTML Comment Box (`htmlcommentbox.com`), posts a balloon-style note on the site.
- ✔ Review comments and suggestions about your site that are sent to the webmaster.
- ✔ Tally customer service requests for products or problems with order fulfillment.
- ✔ Drop in to your blog, message board, or chat room at random times to see what's happening.
- ✔ Make it easy for customers to send you new product ideas or comments on current offerings.
- ✔ If you allow reviews on your own site, read them.

Feedback can be viral, too, especially the negative kind. After your problems are posted on the web, especially via social media, you're exposed forever. Be proactive.

Chapter 6

Improving Results with Analytics

*W*eb analytics is the art of using traffic and sales statistics to understand user behavior and improve the performance of your site. In the best of all possible worlds, analytics is part of a continuous spiral of feedback and quality improvement.

Before getting mired in the details of web analytics, think about your most critical statistics — your financial reports! If you have a business site, the most important number to know is whether the site is providing a return on your investment. If you aren't making a profit, it doesn't matter whether you have a fantastic amount of traffic, a soaring conversion rate, or revenue through the roof.

In this chapter, I discuss the importance of measuring statistical results, which the web marketing world calls *analytics,* for your business, your website, your online store, and social media channels.

Preparing Financial Reports to Track Web Results

As part of planning your site, talk to your bookkeeper or accountant. Although this conversation is obviously critical for a site that sells online, it's equally important for tracking costs on a nonsales site. Unless you have a small, strictly informational site, ask your accountant to

✔ **Set up your website as a separate job in your accounting software.** You can then track costs (and revenue, if appropriate) attributable to the site. In other words, operate your site financially as though you're opening a new, bricks-and-mortar location and need to know how it performs. Your website is, indeed, a new cost center and — with some hard work and luck — a new profit center.

✔ **Segregate online advertising expenses from other marketing and advertising costs in a unique cost category.** If you sell online, separate online shipping and handling costs from offline shipping and from product revenue. Track whether you're losing money on shipping, one of the most common problems e-tailers (retail businesses that sell online) have.

✔ **Decide how to allocate labor, benefits, and overhead costs to your website.** Although cost of goods might be obvious, cost of sales is not.

✔ **Determine how development costs will be amortized over a specified time frame.** If you're having trouble calculating your return on investment (ROI), remember that bookkeepers and accountants compute this amount for their entertainment.

✔ **Become familiar with your site goals and objectives, help measure financial results, and prepare a custom report monthly or quarterly.** Request more frequent reports as revenue rises or if you need more detailed tracking.

✔ **Review your web and store statistics software to see which data should be fed into the accounting system.** If you already have an integrated inventory, point-of-sale (POS), and accounting system, this task might be semiautomatic.

Your financial reports are worth the effort only if you use them. Watch your profit number like a hawk to ensure that your projections are on track — or as an early warning sign that revenues and expenses are getting out of hand. Act as soon as you identify a problem, because it won't solve itself.

Now, and only now, are you ready to use web analytics to improve your marketing and your website.

Tracking Website Activity

The basic principle "You can't manage what you don't measure" applies doubly to websites. You must know whether your website or other elements of your web presence are losing or gaining traffic; whether visitors boogie away after less than a minute; or whether anyone is bothering to call, e-mail, or buy. Otherwise, you have no clue what problem you need to solve, let alone how to solve it.

Fortunately, computers excel at counting. In fact, that's what they do best. All sites need traffic statistics; if you sell online, you also need sales statistics. Unless you have a huge site, pay attention to only a few key statistics, as detailed in the later section, "Which statistics to fret over."

The Google Analytics dashboard in Figure 6-1 shows an example of the types of statistics you can gather for both your website and social media pages.

You can find more information about web analytics from the list of information resources for web analytics in Bonus Chapter 2 on the Downloads tab at www.dummies.com/go/webmarketingfd3e.

Ask your developer or web host which statistical packages are offered for your site. Unless you have a fairly large site or need real-time data, one of the many free statistical alternatives, such as Google Analytics, should work well. Review your choices to select the best fit for your needs. Do the same thing with sales analytics (sometimes called *store statistics*), which usually are bundled with store builder or shopping cart software. If your developer or web host tells you that statistics aren't available or that you don't need them, find another developer, host, or storefront package.

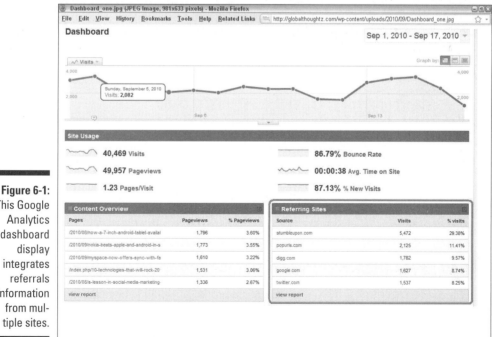

Figure 6-1:
This Google Analytics dashboard display integrates referrals information from multiple sites.

Courtesy of Buzzom.com

A list of free statistical packages is included in Bonus Chapter 2 on the Downloads tab of the book's companion website.

Identifying Which Parameters to Measure

When you read articles about web analytics, you might see the term *key performance indicator* (KPI). KPIs differ slightly for every business and website. A lead generation site and a retail site both care about the most important statistic: conversion rate. However, requests for a quote might be a KPI for a B2B lead generation site. For a retailer, number and average value per sale are more important. Because you calculate the conversion rate, you must decide which factors are essential to measure.

Ignore hits. A *hit* is any file that's downloaded as part of a web page. In other words, every image is a hit; every text file is a hit. Hit rates usually overstate the number of visits to a site by a factor of 10 or 12. As I mention in Chapter 5, never put a visible hit rate or visitor counter on your site.

The following three sections address some general web statistics that are worth attention but might not apply to your business. After you decide which web statistics truly matter, monitor whichever ones best support your needs.

Which statistics to fret over

Of the many, many statistics that are available, the following key parameters provide valuable information for every business. Compare them by month or week, depending on the statistical package you use. Sites with heavy traffic justify daily, or even hourly, reviews.

Some packages might use slightly different terms but measure the same elements. (These definitions apply to whichever time frame you choose.) This list describes the key statistics to track:

- ✔ **Visits:** The number of distinct *user sessions* that take place; in other words, the number of times your website is viewed. It's your total traffic to the site. Different stat packages may define a new visit after different frames; many users go back and forth among websites several times. Most statistical packages delete visits made by search engine spiders or robots because these devices artificially inflate the number of visits.

- ✔ **Unique visitors:** The number of user sessions from different computers. (Stats can track users' IP addresses but not who's sitting at the machine.) This number is smaller than the total number of visits; the difference represents repeat visits, which are extremely valuable. To assess your success in drawing people back to your site, you might want to track repeat visits as a percentage of all visits.

- ✔ **Page views:** The total number of distinct web pages downloaded — that is, displayed on the screen.

- ✔ **Page views per visit:** The number of pages shown divided by the total number of visits. The more pages viewed, the longer the user is on the site and the *stickier* your site is. If more than half your visitors leave before viewing two pages, you have a problem capturing viewers' attention and interest. This key parameter correlates roughly to time onsite. Time measurement can be misleading, however, because it doesn't consider what happens if people leave a browser window open when they go to lunch or leave at the end of the day.

- ✔ **URLs viewed:** The number of times each individual page of your site is viewed (downloaded). It's helpful to know not only which pages are popular but also which ones aren't. The latter might be caused by lack of interest or perhaps a lack of contextual links or calls to action that pull someone to that page. This statistic is handy to count thank-you pages for contact forms or other pages that are part of your conversion equation.

- ✔ **Referrers:** The websites or pages that generated links to your site. Some statistical packages include links between onsite pages in this list. If you have an active, inbound link campaign, you can easily see which links are driving traffic your way. You might also discover links from previously unknown sources. To distinguish links from multiple online ads in your analytics, you can always insert /?src=X at the end of the destination URL, where X represents the source of the ad or any other distinguishing feature you want to track.

- ✔ **Search engines:** Which search engines generated links to your site based on appearance in natural search results.

- ✔ **Conversion rate:** A number that's calculated as a percentage. The denominator is total visits; you decide on the numerator, whether it's number of sales, number of contact forms, e-mails or calls generated from the site, or newsletter subscribers, for example.

Unless you have quite a large site, monitoring statistics monthly or quarterly is usually sufficient. You might check more often when you first open your site and whenever you initiate a specific web marketing activity.

Most statistical packages have an administrative setup, allowing your programmer to change the default values for certain statistics. If you don't see what you want, ask! For instance, some packages display the page views for only the 25 most visited URLs. If you have a larger site, set that parameter to display the results for all your pages.

Which statistics to scan casually

The following statistics are less critical than the ones listed in the preceding section but still helpful when you make decisions about your marketing program, site development, or newsletter timing:

- ✔ **Time of day:** The time of day that people visit lets you know whether they're visiting from work (where they usually have faster Internet access) or from home. Watch for a bulge around lunchtime, which is often a good time to release a newsletter. Unless you're publicizing your site locally only, your hours of use extend across four time zones. If you're marketing internationally, use spreads out over time accordingly.

- ✔ **Day of week:** The days of the week also let you know patterns of use, from work or home. Anecdotal evidence shows shoppers browsing from home on weekends and buying on Monday from work. Compare your own patterns of traffic versus sales.

- ✔ **Browser and operating system:** Most statistical packages can identify browser, version, and operating system. This information is valuable during development because you can infer certain characteristics of your user base: The more current these items, the more likely your users also have faster access and higher-resolution monitors. Let this information guide the features you include on your site and the size screen for which your site is optimized.

- ✔ **Length of visit:** Some analytics packages offer length or duration of visit in minutes and seconds (for a sample display). Set a goal to have more than half your visitors stay longer than 30 seconds.

- ✔ **Search string:** Lists of words or phrases that users actually entered into search engines to find your site. If these strings aren't already in your keyword list, add them. You might also want to use them in your keyword list for pay per click ads. Some advanced packages analyze search strings by search engine. Different people use different search engines, and they often use different words or phrases.

- ✔ **Country:** Whether you're already shipping internationally or thinking about it, watch the country statistics. They can indicate either your success in penetrating another market or wherever interest exists.

✔ **Host or site:** This list of host IP addresses of visitors to your site is some-times sorted by state. If you're curious about an address that seems to generate numerous visits, you can find out to whom it belongs. Try click-ing its IP address, copying it into the Address bar of your browser, or submitting it to the Whois database at `www.networksolutions.com/whois/index.jsp` to see who owns it. This data is sometimes used to track someone hacking your site.

✔ **Entry page:** Some packages display how users first arrived at your site. Although your home page is almost always the most frequently used entry page, users might enter on other pages: from a bookmark; from a link provided by someone else; by clicking another URL that shows up in natural search engine results; by clicking a landing page URL in an ad; or by entering a promotion-specific URL that you created. The entry page is a quick way to track entries from offline ads.

✔ **Exit page:** The last page that users view can provide insight into when they've "had enough." In some cases, the exit page is a thank-you.

Take absolute numbers for any statistic with a grain — make that an entire shaker — of salt. Although efforts are made to standardize the meaning of statistical terms, for now they're still efforts. For example, does a new visitor session start after someone has logged off for 24 minutes or 24 hours? Relative numbers are more meaningful. Is your traffic growing or shrinking? Is your conversion rate increasing or decreasing?

To minimize attention on absolute values, focus on ratios or percentages. Suppose that 10 percent of a small number of viewers converted before you conduct a sales-focused ad campaign, compared to only 5 percent of a larger number of viewers afterward — what does that tell you? (It might indicate that your ad wasn't directed tightly on your target market.)

Even if an analytics package lets you set a date range, it may display only 12 consecutive months of data. It doesn't let you review stats for a more useful, 13-month window. This limitation is unfortunate because most sites — even B2B — experience cyclic traffic, especially during the summer and around holidays. For retailers, same-store sales comparing May 2011 to May 2012, for example, are critical. If your stat package has this limitation, download and back up statistics for comparison on your own. You can feed the data into a graphical display by using spreadsheet software.

Some statistics are more useful to your developer than to you. Every quarter or so, ask your developer to review such statistics as bandwidth and HTTP status codes, especially for pages not found.

Special statistical needs

If you have a large site with heavy traffic or extensive reporting needs, free packages might not be enough. You can find hundreds of paid statistical programs by searching online. Solutions that are high-end or hosted generally offer real-time analysis. Independent or integrated social media analytics programs such as Unilyzer in Figure 6-2 or Bango in Figure 6-3, provide information about visitors, stickiness, and time onsite for multiple social media channels.

For a table of some paid statistical packages, see Bonus Chapter 2 on the Downloads tab of the companion website. Several packages are relatively inexpensive, but the ones described as *high-end* can escalate into real money.

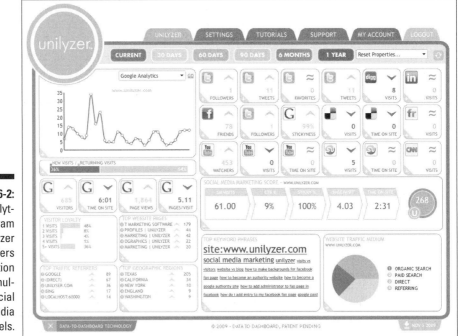

Figure 6-2: The analytics program from Unilyzer offers information about multiple social media channels.

© Eman Bass, LLC Unilyzer is a registered trademark of Eman Bass, LLC. Courtesy of Bango Analytics

Whether you need any of this information depends on your key performance indicators, the complexity of your site, the amount of traffic it receives (you must have enough to make statistical analysis valid), and what you would do with the information if you had it. Don't bother collecting information for information's sake. Stop when you have enough data to make essential business decisions.

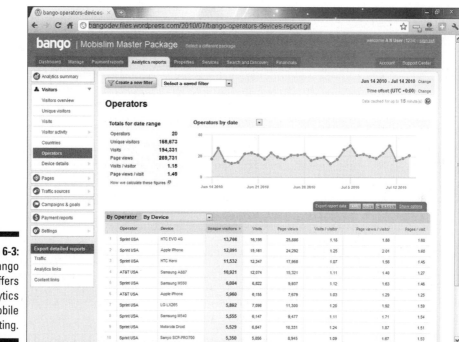

Figure 6-3:
Bango
offers
analytics
for mobile
marketing.

Although it's nice to know industry averages, the only statistics that truly matter are yours. Bear in mind that industry statistics are just as prone to error in absolute value as the stats you collect for your own site. Again, pay more attention to trends and relative values.

Interpreting Sales Statistics

Traffic stats are relevant for all sites, but those who sell online face another challenge. Analyzing what's happening with a cyberstore is just as important as it is for a bricks-and-mortar shop. Business owners who integrate their bricks-and-clicks operations through shared point-of-sale (POS) software, inventory control, and accounting might need to make changes in their reports but have a framework to start with. For store statistics, a *pure-play* (online-only) business must rely on software supplied with its storefront package or custom-developed by its programmer.

If you expect significant sales on a catalog of more than a few products, store statistics are critical. When selecting your storefront package or developer, review the statistics you receive. If you can't get statistics, look elsewhere for a storefront solution.

Here are a few of the statistics to watch for:

- Internal store reports, often by item, include the number of active items, items missing images, and store size.

- In addition to summary sales reports, watch for sales reports broken down by product. Sometimes called a *product tree,* these statistics reflect your store organization, with reports at category, subcategory, and product levels.

- Look for sales reports by average dollar amount and by number of sales.

- You should be able to request order totals for a specific period that you define.

- Sales sorted by day should be available so that you can track sales tied to promotions, marketing activities, and sale announcements.

- Make sure that you can collect statistics on the use of promotion codes by number and dollar value so that you can decide which promotions are the most successful.

- If you use special shopping features such as gift registries, upselling, cross-selling, wish lists, or affiliate programs, monitor the items sold and those on reserve for every activity.

- Sales sorted by customers, to allow for future, personalized correspondence and to see how many repeat versus new customers you have, can be useful.

- If your shopping cart abandonment rate is more than 70 percent, try to identify the step at which shoppers leave. You should know how many carts were opened, compared to the number of completed purchases. Computation can be tricky if your storefront places cookies that allow users as much as 30 days to complete transactions. Statistics that show the contents of abandoned (and active) carts can give you a clue to merchandising or site changes you might need.

- If you haven't used an integrated store builder solution, you might discover that users often enter a completely different website when they link to shopping online. (Watch what happens to the URL.) Only a portion of users who arrive at your HTML site will shift to your storefront, essentially creating an intermediate conversion rate. Be sure that you understand how the store statistical package interprets the number of visitors. You will overestimate your conversion rate if your base is the number of visitors who enter the store itself rather than those who arrive at your site.

Measuring Social Media

Social media measurement takes three forms: analyzing traditional metrics such as numbers of visitors and referrals; monitoring for mentions of your company, brands, products, or employees on social media; and assessing channel-specific performance in terms of user participation or engagement.

Social media *must* be incorporated into your overall analytics review, either in the aggregate or by individual service. Often, analytical metrics treat social media as referrers to your primary web presence and integrate them into funnels to assess conversion rates. You can analyze the effectiveness of individual social media campaigns or obtain a comparative overview of your overall web marketing strategy. You can choose from several tools that combine and sort data from social media, blogs, and your primary website.

In addition to traditional analytics, *monitoring* the incessant chatter of social media has become an essential component of online marketing. Monitoring tools allow you to track and respond nearly in real-time to the ocean of comments, posts, and tweets from others. You use these tools particularly when negative word-of-mouth might affect your reputation or your brand or when positive word-of-mouth might signal a need for your company to gear up its performance. Chapter 19 contains more information on social media monitoring tools.

Finally, every form of social media generates a whole new set of parameters to measure success within a specific medium, often categorized under the term *engagement.* I address these channel-specific metrics in Part V of this book.

Getting Going with Google Analytics

Google Analytics is an excellent free analytics tool for website owners. By April 2011, W³Techs (`http://w3techs.com`) reported that almost half of all websites use this tool to monitor site activity. The upsides for Google Analytics are obvious:

- ✔ It's free.
- ✔ It allows more in-depth analysis than most of the other free statistical packages.
- ✔ You don't need a paid AdWords campaign to take advantage of it.

International Yacht Charter Group sails ahead with Google Analytics

International Yacht Charter Group locates and arranges crewed luxury yacht charters around the world. Because the company prides itself on delivering superb customer service, it's no surprise that it uses Google Analytics to optimize its website to enhance customer experience.

CEO Derek Holding has always paid attention to anything that might indicate a change in client behavior or interest. Analytics provides plenty of data to chew on: from where in the world site visitors are located to what they're searching for, which pages they view, and for how long they view them. Holding also reviews sophisticated items such as bounce rate and other internal measures. Because the purpose of the site is lead generation rather than online sales, he doesn't use goals and ROI data as much as an Internet retailer might.

Holding doesn't measure his company's statistics for their own sake. "We constantly change our site using data from analytics. We are never finished," he notes. "We rarely make any change without the use of data or knowledge of what any change may do to our traffic, online positions, and lead basis."

Although the volume of data available by way of analytics may look daunting, Holding asserts that online data — though different in terminology — is the same data that traditional marketers know and love from offline. For him, analytics is merely another reflection of every marketer's need to understand his audience.

"Many companies believe that a good-looking website is the most important thing, just like a great physical storefront in a mall is important," he acknowledges. "But there's hundreds of years' experience in how to make physical stores work inside. Companies should not throw out that knowledge when planning their website if it is to do the same job."

But Google Analytics also has a few downsides:

- ✔ You can easily drown in data and become so paralyzed by information that you don't take action.

- ✔ It allows less in-depth analysis or audience segmentation than the large, high-end solutions.

- ✔ You have to tag every page of your site with a small piece of code that Google supplies.

Completing the tagging task isn't as bad as it sounds. If you use a `server-side include` (SSI) file or a template, you can place the Analytics code just once and it then appears on all pages. For more information on this topic, see *Web Analytics For Dummies,* by Pedro Sostre and Jennifer LeClaire (John Wiley & Sons, Inc.).

Like all other statistical packages, Google Analytics allows you to see your traffic, pages per visit, and referrers. Unlike many other low-end packages, you can easily set specific time frames, review time-onsite, and see paths through the site.

Analytics integrates easily with Google AdWords. By combining performance reports, for example, you can see how paid search terms correlate with paths through the site or how landing page characteristics may predict which users will take advantage of a special offer in your ad.

Web analytics, from Google or anywhere else, are valuable only if you use them to improve the users' experience on your site and your bottom line.

Diagnosing Conversion Rate Troubles

Without a doubt, the conversion rate is the key statistic to watch. Depending on the nature of your site, your product or service, and your sales cycle, a reasonable conversion rate will probably fall into the 1 to 3 percent range, consistent with recent statistics from Fireclick (`www.fireclick.com`). However, rates may vary substantially by the type and cost of the products or services you sell.

If traffic to the site is good but your conversion rate doesn't hit the mark you established in your financial projections, you have three possibilities to address: your audience, your website, or your business fundamentals, including merchandising. Web analytics can help you determine the source of the problem and the solution. It's the ultimate proof of management by measurement!

Many online merchants consider analytics most valuable for improving conversion rates, reducing the rate of shopping-cart abandonment, and enhancing both natural and paid search marketing. By using a detailed funnel display to specify intermediate goals, as shown in Figure 6-4, you can diagnose specific pages needing improvement within the conversion process.

A conversion problem with the wrong audience

If you see a fair amount of traffic coming to the site (total visitors) but the conversion rate and repeat visitors are low, you might have the wrong audience. Look at pages per view or time onsite. If these numbers are high, you have the right audience. But if these parameters are less than two pages per visit or less than 15 seconds (or both), you have a high *bounce rate* (the percentage of visitors who leave after quickly viewing a single page. In this case, the problem is with either the audience or the website. Check referrers, search engines, search terms, and entry pages to see how people arrive at your site.

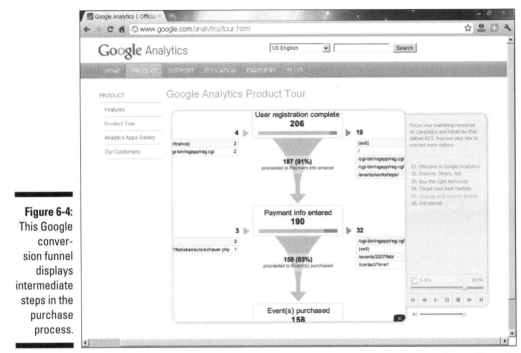

Figure 6-4:
This Google conversion funnel displays intermediate steps in the purchase process.

Of course, every site has bounces. For most transaction-based sites, a reasonable bounce rate is 20 to 50 percent. However, if users are seeking information that's found on a single page (such as a phone number or an article), the bounce rate may reasonably be as high as 60 to 70 percent.

Look at the ratio of people who reach a page with a Buy Now or similar call to action compared to the number who enter the site. If fewer than 60 percent reach an offer page, perhaps you're pulling the wrong audience or attracting traffic from inappropriate search terms or referral sites.

Be sure that you have defined your target audience correctly and narrowly. "Everyone over 25 who uses a computer" isn't a well-defined market! To determine how successfully you're reaching your market, segment it into smaller slices and target only one segment at a time. If you're running ads, they should be specific about your products and services so that the ads attract people who are likely buyers. Be sure your keywords and text are adequately focused to draw your target market.

Fix these problems and watch the results. If these changes don't work, the difficulty might be with the site itself.

A conversion problem with the website itself

Website problems show up in many ways. If you're drawing the right audience (high pages per visit and time onsite) but users leave without fulfilling the objective you've established, you might have trouble with the site itself. Compare the lists of entry and exit pages. If they're close to the same, your visitors might have trouble with navigation.

Ask your programmer to look at the HTTP error codes and browsers that are used to see whether you've designed a site that's appropriate for users' browsers, operating systems, monitors, and access speeds, as discussed in Chapter 3. Check the download time on your site to ensure that entry and catalog pages load quickly. If you have added new features, such as video or animation, without assessing site performance, have your programmer run a link verification program such as Xenu's Link Sleuth (`http://home.snafu.de/tilman/xenulink.html`) to ensure that links are working and that your site has no *orphan pages* (pages no one can open). The programmer can recheck syntax, monitor the display at different resolution sizes, and check browser compatibility.

Experiment with your onsite search function to ensure that it produces complete and relevant results. Then review the checkout process to see whether the pages load quickly and determine whether the process is cumbersome or confusing. Find out whether your site requires registration before purchase or has a broken cart or faulty account login, and find out whether all payment options are working properly.

If the site is functioning correctly, take a look at your text and navigation and ask whether the landing page for a search term or ad takes people directly to the appropriate product or service or strands them on the home page and whether the content quickly answers the question, "What's on this site for me?"

Did you include calls to action so that users know what to do? How many clicks are required to reach an offer (Buy Now) page? Are directions clear? Does the shopping process meet users' expectation for speed and ease of use? Test, test, and retest!

Observe people who've never used the site as they figure out how to locate information and complete a transaction, whether it's a sale or an inquiry. Check your onsite search function to see what people are looking for. If they can't find what they're looking for (and what they want fits with what you offer), you might have navigation, content, or product issues. See what happens after you address these concerns.

A conversion problem with business fundamentals

If your target market arrives at a well-designed, well-functioning website and still doesn't convert, you have to go back to basics. Are you offering the product or service they want, at a price they will pay? Are at least 30 percent of your visitors adding items to a shopping cart? Are more than 75 percent of those carts abandoned before reaching the first page of checkout?

Your conversion funnel statistics might tell you whether you need to modify your product or service offerings.

Here are some additional questions to ask yourself:

- ✔ Do you have enough merchandise on the site for selection purposes? Do you offer enough product options or features?

- ✔ Are your product prices competitive? What about shipping prices? Is the sales tax unexpected? Is using a promotion code complicated?

- ✔ Are you positioned correctly against your competition? Do you have a clearly stated value proposition that sets you apart from your competition? Are your expectations correct?

- ✔ Are your viewers researching online but buying offline from you or others? (If so, you might see multiple visits from the same user.)

- ✔ Are you reaching people at the right point in the sales cycle? (Again, you might see multiple visits from the same user.)

- ✔ Are you reaching the right decision-maker? Most B2B efforts close offline.

- ✔ Does your mobile site, if you have one, meet all the criteria for ease of use and easy purchase by phone?

- ✔ Do elements of your social media drive appropriately qualified prospects to your site?

- ✔ Are you effectively integrating your sales efforts with the rest of your social media and other web marketing for follow-through? A website can't follow up on leads for you!

International Yacht Group, described in this chapter's sidebar titled "International Yacht Charter Group sails ahead with Google Analytics," uses web analytics continuously to monitor performance and improve site operation.

Part III
Maximizing Your
Online Success

The 5th Wave   By Rich Tennant

"Just how accurately should my website reflect my place of business?"

In this part . . .

After you have an effective website, how do you drive traffic to it? Part III covers the essential components of online marketing, using word-of-web techniques to let your target market know that your site exists and why they should visit it. Considering the millions of competing websites, you need agility, persistence, and patience to grab the attention of your target market. Most important, diversify your web marketing approaches.

People arrive at websites in only three ways: use a search engine, click links from other pages, or enter a URL on the Address bar after learning about the site elsewhere. Search engines are critical parts of your web marketing mix, though not sufficient on their own. Chapter 7 shows you how to optimize your site for search engines to gain the visibility you need.

Chapter 8 reviews techniques — sometimes free or cheap — to leverage other online resources to promote your own site, as a form of marketing jujitsu. From posting online press releases or conducting training seminars online to conducting the vital inbound link campaign, you can select online-only techniques for site promotion. Like everything else that's web-based, these techniques evolve as the Internet changes.

E-mail is one of the most effective online techniques. Chapter 9 covers best practices for breaking through the e-mail flood with messages and newsletters that generate business without becoming spam. E-mail techniques range from simple, free signature blocks to expensive, multisegmented newsletter campaigns.

Chapter 10 explores a new avenue for web marketing — the explosive growth of mobile phones and tablet computers. This growth offers web marketers unique opportunities to reach markets on the move, at the exact moment your prospects search for your product or service. You'll find innovative ideas including text messaging campaigns, mobile search marketing, payment acceptance by phone, and specially designed sites optimized for smartphones and tablets.

Chapter 7

Mastering the Secrets of Search Engines

*P*eople ultimately arrive at websites in only three ways: They use search engines, link from other locations online, or enter URLs directly in their browsers. Social media notwithstanding, 87 percent of users on average still use search engines to find information, according to the December 2010 release of the "Generations 2010" report from the Pew Internet & American Life Project.

Given that fact, search optimization remains essential to everyone's online marketing strategy. In this chapter, I explain how to optimize your site for search engines without making yourself either obsessive or paranoid.

Although search engine optimization (SEO) is essential, it isn't the only arrow in your online marketing quiver. Rather than try to achieve top ranking on all search engines for all keywords — especially if you have a B2C site — I recommend putting a reasonable level of effort into search engine marketing and allowing time for other online methods as well.

Recognizing the Value of Search Optimization

Even for online retail sales, search engines remain consumers' primary method of locating sites (see Figure 7-1). As Compete reports (www.compete.com) in its online shopper intelligence study in February 2010, consumers remain heavily dependent on search engines when researching purchases. The report also noted that online shopping behavior varies significantly by industry sector.

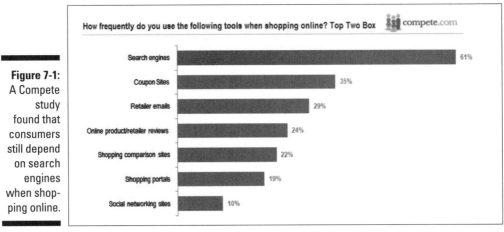

Figure 7-1: A Compete study found that consumers still depend on search engines when shopping online.

Courtesy of Compete.com — Driving digital intelligence

In its study published about a year later, "How Consumers Find Websites in 2010," Forrester hypothesizes that social media may be gaining at the expense of paid advertising, not at the expense of search, especially with younger buyers.

Most businesses should still designate search engine optimization as a technique on their Web Marketing Methods Checklist (see Chapter 2). You can download a copy of this form from the Downloads tab of this book's companion website at www.dummies.com/go/webmarketingfd3e.

With competition from more than 266 million registered websites worldwide in December 2010 (of which 108 million are .com or .net sites), you might think you need either a miracle or a million dollars to be found in search engines. Although barely half of registered names are active, a site that doesn't appear in the first page of search results remains practically invisible.

Search engine jargon

This list can help you master the terminology you see when you read about search engine optimization:

- **Natural,** or **organic,** search results are produced by a search engine's rules (its *algorithms*) when indexing unpaid submissions.

- **Paid** search results are those for which a submission fee or bid has been paid to have the website appear in sponsorship banners at the top of a page, in pay per click (PPC) ads in the right margin, or, in some cases, at the top of the list of search results. Chapter 11 covers these paid techniques.

- **Search engine marketing (SEM)** combines both natural and paid search activities.

- **Search engine optimization (SEO)** is the process of adjusting websites and pages to gain higher placement in search engine results.

- **Search engine results pages (SERP)** display links to sites in response to search queries entered by users.

- **Spiders, crawlers, and robots (bots)** are automated programs used by search engines to visit websites and index their content.

Indeed, an Optify study in 2010 of all Google searches in the United States showed that "60 percent of clicks are generated by the top three SERP (search engine results page) results while the average CTR (click-through rate) for the top spot is 36.4 percent." That makes ranking near the top of the first page of search results far more valuable than appearing on any other page. Sobering, isn't it? (For more details, see `http://marketingprofs.com/charts/print/2011/4856/serps-the-benefits-of-being-no-1`.)

Marketers recognize appearance in search results as a factor important enough that search engine optimization remains a vital area of spending for online marketing, second only to improving websites. (For details, see `www.marketingsherpa.com/article_print.html?id=31817`.)

Determining Who Uses Search Engines

Several studies offer the following interesting insights into the population of search engine users:

- The higher a user's educational level, the more likely he or she is to access a search engine.

- The higher a user's household income, the more likely the user is to access a search engine.

✔ The younger the user, the more likely he or she is to use a search engine.

✔ A user who has a high-speed connection at home is far more likely to use a search engine than a user with a dialup connection.

✔ Rather than try to compete in all sectors, Bing focuses on specific market segment populations, such as people interested in shopping, travel, and sports.

✔ Yahoo! and Bing attract slightly older users than Google. Yahoo! attracts a higher percentage of female users.

Table 7-1 compares the demographics of U.S. users of Google, Bing, and Yahoo! search.

Table 7-1	Demographic Comparison of U.S. Users for Google, Bing, and Yahoo! from March 2011 Estimate		
Demographic	*% Google Users*	*% Bing Users*	*% Yahoo! Users*
Gender			
Male	50	50	48
Female	50	50	52
Age			
3 to 12	5	4	4
13 to 17	15	14	10
18 to 34	36	37	37
35 to 49	26	26	29
Over 50	18	19	21
Ethnicity			
African American	9	13	11
Asian	5	5	6
Caucasian	74	68	71
Hispanic	10	12	10
Other	1	1	1
Income			
$0 to $30,000	15	15	17
$30,000 to $60,000	24	24	25
$60,000 to $100,000	29	29	28
More than $100,000	32	32	30

Demographic	% Google Users	% Bing Users	% Yahoo! Users
Education			
No college	44	51	45
College	40	35	40
Graduate school	16	14	15

Source: Quantcast.com

Not all search engines are created equal! Focus your optimization efforts on the search engine used by your target market.

Figuring Out Which Search Engines You Need

Here's a piece of good-news-bad-news. Only three sites — Google, Yahoo!, and Bing — generate 95 percent of the more than 17 billion monthly searches in the United States alone:

Site	Search Percentage
Google Sites	65.4
Yahoo! Sites	16.1
Microsoft Sites (Bing)	13.6
Ask Network	3.2
AOL, Inc.	1.7

comScore qSearch: Explicit Core Search Share Report, February 2011, Total U.S. — Home/Work/University Locations

Google and Yahoo! together supply the results shown on the two minor search engines (Ask.com and AOL). To further complicate matters, in August 2010, Bing started powering part of the Yahoo! natural search and took over ongoing research into its search algorithms as well as the Yahoo! paid advertising program.

You can obtain maximum visibility for your site by submitting to only the top three search engines. It makes sense, however, to submit to 10 to 50 well-qualified, specialty directories used by your target market (see Chapter 8) to obtain inbound links.

Ignore spammy e-mails promising submissions to hundreds or thousands of search engines. Those trivial search engines get little traffic, and the process might even harm your standing in the primary search engines. Also, delete any e-mail messages guaranteeing number-one search engine rankings. No legitimate SEO company makes this claim. Generating a number-one ranking on a keyword that's rarely used is *always* possible.

Ranking by itself yields no profits. You can make money only after a search engine delivers qualified visitors to your doorstep.

Visit these URLs to start the submission process by hand:

- ✔ `https://www.google.com/webmasters/tools/submit-url`. Google feeds four other engines. For rapid indexing of new sites or new, time-dependent content, try Google's new Fetch as Googlebot URL submission tool at `http://googlewebmastercentral.blogspot.com/2011/08/submit-urls-to-google-with-fetch-as.html`.

- ✔ `http://search.yahoo.com/info/submit.html`. Yahoo! feeds three other engines.

- ✔ `www.bing.com/webmaster/SubmitSitePage.aspx`. Bing, the lone wolf, neither receives nor feeds other engines.

You can find much more on this topic in *Search Engine Optimization For Dummies,* by Peter Kent (John Wiley & Sons, Inc.).

The Google brand network is your choice for an older, business-oriented, slightly wealthier audience.

With so much attention showered on social media traffic, especially to Facebook, it's easy to confuse visits with searches. By September 2011, the Experian/Hitwise list of "Top 10 visited US websites" showed Facebook, with a 10.2 percent share of weekly *visits,* overtaking Google (7.4 percent) and its property, YouTube (3.0 percent); assorted Yahoo! properties fill in positions 4, 5, and 6 for traffic. (For updates, visit `www.hitwise.com/us/data center/main/dashboard-10133.html`.)

Most people visit Facebook to keep up with their friends and family by posting messages, photos, and videos; they do not go to Facebook to search. Although people visit other sites as a result of recommendations from friends, advertising, or direct messages from businesses, this referral activity is relatively small compared to other Facebook activities.

Social networking is another component in your search marketing strategy, but it by no means replaces the need to optimize your website for Google and other search engines.

By early 2011, eMarketer reported on a study showing that a combination of search and social media may substantially increase CTR over the CTR of search alone. Product review sites are most often used in concert with search, followed by Facebook, video sharing sites, and Twitter. (See `www.emarketer.com/Article.aspx?R=1008282`.)

Building a Search-Engine-Friendly Site

Search engines apply sophisticated algorithms to produce relevant results quickly. As smart as they might seem, computers are dumb. To produce good data, they need good input. A well-structured, search-engine-friendly site allows search engines to crawl or spider your site easily. (To see what these creepy-sounding terms means, see the sidebar "Search engine jargon," earlier in this chapter.) As many as half of all sites are so badly structured that search engines never "see" them in the first place.

Planning a search-engine-friendly site from the beginning or during redesign is much easier than trying to retrofit it.

Sites structured with frames or dynamic pages from databases give search engines indigestion. On the other hand, footers, site indexes, and XML feeds are like dessert: Search engines eat them up!

By looking at developers' portfolios and lists of services, you can tell whether they're familiar with techniques for search engine friendliness. If not, ask them to read this section of the book and visit the resource sites in Table 7-2. If they can't or won't do it, you might want to ask an SEO company to assist your developer — or find another developer.

Table 7-2	Search Engine Resources	
Name	*URL*	*What You Can Find*
Digital Point	`http://tools.digital point.com/tracker.php`	Search engine position tracker
Google Webmaster	`www.google.com/support/ webmasters/bin/answer. py?answer=35769&hl=en - 1`	Guidelines and suggestions for site optimization

(continued)

Table 7-2 *(continued)*

Name	URL	What You Can Find
ipl2	`www.ipl.org/IPL/Finding?Key=search+engine+directory&collection=gen`	Search engine directory
LLRX.com	`www.llrx.com/llrxlink.htm`	Legal search engine specialty directory list
Marketing Sherpa	`www.scribd.com/doc/47092434/2011-Search-Marketing-Benchmark-Report-SEO-Edition-Excerpt`	Free excerpt from "2011 Search Marketing Benchmark Report"
Pandia Search Central	`www.pandia.com`	Search engine news
Refdesk.com	`www.refdesk.com/newsrch.html#type`	Search engine directory
Search Engine Guide	`www.searchengineguide.com/marketing.html`	Search engine articles, blog, marketing advice
Search Engine Journal	`www.searchenginejournal.com/seo-best-practices-for-url-structure/7216`	URL best practices
SearchEngineWatch (ClickZ)	`www.searchenginewatch.com`	Articles, blogs, forums, SEO articles, tips, and tutorials
SEOmoz	`www.seomoz.org`	SEO resources, blog spam detector, membership
WebPosition	`www.webposition.com`	SEO, submission, and page rank reporting software; optimization suggestions
WordPot	`www.wordpot.com`	Keyword suggestion tool
Wordtracker	`www.wordtracker.com`	Keyword suggestion tool

Understanding site structure

Many of the articles described in Table 7-2 discuss search-engine-friendly structure. They also cover techniques for using JavaScript and cascading style sheets (CSS) that don't make search engines hiccup. Requirements for "friendliness" change over time as technology and search algorithms improve.

To ensure the best results in search engines, avoid using these techniques on your site:

✔ **Don't place words within images.** Graphics are invisible to search engines.

✔ **Don't use text that isn't in standard HTML format.** To be accessible, any content you embed in rich media such as Flash or video should also be available in text format. Though Google can crawl the text content of Flash files, some structure and context may be missed. The graphics in your header usually don't cause a problem.

✔ **Don't place content in frames.** When you use *frames* — the old-fashioned method of programming that places multiple web pages and URLs within one page — they may not be properly indexed. Though Google may partially support frames, many other engines don't support them.

✔ **Don't place content on dynamic pages.** Some *dynamic* pages, which are composed on the fly from a content database, may not be indexed by search engines.

✔ **Don't try to outsmart a search engine.** Playing games to outsmart search engines is likely to come back and bite you. Your site can be blacklisted for spamming search engines.

Avoiding splash pages

A *splash page* is a graphics-intensive or multimedia home page that delivers a nice "Wow!" response. Your developer might make money creating a splash page, but that doesn't help you. Unless you're a design or entertainment company, a splash page might earn you nothing but aggravation from your target audience.

A splash page can cost you dearly in search engine ranking because it can inhibit a crawler's ability to index your site. Moving multimedia elements to another page on your site where users can choose to view them is much better than forcing users to spend time viewing unwanted elements. If you insist on using a splash page, try adding these elements to soften the effect:

- ✔ **A Skip This Intro link:** Place this link in the upper-right corner, or elsewhere high above the fold, to make it highly visible.

- ✔ **An <alt> tag:** Incorporate into the splash page this tag (known as *hover text*), which is roughly equivalent to the first paragraph of text on the home page.

- ✔ **A paragraph of text in the source code:** If possible, place the paragraph above the call to Flash or a graphical image. It doesn't matter where it appears on the screen.

- ✔ **An entry page:** Convert your splash page to an entry page by including a navigable footer or main-level navigation (or both).

- ✔ **A splash page with an original name:** Give the page a name that's different from your main URL. Submit the home page, rather than the splash page, with content as the primary URL for search engines.

Using search-engine-friendly URLs

As a developer builds your site, she assigns names to your pages. This task is easy on small sites, but sites with thousands of pages become overwhelming. Instead, developers often use content management or storefront systems that automatically generate URLs for dynamic pages pulled from databases, such as product catalogs. Unfortunately, search engines are better at crawling static pages; they might have trouble with or ignore dynamic pages.

Rather than use arbitrary filenames, include different keywords in URLs for different pages. For example, the URL for a bakery site might be `www.YourBakery.com/storefront/fresh_breads.html`. Putting a few (no more than three to five) keywords in the filename portion of a URL (after the last `/`) is more helpful than having keywords in the directory or subdirectory name (where `storefront` appears in this example).

The length of a URL doesn't matter to a search engine, but shorter is better — 2007 research from Marketing Sherpa shows that short URLs attract twice as many clicks! Although domain names themselves aren't case-sensitive, the portion of a URL that follows the top-level domain (after `.com`, for example) may be. Keep it simple with all lowercase characters. Using symbols in a URL can cause major headaches. If you use too many, the URL becomes practically toxic to search engine crawlers. Compare the number of characters — other than dash (—), underscore (_), letters, or numbers — in the "bad" and "good" versions of URLs in the examples in the following paragraph. To avoid problems, limit symbols such as `%`, `&`, and `=` to no more than three (definitely a case of "less is more"). Many systems also generate unsearchable URLs when they initiate an onsite search, tracking code, or session identification number (or *token*).

The best URLs are short, static addresses using only lowercase alphanumeric characters, hyphens, and underscores. Compare these URLs:

```
www.badproductURL.com/cgi-bin/shop.pl?shop=view_category&
category=bolts%20carriage&sub_category=&group=2&wholesale=
```

```
www.goodproductURL.com/browse/4396.htm
```

```
www.betterproductURL.com/gifts/heart-pins.htm
```

```
www.badcontentURL.com/Regional/web/Content.
jsp?nodeId=160&lang=en
```

```
www.goodcontentURL.com/incentives/Tax_Credit_1_2_2.htm
```

```
www.bettercontentURL.com/incentives/tax/credits
```

```
www.badsessionID.com/index.htm?&CFID=1180599941&CFTO
KEN=37702390
```

```
www.goodsessionID.com/gp/yourstore/ref=pd_irl_gw/002-
9876543-1234567
```

```
www.bettersessionID.com/onlinestore/123
```

Surprisingly, some of the worst violators of this guideline are expensive, enterprise-level content management systems for large, database-driven websites. (For shame!) Those software manufacturers should know better.

Fortunately, several solutions exist to solve the problem of unfriendly URLs. The most common is the Apache Module Rewrite. Ask your developer to visit `http://httpd.apache.org/docs/current/mod/mod_rewrite.html` to see how to convert plug-ugly URLs on the fly into ones that are search engine friendly. As I discuss in the "Taking advantage of footers" section, linkable footers, site indexes, and XML site maps can also help resolve this issue.

Taking advantage of footers

Placing a linkable footer in HTML text at the bottom of every page of your site is extremely helpful to search engines, especially if your navigation appears as graphical elements. At the same time, it's helpful to humans, who can navigate to another section without scrolling back to the top. Include a copyright, street address, phone number, and linkable e-mail address, too. Although you display the same information on your Contact Us page, the easier you make it for users to find contact information, the better. In this example, the underlined text represents links — the date in the footer changes automatically:

This site last updated Aug 28, 2011 ©2000-2011 HotShot Co.

Street Address | City, State, Zip <u>E-mail Us</u> or call 800-123-4567

<u>Home</u> | <u>What's New</u> | <u>Local Business</u> | <u>Links</u> | <u>Site Index</u> | <u>Contact Us</u>

For simplicity, ask your developer to put the footer in the cascading style sheet (CSS).

Creating a site index

A *site index,* such as the one at `www.kylezimmermanphotography.com`, shown in Figure 7-2, is a linkable outline of your website. If your website follows the outline you wrote during the development process, this index will look almost the same.

Your site index should allow access to at least the third tier of internal pages so that users don't have to hunt for pages. Indexes are critical for large, information-intensive sites and for sites that don't have well-formed URLs.

Search engines use the site index as a path for their robots, eventually reaching all internal pages listed there.

Figure 7-2:
A linkable index gives users easy access to items on the second and third tiers of the site.

Courtesy of Kyle Zimmerman Photography

Creating a site map

If you have a large site, ask your web developer to convert your site index to a site map in XML and submit it to Yahoo! and Google. Site maps allow search engines to identify dynamically generated pages as well as static ones.

A Real Simple Syndication (RSS) feed for your Google site map automatically notifies Google whenever your site content changes. RSS is excellent for a large site or for one with a continually updated product or information database that already has a feed. Give the links in the following list to your developer if he or she isn't familiar with the site map process:

- Information about Google site maps: `www.google.com/support/webmasters/bin/topic.py?topic=8476` and `www.google.com/support/webmasters/bin/answer.py?hl-en&answer=34634`

- Information about Yahoo! site maps: `www.antezeta.com/yahoo/site-map-feed.html` and `http://help.yahoo.com/l/us/yahoo/search/siteexplorer/manage/siteexplorer-37.html`

- Information about Bing site maps with Silverlight: `http://onlinehelp.microsoft.com/en-us/bing/gg132930.aspx`

- Information about Bing site maps without Silverlight: `http://onlinehelp.microsoft.com/en-us/bing/gg132933.aspx`

- Free site map generator for Google, Yahoo!, and Bing: `www.xml-sitemaps.com`

- Resource for site map generators: `www.vbulletin.org/forum/showthread.php?t=100435Optimizing for Google`

Google accounted for more than 65 percent of all explicit searches in early 2011; with Yahoo! sites at 16.1 percent and Microsoft sites at 13.6 percent, Google won't lose its search engine dominance any time soon. It makes its own rules for ranking sites in search results and changes them often. Some changes result from its own, continuing research or from competitive pressures. Google also shakes things up to prevent large, well-funded companies from dominating results permanently or to counteract the dynamic of people gaming the system to enhance search engine results.

Site relevance, as a human being would determine it, guides the Google approach to search results. This approach puts extraordinary pressure on sites to obtain inbound links from related sites. In theory, a site that's well designed from a human perspective and well connected with other sites does well on Google. That's the theory, anyway. The following sections detail some best practices to help you compete against all the other sites struggling for the same level of visibility.

Set reasonable expectations for your search marketing efforts. Your goal is to have some pages of your website appear on page 1 of search results for some of the search terms that real people use. You *don't* need to have every page appear on page 1 results for every keyword. Decide which search terms are the most critical for you, especially if you have a limited time to devote to SEO and have no funds to hire someone to help.

Dealing with delays

Call it a time-out. Call it isolation. Call it bad site structure. Whatever the reason, you may experience a frustrating delay while getting a new site indexed by Google. Although Google indexes most new sites somewhere between four days and four weeks of their debuts, indexing may take longer if

- ✔ The site has no inbound links.
- ✔ The content isn't easily *crawled* (it isn't search engine friendly).
- ✔ The pages don't link to each other well.

Type your URL into the Search box at www.google.com; if your site appears in the results, Google has indexed it. If not — and it has been more than one month since you originally submitted it — resubmit your URL at www.google.com/addurl/?continue=/addurl. Buying ads (PPC) can provide a presence on search engines until your site is ranked. However, a less expensive solution helps start the Google clock ticking: Have your developer post, fairly quickly, a two-page, search-engine-friendly website with several inbound links after you buy the name.

Write several paragraphs about your products or services for the home page and prepare a second page with contact information and a little about the company. Add search terms and good page titles to the meta tags (see the section "Optimizing for Yahoo!, Bing, and Other Engines with Meta Tags," later in this chapter). Then submit your preliminary site to the three primary search engines.

To be especially productive, start collecting e-mail addresses to notify subscribers when the site is open. Then offer a thank-you promotion for early sign-up.

The standard Under Construction notice or icon that contains no other content not only is a wasted marketing opportunity — it can also prevent your site from being indexed.

The Under Construction announcement for Hyperlingo (www.hyperlingo.com), a language translation site, includes a call to action to sign up for its e-mail list or to help with testing, as well as links to follow on Twitter and Facebook or to share the site with a friend, as shown in Figure 7-3. This approach to an Under Construction notice, which is used while a new site is under development, works equally well for a new version of an existing website.

Figure 7-3:
The Under Construc-
tion page at Hyperlingo collects addresses for its e-mail newsletter.

Courtesy of Hyperlingo.com, Hyperlingo ™

Even if you have an existing site, Google might spend a few weeks fully indexing a redesign. Usually, you see your home page first and other pages follow over time, depending on the size of the site. Because Google now indexes constantly, you don't have to wait for a fixed period. In any case, it takes at least four to eight weeks for your link requests to bear fruit, so your Google search engine ranking might rise more slowly than you want.

Improving your Google PageRank

Google's top secret! Google ranks pages for web relevance or importance on a scale of 1 to 10, where 10 is the top. To see the PageRank for your site, or any other, you must download and install Google Toolbar from the URL listed for *PageRank information* in Table 7-3.

Table 7-3	Google Resource Links
What You Can Find	*URL*
Add site instructions	`www.google.com/support/` `webmasters/bin/answer.` `py?answer=34397&ctx=sibling`
Content submission instructions	`www.google.com/submityour` `content/index.html`
Crawl statistics	`www.google.com/support/` `webmasters/bin/answer.` `py?answer=35253&query=crawl%20` `statistics&topic=&type=`
Domain preference tips (with or without the characters *www.*)	`www.google.com/support/` `webmasters/bin/answer.py?hl=en&a` `nswer=44231&from=44232&rd=1`
Fetch as Googlebot	`http://googlewebmastercentral.` `blogspot.com/2011/08/submit-` `urls-to-google-with-fetch-as.` `html`
Google Maps	`http://maps.google.com`
Google-friendly site tips	`www.google.com/support/` `webmasters/bin/answer.` `py?answer=40349&ctx=related`
Google Places	`www.google.com/places`
Google product list	`www.google.com/options`
Guide to index search statistics	`www.google.com/support/` `webmasters/bin/answer.` `py?answer=35256&query=crawl%20` `statistics&topic=&type`
PageRank information	`www.google.com/corporate/tech.` `html www.google.com/support/` `webmasters/bin/answer.` `py?answer=34432`
Site map information	`www.google.com/support/` `webmasters/bin/answer.py?hl=en&` `answer=156184&from=40318&rd=1`
Toolbar download	`www.google.com/toolbar/ie/` `index.html`
Webmaster Central	`www.google.com/webmasters`
Webmaster guidelines	`www.google.com/support/` `webmasters/bin/answer.` `py?answer=35769`

The PageRank appears in both graphical and text form when you hover the mouse over the PageRank index on the Google Toolbar, as shown in Figure 7-4. Google and the U.S. federal government portal (at www.usa.gov) are two of the few sites ranked as 10. The rankings aren't linear, however: Every point is roughly ten times as "relevant" as the number below it — like earthquakes!

Figure 7-4:
Google Toolbar shows PageRank in both graphics and text. Ranking is by page, not by site.

Courtesy of Google, Inc.

If your site rank seems either unusually high or low or it suddenly falls to zero, click the Reload button on your browser or check again in a few hours. Google PageRank sometimes varies erratically from day to day, or even from hour to hour.

The PageRank algorithm, which involves more than 200 variables, is a closely held secret. More than the simple link popularity described in Chapter 8, the Google PageRank appears to be affected by the following criteria, among others. These factors generate extra value:

✔ Links from related sites with a high Google PageRank.

✔ Links from .edu, .gov, and .org websites.

✔ Links from blogs and press releases.

✔ Relevant text surrounding inbound links; this favors annotated or contextual links and pages with fewer than 60 links per page.

✔ Outbound links to other highly ranked, relevant sites (sites that share at least one other search term).

✔ The size and complexity of your site. Information-intensive sites seem to do better, though Google doesn't index the "deep web" (information in databases) content of academic or trade journals, phone books, or other databases.

- ✔ A Google site map, though badly structured sites might diminish PageRank.

- ✔ Sites that have been around longer than newer ones, so be patient.

- ✔ Sites with newer content tend to have higher rankings.

- ✔ Sites that appear within the top ten results for local (map) searches. See the section "Submitting to Specialty Search Engines and Directories," later in this chapter.

- ✔ Visible title and ALT tags (as I discuss later in this chapter, in the section "Optimizing pages") with search terms versus other meta tags.

- ✔ Contents of surrounding pages, if they're related.

- ✔ Using search terms in subheads, navigation, and links because Google analyzes the difference in font size, style, color, and placement.

- ✔ Site traffic, number of visitors, and page views.

And the following factors diminish PageRank:

- ✔ Links from link farms and other poor, inbound link sources.

- ✔ Unethical black hat techniques. The sites might be not only diminished in rank but also banished.

Finding Google-qualified inbound links

Start your search for inbound links with Google, as described in Chapter 8. Type **link:www.*SomeDomain*.com** (and replace *SomeDomain* with the domain name you want) in the Search box at competitors' sites and sites that appear at the top of Google results on shared search terms. As you review the list, target those with a PageRank of 5 or more for your requests.

Not all web developers have the skills or staff to handle SEO or to manage a custom, inbound link campaign for good Google ranking. If this task is too time consuming to handle inhouse, look for an SEO company to assist.

Your web developer is still the key to developing a well-structured, clean site with a footer, a site index, good URLs, and a site map. The developer must also avoid elements that Google doesn't like: hidden links, hidden text, *cloaked* pages (readers see one page, and search engines see another), or sneaky redirects. For more information, refer to the pages for Google-friendly sites and submission guidelines listed earlier in Table 7-3.

Making adjustments for Google dances

When Google adjusts its algorithm, sometimes called a *Google dance,* the SEO community shimmies. As in a game of musical chairs, some sites gain in search engine results and others lose when the music stops. For example, the February 2011 minuet called Panda caused low-quality sites such as eHow and Answerbag (sometimes called *content farms*) to lose position on SERPs in favor of higher-quality sites with original content.

You might notice changes early if you regularly check your site standing in Google or if you sign up for a newsletter from a search engine resource site listed earlier in Table 7-2.

If you lose position, don't panic. Use the Google resource links listed earlier, in Table 7-3, for crawl statistics information and check the entry labeled *Guide to index search statistics* to gain insight into what specifically has happened to your site. Read whatever material you can about how to reoptimize your site or find additional links. Make adjustments and resubmit to Google manually, with a new site map, or via RSS.

Optimizing for Yahoo!, Bing, and Other Engines with Meta Tags

Unlike Google's emphasis on inbound links, most search engines rely on internal consistency between site content and keywords to produce search engine results. A *hierarchical directory* is organized by fixed subject area, such as the yellow pages or books on library shelves, rather than arranged on the fly by relevance in response to a search request.

Using human editors to review and assign sites to categories, Yahoo! and the Open Directory Project (www.dmoz.org) were eventually overwhelmed by the explosion in the number of websites. Unable to compete with the more powerful Google search algorithms, Yahoo! shifted to Microsoft Bing search technology in 2009 and dropped its paid inclusion program. The Open Directory site has fallen years behind in its indexing, though some diehards insist on its value.

Essential in the early days of the web, a long set of *meta tags* provided a structured description of a website for directory purposes. Meta tags appear at the beginning <head> tag of the code on every web page to provide information to browsers and search engines. Most meta tags are no longer necessary, but three retain value: title, page description, and keyword.

As search algorithms improve, even these meta tags carry less importance for ranking purposes. However, they can provide an edge in some cases, and they help you structure content in a practical way.

You can easily see meta tags for any website: Just view the source in your web browser. Simply right-click a web page and choose View Source in Internet Explorer or View Page Source in Firefox. Alternatively, use the browser toolbar. Choose View➪Source in Internet Explorer or View➪Page Source in Firefox. The meta tags should appear near the top of a separate window, as shown just below the `<head>` tag at `http://guidedimagerydownloads.com`, shown in Figure 7-5.

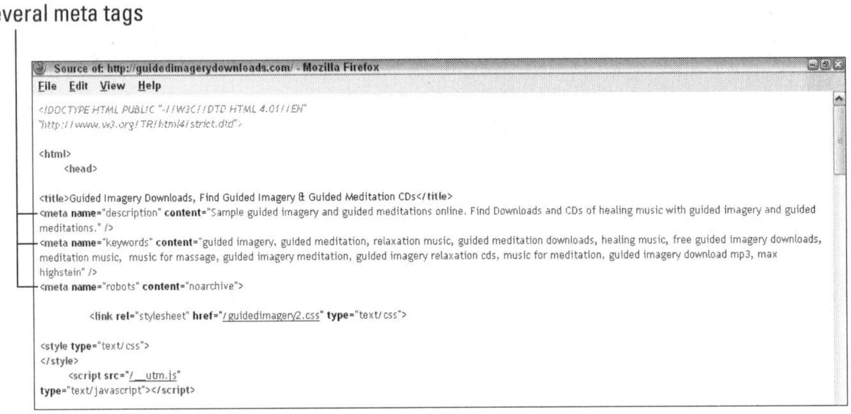

Several meta tags

Figure 7-5:
Check out
the title,
keyword,
and page
description
meta tags
for this site.

Used by permission, www.guidedimagerydownloads.com

Using meta tags

Because meta tags are not as important in search engine ranking as they used to be, limit how much time you spend on them. If tags for a page relate to its content, they're more likely to yield benefits in search engines.

Repeat no more than the same four keywords (or search terms) in several locations on a page, and optimize a different page for another four keywords. (Effective tags include keywords, but you can't optimize one page for all key-words that apply to your site.) If you do this correctly, a page from your web-site will appear in results for most commonly used search terms.

Title meta tags

The *title tag,* likely the most important tag still in use, appears above the browser toolbar when the site is displayed. Keep the title tag to no more than

TIP

6 to ten words, or fewer than 70 characters, including one or two of your terms for that page.

Use a different title tag on every page.

The title tag *Guided Imagery Downloads, Find Guided Imagery & Guided Meditation CDs* appears above the browser toolbar on the home page at `http://guidedimagerydownloads.com`, as shown in Figure 7-6. Note that various terms from the keyword tag shown in Figure 7-5 appear in the text links as well as in the title tag.

Years ago, when site navigation was more of a problem, the title tag often repeated the page name, much like the header in a book shows a chapter title. This repetition is no longer necessary, and page names such as About Us are meaningless for search engines. Instead, insert one or more of your selected keywords in the title tag.

Because different search engines may truncate the title tag at different lengths, place your keywords first, followed by the company name — not the other way around. Your company name appears in so many places on your site that it doesn't matter if it's trimmed off.

Title tag   Text links with search terms

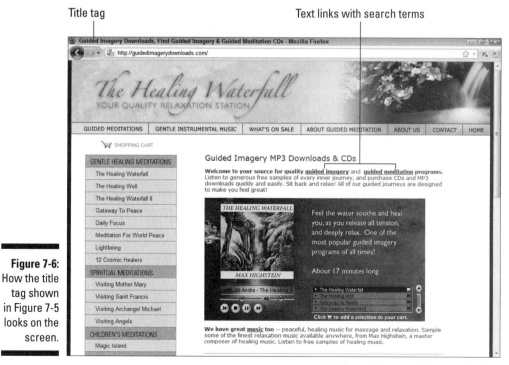

Figure 7-6: How the title tag shown in Figure 7-5 looks on the screen.

Used by permission, www.guidedimagerydownloads.com

Page description meta tags

The source of the text that appears in search engine results is all or a portion of the page description tag or the first paragraph of text, as shown in Figure 7-7. Google search results for the term *CDs healing music guided imagery* yield the Guided Imagery Downloads site on the first page. The entry, which includes the page title, pulls from the page description shown in Figure 7-5.

Figure 7-7:
Part of
the page
description
meta tag for
the home
page in
Figure 7-5
appears in
the search
results.

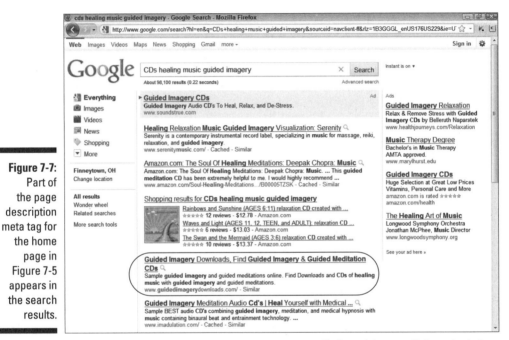

Used by permission, www.guidedimagerydownloads.com

Again, different search engines truncate this tag at different lengths, ranging from 150 to 255 characters, including spaces. A good compromise is 200 characters. Use your four optimized search terms in the description, placing them as close to the beginning as possible while keeping the text readable. Don't keep repeating the same keywords, which is considered spamming.

Use the page description tag as a marketing opportunity. If you're clever, include a call to action, a benefits statement, or a teaser in the description to encourage a searcher to click from search engine results to your site.

Keyword meta tag

Although not as important as it used to be, the keyword tag is a helpful way to organize your optimization work. Again, different search engines truncate this tag at different lengths. Place at the beginning of the tag the four keywords you elect to optimize; put your company name and least important terms at the end. This list describes a few other guidelines to keep in mind:

- **Limit the list of search terms to 30; shorter is better.** You can spread out other search terms on other pages. Some sources suggest keeping this tag between 200 and 500 characters.

- **Make sure your keywords are relevant to your pages' content.** It's best to include at least some of your search terms in the first paragraph.

- **Keyword phrases are more useful than single words.** Earning a page 1 appearance on most single words is next to impossible.

- **Commas are no longer needed to separate search terms but are helpful for you to read what you've done.** Search engines consider reversing the order of words within a phrase, or scrambling words among terms, to find possible combinations. This task can be especially helpful for regional sites where you want to specify the location and type of business, such as *manhattan delis*, *manhattan restaurants*, *manhattan coffee shop*, or *manhattan dining*. However, when several words are listed individually, they may not produce as high a result as when they appear as a phrase.

- **Articles and prepositions aren't necessary.** Examples of articles are *a, an,* and *the;* examples of prepositions are *by, from, on,* and *to.*

- **Use all-lowercase words to encompass all forms of capitalization.** If you capitalize a word in the keyword tag, capitalization is required for a match.

- **Plurals include singulars, as long as they're formed from the same root without changing spelling.** For example, a search for the term *plants* includes the term *plant,* but a search for the term *companies* doesn't include the term *company.* The same principle holds true for gerunds and past tense.

- **Phrases with spaces include the same term without spaces.** For example, a search for the term *coffee shop* includes the term *coffeeshop,* but not vice versa.

- **If a multiword phrase must be kept intact for identification, insert quote marks around it.** Examples are "*days of our lives*" and "*santa fe.*"

- **When results are established, sites with keyword phrases that exactly match the entered search request (the *query string*) generally precede those where other text separates the words within the search request.** You can see this for yourself by entering a multiword search phrase and reviewing the results.

Google rarely uses the keyword tag; other engines even ignore it. Instead, they derive important keywords by the frequency with which they're used (as long as they aren't abused) and by their location on the page. The keyword tag is useful, however, as a way of tracking which pages you optimized for which search terms. Otherwise, you probably need to build another spreadsheet.

Choosing good keywords

Selecting the right keywords for your site is more art than science. The best search terms are ones that people actually use — and ones on which there's limited competition. At least give yourself a chance to appear on page 1. Phrases are almost always better than single words, except in highly specialized applications with their own terminology.

People's brains all work a little differently. You might think the search terms you would choose are so obvious that everyone else would use the same ones. It isn't so. Ask random friends or customers for the search terms they would use to research a topic such as tires or to find your website. You might be surprised.

Finding words

When choosing keywords, start by reverse-engineering competitors' sites and sites that appear in the first three positions on obvious search terms. View the source for their pages and make a list of the keywords they use. Brainstorm other terms from your text. Then use this list as input for one of several tools that identify good search terms and suggest alternatives.

Don't use search terms that aren't relevant to your site. Companies have won legal cases against sites that use trademarked terms in their keyword lists, hoping to divert traffic from the trademark owner's site. If you're an authorized dealer for a trademarked product, review your distribution agreement. It generally specifies where and how you can use trademarked terms. As for *supercalifragilisticexpialidocious* — forget it, Mary Poppins. It already appears on 437,000 pages.

Visualizing keywords in a cloud

Have you seen a paragraph of alphabetically sorted words appearing to the side of a blog or website, with the type set in different sizes and faces? These *tag clouds* are sets of keywords used to index the content on a page, using a visual metaphor to designate their relative importance. The larger and bolder the term, the more frequently it is used, either within the content or as a search term. Brainstorm good ideas for keywords by looking at the largest, boldest tags on a competing or compatible blog or news site.

Using keyword tools

You can choose from several keyword suggestion tools that are free, at least for a trial. Google's tool is available without having an AdWords account, at `https://adwords.google.com/select/KeywordToolExternal`. In addition to receiving synonyms and related ideas, you can find the relative frequency that a term has been used on Google over the past year and the relative number of AdWords competitors for that term.

REMEMBER

The frequency with which search terms are used varies by season, holiday, news, or entertainment event.

Two other keyword suggestion tools are Wordtracker (`www.wordtracker.com`) and Wordpot (`www.wordpot.com`). Wordpot, shown in Figure 7-8, displays lists of the exact and total daily usage of search terms. Options on the right let you select the breadth of synonyms to incorporate and specify which search engines to assess.

Results from Wordpot, Google, and other keyword suggestion sites listed previously, in Table 7-2, may vary for two reasons. Different search word suggestion tools estimate each variant separately (such as singular or plural, past or present tense, or with or without spaces or punctuation). In addition, the tools work from a different database of searches, collected over different time frames and from different audience profiles.

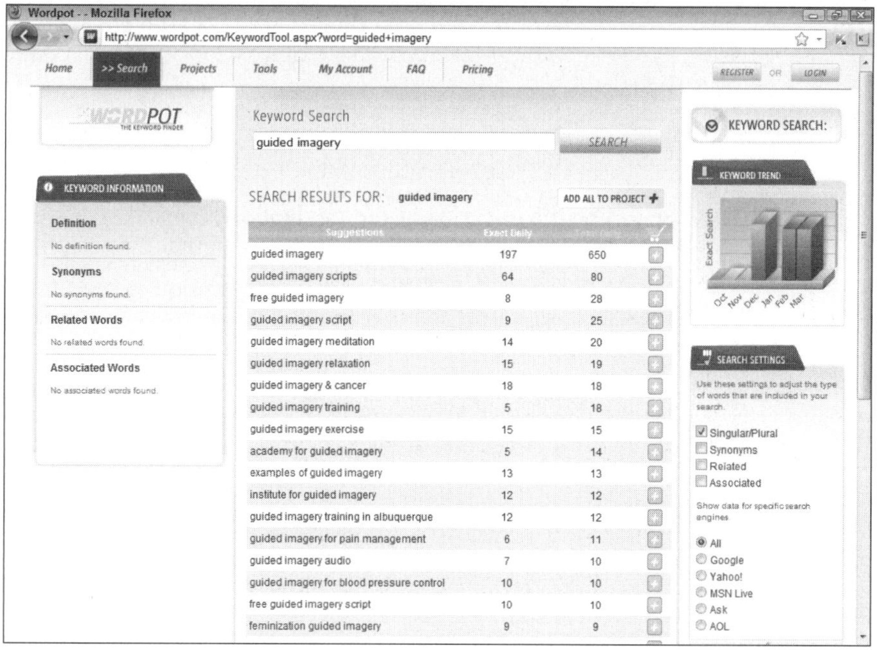

Figure 7-8:
Enter a keyword on the Wordpot site to receive a report suggesting other search terms.

Courtesy of wordpot.com

As with just about every statistic on the Internet, don't worry about absolutes — relative values are the ones that matter. The relative frequency of use of different terms is far more important than the actual number.

None of these numbers can tell you whether these terms are appropriate for your audience or whether *your* audience would actually use them. That's where the art — and some marketing judgment — enter the process.

Always test suggested keywords by entering them back into a search engine. Every once in a while, you'll be surprised to find that a keyword yields a completely different type of business than what you expect.

Some web developers can help with keyword selection, but many can't. Look for assistance from copywriters experienced in optimizing text for the web or from SEO companies.

Optimizing pages

Unless you're part of a huge company, optimize your site only for the search engine your audience is most likely to use. If you already have a site, check your traffic statistics (see Chapter 12) to see which engine generates the most traffic.

Search engines usually specify their preferences on advice pages for webmasters, or you can find the preferences in the search engine resource sites listed earlier in Table 7-2. Follow these tips for keyword placement to prime your pages:

- ✔ **Use keywords in your page URLs.** For example, use `www.dummies.com/web-marketing` rather than `dummies.com/123456`.

- ✔ **Use keywords as terms in the navigation.** This advice doesn't help if your navigation consists of graphical elements.

- ✔ **Include the same four primary keywords you selected for optimization in the first paragraph of text for that page.** It's the only paragraph that most search engines scan.

- ✔ **Use the same four keywords in the ALT tags.** These tags appear in the form of a small text box whenever a user hovers the mouse pointer over a graphic or photo. Descriptive ALT tags make websites accessible for the visually impaired, but you can usually work in one or more of your terms.

✔ **Use keywords as part of the link text rather than the phrase *Click here*.** Doing so not only improves search ranking but also makes the text more readable.

✔ **Some search engines use cues from the HTML code to distinguish text that appears in headlines or subheads; they're usually a different size or color, or both.** If keywords appear in HTML headings at the H1 (main) or H2 (subhead) level, you might get "extra credit" in some engines.

✔ **Have your developer put meta tags at the top of the source code.** Make it easy for search engines to find what they're looking for.

✔ **Text should be the first page content that search engines see.** If a photograph appears to the left or right or above the first paragraph of text on the screen, have your developer rearrange the source code so that the text appears first in the code.

Don't sacrifice human readability and comprehension when trying to use search terms. People buy — search engines don't. Because you're probably the person responsible for reviewing, if not writing, the copy, you're responsible for assessing keyword use. Your developer usually doesn't get involved, though an SEO company certainly will.

You might read about *keyword density* or *keyword ratio.* These terms refer to the percentage of keywords versus the total text on the page. As long as you avoid nasty techniques such as *keyword stuffing* (the excessive use of keywords on a page), you should be okay. If the keyword ratio approaches 20 to 25 percent, most search engines become suspicious. You don't have to measure! It's next to impossible to write text densely stuffed with keywords that also makes sense to a human being. If you write good copy, you're fine.

Avoid using black hat techniques, such as *magic pixels* (links, measuring 1 x 1 pixels, that aren't visible onscreen) or *invisible text* (consisting of keywords written in the same color as the background). These techniques will get you dropped from search engines. If you write an informative website that's useful to people, you don't need black magic for SEO. You'll have all the magic you need.

Bing uses its own technology to index the web. In the past, its algorithm didn't seem as accurate or as fast as other search engines and tended to reward home pages in the results. Recently, Bing claims to have made changes to improve its indexing speed and to produce more relevant results for users by focusing on appearances in social networks and emphasizing areas of interest, such as health and cars, to its search users.

Submitting to Specialty Search Engines and Directories

Just because you've knocked off Google, Yahoo!, and Bing doesn't mean that you're done. Now it's time to locate specialty search engines and directories that your target audience uses. Take advantage of the search engine directories listed earlier, in Table 7-2, or simply search for directories and search engines by subject.

Use Google Toolbar or Alexa to quickly assess the PageRank and traffic for these specialty search engines. Bother only with engines that appeal to your target audience and that seem to be maintained.

You'll find that tracking your search engine and directory submissions is easier if you create a spreadsheet corresponding to the one you build for link requests, as described in Chapter 8. A few directories and search engines accept e-mail applications, but most have online forms that are similar to the one at the Open Directory (www.dmoz.org) or slightly more complicated.

Don't worry about submitting to a meta search engine such as Metacrawler (http://metacrawler.com) or Dogpile (www.dogpile.com), because you can't! These search engines compile results from the other primary search engines. Don't confuse meta search engines with *meta indices,* which are directories of other directories.

In addition to submitting to vertical market, industry-specific, and application directories or search engines, include these essential generic directories:

- ✔ Yellow pages and white pages
- ✔ Maps and local directories, especially if you have an office or bricks-and-mortar storefront
- ✔ General business, trade association, and professional membership directories
- ✔ Directories for images, audio, video, and multimedia, if appropriate

For tables listing some of the resources in the preceding bulleted list, see Bonus Chapter 3 on the Downloads tab of the book's companion website. Look for three tables titled "Basic, Free Directories," "Free Business Directories," and "Audio, Video, Multimedia, and Image Directories."

If your website uses any of the following elements, submit it to the appropriate directories:

✔ Chat, message board, or other online feature directories — for example, coupons or contests (see Chapters 6 and 8)

✔ Public calendars and live event directories (see Chapter 10)

✔ Shopping search engines, such as Google Product Search or Shopzilla (see Chapter 12)

✔ Directories of social sharing sites for blogs, photos, podcasts, and videos (see Chapter 14)

Google Places (www.google.com/places) is the new substitute for Google Local. Even if you have no website, you can create a free listing that appears on Google and Google Maps. Your listing can include video, photos, and more. It's free, it's easy, and it's a great way to get started. For more information, see www.google.com/support/places/bin/answer.py?hl=en&answer=143059.

Maintaining Your Ranking

After you achieve a good search engine ranking, you don't get to snooze. First, another company will fight for that position. Second, circumstances are forever changing. Inbound links come and go, and search engines tweak their algorithms or buy another company's technology. You need to be vigilant to maintain your ranking.

You must update content on your site to remain appealing to search engines, as I discuss in Chapter 6.

Checking your ranking

For most small sites, a quarterly review of search engine ranking, link popularity, and link requests is fine. If you read about a Google dance (see the earlier section "Making adjustments for Google dances"), have a large site, or run a significant SEO effort for natural search, you might want to run reports more often.

This list describes some techniques for taking a closer look at how to perform these tasks:

✔ **Check your site's search engine ranking.** You can use the link for the *Guide to index search statistics* entry in Table 7-3 to check your ranking on Google. That strategy might be enough, depending on your user base.

Or, purchase software such as Web Position (`http://webposition.com`) or Search Engine Tracker (`www.netmechanic.com/products/tracker.shtml`) to check your standings automatically for multiple keywords on multiple search engines.

✔ **Run a link popularity report to be sure that your inbound links are solid.** You might find that about 25 percent of sites disappear over a two-year period. If you discipline yourself to request ten new inbound links every quarter, you'll do fine.

✔ **Check your spreadsheets for successful link requests and directory or search engine submissions.** If your site isn't found on a requested location after three months, resubmit. If your site still isn't posted after two requests, replace the request with a new one.

EarthKind is search kind

EarthKind, Inc., is a manufacturer, wholesaler, and retailer of the first natural rodent repellent approved for indoor use by the U.S. Environmental Protection Agency. From its beginnings in 2000, this North Dakota–based firm has grown in all directions. Direct online retail sales represent 20 percent of its business, but EarthKind also uses its website (and high search engine ranking) to help drive foot traffic to retail bricks-and-mortar stores that carry its product.

"We target anyone who wants to keep rodents out of their property, which is about 30 percent of the population," explains CEO Kari Warberg-Block. EarthKind's approach to SEO is pragmatic and customer-centric. Although it uses many of the standard, keyword research tools to select good search terms, its process, says Warberg-Block, is "mostly good old-fashioned reading into how our customers talk."

The SEO process helps the company focus on customer problems. "Looking at *Long Tail* [rarely used, but important] search terms gives great insight into the dire situation and frustration consumers are facing with rodents. We then use that information to create new content that answers those questions. It's led to increased sales, so we're hopeful that's a sign we're adding value."

Tactically speaking, EarthKind optimizes its home page for its best *Short Tail* [high-frequency] keywords and optimizes deeper pages for the long-tail ones. "Any page that supports a sale gets optimized to some degree," Warberg-Block explains. Sales, naturally, are the driving statistic in determining whether its SEO works. "Traffic is nice, but 1,000 visits with no conversion could mean we're pointing in the wrong direction," she notes.

Recently, EarthKind began expanding its optimization strategy beyond its website. Warberg-Block writes helpful articles with keyword-filled headlines that she publishes with Cambridge Healthcare Media Group (`chimediagroup.com`), which publishes and promotes white papers, and PRWeb (`www.prweb.com`). The company also posts videos on YouTube to illustrate the articles and uses the same keywords in naming the videos. EarthKind began using Facebook in 2010, mainly for fun and networking, and started monitoring Twitter conversations. Both outlets also provide opportunities to forward helpful articles to people who mention that they have mice problems.

Because of EarthKind's policy of hiring people with developmental disabilities, the company won a Business Partnership Award from the state of Minnesota. As an unexpected benefit, it has acquired many links from `.gov` and `.edu` sites that help increase its Google PageRank. But Warberg-Block sees far more value from this activity: "This type of thing trumps anything paid we do online. It's about the integrity we display as a company to our customers."

"Don't be afraid to test," she suggests. "Failure is a foregone conclusion, but that one success out of ten attempts more than makes up for the others. Many businesses, large and small, get hung up on the data and look to minimize risk. Find an acceptable level of risk and get started — a year from now, you'll be in a fantastic position."

Resubmitting your site

If your site appears high in search results, you have no reason to resubmit to search engines. If your search engine ranking drops for no reason, run the report again a few days later to confirm the results. Resubmit to the three main engines.

If you change or add new pages to your site, submit one of those URLs to the three primary search engines. This action triggers your site to be "spidered." Better yet, send a new site map to Google and Yahoo! or ensure that the RSS feed for your site map is working.

To keep the workload reasonable, spread out the task of optimizing additional pages for different keywords. Tweaking text, adding longer product descriptions, revising meta tags and ALT tags, or rearranging the placement of keywords on a page all gradually improve search engine ranking.

Optimizing Social Media for Search

Google indexes social media under its Real Time search category, in reverse chronological order, as well as under its full search results. The more search-engine-friendly components of your web presence you have, the more likely your business will claim a significant amount of SERP real estate. (To read a little about SERP, see the earlier sidebar "Search engine jargon.")

Fortunately, ensuring that your social media channels are properly constructed isn't difficult. Follow these guidelines:

✔ **Core search term consistency:** Use the same six to eight core search terms as tags or keywords on every profile or blog and on every main entry for all social media channels.

✔ **Page description meta tag:** Adapt the meta tag from your home page to become the first sentence of your social profile on every channel.

✔ **Specific search terms:** Select terms from your keyword list as tags on individual posts, as Twitter hashtags, within the item title, and as part of the description of photos and videos.

✔ **Optimized ALT tags:** Whenever possible, include these elements for photos, graphics, and any other type of rich media you upload.

✔ **Term placement:** Because the same search terms are likely to be used by the internal search function on the social media service, be sure that the term also appears within the content.

✔ **Posting frequency:** To appear near the top of reverse chronological postings (most recent is at the top), make it a habit to post often.

For more specific information on optimizing social media for search engines, see Part V of this book.

EarthKind (shown in Figure 7-9), a retailer and wholesaler of natural rodent repellent, believes in the value of SEO. As described in the sidebar "EarthKind is search kind," EarthKind uses search engine optimization as a cost-effective technique for acquiring highly qualified prospects and turning them into customers. Its techniques direct customers to both its online store and to other bricks-and-mortar stores that carry its products.

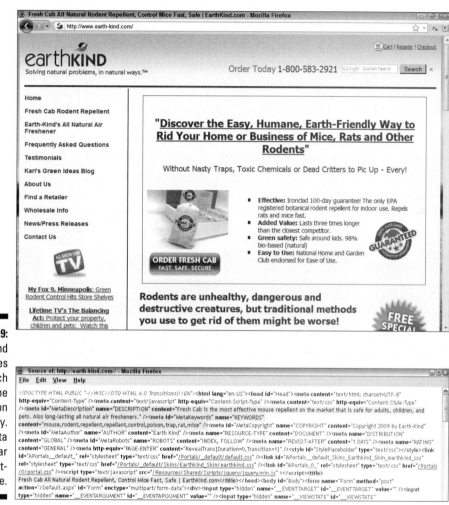

Figure 7-9:
EarthKind (top) uses search engine optimization effectively. Its meta tags appear in the bottom image.

Courtesy of FRESH CAB; EARTH-KIND

Chapter 8

Marketing with Online Building Blocks

In This Chapter

▶ Leveraging the influencers

▶ Proposing to the press

▶ Powering inbound links

▶ Using webinars to generate leads

Chapter 5 covers traffic- and community-building techniques deployed on your site to encourage repeat visits and extend visit length. By comparison, this chapter covers techniques that use other resources on the web to drive traffic to your site. Think of it as online jujitsu. You can increase traffic, inform your target audience, and get folks talking to each other — about your products, services, company, and website — by using these word-of-web methods:

- ✔ E-fluentials
- ✔ Press releases
- ✔ Inbound links

These methods all offer free or relatively inexpensive options, stretching your marketing budget.

Simply mark the methods that seem most useful for your target audience and business sector on your Web Marketing Methods Checklist from Chapter 2. You can download the form from the Downloads tab at `www.dummies.com/go/webmarketingfd3e`.

In Part V, I discuss using various forms of social media to improve search engine results and build traffic to your site with consumer-generated media, videos, blogs, word of mouth, peer recommendations, and viral marketing.

Word-of-web methods work better for reaching tightly targeted market segments than they do for mass marketing or volume traffic. Your site should be live and functioning properly before you drive significant traffic to it. At that point, allot about half a day per week for online marketing.

Incubating the Influencers

Word of web includes third-party sites that collect opinions, product reviews, and vendor ratings; it also includes those who operate online focus groups. Marketing folks speak frequently about the importance of reaching the 10 percent of any audience that charts the course for others.

These electronically (online) influential — or *e-fluential* — folks can do great good, or great harm, on a message board, blog, social network, or consumer review site. They are often early adopters of emerging media and pay close attention to advertising. With a little forethought, you can take advantage of third-party review sites to promote your product, service, or company.

For a few examples of the dozens of these e-fluential sites, see the table titled "Review Sites that Influence Purchases" in Bonus Chapter 3 on the Downloads tab of the companion website.

Many e-fluentials now focus on blogs and social media services. Select blogs with current postings that rank highly for the number of views in directories such as Technorati. On Twitter, look for people with many followers and whose posts are frequently retweeted. On Facebook, look for pages where plenty of people have clicked the Like button and engaged in lots of dialogue. In all cases, watch for a while to see whether the writer routinely recommends or reviews items. You can always search for writers' biographies to ensure that they have good reputations or check their visibility on sites such as Social Mention (http://socialmention.com).

As of 2010, bloggers must legally disclose gifts, products, or payments that influence their opinions.

One caveat: Don't do the talking yourself. Internet users have decent "spin detectors." They can distinguish whether an actual customer or your marketing department wrote a review. Instead, ask satisfied customers or clients whether they would post their comments on one of these sites or give you permission to post a comment in their name.

Posting existing testimonials elsewhere is an easy way to leverage their power. You can offer a small token of your appreciation or a discount coupon to thank good customers for their business and their time.

Promoting with Press Releases

Unlike the influencer category of online promotion, the press release isn't a form with consumer-generated content. However, press releases build interest online when they're repeated on multiple sites, thus conveying information cost-effectively. Figure 8-1 shows how Mobile Tech News (at www.mobiletechnews.com) displays press releases from other sources.

Whenever your company appears on a third-party site or whenever a journalist writes about your site, you gain relevance and credibility from an objective source. You're working on your 15 minutes of fame!

Search engines love press releases almost as much as they love blogs. Because press releases often appear on popular sites, such as Yahoo! News (http://news.yahoo.com) and Google News (http://news.google.com), they earn extra points with inbound links to your site. Use keywords in the headline or lead sentence to make it even likelier that your rank will rise in search engine results.

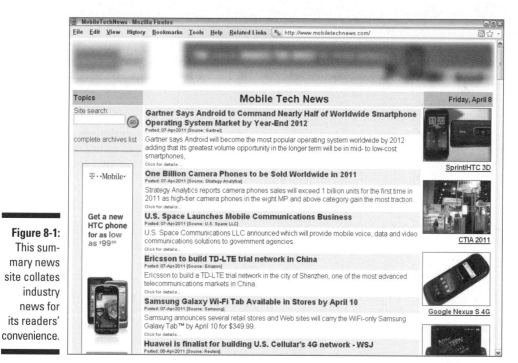

Figure 8-1: This summary news site collates industry news for its readers' convenience.

Courtesy of MobileTechNews

Perking along with press

The unique, online-only travel site Insider Perks (www.insiderperks.com) first entices travelers with videos and then books reservations and sells travel accessories online. As Brian Searl, its founder and CEO, puts it, "We're connecting travelers with people and places they never dreamed possible. We're changing the way you travel, one video at a time." Launched in March 2009, the site targets travelers who like to research destinations before booking.

Recognizing the need for immediate visibility of the site, Searl started distributing press releases, only two months after launch, by using services such as PRWeb (www.prweb.com). Although PRWeb remains its primary distribution channel, Insider Perks sometimes uses PRNewswire to target local markets or PitchEngine to disseminate information quickly that isn't big enough for a release.

Searl, who writes all the press releases himself, takes full advantage of social media, posting primarily on Facebook and Twitter. "But," he notes, "we publish to as many niche sites as possible."

Perhaps it's this consciousness of the social media consumer that leads to Searl's unusual advice: "Try and talk to your audience as a person. Many people write press releases directed at the media but fail to realize that they can easily show up in Google when someone looks for your company name. If you target consumers as well, more people will click through."

Of course, you can also post your press release on your own site, perhaps on your Media Room page, along with coverage you receive.

Online press releases have three audiences:

- ✔ **Automatic:** Many sites now automatically publish press releases from specific distribution sources (that is, they accept electronic RSS feeds) without human review. In this case, your target audience becomes the immediate consumer of your release.

- ✔ **Industry specific:** Readers of blogs that aggregate industry-specific news are intense consumers of news releases. Distribute or post your release on as many subject-related blogs as possible. Check blog directories such as Technorati and others that appear in Chapter 14 to identify sites that accept press releases.

- ✔ **Intermediary:** Like traditional press releases, online press releases run through an intermediary audience of editors or journalists who decide whether to place your headlines and links on their sites and, potentially, reproduce the information in print publications.

Online readers rarely see the complete release at first glance. They see only the headline and perhaps the first line (the *lede*) or a summary. Because you must convince readers to click through to the full release, writing an effective release becomes doubly tricky.

Writing an effective release

The principles of writing for the web, covered in Chapter 3, apply to writing press releases as well. As always, be sure to

- **Keep it short.** A good maximum length is 400 words.
- **Include a dateline.** It should include your city and the day of release.
- **Use active voice.** It enlivens text when the subject of a sentence performs an action.
- **Write an intriguing headline.** The headline should be no longer than ten words.
- **Write a lead that "hooks" your readers.** Make them want to read more of what you write.
- **Cover the basic elements — the "five Ws (and one H)" — of journalism.** Tell readers who, what, when, where, why, and how.
- **Conclude with a standard *cut* paragraph about your company.** This descriptive paragraph can easily be deleted for space.
- **Spell-check and proofread your work.** Accuracy counts.
- **Test all links before posting.** Use as many links as allowed, taking readers to pages with additional detail about the topic of the release, not just to your home page.
- **Add your contact information.** Provide your name, phone number, and e-mail address for additional information.
- **Specify the end of your release.** Type ### or -30- to designate that you're finished.

Figure 8-2 shows an informative press release from Pizza Fusion. Note the dateline at the top, search terms in the headline and text, basic journalistic elements in the first paragraph, and contact information at the bottom. For additional information on preparing a good press release, visit `http://advertising.about.com/od/pressreleases/a/pressreleases.htm` or `www.publicityinsider.com/release.asp`.

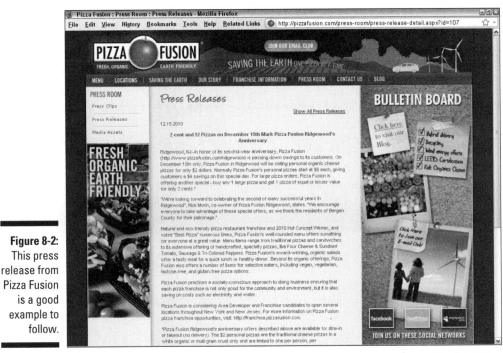

Figure 8-2:
This press release from Pizza Fusion is a good example to follow.

Courtesy of Pizza Fusion Holdings

Distributing releases through social media

Social media outlets offer many more channels for distributing press releases, as well as the opportunity to enhance your release with rich media, such as podcasts, video, or Flash, and to include social sharing options. You can find a template for a social media press release, shown in Figure 8-3, at www. shiftcomm.com/downloads/smprtemplate.pdf. (Todd Defren of Shift Communications developed this template.) For an example of a social media release, look at Figure 8-4, from the home-staging service Sundaybell. Its press release (which is in social media format and distributed via PitchEngine) incorporates a logo, a video, a Twitter pitch, and social media links.

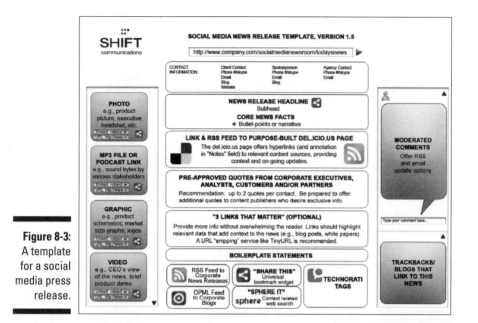

Figure 8-3: A template for a social media press release.

Courtesy of Shift Communications LLC

Figure 8-4: This press release incorporates a logo, a video, a Twitter pitch, and social media links.

Courtesy of pitchengine.com

Distributing your release

Because press releases are marketing materials, you must consider your target market. Depending on your topic and audience, a good distribution network might include both online and offline outlets, including

- General-interest magazines
- Journalists who write about your subject
- Newspapers
- Nontraditional media outlets (for example, text messaging)
- Publications specific to a particular industry (sometimes called a *vertical market*)
- Radio, cable, and broadcast TV
- Social media news services
- Web-only sites

If you already have a public relations or advertising agency, your contractors can help you with writing and distribution. Otherwise, you can decide whether you're looking for B2C or B2B outlets, or both, and whether you want local, regional, national, or international distribution. It all depends on how large a megaphone you want and how much you can afford.

Although you can distribute a release yourself, especially to local press, it's much easier to select an online distribution network that can target the industry sectors you want. To begin, research distribution networks for traditional press releases. Rates, formatting, and other requirements vary widely by network, so select one that fits your budget as well as your needs. Ask whether you can add your own, existing list of journalists, trade industry publications, and websites that accept press releases. What? You don't have an existing list? Start one now.

Explore links to distribution networks and resources for traditional press releases and for social media press releases in Bonus Chapter 3 on the Downloads tab of this book's companion website.

Social news services for traditional press release distribution generally post stories, topics, or links to releases suggested by their members under appropriate topic categories. Not all allow you to nominate your own release, but you can always find a friend or colleague to post a recommendation for you. (Be sure to return the favor.)

Most of these sites rank stories by the number of people who Like them or who rate them highly by pressing the Thumbs Up button, for example. Their popularity then determines where the story will appear on a results page. (With luck, you have a lot of friends!) In any case, many social news services help with your standing in general search engine results and offer additional opportunities for readers to share your story elsewhere. For more on integrating social news services into your online marketing program, see Chapter 19.

Schedule your release based on its time dependence and when your target audience will be available to view it. Because many releases arrive in journalists' inboxes through Real Simple Syndication or e-mail, consider scheduling date-independent releases as you would a B2B newsletter: on Tuesdays or Wednesdays, either early in the morning or midday.

In addition to distributing your release all around the web, be sure to post it on your own site, blog, or social media pages (or all three).

The life span of your release might extend long after your initial distribution. Print outlets might publish your release anywhere from several days to several months after you distribute it. Be sure that its contact information will still be accurate! For more information about working with the press, check out the Internet Press Guild at `www.netpress.org/careandfeeding.html`.

Insider Perks (at `www.insiderperks.com`), shown in Figure 8-5 and profiled in the earlier sidebar "Perking along with press," uses press releases successfully to spread its message. In the figure, Insider Perks offers a full page of material for media outlets at `www.insiderperks.com/media`, including logos, graphics, and videos as well as press releases and fact sheets.

Figure 8-5:
This enchanting travel site offers a full page of material for media outlets.

Courtesy of Insider Perks, Inc.

Connecting with Inbound Link Campaigns

Links from other sites to yours not only yield visits from prequalified prospects but also enhance your search engine ranking. Google, in particular, factors the quantity and quality of inbound links into search engine results. (See Chapter 7.) Good link campaigns are time consuming but valuable for every website seeking new business. They're critical for B2B companies, which usually derive more traffic from Google than they do from other search engines.

When you request an inbound link, you may have to offer a return link, also known as a *reciprocal* link. Try to offer reciprocal links only to sites that have a Google PageRank of 5 or higher. To see the PageRank while you browse, download Google Toolbar from www.google.com/toolbar/ie/index.html.

Some websites might charge for links. If they charge what seems like a lot of money, shift them to your paid-advertising category. In addition to finding links from search engines and all the types of sites listed in this chapter, you can obtain free and often nonreciprocal links from these sources:

- ✔ Industry-based business directories
- ✔ Yellow pages and map sites
- ✔ Local business directories
- ✔ Colleagues
- ✔ Trade associations
- ✔ Other organizations you belong to or sponsor
- ✔ Suppliers, including your web development company and host
- ✔ Distributors, clients, customers, or affiliates (ask!)
- ✔ Award sites such as the Webbys (www.webbyawards.com)
- ✔ Sites to which you contribute content
- ✔ Sites such as www.mycontentbuilder.com or www.isnare.com for content distribution, or search for e-zine directories such as www.zinos.com/f/z/author_signup.html or www.zinebook.com.
- ✔ Sites that list you as an expert (for example, www.prleads.com or https://profnet.prnewswire.com/ProfNetHome.aspx)
- ✔ *Meta indexes* (sites with master lists of directories)
- ✔ Related, but not directly competing, businesses

Evaluating link popularity

Link popularity, a count of how many sites link to you, measures your visibility on the web. Links are search engine specific, so only other sites that are indexed by the same engine appear on the list of inbound links. Start by entering **link:www.*yourdomain*.com** into the search field of a target search engine. (Some search engines prefer **linkdomain:www.*yourdomain*.com**.)

Additional link checkers are included in the resource table "Inbound Link Resources" in Bonus Chapter 3 on the Downloads tab of the companion website.

You might discover that other sites have linked to yours without your knowledge, which is usually okay. You will also find that Google usually displays far fewer inbound links than other search engines, although it "knows" that others are there. You can find more about selecting links specifically for Google in Chapter 7.

Figure 8-6 shows a partial page of inbound links on Google for the International Fund for Animal Welfare (`www.ifaw.org`). Its link report shows some of the inbound links from other sites that are in the Google database. The total number of found links, including internal ones, according to Google, appears in the upper-left corner (118,000 results).

A sample link-request e-mail message

Dear Colleague,

I am requesting a link on behalf of YourDomain.com, a new, online gallery that focuses on highly collectible and one-of-a-kind pieces by renowned artists and artisans. We offer serious art lovers and collectors the opportunity to acquire unique contemporary art. The site contains artist biographies, an explanation of art media, and a calendar of statewide art events and studio tours.

I believe that our site would appeal to the same audience that visits yours. Please consider adding a link to `www.YourDomain.com` on your site. I would appreciate your letting me know whether you are accepting new links and when the link has posted.

For your convenience, I have provided a title, a description, and some keywords as well as the code for an HTML text link.

Thank you for your time and consideration.

Signature Block

Found links

Search request

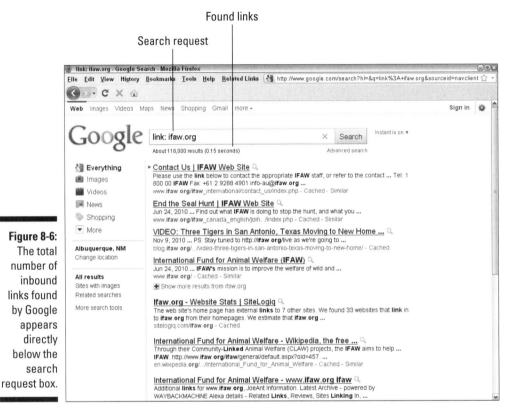

Figure 8-6:
The total
number of
inbound
links found
by Google
appears
directly
below the
search
request box.

Implementing a link campaign

When putting together your link campaign, try for at least 50 inbound links, which you request by e-mail or submit by hand. The more links the merrier, as long as they're from valid sites. Follow these steps:

1. **Start your search for inbound links.**

   Enter one of your keywords in a search engine such as Google to see which sites appear at the top of its results. Then run an inbound link check by using one of the tools discussed in the preceding section for the top two or three sites to see a list of possible targets.

2. **Run a report on inbound link popularity on several of your competitors to get ideas.**

3. **Research the sources of free links in the bulleted list at the beginning of the section "Connecting with Inbound Link Campaigns" as well as other search engines, business directories, and meta indexes.**

You can research links while your site is under development, but don't make any requests until the site is live.

4. **Visit every site to ensure that it's relevant and that your target audience would visit.**

   This way, any referred traffic is prequalified.

5. **Look for directions such as *Add your URL* to see whether to request a link by e-mail or fill out a form on the target site.**

   You might need to look at the footer or site index to find out how to add your link.

6. **When you're ready, start your link requests.**

   Blind-copy 30 or so e-mail requests to save time, using a message such as the one in the nearby sidebar, "A sample link-request e-mail message." Insert your website name and link request in the Subject line. If you're willing to offer a reciprocal link or if you already have a good Google PageRank or a significant amount of traffic, add that information to your message.

7. **Submit onsite requests manually.**

   Some sites ask only for a site's URL; others ask for a page title, description, keywords, contact information, or more.

8. **Do your follow-up homework. Check your e-mail for responses from websites.**

   Some responses ask you to confirm that you're a real person by asking you to click a link or e-mail back. Others might request reciprocal links before they post yours. Only a small fraction of your link requests is likely to respond.

9. **After six to eight weeks, check to see which links have posted. Make a second polite request and check again after another two months.**

   If a site still hasn't posted your link after two months, find a substitute.

Unless you request otherwise, most inbound sites link to your home page. If your site is segmented by target market or product, segment your requests for inbound links to match. Provide the URL for the correct internal page rather than for your home page. Most sites post your link on their own Links or Resources pages. From a search engine point of view, links from other content pages usually carry greater value.

Link campaigns involve a lot of detail. To keep track, create a spreadsheet to track your efforts, with columns for these details:

✔ Site name

✔ Appearance URL

✔ Submission URL or e-mail address

- Date of submission
- URL of page you asked others to link to
- Whether a reciprocal link or payment is needed
- Date the link was checked

To make your life easier, purchase software programs such as those from Raven (or others in the "Inbound Link Resources" table in Bonus Chapter 3 of the Downloads tab on the companion website) or look for a search engine optimization (SEO) consultant or an online marketing company to find links and manage your link campaign.

Differentiating between nice links and naughty ones

Some search engines count every link, regardless of its source. However, Google and other engines have criteria for legitimate links. (In Chapter 7, I discuss other criteria that Google uses to establish ranking in search results.)

A "nice" link comes from a site that

- Is on the same search engine as yours.
- Shares at least one keyword or search term with yours.
- Has text content on the page, not just links. (The text can consist of one-line link annotations.)

Both a gray market and a black market exist for selling links to enhance search engine ranking — avoid the temptation. The links that are offered probably don't qualify as "nice" in the first place.

Most "naughty" links aren't evil, but they don't do you much good because some search engines ignore them. Avoid the following types of sites:

- **Link farms, or free-for-all (FFA):** They randomly link thousands of sites and can get you bounced from search engines. (Okay, these sites are close to evil.)
- **Multilink pages:** These sites have more than 50 or 60 links per page.
- **Web alliances or rings of related sites:** These sites exchange links among the members of the group.
- **Link exchanges:** They automatically arrange links between two sites rather than allow two individual companies to establish reciprocity. Because the offered links frequently originate from totally unrelated sites, these automated exchanges might be a waste of time. Usually, you must post two links for every one you receive.

Following external and reciprocal link protocol

It has become standard operating procedure to have a page for external (or *outbound*) links on your website. Often named Links or Resources, this page displays reciprocal links and convenient links to sites with additional information.

Google, which incorporates outbound links as part of its algorithm for ranking search engine results, prefers sites whose outbound links demonstrate a broad relation to cyberspace. The better structured your own links page, the better the offer you can make when you request a reciprocal link from others. To help structure your links page, try to follow the principles described in this list:

- ✔ **Limit the number of external links.** If you have more than 50 or 60 per page, organize them by topic and start another page.

- ✔ **Summarize the content of your links.** Insert one line of text below every link for its summary.

- ✔ **Include educational (.edu), government (.gov), and not-for-profit (.org) sites among your outbound links, even if they don't link back to you.** By adding objectivity and credibility, these links generate goodwill among your customers and extra value toward the Google search engine ranking.

These principles are visible on the links page for Wanderlust Jewelry (at www.wanderlustjewelry.com), shown in Figure 8-7.

Links from your site that originate on a regular text page are even more valuable to offer, but you don't want to draw visitors away from your message and calls to action. Think about internal HTML pages where outbound links might appear without distraction, such as testimonials, success stories, client lists, or lists of retailers.

Generally, you can link to another site without obtaining permission, as long as the other site appears independently. Occasionally, you'll come across a site such as Forbes (at www.forbes.com) that requires permission. (Use the request form on the site.) This situation is unlikely, except with large corporations. If you aren't sure whether you can link, look around a large website for the media, legal, or public relations section for directions.

Don't open other sites within a frame on your site without prior permission from the owner of the other site. (Frames aren't search engine friendly — you shouldn't use them anyway.) Don't make it appear in any other way that someone else's content belongs to you.

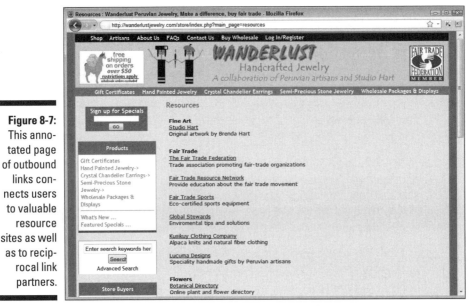

Figure 8-7: This annotated page of outbound links connects users to valuable resource sites as well as to reciprocal link partners.

Some external sites might refuse to link unless your link page is accessible from the navigation, not just from other pages. That's your call. You can easily include a Links or Resources page in your site index at the beginning of the development process. If the page is an afterthought, decide whether it's worth the cost and hassle to modify the navigation. As a simple alternative, include the Links page as an option in a linkable footer.

After you start a link campaign, your inbox might fill with requests from other sites asking you to link to them. Evaluate every one strategically for the value the link brings, such as a high Google PageRank or your target audience. You're under no obligation to post other links unless you have promised reciprocity.

Be leery of requests from sites that ask visitors to vote on your site popularity, charge for links, or otherwise get you in trouble with search engines. Some of these are truly scams: They return afterward to ask for payment, similar to the way fake yellow pages bills are sent in the mail.

Qualifying Leads with Webcasts, Web Conferences, and Webinars

In the instant-gratification world of the web, you rarely have a chance to interact with prospects or customers for more than a few seconds, let alone minutes. All three web education methods (webcasts, web conferences, and webinars) allow you 15 minutes or more of uninterrupted user contact. How can you pass that up, especially when you compare the costs of traveling and staging live events in multiple locations?

These content-driven techniques work well in B2B environments, where you can adapt them for free product demonstrations, market research presentations, or teaching sessions in exchange for contact information. They're useful for building brand awareness, positioning your company as a leader, and generating sales leads. Don't poison the well with overt marketing or hard sales pitches.

Segment leads by including on the sign-up form a question about registrants' levels of interest or decision-making timeframes.

Comparing options

Webcasts, web conferences, and webinars all run in a browser environment. The combination of increased broadband access and the inclusion of streaming media within browsers make these methods much more accessible than they were in the past.

Webcasts

Generally, a *webcast* refers to a live, video broadcast online. Inherently passive, a webcast is delivered from one speaker to many listeners, often 50 or more. Of the three techniques, webcasts work best in a B2C environment for concerts, lectures, dance, comedy, theater, performance arts, sports events, entertainment, and events of educational or training content. Depending on its audience and purpose, you can promote a webcast like any other online event. Webcasts are often recorded for future replays on any of the video services, such as YouTube. (See Chapter 14 for more information on video sharing.)

Web conferences

A *web conference* works best with a small-group presentation that's data or document driven. Web conferences support two-way interaction, such as in an online focus group or a presentation near the close of the sales cycle. Conferences generally involve a combination of two-way audio teleconferencing, live desktop-based whiteboards, PowerPoint presentations, and instant messaging or chat software. For example, Vyew, shown in Figure 8-8, offers "groupware for bridging time and space."

Webinars

A *webinar* is more complex than a webcast or web conference, mixing and matching such multimedia components as a one-way audio conference, a video conference (sometimes a talking head, which is more useful for product demonstrations), PowerPoint or whiteboard presentations, live polls or surveys, and one-way instant messaging for participants to submit questions.

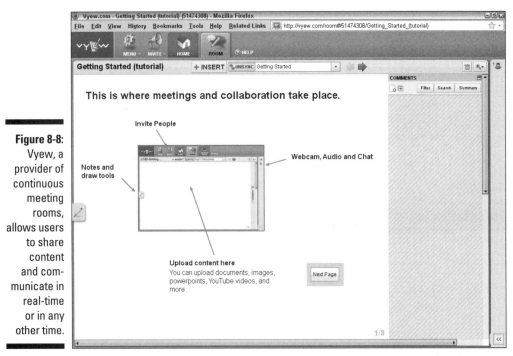

Figure 8-8:
Vyew, a provider of continuous meeting rooms, allows users to share content and communicate in real-time or in any other time.

Designed to reach a large number of participants over a widespread geographical region, webinars generally require a sequence of activities in order to be successful: promotion, registration, confirmation e-mails, reminder e-mails, thank-you messages, and feedback surveys. Consider these elements as premium branding and lead generation opportunities.

Planning a webcast, webinar, or web conference

Before planning webinars or web conferences, participate in a few to see how other businesses use them. Figure 8-9 shows a webinar in progress from HubSpot, using the Citrix GoToWebinar software.

For resources on webcasts, web conferencing, and webinars, search some of the sites listed in Bonus Chapter 3 on the Downloads tab of the companion website.

Chat box

A third of companies have no
the ROI of their mobile marketi
only 24% say it performed as w
better than expected.

41% THEY WILL BE REQUIRED TO SHOW A POSITIVE ROI TO CONTINUE

23. How do you rate the ROI of
your existing mobile marketing
campaign(s) as a whole?

EXCEEDED EXPECTATIONS	**8**%
PERFORMED AS EXPECTED	**16**%
WE HAVEN'T MEASURED IT	**34**%
PERFORMED WORSE THAN EXPECTED	**5**%
FAR BELOW EXPECTATIONS	**5**%
I DON'T KNOW	**29**%
NET EXCEEDED EXPECTATIONS/ PERFORMED AS EXPECTED	**24**%

BASE: COMPANY CURRENTLY HAS/PLANS A MOBILE STRATEGY

24. Will m
be requ
to be fr

41% YES, WE WILL NEED TO
RETURN TO CONTINUE

31% NO, ALTHOUGH WE WILL BE
MEASURING AND TRACKING ROI

13% NO, WE WON'T BE TRACKING
ROI AT THIS TIME

14% DON'T KNOW

KingFishMedia

GoToWebinar Viewer

File View Help

Audio

Audio Mode: Use Telephone / Use Mic & Speakers

MUTED

Audio Setup

Talking: Gordon Plutsky

Questions/Chat

Audience Question
Q: Can we get/download the presentations slides?
A: Yes, the recording and slides will be sent out!

Can you think of any service applications for a B2B company using mobile apps?

Send

Free Webinar: How Companies Adopt and
Measure Mobile Marketing
Webinar ID: 616-935-033

GoToWebinar™

citrix

Talking: Gordon Plutsky

Figure 8-9:
A webinar
in progress.
Note the
control
panel and
chat box on
the right.

Courtesy of Hubspot

Expect falloff to occur from registration to attendance. Perhaps only one-third to one-half of preregistrants show up, depending on how targeted your audience is and how specialized your topic. Of those, you'll probably find that only 5 to 10 percent are close to sales ready. Step softly in these environments! Use these opportunities to build credibility and trust, establish relationships, and answer questions fairly.

Offer an on-demand recording of the event to everyone who registers. Then post a link to the recorded webinar on your site for others to download. You'll get views from people who registered but couldn't participate, repeat views, and new visits from those who missed the presentation.

Figure 8-10 and the sidebar "Educating online for a cure" demonstrate how the PKD Foundation made creative use of webinars to provide essential information while boosting its membership.

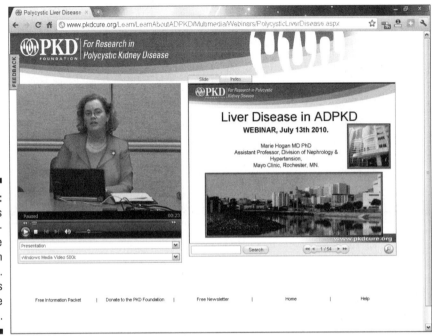

Figure 8-10:
This webinar-on-demand, like others from PKDcure.org, helps educate the public.

Consider these hints for planning webinars or web conferences:

- ✔ **To increase attendance, focus on high-quality, relevant content.** If what you offer is useful and appealing, you'll find an audience.

- ✔ **Ensure that your promotion clearly answers the question "What's in it for me?"** Be sure to list your live events in web event directories — refer to the resource list in Bonus Chapter 3 on the Downloads tab of the companion website. Consider paid banner advertising or newsletter sponsorships to promote your web learning event.

- ✔ **Get more mileage from the level of effort that's applied!** Archive any of these events on your site and make them easily available on demand. This strategy also saves staff time downstream.

- ✔ **Use a survey package (such as StellarSurvey, SurveyMonkey, or Zoomerang) to obtain feedback after the event.** You might want to share some or all of the feedback with participants in a final, e-mailed, thank-you note. Of course, include contact information for the future.

Unless you have a large company or plan frequent webcasts, webinars, and conferences, you probably prefer not to purchase and install software. Look for third-party providers to handle the real-time events. Simply search for them or start with the companies listed on the companion website. Your developer can easily post your archived media on your site, of course.

Educating online for a cure

Founded in 1982 in Kansas City, Missouri, the PKD Foundation is the only nonprofit organization worldwide dedicated to fighting polycystic kidney disease (PKD) through research, education, advocacy, support, and awareness. Launched in 2000, the website `www.pkdcure.org` offers 24/7/365 access to the PKD Learning Center, including webinars directed to PKD patients, their family members, and anyone else who wants to learn about this disease.

Dave Switzer, director of marketing and communications, explains that the foundation began using the free webinars in October 2008 as a way to spread information far beyond the attendance at their annual national convention. Webinars cover such topics as nutrition, dialysis, kidney transplantation, pain management, emotional impact, and more.

The initial webinar took a fair amount of time to set up, given the learning curve. The live Q&A session, combined with video and presentation elements, required higher-end technology than expected, Switzer recalls. With experience, the process became a little easier. Switzer expects costs to fall dramatically when the foundation finishes migrating to a newer, web-based system.

Traditionally, Switzer starts promoting webinars one month in advance on the site and by e-mail so that people can "save the date." He follows up with a reminder one week out, and another on the day of the event to those who have registered. He also promotes the webinars in monthly, national e-newsletters and in chapter e-newsletters to local groups. The PKD Foundation maintains a social media presence on Facebook and Twitter, where he interjects information about activities and events such as the webinars.

Switzer tracks the number of attendees, the knowledge of the subject matter before and after the webinar, the number of people who watch live, the number who watch the recorded version, and whether they felt the topic was presented in a manner that was easy to understand.

"Webinars are an excellent tool to share information in an interactive format," he says, "but they work best when there is an opportunity for viewers to ask questions so they can feel engaged." Switzer offers a litany of do's and don'ts: Don't spend too much on technology. Do make sure to provide enough advance promotion of your webinar. Don't worry about having a presenter onscreen — a talking head isn't too exciting! Most of all, do decide which stats you want to track before you get started so that you can monitor whether you're truly reaching your goals.

Chapter 9

The Art of E-Mail Marketing

*S*ome 294 billion e-mail messages were flooding inboxes every day in April 2010; that's 90 trillion messages in a year! As many as 90 percent were *spam* (unwanted, unsolicited e-mail); some were filtered out and most of the rest were deleted without being read. The rest were sent by about 1.9 billion legitimate e-mail users. Getting prospects or customers to notice your message in the midst of this deluge takes a bit of effort. Fortunately, you can master some best practices for breaking through with e-mail messages and newsletters that generate business, build relationships, and encourage customer loyalty.

Good e-mail messages start with informational From and Subject lines and follow through with interesting content, links to your website and other social media, and calls to action. These messages have a purpose and, in the best of all worlds, are directed to a specific audience. Of course, any e-mail messages distributed to a group should be addressed only to recipients who *opt in* (specifically and positively give you permission to send them e-mail messages), and they should comply with the federal CAN-SPAM Act of 2003 and its updates (http://business.ftc.gov/documents/bus61-can-spam-act-compliance-guide-business).

E-mail techniques range from simple, free, signature blocks to expensive, multisegmented, newsletter campaigns, all of which I address in this chapter. On your Web Marketing Methods Checklist (see Chapter 2), you might want to check off the techniques you plan to use. You can download the form from the Downloads tab of the companion website, at www.dummies.com/go/webmarketing3fde. For more information on e-mail marketing, see *E-Mail Marketing For Dummies,* by John Arnold (John Wiley & Sons, Inc.).

Using What You Already Have: Free E-Mail Tools

In the rush to benefit from advanced technology, business owners often forget about basic, one-to-one, e-mail marketing tools. That's a shame because these tools are free with services you already have. As I explain in more detail in the following sections, signature blocks are primarily for branding, blurbs save time by offering customer support, and autoresponders help maintain a relationship with prospects or customers. All three are components of good customer service.

Branding with signature blocks

As shown in Figure 9-1, a *signature block* is the e-mail equivalent of a business card or letterhead. A signature block should appear at the bottom of *every* business e-mail you send out. A good signature block includes a marketing tag, all your contact information, and live links to your website and social media pages.

Figure 9-1:
A sample signature block with links to social media.

Jan Zimmerman, Author
Web Marketing For Dummies
Social Media Marketing All-in-One For Dummies
Strategic Web Marketing and Site Management
Watermelon Mountain Web Marketing
4614 Sixth St. NW
Albuquerque, NM 87107
t: 505.344.4230
f: 505.345.4128
e: info@watermelonweb.com
w: http://www.watermelonweb.com

Courtesy of Watermelon Mountain Web Marketing www.watermelonweb.com

Your company name and marketing tag provide name recognition and branding. The block offers consistent, easy access to all your contact information, including (at minimum) your phone number, fax number, street address, e-mail address, and website address. Some signature blocks include business hours, a link to a map, or a link to a current special offer or event, as well as linkable calls to action to visit elements of the company's social media presence.

Almost all e-mail programs (sometimes called e-mail *clients*), such as Outlook, Outlook Express, Gmail, and Eudora, allow you to set up signature blocks. In other words, they're free! To set up a signature block, look on the toolbar in your e-mail program for a menu option named Tools⇨Options or (similar), or use the Help feature to look up instructions.

Display the website address in your signature block as a live link. Most e-mail programs create the link automatically if you start the URL with `http://`.

Letting autoresponders do the work

You've probably received many autoresponder messages without realizing it. *Autoresponder* messages are sent automatically in response to e-mail or as part of the cycle of activity on a website. You set up the former type in your e-mail program, usually by creating a message rule. (See the Help feature in your e-mail program.) The standard out-of-office message is perhaps the most common use of this type of autoresponder. Web-based autoresponders, such as the one for Sewing Patterns, shown in Figure 9-2, are often generated when users submit forms or make purchases.

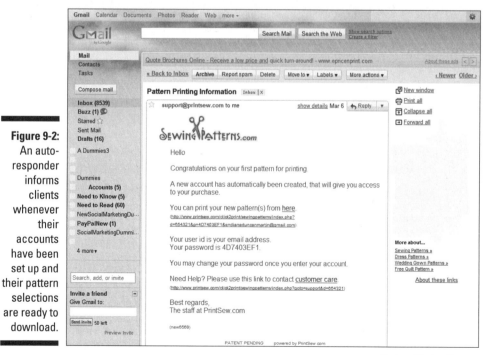

Figure 9-2: An auto-responder informs clients whenever their accounts have been set up and their pattern selections are ready to download.

Courtesy of Sewingpatterns.com

These autoresponder messages are useful when you want to

- ✓ Welcome users to a newsletter, perhaps with a coupon for an initial purchase.
- ✓ Acknowledge a request for information or technical support.
- ✓ Confirm a purchase.
- ✓ Indicate that an item is in production or has shipped.
- ✓ Send a survey for feedback on customer service.
- ✓ Say thank you and inquire about customer satisfaction.

Because users can't reply to web-based autoresponder messages, include a live e-mail address and phone number in your message. Simple autoresponders are usually included in hosting packages. Tell your developer which autoresponders you want to send and when. Ask whether you can personalize these autoresponders with a salutation (such as "Dear Jane") that draws the user's name from an order or information request form.

If you need multiple, timed autoresponders, you can use shareware, purchased software, add-on features offered by many e-newsletter vendors, an autoresponder included with your storefront package, or a third-party provider's web-based service, such as the one at www.ecoursewizard.com. Given the sensitivity to spam, just don't overdo it. See www.thesite wizard.com/archive/autoresponders.shtml for more information about autoresponders.

An e-mailed autoresponder doesn't serve the same function as a Thank You page on a website. You still should provide immediate feedback online whenever a user successfully submits a form or places an order.

Speeding response time with packaged blurbs

Blurbs are prepackaged e-mail responses used to respond quickly to customer requests for information. You merely supply a salutation or insert other personalized information. The 80/20 rule applies: Of the e-mail inquiries you receive, 80 percent cover the same 20 percent of topics. Blurbs that cover 80 percent of your e-mail responses cost nothing more than the time to write them.

Prepackaged blurbs, such as the one shown in Figure 9-3, help you manage your inbox and respond to e-mails within one business day. Save blurbs as drafts in your e-mail program and copy them to a new message as needed. Always include a salutation ("Dear John") and an invitation to call or e-mail for additional information.

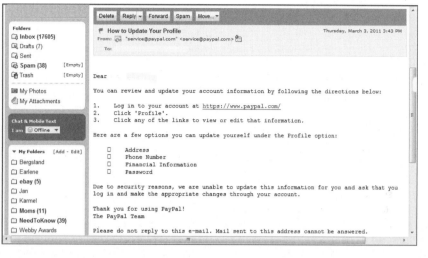

Figure 9-3:
This
blurb from
PayPal was
received in
response to
an inquiry
about how
to update a
profile.

Although you can send blurbs as attachments, recipients are more likely to open and read simple e-mails.

Possible topics for blurbs include

- Items from the FAQ (frequently asked questions) section of your website
- An abbreviated corporate "backgrounder"
- Copies of recent press releases
- Troubleshooting replies to common problems

Getting the Most Out of E-Mail Messages

As Chapter 5 notes, "Marketing is only part of a business, but all of a business is marketing." This statement includes e-mail correspondence with your customers.

Ignore at your peril the marketing value of the messages you send to prospects, customers, vendors, and other people. Your time-critical messages might end up in someone's deleted mail folder, lost, forlorn, and unread. They might be so poorly written that they turn off the recipient or have such large attachments that the recipient's e-mail program discards them as spam.

Send PDF files or attachments larger than 100K only to people that you know can receive them. Ask before you e-mail. For alternative methods, you can post the material on your website and send your recipients a link, send the documents by way of online signature services such as EchoSign (www.echosign.com), or — gasp! — fax them electronically via efax.com.

E-mailing like a pro

Here's some advice to keep in mind when you compose e-mail messages:

- ✔ **From line:** The From line is the first criterion that recipients use in deciding whether to open a message — which makes your e-mail address a marketing decision. Select text that customers will recognize, such as your full name or a phrase such as *CustomerService@YourCompany.com*.

   At this point, every good web host offers free e-mail addresses with your web domain name (*@yourdomain.com*), which you should use for branding and name recognition. You can access these addresses directly by using your e-mail program or have them forwarded to your regular e-mail account. Your developer or host can help you set them up.

   To appear professional, don't reply from or otherwise display your regular Internet service provider (ISP) e-mail account (for example, @aol, @hotmail, @gmail, or @comcast) or send business e-mail containing advertisements. Most e-mail programs let you define the From address that's displayed in recipients' inboxes. If you have any difficulty, ask your ISP.

- ✔ **Subject line:** Recipients use the Subject line as their second criterion in the ruthless game of Toss or Read. Be succinct and factual; this isn't the place for cute tricks. Keep the Subject line to fewer than 50 characters, which is the maximum length of the standard subject display. Shorter is better anyway; several studies have shown that shorter Subject lines are more likely to be opened and to generate clicks. If your e-mail address doesn't include your company name or function, put it in the Subject line: *Your Tech Support Reply from ABC Products,* for example. If appropriate, put an event name or a meeting date in the Subject line.

- ✔ **Message text:** In the text itself, quickly identify yourself, the nature of your relationship with the recipient (or the person who referred you), and the purpose of your message. Also, keep your messages business-like in appearance. Save the fancy fonts and bright colors for your personal e-mail. If you include a small logo, remember that some people suppress images in e-mail. All these directives hold true for autoresponders and blurbs as well as for e-mail messages.

   E-mail messages, autoresponders, and blurbs are standard forms of business correspondence. Always check them for clarity, formatting, spelling, and other essential principles of good writing. Send them to yourself or others to test whether they look right in different e-mail clients. Put the most important information at the top in case someone views messages in Preview mode.

Keep separate accounts for your business and personal e-mail. Many people keep a third e-mail identity for newsletters and other correspondence from websites to which they've given their e-mail address.

Sending bulk or group e-mail

All the e-mail techniques discussed so far in this chapter deal with one-on-one marketing. *Bulk* e-mail is a free technique that lets you send e-mail to small groups of users who share a common interest.

The simplest setup for bulk e-mail is to create a *group* in your e-mail program and add addresses to it. Rather than enter individual names in the Address field of the message, you enter the name of the group. (See the Help feature in your e-mail program for details.)

Because of concerns about spam, some ISPs don't let you send bulk e-mail to more than 50 to 100 names at one time. To work around this limitation, you can buy inexpensive software to handle bulk mail. Here are a few suggestions to get you started:

Software Name	*URL*
LmhSoft e-Campaign 8	`www.lmhsoft.com`
G-Lock Software	`www.glocksoft.com/easymail`
GroupMail	`www.group-mail.com/asp/common/default.asp`

For more options, search for *group e-mail software* at your favorite search engine. As a cheaper solution, consider using free Yahoo! Groups (`http://groups.yahoo.com`) or Google Groups (`http://groups.google.com/?pli=1`).

These methods are all easy, but rather old-fashioned, alternatives to sending a special newsletter to a small subset of your commercial e-mailing list. Group e-mail is useful to

- ✔ Notify registrants in a course, conference, or program or another type of event.
- ✔ Communicate with dealers, distributors, or franchisees.
- ✔ Send routine service reminders or product recalls.
- ✔ Remind customers of appointments or item pick-ups.
- ✔ Distribute information to journalists.
- ✔ Communicate with committees, board members, or employees.
- ✔ Announce availability of products on back order.

Rolling Out E-Mail Newsletters

Offering deals on the latest digital cameras? Directions for cooking with organic beets and carrots or perhaps some last-minute tax tips? Suggestions for stain removal or the latest news on the Rockabilly Roller Derby? Do you have the buzz on what Carrie told Mary, who left Barry, who used to be with Gary on a soap opera?

Whatever their interests, passions, or buying habits, consumers can sign up for e-mail newsletters to sate their desires. As an e-mail marketer, you must find the people who want your special offers, hot gossip, or the latest news delivered to their electronic doorsteps; get them to sign up for your distribution service; and then encourage them to follow through with a click to your site.

The newsletter shown in Figure 9-4 from FaveCrafts, a retailer of discounted craft supplies, illustrates how a company can use a newsletter to let customers and prospects know about special offers and new products. Their newsletter includes links to specific products and linkable navigation across the top that take users to featured categories on the website.

Links to their website

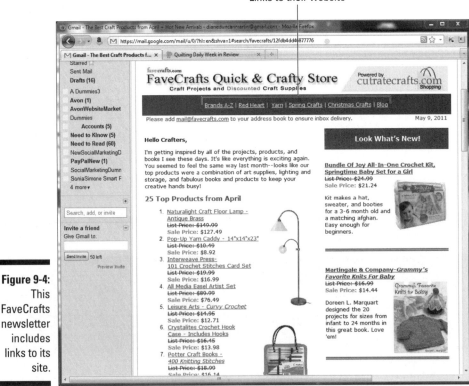

Figure 9-4: This FaveCrafts newsletter includes links to its site.

Courtesy of FaveCrafts.com, CutRateCrafts.com

Compared to other forms of online advertising, online newsletters have a fairly high *click-through rate* (CTR), which is the percentage of people who see an ad and click through to the website. Although banner ads routinely draw less than 0.5 percent of viewers to a site, online newsletters average 4 to 5 percent depending on the size and quality of the list. To be successful, you need a good newsletter that's sent to the right audience at the right time.

E-mail is on its way o-u-t among the young! If you're aiming at a demographic younger than 25 years old, e-mail might be too old-fashioned for marketing communication. For this population, use social networking (see Part V) or text messaging (see Chapter 10). By comparison, Internet users older than 40 prefer e-mail newsletters.

Improving the efficacy of your newsletter

The more targeted your newsletter and its audience, the more likely it will be successful. Before creating and distributing an issue of your newsletter, define its objective and its target audience. Is it to make sales? If so, which segment of your customer base is interested in the products you display?

Figure 9-5 shows a product-driven newsletter from Daily Grommet, a consumer-driven online marketplace that sends a short, graphically enticing newsletter to its subscribers every day as a way to focus attention on a new find. Note the Follow Us icons for Facebook and Twitter and for sharing by e-mail.

If you're moving a prospect along the sales cycle, for example, provide the information customers need next to make a purchasing decision. Or, if you're trying to recover customers you haven't heard from in a while, provide an offer that will bring them back.

Another consideration is whether you eventually want to accept advertising or paid sponsorships for your newsletter. This decision affects your newsletter design and implementation.

Analyzing statistics related to your newsletter objective is just as important as analyzing statistics on your website. If the purpose of your newsletter is branding, track growth in the number of subscribers. If your purpose is sales, measure the sales conversion rate and profitability.

A few terms of the trade define what success means. A good newsletter service provides the following statistics: bounce rate, open rate, unsubscribe rate, click-through rate, and A/B testing. Read on for more information about measuring your newsletter's success.

Bounce rate

The *bounce rate* is the percentage of addresses that can't be delivered for various reasons. Most services provide a breakdown. Review the list of bounces for typos and poorly formatted e-mail addresses. Some list management services do this automatically before sending, and others test all addresses with a signal to confirm that addresses are valid (a process called *pinging*) before sending an e-mail. Obviously, the lower the bounce rate, the better.

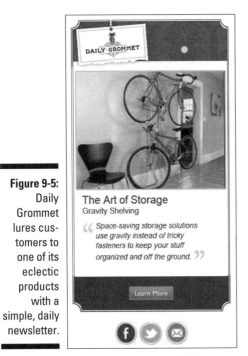

Figure 9-5:
Daily
Grommet
lures cus-
tomers to
one of its
eclectic
products
with a
simple, daily
newsletter.

Courtesy of DailyGrommet.com

Open rate

The *open rate* is the percentage of *delivered mail* (that is, names sent minus bounces) that readers open. You can't guarantee that recipients *read* the messages they open, but you can guarantee that the messages have been opened (clicked on and displayed in the Preview box or main window). The better your From and Subject lines, the higher your open rate. Open and click-through rates vary widely by time of delivery, the size and source of your list, and industry, as shown in Figure 9-6. The figure, from MailerMailer, an e-mail service provider, displays open rates and click-through rates by industry based on the 2010 results for MailerMailer clients. Rates as high as possible are desirable.

Open Rate by Industry

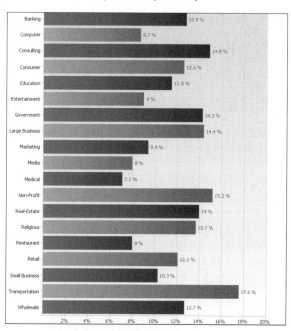

Click-Through Rate by Industry

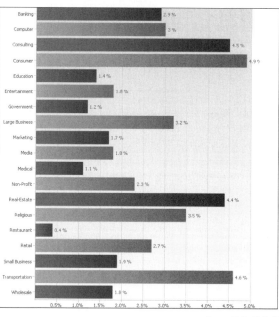

Figure 9-6:
The e-mail service provider Mailer-Mailer offers open rates by industry for 2010 (top) and click-through rates by industry (bottom).

Source: MailerMailer®

Unsubscribe rate

The CAN-SPAM Act of 2003 now requires an option to unsubscribe with a single action in all e-mail newsletters. People usually click a link to unsubscribe. Everyone on your list should already have opted in, either online or offline.

Strive for a low unsubscribe rate. To reduce this rate, segment your list by interest area or incorporate a *double opt-in process* (subscribers receive an e-mail asking them to confirm their registration by clicking a link; only then are they added to your distribution list). These practices may, however, depress your sign-up rate. Again, this rate varies widely based on the quality of your list.

Click-through rate

The *click-through rate (CTR)* is the number of links to your website divided by the number of opened newsletters. To reach a higher CTR, make sure you have a good match between your newsletter and your target audience, even if it means sending a different message to different segments of your list.

CTR also depends on the quality of your headline, offer, and content and the number of links you have in your newsletter. Studies show that the more links newsletters have, the higher their click-through rates.

Include at least one link for every text block and one link for every image.

Some newsletter services give you two CTR rates: total clicks and clicks from unique users. Then you can tell how many readers clicked through more than once. Whatever your specific objective, you must drive your readers to your website to complete a purchase or to find more information. Strive for a CTR as high as possible.

An intriguing report by MailerMailer (at www.mailermailer.com/resources/metrics/daily-rates.rwp) indicates that smaller lists tend to perform better in terms of open rate but that the results vary significantly by industry. This finding indicates the value of segmenting your list by interest or purchase history after you reach approximately 2,000 names.

E-mail lists age rapidly because users often change providers or abandon addresses to avoid spam. Rented and public lists are less effective than your own. Thus, the older your address list, the higher the bounce and unsubscribe rates, and the lower the open and click-through rates.

A/B testing

It's surprisingly difficult to predict how people will respond to even slight changes in phrasing on promotional material. *A/B testing,* a technique drawn from direct mail marketing, lets you analyze different elements of your newsletter to maximize its effectiveness. In an A/B test, you send slightly different versions of your newsletter to a representative sample of your audience. Because you can test your e-mail with as few as 25 recipients, testing is feasible even for small businesses. You can separately test these elements:

> From line
>
> Subject line
>
> Headline
>
> Product selection
>
> Time of delivery
>
> Offer

Change only one element at a time! If you don't control the variables, you can't distinguish which element accounts for the results you get.

Creating an effective newsletter

Like everything else in web marketing, creating a good newsletter can take more time than you expect. Allow a learning curve, starting out with a slower schedule than you might eventually adopt.

Your newsletter must comply with the CAN-SPAM Act of 2003 and its updates. Some states have additional antispam laws. In spite of laws and better filtering software, the amount of spam that reaches users' mailboxes hasn't leveled off. Spammers seem to find new ways to evade the filters as fast as the filters are improved. Commercial newsletter services require you to meet CAN-SPAM requirements to retain their own viability.

The From and Subject lines are the key to increasing the open rate for your newsletter — in particular:

> ✔ **Don't forget branding.** Include your name, company, product, and service (whatever readers will most recognize as your brand) in either the From or Subject line. After the From line is established, use it consistently.
>
> ✔ **Entice the subscriber.** Insert in the Subject line a benefit or another reason for opening the message. You're more likely to receive a response to an e-mail titled *November Savings from Your Company* than one titled *Monthly News from Your Company*. Of course, *a good offer* always works, such as *2 for 1 Dinner Coupon*.

> ✔ **Be honest.** Don't trick people into opening your e-mail with a misleading Subject line.
>
> An accurate Subject line is a legal requirement.

✔ **Create a sense of urgency.** Incorporate time-dependent phrases or other words of urgency to encourage opening your newsletter promptly, such as the name of the month or terms such as *this week, now, important recall notice,* or *exclusive offer.*

✔ **Don't overdo it.** Avoid using punctuation in the Subject line, especially exclamation points. Don't use all capital letters either; they trigger spam filters.

✔ **Keep it short.** Limit the Subject line to 50 characters, including spaces. Restrict most newsletters to no more than two scrolling pages.

The length of your newsletter may vary according to its purpose and audience. An informational newsletter, for example, might be longer than one designed to drive customers to your site to buy. Place an internally linked table of contents at the top of a long newsletter to direct readers directly to articles of interest.

Try to use a headline that grabs attention. Just as with your website, you have only a few seconds to catch your reader's attention and answer the question "What's in it for me?" Users who skim their e-mail in a preview pane might see only several inches of material on the screen. Keep the most important information at the top, before any scrolling is needed. In other words, shorter is better.

When putting together your newsletter, follow the same design and writing principles that you would use for a page on your website (see Chapter 3), as described in this list:

✔ **Emphasize your brand.** Consistently include your logo or header graphic, or both elements, for branding purposes.

✔ **Use small photos.** Be sure to resize your photos for the web so that they download quickly.

✔ **Accommodate subscribers who use text-only e-mail.** Provide vivid descriptions as alternatives to photos, because users might suppress image delivery in e-mail.

✔ **Provide relevant content.** Match your content to your audience. You may see better results if you segment a large address list and send somewhat different versions of your newsletter based on interest area or past purchase history than if you try to make one newsletter do everything.

Use teaser lines or incomplete paragraphs with links to the appropriate pages of your website. This strategy is far better than putting too much information in the newsletter. In fact, your newsletter should have at least 20 assorted links to your site, some of which are for content or products and some of which are for best practice functions I describe in the section "Following best practices," later in this chapter.

Links should take viewers as close as possible to the desired call to action. For example, link a promotion to its product detail page to prompt subscribers to purchase an item. The Daily Grommet newsletter (refer to Figure 9-5) demonstrates this concept.

Selecting a method of distribution

Options for creating your newsletter are much like those for creating a website. Your choice depends on ease of use, cost, the size of your mailing list, and the skills of your support staff. Here's a rundown of your distribution options:

- ✓ **Ask your web developer to develop a custom solution.** Your developer can design an HTML template that lets you change content for every issue. He or she can also set up your website to collect subscribers' e-mail addresses and arrange with the hosting company to provide list management services. Be sure to include these tasks in your request for proposal (RFP) if you want to use this alternative.

- ✓ **Use a one-stop solution that offers templates, list management, and distribution.** Constant Contact, whose template site is shown in Figure 9-7, offers this type of solution. For small companies, this approach is generally the easiest and least expensive. These third-party solutions generally require that your developer place a small chunk of code on your site that links to your sign-up page. After that, you handle most tasks from third-party servers.

- ✓ **Purchase HTML newsletter template software and arrange for list management services on your own.** This solution generally works for larger companies that need more-sophisticated options and have the technical support staff to implement them. You can find a list comparing providers at www.tamingthebeast.net/tools/autoresponder-software.htm.

For providers of e-mail template or hosting solutions or list management services, see Bonus Chapter 3 on the Downloads tab of the book's companion website.

The success of your newsletter is 40 percent due to finding the right audience, 40 percent due to making the right offer, and 20 percent due to creating the right design (the newsletter content and appearance).

Figure 9-7:
Constant
Contact
offers
one-stop,
template-
based
newsletters,
list manage-
ment, and
distribution.

Courtesy of Constant Contact, Inc.

Choosing HTML or text

Because HTML newsletters contain graphics, icons, and fonts, they're more visually appealing than plain text. Because these newsletters are slower to load, some users with slow connections might suppress photos or elect text-only e-mail. Others might block HTML e-mail to protect against viruses. As broadband use expands, HTML newsletters are becoming more prevalent. Your best bet is to offer both and compare the open rate and click-through rate for the two versions.

Following best practices

E-mail represents an increasing percentage of online advertising spending. With this emphasis, e-mail companies have studied best practices to achieve a high CTR while complying with all the legal requirements of the CAN-SPAM Act.

Here are the best practices that you're legally obligated to follow:

✔ **Include your company's street address or P.O. box and phone number in your newsletter.**

✔ **Include a link to unsubscribe or opt out with a single click.**

✔ **Provide a link to your privacy policy.** Don't share your lists with a third party unless you give notice to subscribers and obtain consent from them.

These best practices create a customer-friendly or high-quality newsletter:

✔ **As always, proofread *everything*, including the From and Subject lines, and test all links.**

✔ **Send preview copies of both HTML and text copies to yourself and others.**

✔ **Tell people how often the newsletter will arrive and when.**

✔ **Provide a place for subscribers to indicate their name, areas of interest, job title, or type of newsletter they want, especially if you have more than one newsletter.** For example, some readers might be interested in events or new products; others in sales or discounts.

✔ **Require only a few fields in this subscriber profile.** A sign-up form that's too long discourages subscribers.

✔ **Include a link that allows subscribers to change their profiles easily.**

Best practices for marketing and growing your subscriber base appear in this list:

✔ **Send a welcome message to new subscribers.** Include a coupon (or promotion code), if appropriate. Remember to update your online store with the promo code and its start and end dates.

✔ **Send your e-mail only to the people who have agreed to receive it.** When feasible, use a double opt-in process (which I discuss in more detail in the previous section, "Unsubscribe rate").

✔ **Include a link to forward the e-mail newsletter to a subscriber's friend or colleague.** Place it near the top of the newsletter, if you can.

✔ **Provide a direct link to the Subscribe page for people who've received a forwarded e-mail.** This strategy is especially important as a call to action in a newsletter sent to a rented list of e-mail addresses (a *rental list*). One of the most important goals of sending a newsletter to a rental list is to acquire some of those names for *your* list.

✔ **Restate your privacy policy and the benefits of subscribing.** Place this information immediately above the subscription form on your web page.

- ✔ **Post sample newsletters on your website.** Potential subscribers can then preview them.

- ✔ **Include a link to subscribe to your newsletter.** Place the link on all your social media pages.

- ✔ **Post excerpts from your newsletters on your social media pages.** Then invite readers to share the newsletters with their friends.

- ✔ **Save testimonials that praise your newsletter.** Get permission to post them on your subscription page.

Deciding on timing and frequency

Companies have researched the best day and time, though results fluctuate, time of year, and list size for newsletter distribution. Aggregate data for day of week and time of day for 2010 from the e-mail provider MailerMailer are shown in Figure 9-8. (See www.mailermailer.com/resources/metrics/2011/daily-rates.rwp.) Although this data suggest that Sunday e-mail releases produce the best results, and that Tuesday, Wednesday, and Thursday have the worst click-through rates, aggregate data may not apply for you. Test delivery schedules with your specific target market.

This list describes some timing guidelines for B2B and B2C newsletters:

- ✔ **B2B:** B2B newsletters generally do best on Tuesday or Wednesday afternoon. Distribute them at midday when workers often try to catch up on e-mail but have already cleared out their overnight accumulation.

  No across-the-board averages matter more than your own experience. Review your own site statistics for the most popular time of day and day of the week for visitors to your site. (See Chapter 6 for more on web statistics.)

- ✔ **B2C:** B2C newsletters typically see higher open and click-through rates before or after the workday — if people are logging in from home. You might find a higher open rate for B2C e-mails sent over the weekend, simply because your message has less competition. Experiment to see what's best for you. Remember that many people research purchases from home on the weekend but wait until Monday or Tuesday to make their purchases from work. CyberMonday, the first workday after the long Thanksgiving holiday, is the best-known example of this phenomenon.

The ideal frequency of mailings depends on your audience and the purpose of your newsletter. Recipients don't like being flooded with messages from a single source unless they receive time-critical news (for example, drug alerts for physicians).

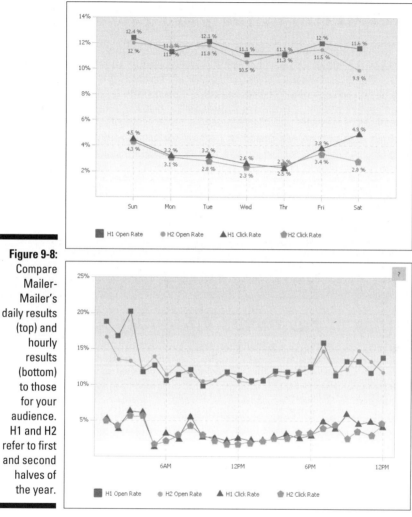

Figure 9-8:
Compare Mailer-Mailer's daily results (top) and hourly results (bottom) to those for your audience. H1 and H2 refer to first and second halves of the year.

Source: MailerMailer®

Only you can decide whether you should be mailing daily, weekly, monthly, quarterly, or semiannually. If you segment your list, you can send out newsletters often but reduce the number going to any particular group of recipients.

Your audience is always the most accurate source of information. Ask them what frequency they want.

The book's companion website has more newsletter resources in Bonus Chapter 3 on the Downloads tab.

Finding Subscribers for Your Newsletter

As soon as you begin planning your website, start collecting e-mail addresses. Begin with your e-mail address book: friends and family members; your banker, accountant, or attorney; and investors, business advisors, vendors, members of local media, government officials, or other community leaders. Those in the media or government positions are obligated to communicate with the public.

As a matter of courtesy, ask the folks previously listed, and any others that you add to your newsletter list, to opt in by clicking a confirmation link within your newsletter. The confirmation link should take users to a screen that allows options for selecting types of e-mail (such as HTML or text) or choosing interest areas (or both), just as you ask new subscribers to do.

Your e-mail address list is gold! Building a good list of e-mail addresses is critical to recovering your investment in an e-mail newsletter program. Be sure to back up your address list along with other valuable files and store a copy offsite.

Mailing to customers and prospects

After you add e-mail addresses to your list of customers and prospects, as described in the preceding section, review the list to make sure you have permission to e-mail them according to the list in this section. You might use contact management software — such as ACT! (available at www.act.com) — or perhaps you have an Excel file or another database file for print mailings. The CAN-SPAM Act lets you send at least one e-mail to individuals who have a pre-existing business relationship, such as one of these:

- Existing customers and clients who've purchased within the past 13 months
- Dealers and distributors
- Prospects who have requested information
- Respondents to a questionnaire or survey
- People who have signed up on your website to receive a white paper or other download
- Members of professional organizations to which you belong

Use that e-mail to request explicit permission to send further e-mails and provide a link to opt-in.

Keeping your address list up-to-date

Starting a newsletter is a useful opportunity to clean out and update your e-mail address list. Any e-mail addresses that have been in your database for more than a year are suspect, on the surface. Here are some ways to keep your address list up-to-date:

- ✔ Send everyone in your database a bulk e-mail asking for opt-in e-mail confirmation, and then delete addresses that are no longer valid.

- ✔ Most list servers and template newsletters automatically test subscriber e-mails to make sure addresses are current. Delete the bounced addresses from your list.

- ✔ If you have a list of print addresses without e-mail, send a prepaid business-reply postcard announcing your newsletter. Be sure to request opt-in permission and an e-mail address on the reply card, and provide a link to sign up online.

Most providers of e-mail services segregate undeliverable e-mail addresses before sending your first message, or they record them as bounces. This strategy keeps your newsletter list up-to-date, but your base contact list might now be out of sync. You might need to delete undeliverable e-mail addresses from your source file as well.

Maintaining and grooming your list is an ongoing process. Between mailings, add new names to your list and review blocked or otherwise undeliverable ones.

What about e-mailing to that carton of business cards you collected at trade shows and networking events? If you didn't get permission to add them to a newsletter list when you acquired them, you must send a confirmation link or postcard to obtain an explicit opt-in.

Collecting new names

You can collect new e-mail addresses offline at networking events and trade shows and whenever you have live customer contact. Verbally ask permission to send a newsletter, noting the date, event, and response. Or post a sign above the business card collection bowl or headline the electronic sign-in on your tablet computer, saying something like, "Get the latest product news and special offers! We'll add your e-mail address to our newsletter list." Sweeten the pot by also drawing from those names to receive a prize. When speaking at an event, provide a newsletter sign-up mechanism.

Of course, another important place to request e-mail addresses is at your bricks-and-mortar store, especially at checkout. If you aren't equipped to add an e-mail address at the register, offer a collection bowl for cards or a guest book. And, consider offering customers a free item in exchange for signing up.

Take advantage of other opportunities on your website and social media pages to collect e-mail addresses:

- ✔ Request an e-mail address when offering visitors a free case study or white paper to download; offer newsletter sign-up as a check box.
- ✔ Place a newsletter opt-in check box on the same form that customers fill out when purchasing online.
- ✔ Put a newsletter opt-in check box on any submission form: Name it Contact Us, Tech Support, Demo, Sales Call, or Request for Quote.

Ask your developer to collect these e-mail addresses automatically in a database that you can access easily. They probably can be added to your list only if the developer has integrated the list server. If you're using a third-party solution or if the onscreen forms are e-mailed to you from the website, you must upload these addresses manually to your newsletter list.

Of course, there's an art to the newsletter sign-up form. Try to get more than an e-mail address, but make most fields optional. If you have a B2B company, the user's job title and company name are valuable, as well as the urgency of the need. For a B2C company, specific areas of product interest are helpful to know.

Growing a list of qualified addresses is an essential objective for any site that intends to use e-mail marketing. Make it easy for site visitors to sign up from any page by placing the call to action in the navigation. You might choose to display a simple e-mail text box or a link to a second page that has room to display options, ask for additional information, provide a reminder of your privacy policy, and summarize the benefits of signing up. Try to phrase the sign-up navigation link to convey benefits — for example, *Sign Up for Savings* or *Get Product News.*

Renting e-mail subscribers

Legitimate e-mail list brokers rent opt-in lists of both B2B and B2C audiences. These lists generally consist of magazine or e-zine subscribers, members of organizations, or people who participate in surveys and free offers in exchange for providing their e-mail addresses.

Do *not* use lists from friends or businesses whose users weren't notified that their names could be sold, exchanged, or rented — or from disreputable brokers who offer names at a bargain rate. All you buy is trouble at a discount price.

Although a highly targeted rental list isn't the best way to acquire new names, it's still worth the search. Some brokers specialize in B2B versus B2C or in certain vertical industry segments. Technology professionals are particularly hard to reach by using rental lists.

The more targeted the list, the more you pay per address, just as with any other advertising audience. Estimate your costs at 25 cents per name on a B2B list, though prices might range from a nickel on a B2C list to 50 cents or more for a tightly drawn demographic such as wealthy residents who own dogs. You must usually rent a minimum number of names, depending on the source.

Rental lists generally have lower open and click-through rates than your own, highly prequalified list of names, so don't be surprised if success rates are half those for your own list. List rental rates are falling, so it's worth negotiating, especially after a first test mailing. Or, rent the list multiple times to bring down the price per name.

Run the numbers to be sure that your expected return will offset the cost of list rental and newsletter preparation. Because of the cost, you might want to perform A/B testing (see the earlier section "A/B testing") with your own list first to ensure that you're sending out the best possible newsletter.

If you use a free list, be sure to review the rules for allowable content. Some lists constrain the content or form of e-mail sent to members. Information about every list is available online. For more general information about how to select a mailing list, see Name-Finders at `www.namefinders.info/dmr`.

Working with a list rental house

When you rent a list of e-mail addresses, it truly is *rent*. You don't receive the names. Instead, you deliver your HTML and text e-mail newsletters to the rental house. The rental house confirms that your newsletter meets its requirements, adds code to links to track open rates and CTR, and sends out a trial blast to you and several other people (known as *seed names*). You select the date and time for the actual e-mail blast.

When you request a particular audience, the mailing house sends you a *data card* (a page describing the detailed demographics, source, and available sorting criteria) for every possible list that meets your needs. Data cards can be a little hard to interpret, so ask plenty of questions.

Newsletters put Boston Duck Tours in the swim

The famous Ducks of Boston neither waddle nor swim. They are the World War II–style amphibious vehicles that Boston Duck Tours uses to provide a fully narrated, land-and-water tour of Boston. Since its founding in 1994, the firm has grown to a 28-duck, 130-employee tourism phenomenon.

The company relies primarily on word-of-mouth, its brightly painted ducks, and its web presence to promote its tours. Online since 1996, the company updated its site in 2006 and added e-mail newsletters as a marketing technique in April 2005.

Driven by concern about the cost of paper mailings, Boston Duck Tours saw many benefits beyond cost savings from e-mail newsletters, according to Bob Schwartz, its director of marketing and sales. He ticks off the ability to track who truly pays attention to the company's message, an easy way to promote different specials to different segments of its mailing list, and the value of e-mail analytics to understand exactly what people like and don't like.

Duck Tours acquires e-mail addresses from past guests and groups and opt-in options on their online marketing campaigns and website (at www.bostonducktours.com). Schwartz divides the list into 14 segments, such as senior groups, schools, college, Boy Scouts and Girl Scouts, and hotel sales, each of which receives two customized messages per year. "[When] sending e-mails more than two to three times per year, our unsubscribe clicks grow tremendously and our openings and CTRs (click-through rates) drop."

As a matter of best practice, Schwartz studied results until he determined that the best times to send Duck Tours' newsletters are Tuesdays and Wednesdays from 10 to 10:30 a.m. "E-mails from the day [or] night before have usually been opened already and we can have more of the guests' attention," he explains. "If I sent it at a time that they were going through and deleting a bunch of spam messages (3 to 5 p.m.) or (9 to 10 a.m.), mine could possibly get lumped in accidentally with spam messages." Pinpointing the right time and frequency pays off: Boston Duck Tours typically sees a 20 to 25 percent open rate and an average 15 to 20 percent CTR, both well above the average for the tourism industry, according to data from Constant Contact.

Schwartz finds the newsletter campaigns themselves "extremely easy to put together." A user of Constant Contact, he spends a maximum of four hours per month on the task. "Coming up with a great idea for the campaign is the most important and time-consuming aspect," he acknowledges, aware that sending a newsletter that doesn't appeal to a specific target audience can cost him their interest forever.

Schwartz advises others that "throwing money at new marketing initiatives can be a waste of money if you don't carefully examine how to track your ROI. This is easily done through new web-based e-mail marketing websites that are out there."

In addition to a minimum number of names and the cost per name, you might be charged for every subselection or sort you request (for example, by zip code, gender, age, or time since last purchase). Some companies also charge a transmission fee or a setup fee (or both). All charges and minimums vary by broker and by list. Negotiate. When you're ready, the company sends you an *insertion order* (a form used to place an advertisement) to sign.

The e-mail house asks you not only for your seed names but also for everyone who has been permanently removed from your list — to eliminate those names from their lists. To avoid any possible duplication, you can also send names with matching profiles to remove from the list you're renting. Why pay to send the same newsletter to someone who has already received it? Generally, rental houses mail to more than the number in your contract to allow for undeliverable addresses. If the number that's sent ends up below the number on your contract, reputable dealers send a "make good" mailing on request.

One objective is to convert rental names to your subscribers, so at the top of the newsletter you're sending to rental names, incorporate a linkable invitation to join your list. Make other text changes to accommodate the possibility that these recipients, unlike your own carefully gathered names, have never heard of your company, product, or service.

Allow a week or more to establish an account before sending your first blast with a particular broker. This strategy gives you time to work out any kinks in your newsletter, formatting, links, or list. After the blast, track your open rate, CTR, and other criteria. Compare them to the results of your own list. Remember that people usually need to see your brand seven times to remember you!

Third-party template newsletters can't be sent to rental houses, because their newsletter code isn't self-standing. You (or your developer) must create new HTML and text versions, or else you have to pay the mailing house to create them for you.

A newsletter program can either serve as an independent marketing vehicle or carry another marketing effort on its back. For example, by segmenting its list into 14 strategic submarkets, Boston Duck Tours (shown in Figure 9-9 and discussed in the nearby sidebar, "Newsletters put Boston Duck Tours in the swim") can target special offers in its newsletters to different audiences.

Figure 9-9:
Boston
Duck Tours
uses its
newsletters to offer
special
discounts to
various segments of its
mailing list.

Integrating E-Mail with Social Media

People who use social media are still committed users of e-mail, according to
"View from the Social Inbox 2010," a study published by the marketing agency
Merkle (www.merkleinc.com/news-and-events/press-releases/
merkle-releases-view-social-inbox-consumer-email-and-social)
and described in this list:

✔ Of social networkers, 42 percent check their e-mail four or more times
per day, compared to just 27 percent of those who don't use the current
top social networking sites.

✔ Of social networkers, 63 percent use the same e-mail account for their
social networking messages and the majority of their permission-based,
e-mail.

✔ Of Facebook, MySpace, and Twitter users, 20 percent have posted or shared something from permission e-mail to their social accounts by using the Share option.

With numbers like these, you have every reason to integrate e-mail with social media to attract new subscribers, find new followers for your social media presence, and obtain content ideas for both outlets.

Gaining more subscribers

Cross-promotional opportunities to gain newsletter subscribers abound in social media. Always include subscription links on your blog, in other social media pages, and in your signature block. You can preview topics on Facebook or tweet about your newsletter release to entice friends and followers to sign up. Don't forget to link to an archived newsletter so that people can view a sample.

Adding more followers and connections

In a parallel fashion to gaining more subscribers, use your newsletter to drive traffic to social media outlets, with Follow Us links and social sharing buttons on each of your newsletters. (See Chapter 19 for more about these tools.) You can even use your newsletter to announce a special offer or contest that's available only to social media participants. All these techniques make it more likely that you'll catch your fish in your online net.

Finding and sharing content

Ah, a life full of repurpose! Just as you can cross-promote between e-mail and social media, you can reuse content in both places or dip into one well to fill the other. Some of the solutions are as easy as using a distribution tool (see Chapter 19) to post your newsletter content automatically to social media channels. Or, use your newsletter content as a contribution to a Facebook or LinkedIn group.

To transport content in the other direction, mine other people's posts on your own social media pages and follow social media groups to spark ideas for your newsletter, detect trending topics, and pick up industry news. To get ideas, try social media tools such as Google Alerts, Social Mention (at `http://socialmention.com`), Twitter Search, or social news outlets such as Digg or Reddit.

Google Insights (at www.google.com/insights/search/#) shows the time of day, day of week, and time of year when specific search terms are popular. Take advantage of this type of market intelligence to schedule topical e-mail newsletters.

Include the same industry-related or topical keywords and tags in both your social media sites and newsletters or newsletter announcements that may be reposted online.

Chapter 10

Figuring Out Mobile Marketing

Mobile marketing includes standard feature-based cellphones, smartphones such as the iPhone and Android models, PDAs (personal digital assistants) such as the BlackBerry, and tablet computers, which can use either the cellular network or Wi-Fi for wireless Internet access. Because of rapidly advancing technology, mobile devices offer multiple options for the astute online marketer: text messaging (also known as *short messaging service, or SMS*); mobile search, pay per click (PPC), and display advertising; coupons and pay by phone technologies; and specially formatted websites for smartphones and tablets.

Whew! That's a lot of technology in the palm of your hand. In this chapter, I discuss how to market to people on the move by taking advantage of mobile devices.

Decoding Mobile Jargon

Sometimes, it's difficult to distinguish one category of handheld mobile device from another. The lines blur as manufacturers compete by adding capabilities. For the purpose of writing this chapter, I categorize devices this way:

✔ **PDA:** The handheld PDA helps people organize their lives by using various software tools, such as calendars. Originally used for exchanging e-mail and browsing the web, newer versions add phone capabilities. Although this older, network-independent device may be on its way out, it still has millions of users.

✔ **Standard cellphone:** Sometimes known as a *feature* phone, it uses a telephone-style keypad and a small display screen for voice calls and text messaging and for shooting and sending photos and videos. Some newer models include e-mail, instant messaging, GPS, and limited web searching.

✔ **Smartphone:** The iPhone (from Apple) and Droid (from Google and many other manufacturers), for example, combine web browsing and PDA functions with feature phone capabilities and larger screens. The use of the keyboard and touch interface makes it almost an extension of a desktop computer; a smartphone can be used to create documents and spreadsheets and connect with social networking sites. The iPhone incorporates the music capabilities of the iPod as well. Smartphones are gobbling market share from feature phones and PDAs.

✔ **Tablet computer:** A tablet such as the Apple iPad marries the functionality of a smartphone that has an extra large screen with a netbook computer. Like a smartphone, a tablet responds to touch commands as well as to keyboard input. Its high-resolution screen and high-speed web access make it an excellent choice for displaying videos. Like desktop computers, tablets now have USB ports and external storage. Special software applications (or *apps*) are developed for both smartphones and tablets.

As a marketer, what you need to know is that all these devices offer incredible marketing opportunities to reach consumers with the information they seek — at the moment they seek it. The marketing techniques you select may depend on the devices your target market uses.

The terms *3G* (third generation) and *4G* (fourth generation) refer to the speed and underlying technology of the cellular networks that enable smartphones and tablet computers to access the web. 3G supports voice and video and works well for people who download (at 14 Mbps) more than upload (at 5 Mbps); 4G offers full Internet-style services at high connection speeds (100 Mbps to 1 Gbps), even from moving vehicles.

Harvesting Leads and Sales from Mobile Phones

Mobile users check e-mail, weather, traffic, maps, directions, and headlines. They also search for companies and products (especially local ones), review entertainment schedules, access social media sites, watch videos, check review and ratings sites, and play games online. It shouldn't be surprising to find that the two most popular mobile phone websites in the United States in June 2011 were (according to MarketingCharts) the social gaming sites MocoSpace (`http://mobi.mocospace.com`) and WeeWorld (`http://talkingweemee.weeworld.com`), accounting for more than 30 percent of visits between them.

Multiplying the effect of mobile marketing

You can find as many applications for mobile marketing as you can imagine. Keep in mind the areas described in this list, whatever the device or market segment you target:

- **News and updates:** Distribute this type of information to your customers, the people on your prospect list, and your newsletter subscribers.

- **Emergency information:** Warnings range from product recalls to weather hazards.

- **Comparison shopping:** Provide information so that shoppers can compare by price and feature.

- **Local business announcements:** Announce coupons, deals, and special offers, for example.

- **Customer service improvements:** For example, you can let customers make reservations (as does MacCallum House, as described in the nearby sidebar "Smartphones pull smart guests to MacCallum House") or find out when an order is ready for pick-up.

- **Event publicity:** Consider providing real-time logistical information.

- **Integration of mobile marketing and social media:** Post updates on-the-fly and use geolocation services such as Foursquare (described in Chapter 18).

- **Payments accepted by mobile phone:** Customers can pay with their mobile device at the moment they're ready to buy.

- **Leads you collect by offering a product or service in return:** You can offer a free app or an estimate, for example.

Don't let the obvious B2C value of mobile devices fool you: Mobile marketing has a place in B2B strategies as well. Some of the earliest adopters of new technology are businesses seeking improved productivity or a competitive edge. In fact, more than 49 percent of small businesses already use smartphones.

Measuring mobile phone use by the numbers

The Nielsen Company's 2010 Media Industry Fact Sheet estimates that, of the more than 223 million U.S. mobile phone users over the age of 13, 16.7 million already access the web via cell networks. Webtrends even projects that the number of mobile Internet users will exceed that of desktop Internet users by 2014.

The shift of users from feature phone to smartphone has been stunningly fast. By the first quarter of 2011, 54 percent of all new mobile phones sold were smartphones, with Nielsen predicting that half of all American mobile phone owners would have smartphones by Christmas 2011. The market share of smartphone operating systems is shown in Figure 10-1. Generally speaking, the Apple market share is increasing, the BlackBerry share is decreasing, and Android phones are more popular than the iPhone among most recent buyers.

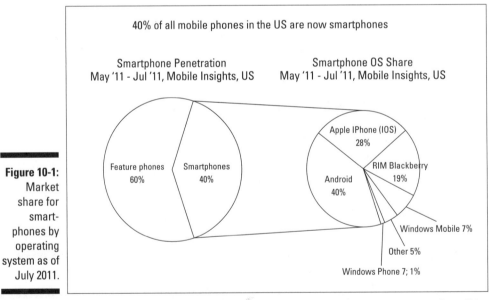

Figure 10-1: Market share for smartphones by operating system as of July 2011.

40% of all mobile phones in the US are now smartphones

Smartphone Penetration
May '11 - Jul '11, Mobile Insights, US

Smartphone OS Share
May '11 - Jul '11, Mobile Insights, US

Feature phones 60%

Smartphones 40%

Apple IPhone (IOS) 28%

RIM Blackberry 19%

Android 40%

Windows Mobile 7%

Other 5%

Windows Phone 7; 1%

Source: Nielsen

Market share for smartphones, a highly competitive measurement, changes often. Check current statistics before you make a decision about targeting particular users.

About 55 percent of smartphone users are male, and 45 percent female, with the highest usage level by those younger than 50. Not surprisingly, smartphone ownership skews toward higher-income users, but that situation will change as prices decrease.

The Nielsen report shows that the smartphone user population is more diverse overall than the cellphone user population. Minorities comprise 35 percent of smartphone users, compared to 21 percent of feature phone users. Think about it: Smartphones are a comparatively inexpensive bridge across the digital divide.

The MacCallum House Inn and Restaurant in Mendocino, California (shown in Figure 10-2), takes advantage of mobile marketing to reach tech-savvy travelers, as discussed in the nearby sidebar, "Smartphones pull smart guests to MacCallum House." Viewers can tap any item on the main menu (Figure 10-3, left) to open a secondary page, such as one that lets them make reservations (Figure 10-3, right).

Figure 10-2:
The primary website for MacCallum House.

Courtesy of www.maccallumhouse.com & www.hoimoonmarketing.com

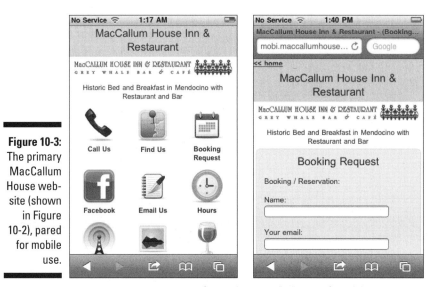

Courtesy of www.maccallumhouse.com & www.hoimoonmarketing.com

Figure 10-3: The primary MacCallum House website (shown in Figure 10-2), pared for mobile use.

Smartphones pull smart guests to MacCallum House

Situated about three hours north of San Francisco, the MacCallum House Inn and Restaurant in Mendocino Village serves tourists traveling to the northern California wine country coast. (See the inn's main website at http://maccallumhouse.com.) Although primarily serving consumers for lodging and dining, the inn also has B2B customers such as vendors of wedding services and business seminars.

As a hospitality and tourism destination, MacCallum House went online early. Its PR agency, Hoi Moon Marketing, originally built the restaurant website in the 1990s, before the restaurant and hotel merged in 2002. Since then, the agency has helped the inn transition into using social media and new technologies. In January 2011, the firm created an optimized mobile site for smartphones at http://mobi.maccallumhouse.com.

Jude Lutge, the PR director of MacCallum House and the cofounder of Hoi Moon Marketing with Julie Vetter, explains that the goal of the mobile site is to ensure that the business is accessible by using whatever devices its customers use. With a target audience composed of the digitally connected crowd from San Francisco and Silicon Valley visiting Mendocino on weekend getaways, Lutge says, "We do not [want to] lose potential visitors who are trying to find lodging or dining in our area from their mobile phones."

Using the mobile site, users simply press a button to call the inn, read restaurant menus, see room photos, send e-mail, connect to the inn's Facebook page, or request a reservation for dinner or lodging. Because staff members field these requests, they have an easy way to measure the number of sales made from the mobile site.

Because web developer Nile Sprague set up MacCallum's .mobi site via the mobile site provider GoMobi (http://gomobi.info/home.html), it works on all phone platforms. A business owner with no programming knowledge can set up a basic GoMobi site, however, says Lutge. She suggests sticking with "a simple solution like GoMobi or good XHTML coding rather than trying to produce something for all devices — they change too fast and the [operating system manufacturers] are working to make all sites visible without custom versions." Code on the inn's primary website automatically sends mobile devices to the `.mobi` site. The link even helps with SEO for the mobile site.

Vetter, of Hoi Moon Marketing, has been watching the development of mobile advertising and promotional campaigns. Hoi Moon will likely include mobile ads in the inn's campaigns when it sees a feasible solution. For now, the agency is confident that its Twitter and Facebook efforts reach many of the inn's mobile users. It uses Wildfire Promotions Builder (at `www.wildfireapp.com`) on Facebook and Twitter, and it uses HootSuite to schedule and monitor social networks. For visibility, the inn runs Google AdWords (PPC); Facebook ads haven't yet been as effective. So far, Vetter hasn't tried text or SMS campaigns.

Lutge adds that the most important tasks are to focus on making your brand visible and engage authentically with your customers wherever they are. "Don't let social media turn into a customer service reaction tool; be proactive."

Following are the URLs for the MacCallum House Inn:

`http://maccallumhouse.com`

`http://mobi.maccallumhouse.com`

`http://twitter.com/maccallum house`

`www.facebook.com/MacCallum HouseInnandRestaurant`

`http://www.facebook. com/pages/MacKitchen- Mendocino/151639068207294`

`www.facebook.com/mendocino villageweddings`

`www.facebook.com/westcoast cocktails`

Reaching People on the Move

Given the power of mobile devices, you have multiple channels for reaching people wherever they happen to be.

- ✔ Mobile e-mail
- ✔ PPC and display advertising
- ✔ Search marketing
- ✔ Social media for mobile devices
- ✔ Text messaging
- ✔ Your own mobile site

The most valuable uses for search-based mobile marketing occur whenever time or geographic constraints affect a pending decision or activity, such as hotels, tourist destinations, restaurants, entertainment, movie schedules, sporting events, traffic alerts, transportation schedules, driving directions, gas stations, appointment reminders, or shopping.

If your business is in one of these market sectors, SEO is critical for success. Even more essential now are the tasks of optimizing your site for search results and submitting it to city directories, mapping sites, and local services such as Local Yahoo! and Google Places.

If your business targets younger, local customers, also consider participating in one or more of the geosocial services such as Foursquare or Gowalla, described in Chapter 18.

On text-enabled feature phones, callers enter a text query by using a keyword and a zip code or address, such as *Chinese food 47110*. They send their message to a special, six-digit number — for example, 466453 for Google. In response, the caller receives a text message with a list of names, addresses, and phone numbers for Chinese restaurants in that zip code.

For users of browser-enabled smartphones (77 percent of whom use search engines), searching is almost identical to the desktop-based search process except that fewer results appear on the (obviously) smaller phone displays before users need to scroll. In Figure 10-4, a mobile search query for the word *pizza* on Yahoo! appears on the left, with one result; additional results appear after tapping to open the next screen, as shown in the middle. Note the paid ad below the Search box on the left. The phone shown on the right side displays typical results for local search on Google Places.

Paid ad

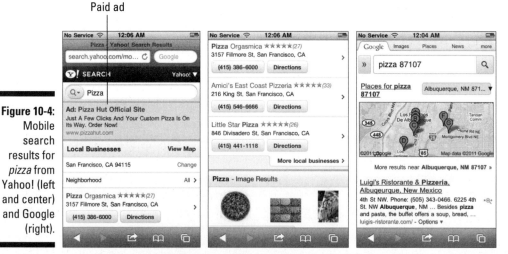

Figure 10-4: Mobile search results for *pizza* from Yahoo! (left and center) and Google (right).

Left and center images reproduced with permission of Yahoo! Inc. © 2011 Yahoo! Inc. YAHOO! and the YAHOO! logo are registered trademarks of Yahoo! Inc. Right image courtesy of Google, Inc.

A search on a mobile device produces listings almost identical to a search on a desktop computer, with two exceptions: The major search engines usually exclude real-time social results on mobile devices, and the sequence of search results may vary somewhat. Unfortunately, the variation may be enough to affect your visibility significantly.

You can deal with these issues by adhering to the same requirements for good SEO that I discuss in Chapter 7: Your well-structured site should be easily crawled, should offer well-indexed, relevant content containing search terms, and should have plenty of inbound links.

You don't need a special mobile site to be found in mobile searches. However, a site designed for mobile devices ensures that your site is mobile-search-friendly and helps a user who clicks your link.

Because 95 percent of smartphone users have searched for local information, try these changes when optimizing to improve your results:

- ✔ Prioritize location-based products and services in your search term selection.

- ✔ Include familiar locations in search terms, perhaps even at the neighborhood or zip code level, such as *nob hill coffee.*

- ✔ Include a phone number in your page description tag to benefit from click-to-call capabilities; 77 percent of smartphone users contact a business within a day of conducting a search, 61 percent visit, and 59 percent call, as noted at `http://googlemobileads.blogspot.com/2011/04/smartphone-user-study-shows-mobile.html`.

- ✔ Submit to all location-based services such as Google Places and Local Yahoo! and local directories.

- ✔ Be sure that the title tag and page description fit within the constraints of mobile search results without using line breaks.

- ✔ If you offer apps or music or other types of downloadable content, be sure to include the words *download* or *app* in your search phrases; this strategy usually spurs Android Market or iTunes results.

- ✔ Create a mobile-friendly version of your site (as I discuss later in the "Developing Mobile Websites" section). Be sure that your street address is on your site.

- ✔ Optimize individual product detail pages because many smartphone users take advantage of their phones to comparison-shop for prices, features, and items in stock.

Bounce rates and click-through rates may vary between desktop and smartphone search results. Review the results separately in your analytics.

Texting As a Marketing Technique

If you've ever watched the blur of teenagers' speeding thumbs, you're well aware that teens, especially females aged 13 to 17, send thousands of text messages every month on their cellphones. It turns out that many other people do, too — about a trillion text messages per year, worldwide.

In an October 2010 report, The Nielsen Company reports that although texting falls off rapidly with age, users as old as 54 still send or receive hundreds of messages every month, making cellphone users appealing targets for specific messaging needs.

These needs may range from requests to text the characters *2HELP* (24357) to make a $5 donation to the Red Cross for disaster relief, to a campaign (triggered perhaps from an online search) encouraging users to text a keyword to your number to receive a special mobile coupon. The coupon or promotional code displays as a text message that they can show to receive a discount for an event admission or purchase.

For a quick, inexpensive way to reach hundreds or thousands of people (especially teens), consider short message service, or SMS, which operates essentially like bulk e-mail by cellphone, as long as you have user permission to send these messages. Companies such as the ones in this minitable offer bulk SMS services:

Software Name	*URL*
Club Texting	www.clubtexting.com
TextBoard	www.text-board.com
Text2VIP	www.text2vip.com

As recently as September 2010, eMarketer forecast (at www.emarketer. com/Article.aspx?R=1008383) that SMS would be "the biggest single mobile advertising format in 2011, with a 38 percent share of mobile advertising spending." However, eMarketer also warns that SMS will decline in importance as smartphone users increase, shifting the spending focus to display and search advertising.

Never send unsolicited text messages to customers' cellphones. Depending on an individual's cellphone plan, a consumer might have to pay to receive text messages; in that case, the customer would be furious to receive spam. As with e-mail campaigns, always enable users to unsubscribe easily.

Implementing a text-messaging campaign

Companies that sell ring tones, screen savers, wallpapers, games, and other mobile content are some of the biggest users of SMS. Stock tickers, horoscopes, sports scores, emergency services, retail offers, weather, price comparisons, and real estate applications use SMS as well.

Because cellphone users are often close to making a purchasing decision or an impulse buy, SMS works well for sales messages, coupons, enter-to-win campaigns, informative messages, subscriptions, and donations. Many large advertisers, such as McDonald's, send promotional messages or coupons with SMS. Customers usually redeem an SMS coupon by showing their stored text message at checkout. Figure 10-5 shows a typical SMS advertising message with a promotion.

Figure 10-5:
A typical text message promotion often includes a specific offer.

Qdoba's better w/ a friend! Bring a pal and get 1/2 off an entree w/purchase of a reg price entree Lmt1 Exp: 9/1 Code:0829BOGOHALF

Courtesy Tetherball360.com

Accessing mobile e-mail

Mobile users have two choices for accessing e-mail on their devices: Use their mobile browsers (just as they would access any web-based e-mail program) or download an app. Apps for e-mail clients generally run a little faster and are designed for touchscreens, but are otherwise similar to their desktop counterparts.

People who are using their devices for e-mail can receive e-newsletters, too. Again, many e-mail companies offer apps that allow their users to subscribe to newsletters from their phones, participate in surveys or polls, and provide feedback. For example, the Constant Contact QuickView for iPhone app (`http://itunes.apple.com/app/constant-contact-quickview/id329744931?mt=8`) lets businesses create short e-mail marketing messages from templates, update subscriber lists, manage campaigns, and monitor results. Rather than ask for text message responses, these apps generally differentiate themselves from SMS apps by including longer messages, graphics, and links to websites.

Advertising on mobile media

In the not-so-distant past, businesses struggled with multimedia messaging services (MMS) to provide static display ads on mobile phones. Now that full HTML browsers are used on smartphones and tablets, all forms of online advertising, from PPC to banners and video ads (but not Flash), are easily implemented.

Given the 2 percent click-through rate on smartphones (compared to 0.5 percent online), mobile display advertising is hot-hot-hot. eMarketer estimates that spending on mobile advertising (encompassing search, display, and SMS ads) will grow nearly 50 percent to top $1 billion in 2011.

Google sorts out the advertising options succinctly at http://adwords.google.com/support/aw/bin/answer.py?hl=en&answer=107516. Feature phones and PDAs with mobile browsers run specially formatted mobile text PPC ads (two lines of text with 12 to 18 characters apiece, plus a display URL with an optional click-to-call button), as shown in Figure 10-6.

PPC ad   Phone number

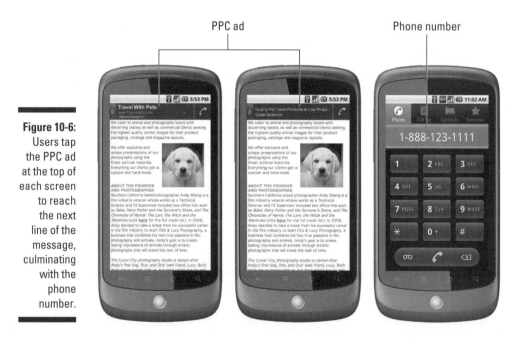

Figure 10-6:
Users tap the PPC ad at the top of each screen to reach the next line of the message, culminating with the phone number.

Courtesy of Google, Inc.

See http://adwords.google.com/support/aw/bin/answer.py?hl=en&answer=83248 and http://adwords.google.com/support/aw/bin/answer.py?hl=en&answer=97525 for more information about mobile image ads. Full HTML browsers on mobile devices show regular PPC and display ads on partner sites for the major search engines. Adjust the display ad settings in your campaigns to fit your needs. Of course, mobile ads can also be served by way of ad networks or individually negotiated ad contracts on the destination sites of your choice.

Benefitting from the click-to-call capability

Take advantage of a crucial option for mobile ads: Add the click-to-call option to autodial your company with a single tap on the user's touchscreen. This option is essential for local ads that encourage viewers to take immediate action. The call generally costs whatever you would otherwise pay for a click.

Mobile ads must link to mobile sites. On Google AdWords, these ads appear only on sites that partner with their mobile ad networks.

Marketing with mobile social media

Users of social media on mobile devices make up a growing and often highly active share of social media addicts. Almost all social media services now offer versions of their sites specially configured for mobile devices.

For links to popular social media sites for mobile devices, visit Bonus Chapter 3 on the Downloads tab of the book's companion website.

For example, the mobile version of Facebook displays a stripped-down home page that focuses on interactivity. Users can view status updates and other messages and post their own updates, comments, videos, and images.

Even Twitter, which has cellphone DNA in its genes, has revamped its mobile applications with an app that gives the page a better, easier-to-use layout, including navigation icons at the top, @replies, a column for the message stream, and search functionality.

Check out your Facebook page and Twitter stream on various phone and tablet operating systems to see how they appear, and then adjust them as needed.

Developing Mobile Websites

PDAs and most smartphones with full web access offer *another* way to promote your site or deliver content such as news, sports, blogs, video, and games. Users can use Wi-Fi or subscribe to a data plan from their cellular providers. Some 40 million consumers now use some type of mobile device for web surfing; about one-quarter of them have paid for items by using their mobile phones, and 13 million have accessed retail sites. A mobile-friendly site that viewers reach is more likely to lead to conversion, so you must design your site in line with the ways that people use their smartphones.

Viewers can access mobile sites while watching TV, riding in a car (*not* while driving), or while shopping in a store. They can see TV commercials and determine where to buy products; conduct competitive research to ask a retailer to match another's price; or search for and download coupons. Increasingly, users are interested in using their mobile phones to scan bar codes and purchase items to avoid long checkout lines.

Most websites designed for use on a full-size screen translate poorly to smaller smartphone or PDA screens. Graphics-heavy sites take too long to download, especially on 3G networks or slower; text-intensive sites are difficult to read; and sites with deep layers of content are often difficult to navigate. Creating a positive experience online (refer to Figure 10-3), is one key to mobile success.

Having a `.mobi` top-level domain (TLD) name or mobile platform isn't necessary in order to create a mobile site. However, purchasing a `.mobi` TLD (such as `http://yourcompany.mobi`) via your domain name registrar or using a mobile subdomain designation (such as `http://m.yourcompany.com`) is a visible cue to your users of your existence as a mobile maven.

Follow the best practices for mobile sites, established by the World Wide Web Consortium (W3C), to ensure your success (`www.w3.org/TR/mobile-bp`).

Special third-party providers develop `dot-mobi` sites and can help you plan a wireless marketing campaign. The only limits are your imagination, your budget, and the presence of your target audience.

A few mobile platforms, along with other mobile marketing resources, are described in the list "Mobile Website and Marketing Resources" in Bonus Chapter 3 on the Downloads tab of the companion website.

Unless you're part of a large corporation or developing an app as a freestanding destination (a game specifically designed for mobile players, for example), you're better off using a standard mobile platform that runs on all phones. Your programmer can also develop a mobile site by using a cascading style sheet; most phones automatically detect the appropriate version.

Keeping up with version changes for all competing mobile operating systems — such as Android (Google), BlackBerry (RIM), and the Apple iOS — is quite difficult. For most small businesses, the process of developing several custom phone apps for a website is time-consuming and expensive and probably not worth the effort.

Measuring Your Mobile Marketing Success

As with all analytics, determining which elements you measure depends on your goals and objectives. Your choices vary based on whether you're measuring the success of a mobile advertising campaign, the sales of a new mobile app, the number of visitors to your site, or the level of foot traffic to a bricks-and-mortar store. Start by outlining your goals and objectives (see Chapter 2) and look at the parameters discussed in Chapter 6.

Apart from mobile apps sold as products, most of the measurements should be familiar to you. You can segment mobile visitors by using the available tools within Google Analytics, for example, to track their behavior on a mobile site or on your regular website (or both). You might want to set up a separate conversion funnel for mobile users. Standard site parameters such as CTR, number of impressions, level of site traffic, number of page views, visit duration, and number of new versus repeat visitors still apply, of course. Watch for variations between mobile and web visitors on conversion rates, newsletter subscriptions, and brand recall. Naturally, you should watch for metrics specific to mobile use, such as

- The use of mobile payment methods, codes, and coupons (discussed in the next section)
- Click-throughs from a mobile site to your regular site
- Click-to-call rate
- Behavioral differences between users of feature phones and smartphones or among users of different mobile phone models

Reading QR Codes

I'd be remiss if I didn't mention two technologies that are poised to further increase the adoption rate of mobile devices: Quick Response (QR) codes and paying with credit cards by phone.

A *QR code*, like the one shown in Figure 10-7, is a two-dimensional bar code that compresses information in an action-ready, digital format. For example, the Cure Starts Now Foundation, which raises funds for brain cancer research, links a QR code in a print ad to a landing page at `http://blog.ovrdrv.com/wp-content/uploads/2011/02/Cone-for-the-Cure-QR-code.jpg`. The landing page offers a coupon in exchange for contact information. Any camera-enabled cellphone can scan a QR code (which can contain a phone number for autodial), send an e-mail, include a link to a website for more information or to view a video, or offer a chance to Like your Facebook page.

Figure 10-7:
The QR code for this book is a link to the book's companion website.

Creating a QR code is free with a generator such as the one at www.qrstuff.com. QR readers are built into the latest smartphones, or users can download free apps for their particular devices from sites such as http://i-nigma.com. Be sure to tell readers the benefits of the code, how to scan it, and where to find a reader application.

Taking Payments on the Fly

For businesses that sell their products offsite (such as street carts, home repair services, or massage therapists), smartphone technology improves basic business productivity by simplifying and verifying payments instantly.

Square (at https://squareup.com) is leading the charge to accept credit card payments in the mobile world. A merchant inserts a simple plastic card swiper into the audio jack to turn a smartphone or an iPad into an electronic register (see Figure 10-8 left). The customer simply sees a digital receipt (center), and signs online (right).

Square, which accepts all types of cards, deposits payments automatically in your bank account the next business day. In 2011, Square charged merchants a flat fee of 2.75 percent, which is roughly competitive with credit card merchant rates for many small businesses. Credit card numbers entered manually via Square cost 3.5 percent plus 15 cents per transaction.

Payments can also be taken through PayPal and other electronic payment services. The customer sees the bill (Figure 10-9, left) and signs into PayPal electronically (right). This process not only speeds up checkout but also reduces lost sales.

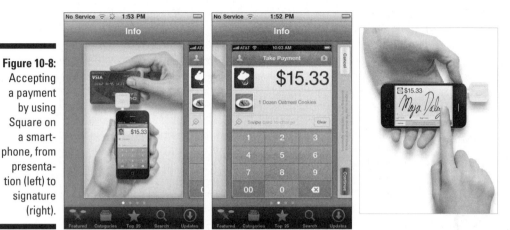

Figure 10-8: Accepting a payment by using Square on a smartphone, from presentation (left) to signature (right).

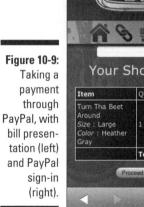

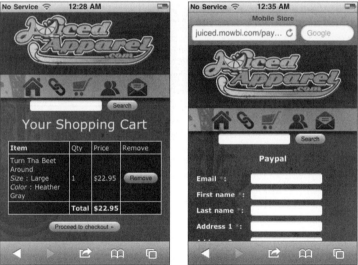

Figure 10-9: Taking a payment through PayPal, with bill presentation (left) and PayPal sign-in (right).

Counting on Tablets

Although the absolute number of current owners is still relatively small, the iPad and other tablet computer models are on the brink of expansion. CNBC reports that the rate of adoption of the iPad, in particular, positions it as "the most quickly adopted non-phone consumer electronics product in history." Given the convergence of high technology with usability, portability, mobility, and affordability, it may represent a true paradigm shift in computing.

According to the Nielsen Company, fewer than 5 percent of American consumers owned a tablet computer in May 2011 (compared to 36 percent who owned smartphones), but those consumers "watch more videos, read and pay for more books, are more willing to watch ads, and are more prone to buy an item after seeing an ad." In other words, businesses are already making money off them.

Considering that Nielsen found that 82 percent of tablet users covet the Apple iPad — with the Samsung Galaxy, Dell Streak, Motorola Xoom, and other models standing in place with a single-digit market share — I focus in this section on the iPad.

The demographics of iPad users are quite similar to those of the smartphone user base. They skew most heavily toward people who are between 25 and 34 years old (27 percent) and trend toward high levels of education and household income.

Making good marketing use of the iPad

In addition to the use of the iPad as a tool to enhance sales productivity and marketing presentations, the device opens new vistas for marketing. Because tablets have full-featured web browsers, users can view websites and ads just as they are. But the iPad offers customers new experiences, such as being able to visualize products in their own environment while providing almost instant feedback for marketers to see how well these experiences work.

As with any new medium, it will take time for creative designers to fully explore the options, from tablet-enhanced sites to iPad-specific apps, which don't require access to the Internet the way a website does. Advertising enhancements, beyond the obvious personalization, localization, and customization, include

- ✔ **Multimedia display advertising:** Full-screen images have interactive components.

- ✔ **E-mail marketing:** This strategy is tailored for the iPad, with its large graphics and touchscreen buttons.

- ✔ **In-app advertising and content for sale:** The mobile ad network provider Mobclix claims that iPad apps may generate five times the estimated advertising revenue of iPhone apps, and people continue viewing ads about six times longer than they do on a desktop.

- ✔ **Search advertising:** As with smartphones, geotargeting is vastly improved; just be sure to optimize landing and video pages for the iPad (remember not to use Flash).

✔ **Video advertising:** The high-resolution iPad screen makes viewing videos more appealing than on smartphones.

✔ **Social media:** Facebook, Twitter, and other social media services have their own apps for the iPad.

You can find a list of inexpensive (or free) iPad apps for social media and mobile marketing in Bonus Chapter 3 on the Downloads tab of the companion website.

Developing marketing-friendly iPad websites

Although most standard websites look fine on an iPad, they don't take advantage of all the features the device offers. In particular, the touchscreen user interface offers opportunities to reconfigure websites for better accessibility and ease of use, as shown in Figure 10-10.

Figure 10-10: Viewers using the iPad app developed by TheFind can simply tap a finger to choose from various catalogs.

Courtesy of TheFind, Inc.

For more guidance in finding design-related iPad apps, check out the resources list in Bonus Chapter 3 on the Downloads tab of the companion website.

Expect your developer to address many issues, such as the fluid width (because the iPad can be held in either portrait or landscape position); the lack of a vertical or horizontal "fold"; the unavailability of hover effects with a pointer or cursor; the need for icons and links that are large enough to touch without interference; the inability to use Flash; and the use of HTML5. To gain a sense of the complexity facing developers, see all the available choices at www.washingtonpost.com/wp-srv/contents/mobile.

Designing a completely new iPad app can be time consuming and expensive. Be sure to get your existing website up and running in the meantime. Tweak it slightly in HTML, if necessary. The Safari browser automatically defaults to the mobile version of a site on the iPad, but other browsers allow users to change the settings to view the full-size version of a site when an iPad app isn't available.

Part IV
Spending Online Marketing Dollars

The 5th Wave   By Rich Tennant

" Good news, honey! No one's registered our last name as a domain name yet! Helloooo Haffassoralsurgery.com!"

In this part . . .

The advertising techniques described in Part IV cost money, but well-designed paid advertising campaigns may produce the short-term boost you need in order to promote your new web presence, increase online visibility, or grow sales.

Consider paid advertising not only for long-term branding but also as an interim technique while your social media and natural search engine optimization efforts take hold.

Pay per click (PPC) ads that appear on search engines, their content partners, and now on social media channels are one of the most cost-effective methods of advertising online. PPC ads are easily targeted for keyword relevance; their conversion rate is easy to measure; and they're excellent mechanisms for generating leads and making sales. Chapter 11 covers the rarely discussed strategic and tactical marketing decisions you should make before spending on PPC campaigns.

Banner ads — those ubiquitous and sometimes annoying hyperlinked graphical ads — are more expensive than PPC, with a much lower click-through rate. As you can read in Chapter 12, they, too, have a place in the web marketer's quiver, particularly for branding. This chapter gives you the tools to select the types of banner ads that best fit your needs and budget, and to identify the most cost-effective publishers to reach your target market.

Chapter 11

Marketing with Pay Per Click Ads

• •

• •

*P*ity all those poor, pre-web marketers who were stuck with coupons, direct mail, or television to connect customer interest in an ad to customer action that takes place later. In contrast, the Internet enables an advertiser to reach a viewer who is actively engaged in a related activity on a website. Better yet, *pay per click* (or PPC) ads on a search engine allow an advertiser to supply answers to a viewer at the moment the viewer is interested in a specific product or service.

This chapter focuses on the marketing strategies and tactics that apply to PPC programs (also called *cost per click,* or CPC), with an emphasis on Google AdWords, Bing/Yahoo! Search Marketing, shopping search engines, social media PPC options, and a few specialty search engines.

Since 2009, Yahoo! and Microsoft Bing have partnered in a search-and-advertising partnership. They share the advertising results and management tools, but both companies retain separate user interfaces for organic and paid searches. When I refer to their joint advertising or search programs, I use *Bing/Yahoo!* in the text. When I refer to the companies as individual entities, I use *Bing* or *Yahoo!* or *Bing and Yahoo!* in the text.

Paying for Presence

The most familiar PPC ads appear on search engines, as shown in Figure 11-1. In the figure, typical PPC ads on Yahoo! are shown in the column to the right of natural search results for the search term *reno real estate;* paid sponsor listings appear above natural search results. These text-only ads, which look like classified ads, appear only if users search for one of your preselected keywords. Facebook, MySpace, Twitter, and other social media channels now also carry PPC-style ads. PPC advertising has proved durable: Spending on PPC ads generated about $11.9 billion in advertising revenue in 2010.

Sponsored ad   PPC ads

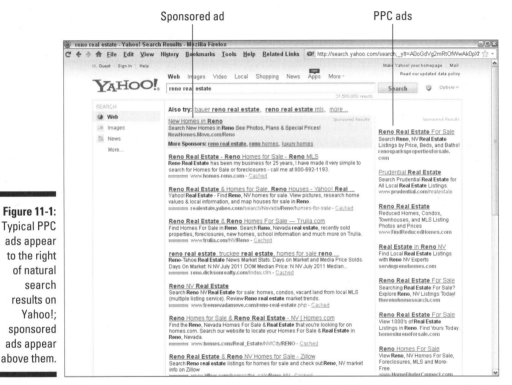

Figure 11-1:
Typical PPC
ads appear
to the right
of natural
search
results on
Yahoo!;
sponsored
ads appear
above them.

PPC-like ads that appear outside search engines may not reach well-qualified prospects. A user who views ads on social media pages or other websites isn't as likely to be nearing a purchase decision as someone who clicks the ads in the rightmost column of a search engine results page.

PPC differs from old-fashioned advertising in these three important ways:

- **PPC ads are displayed on search engines only when users are interested enough to enter a chosen keyword.** The result is a highly targeted audience.

- **Ads that are fed to non-search-engine sites generally use** *contextual targeting.* Results from using this technique are displayed only when nearby content or an internal search includes your chosen keyword. On some social media channels or other non-search-engine sites, you can also target ads based on demographic options, instead of, or in addition to, keywords.

✔ **By definition, the cost of PPC ads is based on the number of click-throughs you receive, not on the number of times your ad is served or viewed.** Those views are called *impressions* in traditional advertising. Variants of PPC, including PPA (pay per action) and the traditional CPM (cost per thousand impressions), now exist.

David Hallerman of eMarketer noted in 2008 that "even though many people are willing to click relevant paid search ads, they prefer organic listings" (www.emarketer.com/Article.aspx?R=1006182). Although organic search listings may receive as much as 70 percent more traffic than PPC results, people who click PPC ads are more likely to be interested in buying products or services than in seeking information.

As a web marketer, it behooves you to use the guerrilla PPC techniques in this chapter as a strategic complement to natural SEO (search engine optimization), described in Chapter 7.

You don't have to place ads on terms and phrases for which your site already appears near the top of search results! Save your budget for competitive search terms when you can't break through on natural searches. As your natural search results improve from using SEO, you may be able to stop paid ads on certain keywords.

Add *PPC* to your Web Marketing Methods Checklist (see Chapter 2). You can also download the checklist from the Downloads tab at www.dummies.com/go/webmarketingfd3e.

For a wealth of additional information on PPC, including detailed implementation directions, check out *Pay Per Click For Dummies,* by Peter Kent.

Devising a Pay Per Click (PPC) Strategy

Under pay per click (PPC) programs, you bid competitively on specific keywords, setting the maximum amount you're willing to pay every time a viewer clicks through to your site. In the past, the ad provided by the highest bidder usually appeared at the top of the list of sponsored searches, with other ads appearing in descending order by bid amount. Now, however, the major search engines consider the quality of the ad and the landing page on the website when assigning appearance.

Premium sponsored positions appear above the natural search results. You can't pay to have ads appear there on Google; the order of appearance rotates and is derived from ad quality. Yahoo! offers these ads through a separate advertising program at relatively expensive monthly rates. The ads are bought primarily by large companies running broad-based branding campaigns.

PPC ads are displayed the same way on other search engines, such as AOL (at www.aol.com) or Alta Vista (at www.altavista.com), that receive their feeds from Google or Yahoo! (See www.bruceclay.com/searchengine relationshipchart.htm to understand which search engines generate or receive results from another.) However, some, such as AOL Search, display only the top few PPC ads in the feed.

Although the number of people who prefer organic search results may be higher than the number who prefer PPC, visitors from PPC ads bring in more money! In a two-year study, Engine Ready (at www.engineready.com) found that conversions from paid traffic were 20 percent higher than those from organic search results and that the average order value was 18 percent higher. These numbers make sense: People who click ads are more likely, by definition, to be buyers than those using organic results to research topics.

As with natural search engine results, your ad usually needs to appear *above the fold* (on the portion of the page the user sees without scrolling), in the top five listings, to have a reasonable chance of being viewed and receiving a click-through.

The top position in the right column of PPC ads may attract more views. You may have more clicks on that ad, but you may receive more conversions from an ad in positions 2 through 5 (above the fold).

Some advertisers stretch their budgets by selecting inexpensive, less frequently used keywords and relying on the long-tail effect to produce click-throughs to their sites. (In the *long-tail effect,* the cumulative value of many low-volume terms may equal or exceed that of a few, high-volume terms.) Your best bet is to experiment.

Requesting a specific position is now more difficult on Google. In a recent round of advertiser interface changes, it removed position preference as an option. Advertisers must now establish a specific rule to raise bids to the level of positions 1 through 5. Google has added the capability of estimating the cost to achieve that prominence.

The limited onscreen real estate on popular search terms puts small businesses with small pocketbooks at a disadvantage on the most popular terms. Scarcity leads to higher prices: The cost of bidding on certain popular search terms has become prohibitive for some and unprofitable for others. In this case, avoid single words such as *gifts,* as keywords. Instead, try using phrases (for example, *children's birthday gifts*) or one of the more narrowly defined keyword options, such as an exact match.

Comparing PPC to other online advertising

Chapter 12 discusses forms of online advertising other than PPC, including banners and newsletter sponsorships. These types of ads generally use a traditional payment model that sets the cost per thousand impressions (CPM), as described in the nearby "PPC terms to remember" sidebar. Others charge a flat fee, often by the month, regardless of the number of impressions or clicks you receive.

Over time, the distinction between PPC and CPM advertising models has become muddied. To appeal to more advertisers, Google and Bing/Yahoo! also offer a traditional CPM model, but only for third-party, content partner sites. These partner sites, which publish contextual ads, may carry CPC- and CPM-priced ads simultaneously. To make the situation more confusing, you can use Google as an ad network to place graphical and video-based banner ads on some of their content partner sites.

A few *publishers* (websites that carry ads) offer a cost per acquisition (CPA) model, but most publishers avoid the uncertainty of CPA ad revenue. From their perspective, a high acquisition rate depends on the quality of the ad text (the creative), the website, and the offer in the ad, all of which are outside their control. All they can deliver is the audience.

In the online world, an *impression* is counted whenever a page containing an ad is downloaded (or *served*). When banner or placement-targeted ads are priced by CPM, you're charged for the impression even if your ad is so far below the fold that few people see it. Using PPC, you pay only when someone reaches your site.

Using content ad partners

The Google AdSense program and Yahoo! Content Match display your ads on other non-search-engine sites. These ads are supposed to appear only if they're related to nearby content on the partner sites, but it isn't always so.

Although you try to target all ads as closely as you can to your desired market, a PPC ad on a search results page is more likely to reach your target prospects at the moment they research an item or consider making a purchase. Ads on content partners are often better suited to branding and increasing visibility. You can see an example of PPC ads at a content partner at SustainabilityNinja (www.sustainabilityninja.com).

The CTR and the likelihood of purchase on content partner sites is usually much lower than the CTR you receive for ads on search results pages. Recognizing that the audience on content sites is "less qualified," both Google and Yahoo! allow you to bid a lower amount if you choose PPC for content partner sites. Take advantage of this option to reduce your costs.

Generic content partner sites are the least focused PPC audience. Although the Google placement or demographic selection options to review and select specific partner sites are more time-consuming, use them, especially for sales-oriented ads. Always preview content sites to ensure that they truly draw your audience.

If you know in advance that you want to place PPC ads on a specific site, check first to see which network it participates in. You must either sign up on that network or make arrangements directly with the publishers (see Chapter 12).

PPC terms to remember

content partner: A non-search-engine site that carries PPC ads via a feed from a search engine or another network.

conversion rate: The number of actions taken or purchases made divided by the number of clicks received.

CPA: Cost per action; the dollar value you pay whenever a visitor completes a predetermined action, such as a conversion, phone call, or newsletter sign-up. Comparable to commission on a sale, CPA can be significantly higher per unit than CPC for an equivalent ad. This pricing is reasonable because the prospect has prequalified by taking an additional action toward purchase. Run projections based on your historical conversion rate to see which is more advantageous.

CPC: Cost per click; the actual dollar value you pay. Some people reserve the term *CPC* for banners that charge by the click and the term *PPC* for sponsored ads on search engines.

CPM: Cost per thousand impressions; allows you to compare costs from one ad venue, or type, to another. If an ad costs $500 for 10,000 impressions, your CPM is $500 divided by 10, or $50. Because most PPC sites also provide the number of impressions, you can compute the CPM for your PPC campaign.

CTR: Click-through rate; the number of clicks divided by the number of impressions. Expect costs for a click-through to be higher than costs for an impression.

landing page: The destination page on your site that viewers see when they click your ad.

paid inclusion: Payment for being listed in a search engine or directory, often for faster review or guaranteed listing. The search engine or directory generally charges a flat annual fee or monthly charge per URL.

placement-targeted ad: A PPC ad posted on an individually selected content partner.

PPC: The pay per click payment method. Compare to *CPC*.

PPA: Pay per action. Compare to *CPA*. Some people use CPA to designate banners that charge by action and use PPA for the equivalent on search engines.

ROI: Return on investment. For PPC, refers to the profit made divided by the cost of the PPC campaign. Computing ROI over a whole program might be more useful than computing it for an individual product. Sometimes, you deliberately lose money or break even on one product (a *loss leader*) to draw customers into a store, only to make more profit on sales of other items that follow.

search partner: A secondary search engine that carries PPC ads via a feed from a primary search engine or another network.

Planning your PPC campaign

As with any other online marketing technique, you need to set goals and objectives for your PPC campaigns. Here are some questions to consider:

- ✔ Are you interested in introducing your site (branding it)?
- ✔ Are you competing for sales on specific goods?
- ✔ Are you trying to capture the interest of prospects researching major purchases so that they visit your store? Or are you selling retail online?
- ✔ How does PPC fit into your overall marketing plan, including offline activities?

If you're an e-tailer (a business selling retail goods online), coordinate your PPC program with merchandising activities continuously to promote your specials, seasonal offers, clearance sales, and new products.

For most businesses, a PPC program is a matter of trial and error. Produce and test multiple iterations of your ads until you find the combination of ad content and search terms that produces the best results. Consequently, a PPC campaign also requires a time commitment to set up and monitor, especially in its early stages — or if it becomes large and complex. Do you have the time?

If you have a limited budget, pause your campaign occasionally and narrow your geographic reach, rather than run it evenly over time and place. In most cases, you gain better visibility and more click-throughs from qualified prospects if you spend more money over a shorter period than if you spend a little bit of money all the time. Use your PPC budget only when it will do you the most good, such as when

- ✔ You first launch your site for greater visibility and branding.
- ✔ You're waiting to get out of the Google sandbox, for link campaigns to kick in, or for search engines to spider new pages.
- ✔ You add important new products, services, content, or features to your site.
- ✔ You can't reach first-page traction in natural search results for a particular keyword.
- ✔ You're trying to reach prospects in a targeted geographical area.
- ✔ You can identify the demographics of the audience you're trying to reach.
- ✔ Your target audience is online during certain hours. (Consult your traffic statistics.)
- ✔ Seasonal campaigns are tied to holiday giving (especially in December, February, and May) or to key points in your own annual sales cycle.

Carrying Out Your PPC Plan

After you've decided to carry out a PPC campaign, you need to decide where to spend your PPC budget. Given that Google provided almost 65 percent of all searches in April 2011 (according to comScore — www.comscore.com) while Bing and Yahoo! controlled another 14 and 16 percent, respectively, your PPC campaign will probably include Google and perhaps one or both of the others.

Choose your PPC venue based on where your target audience searches. According to Alexa (at www.alexa.com), Google, which draws one-third of its search base internationally, has the fewest young users and the fewest without a college education. Considering that most users are likely to browse from the workplace, Google has been an essential pathway to reach B2B customers. In the future, LinkedIn is likely to compete for this audience. The Yahoo! user profile is quite similar to Google's, though more Yahoo! users are likely to browse from home.

The oldest demographic of users prefers Bing, which has the best conversion rates for older users, especially those over 55. Concentrated in the United States, other components of Bing's audience are more likely to browse from school, be less well educated, and have a lower income (both of which correlate to being in school).

Although Google generates more online sales revenue than any other search engine (at least partly because of its vastly larger user base), Bing has, anecdotally, a higher conversion rate for retail and travel purchases.

Your best bet is to try the same ads and search terms on all three search engines — Bing, Yahoo!, and Google — to see which ones work better for you.

Watch your own traffic statistics (see Chapter 6) and the results of your search engine optimization (SEO) campaign from Chapter 7. The source of visitors and the terms they use for a natural search provide invaluable information about the best tactics for your PPC campaign.

PPC features change often. Now that Bing is running PPC for both itself and Yahoo!, their combined operation has become more like Google's. Check both Google AdWords and Bing/Yahoo! Search Marketing regularly for updates.

Google offers its own chart-comparison features at https://adwords. google.com/select/comparison.html, or you can review the differences summarized in the table titled "Search Marketing Comparison of Google AdWords and Bing/Yahoo!" in Bonus Chapter 4 on the Downloads tab of the companion website.

Bidding within your budget

When you assemble your PPC budget, work your numbers backward to set up a budget within your overall marketing plan. Think about how much you can afford to spend and whether you want to spend it all at once or spread it out over a month or year. Every PPC provider has a somewhat different format for estimating results on search terms based on your bid. An example of Yahoo!'s traffic estimation appears on the Set Your Ad Group Bid page in Figure 11-2. Changing your bid or moving the slider on the graph adjusts the projections.

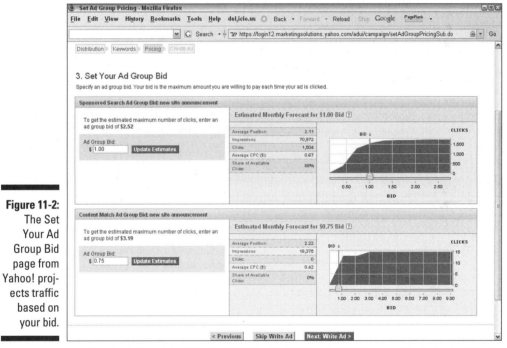

Figure 11-2:
The Set Your Ad Group Bid page from Yahoo! projects traffic based on your bid.

You can easily break the bank on PPC ads, so try these tips to get the most benefit from your PPC spending, without getting sucked into the budget-busting barrel of overbidding:

✔ **Don't bid to win the top position.** In fact, TheNextWeb (at `http://thenextweb.com`) shows that the top PPC ad might attract the highest number of tire kickers. Ads in the second position might draw more serious buyers.

✔ **Remember that Google incorporates quality score and CTR, as well as bid price, in determining ad placement.** (This approach just happens to maximize the revenue that the search engines receive.) Bing/Yahoo! uses these criteria only to provide feedback on ad and keyword relevance.

✔ **Improve your natural search engine ranking.** Why waste money advertising on sponsored searches if you achieve top results for free? Save your money or spend it elsewhere.

✔ **Set geographic limits.** You obviously would limit the range of your ads if you depend on a local population to attend an event or make a purchase in your real-world store. Setting geographical limits can extend your budget, even when you sell nationwide. Look at your sales statistics (see Chapter 6) to see where your past and most lucrative buyers live. Constrain your ads to run in those locations.

✔ **Use your traffic statistics (see Chapter 6) to see which days of the week and times of day your buyers are active.** Constrain your ads to run during those times.

✔ **If you're selling online or have a specific way to monitor viewer activity, set up conversion tracking.** Have your programmer place the required snippet of code on the Thank You pages after a sale or sign-up or on other pages you want to track. Your reports will show what percentage of click-through visitors reach that page and how much your campaign has cost per conversion.

✔ **Be ruthless about dropping keywords that don't convert!** This advice applies especially if you're selling. If your ad is designed for research or for driving people into a real-world storefront, you might want to maintain CTR as your key parameter.

✔ **If you're using PPC for sales purposes, don't bid more than an average sale (rather than a single item) is worth.** As a rule of thumb, spend no more than 10 percent of your average sales amount on advertising if your company is new or 5 percent if you've already built an online reputation. If you estimate conservatively that 2 percent of people who click through to your site will buy, you must pay for 50 clicks to make one sale! For example, if your average online sale is $100, limit advertising (for a new company) to $10. Divide $10 by 50 to calculate an average bid of 20 cents per click. Of course, you can bid more on some words and less on others.

You can always break the "rules" for strategic marketing purposes. Paying more to acquire a new customer makes sense if you have a history of turning first-time shoppers into repeat buyers. Although online sales may lead to offline sales, you can't count on it, especially in the beginning.

Selecting search terms

Selecting the appropriate search terms for an ad is much like selecting keywords for SEO. You might find it helpful to use PPC ads for search terms on which you don't appear on the first page of search results. Bing/Yahoo! offers a search term selection tool that includes historical use. In Figure 11-3, Yahoo! suggests keywords based on synonyms for the words you enter or for words found on your website. From the resulting list on the left, you select the ones you want to use on the right.

Google also offers a search term selection tool based on historical use, as shown in Figure 11-4. The Google Keyword Tool, which is available as you set up your AdWords campaign, offers keyword suggestions as well as detailed projections. You can designate some suggestions as negative keywords to be ignored, as shown in the pop-up. The tool is also available externally at `https://adwords.google.com/o/Targeting/Explorer`.

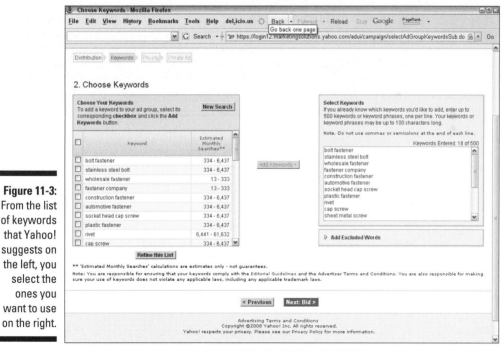

Figure 11-3:
From the list of keywords that Yahoo! suggests on the left, you select the ones you want to use on the right.

Both Bing/Yahoo! and Google let you

✔ Enter terms to search for synonyms

✔ Crawl your pages to suggest terms

✔ Suggest terms based on your current search terms and ads

See `http://advertising.microsoft.com/small-business/` `adcenter-downloads/microsoft-advertising-intelligence` and `https://adwords.google.com/o/Targeting/Explorer` for more information on Bing/Yahoo! and Google, respectively.

As with natural SEO, select targeted search phrases rather than single words. Also, don't select terms that are longer than most users will type. If terms are difficult to spell, you might want to include common misspellings also, such as *O'Keefe* for Georgia O'Keeffe. See Chapter 7 for more suggestions.

If you aren't sure whether to include a search term, use it. Start with too many terms and delete the ones that don't perform; sometimes, a term is successful unexpectedly. You can and should apply keyword ideas you find on WordPot (see Chapter 7) or other keyword suggestion sites, such as `www.nichebot.com` or `www.keyworddiscovery.com`. Don't forget search terms used by existing users, which are usually available in your traffic statistics. (See Chapter 6.)

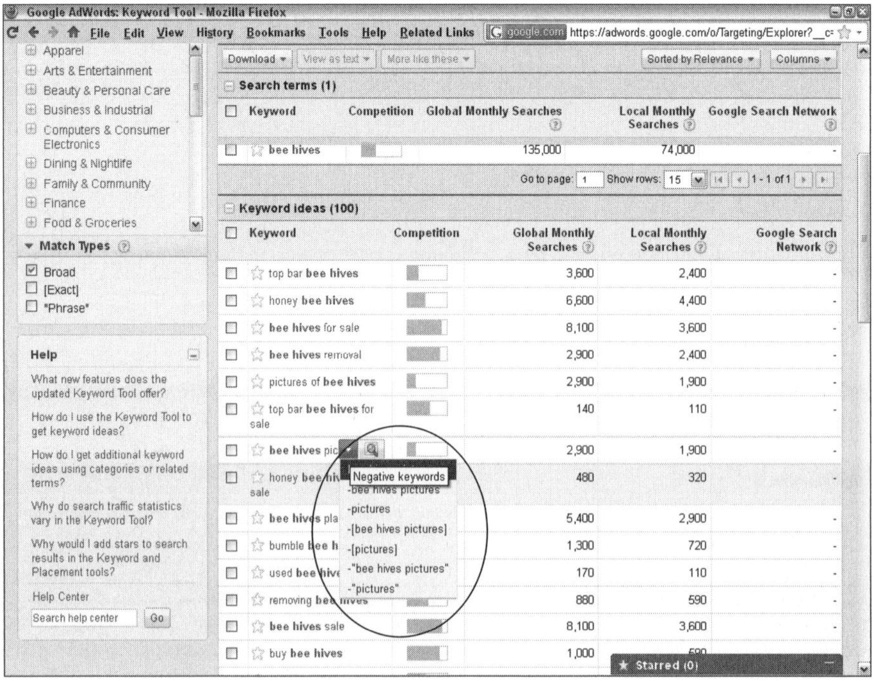

Figure 11-4:
The Google
Keyword
Tool offers
keyword
suggestions
and detailed
projections.

As with regular search term selection, not everyone uses the same words when looking for an item. People from different regions and countries and who use different dialects may use different words to refer to the same item. Are you selling buckets or pails? Is that a stroller or a pram?

Writing a good PPC ad

You might recall this adage about advertising: Successful ads owe 40 percent to the offer, 40 percent to the audience, and 20 percent to the creative element. If you use the right search engine and select search terms that your prospects are likely to use, you have the audience. Now viewers need a reason to click your ad rather than your competitors'.

Most PPC ads include these elements: headline, two lines of text, a visible URL, and an unseen landing page URL. Every search engine sets the specific length of a line, but the same general principles apply across all engines. Tips for writing ads are available on Google and Bing/Yahoo!, or you can find out how to write a good classified ad at a site such as `www.websitemarketing` `plan.com/small_business/classified.htm`. Figure 11-5 shows you the Google ad template.

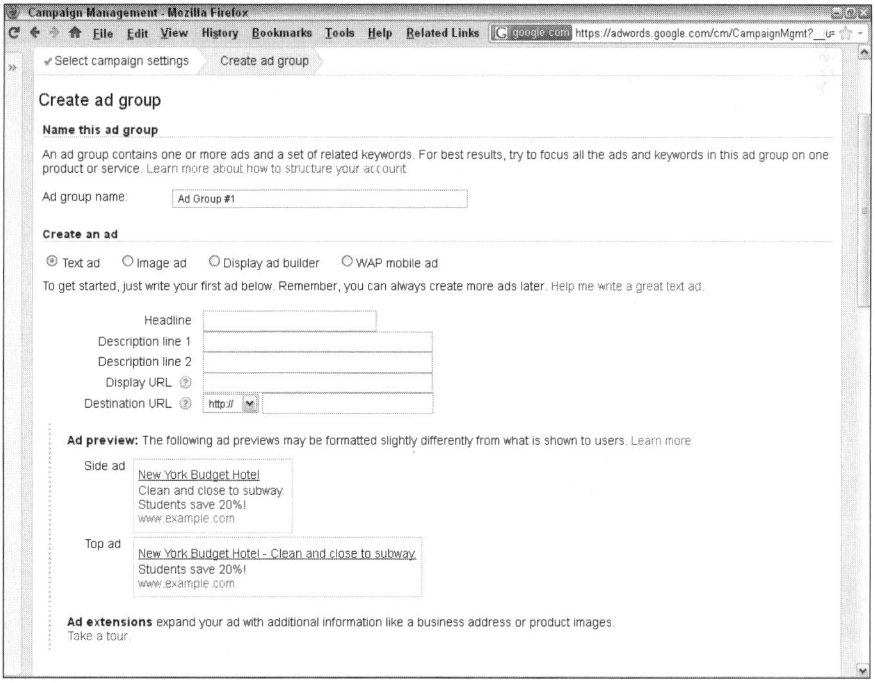

Figure 11-5:
The ad template at Google automatically counts characters in each field to keep you within limits.

[Screenshot of Campaign Management window in Mozilla Firefox showing Google's "Create ad group" template with fields for Ad group name, Create an ad options (Text ad, Image ad, Display ad builder, WAP mobile ad), Headline, Description line 1, Description line 2, Display URL, Destination URL, and Ad preview showing Side ad and Top ad examples for "New York Budget Hotel — Clean and close to subway. Students save 20%! www.example.com"]

Courtesy of Google, Inc.

Both Bing/Yahoo! and Google have additional rules governing word use, punctuation, qualifiers, proper nouns, trademarks, and other characteristics. Because both sites review your ads to make sure that they comply, read the rules for whichever one you use.

Headline

Just as with your website, your ad headline should grab attention quickly. Here are some general guidelines:

- ✔ **Avoid small words.** They often only take up space.

- ✔ **Use words that draw attention.** Examples are *new, exclusive, special, now,* and *save.*

- ✔ **Use search terms in the headline or in the text of the ad — or both.** This strategy might mean writing a lot of different ads!

A small difference in wording might have a big effect on the success of your ad. Try several variations if you don't see a good click-through rate. Run multiple ads on the same search terms, making it easy to test wording. (Only one of your ads at a time will appear for any one of your keywords.) Remember to test changes in only one line at a time!

This type of testing can be applied to offers and the wording of ads, landing pages, keywords, or any other single variable. Just remember to change only one element at a time! Google makes it possible to test landing pages by varying traffic to your original page and alternative versions to see how users respond.

Ask your programmer to check out the following sites to set up testing for ads or to test landing pages, respectively: http://adwords.google.com/support/aw/bin/answer.py?hl=en&answer=62999 and http://adwords.google.com/support/aw/bin/answer.py?hl=en&answer=55589.

Try to keep your text specific to the purpose of the ad by focusing on user benefits. For sales-oriented ads, the more details the better. Include the price or low shipping cost, for example, if either one is a selling point. Also, think about your audience and consider which factors matter to them. You might have several ads for the same product, each oriented toward a different benefit that appeals to a different segment of your market. Test different offers on otherwise identical ads.

These short ads work much better when you deal with only one item or group of closely related items rather than with diverse products. Combining shirts and shoes might work in a print ad, for example, but doing this is difficult online because users can click to only one destination page.

Just as you did when writing text for your site, stick with active voice and second person: *you,* not *we.* Use a call to action in your offer. An imperative verb, such as *enjoy, savor, relax, play, indulge,* or *earn* gives people an immediate reason to click through. Don't waste precious characters telling people to click! When users search for something, they want to know What's-in-it-for-me? on the other side of the action.

Landing pages

Generally, you display the same primary URL on all your ads for branding purposes. However, someone clicking an ad should immediately see a destination, or *landing page,* on your site that is directly related to the ad. A good landing page fulfills the promise that's implicit in your ad, and its content and appearance should be well structured to convert a browser to a buyer. Try to imagine yourself in your viewer's place, looking with new eyes at your site.

Google explicitly includes the quality of a landing page, including download time, when deciding how to rank ads. For more information, see `http://adwords.google.com/support/bin/answer.py?hl=en&answer=46675`.

Here are some guidelines to consider for landing pages:

- ✔ **Have your search terms or synonyms appear in the text or meta tags of your landing page.** This tactic improves landing page quality and thus indirectly improves the ranking of an ad.

- ✔ **If you're selling a single product, the landing page should be the product detail page.** If you advertise related sizes or items, go up a level to a subcategory or category page in your storefront to encompass your offer.

- ✔ **Specify the results of an onsite search as a landing page.** To more closely match a landing page to a group of products you advertise, for example, preset a search for *turquoise earrings.*

- ✔ **Avoid directing people to pages with large photo files or rich media.** Download time is a criterion for assessing landing page quality.

- ✔ **Help visitors land where they want to land!** Don't strand them on your home page, wondering where to find the product you advertised.

Reviewing reports

If you can afford to, put some extra funds into the first week or two of your PPC campaign so that you can see which search terms perform best for CTR and conversion. Watch the results for at least a week to collect representative data, especially if some of your terms are rarely used.

Both Bing/Yahoo! and Google offer reporting tools at various levels of detail. A Google Dashboard and an example of a detailed keyword report appear in Figures 11-6 and 11-7, respectively. If you implement conversion tracking, you can configure these reports to display also the number or value of conversions and cost per conversion.

PPC is an iterative process. Look at your PPC and traffic reports and make changes based on the information you find.

Stick with what works until it doesn't. Then refresh your ads with new content and new offers. Over time, you'll probably discover that a reduced set of search terms works best with a particular ad.

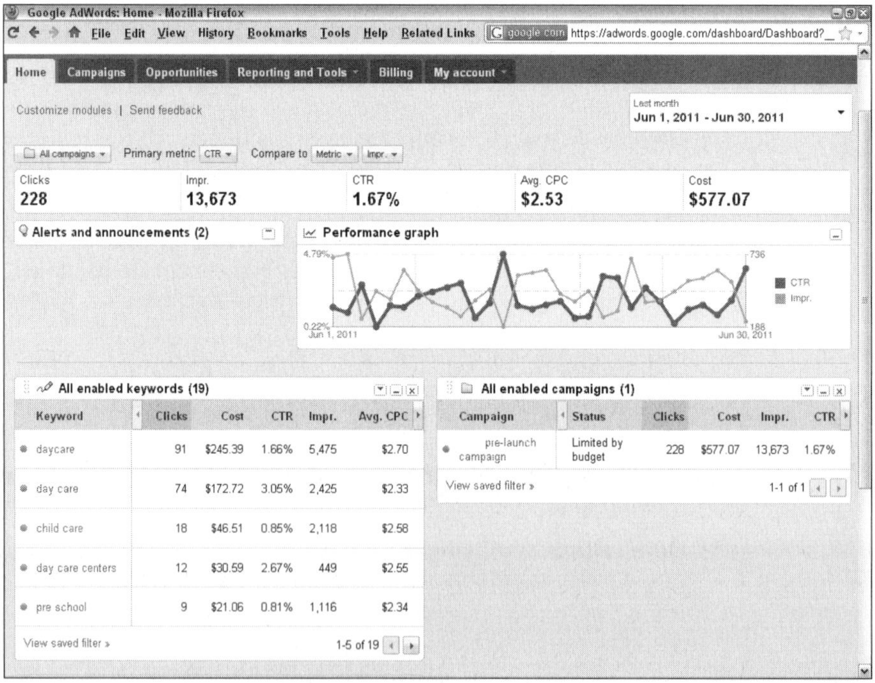

Figure 11-6:
A Google Dashboard provides a graphical overview of AdWords performance.

Courtesy of Google, Inc.

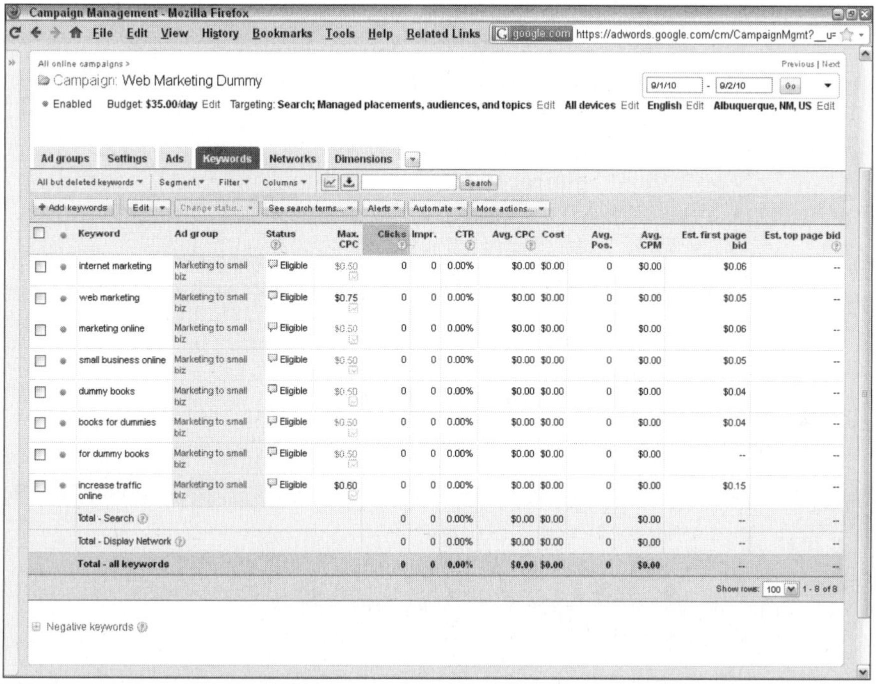

Keyword	Ad group	Status	Max. CPC	Clicks	Impr.	CTR	Avg. CPC	Cost	Avg. Pos.	Avg. CPM	Est. first page bid	Est. top page bid
internet marketing	Marketing to small biz	Eligible	$0.50	0	0	0.00%	$0.00	$0.00	0	$0.00	$0.06	--
web marketing	Marketing to small biz	Eligible	$0.75	0	0	0.00%	$0.00	$0.00	0	$0.00	$0.05	--
marketing online	Marketing to small biz	Eligible	$0.50	0	0	0.00%	$0.00	$0.00	0	$0.00	$0.06	--
small business online	Marketing to small biz	Eligible	$0.50	0	0	0.00%	$0.00	$0.00	0	$0.00	$0.05	--
dummy books	Marketing to small biz	Eligible	$0.50	0	0	0.00%	$0.00	$0.00	0	$0.00	$0.04	--
books for dummies	Marketing to small biz	Eligible	$0.50	0	0	0.00%	$0.00	$0.00	0	$0.00	$0.04	--
for dummy books	Marketing to small biz	Eligible	$0.50	0	0	0.00%	$0.00	$0.00	0	$0.00	--	--
increase traffic online	Marketing to small biz	Eligible	$0.60	0	0	0.00%	$0.00	$0.00	0	$0.00	$0.15	--
Total - Search				0	0	0.00%	$0.00	$0.00	0	$0.00	--	--
Total - Display Network				0	0	0.00%	$0.00	$0.00	0	$0.00	--	--
Total - all keywords				**0**	**0**	**0.00%**	**$0.00**	**$0.00**	**0**	**$0.00**	--	--

Figure 11-7: A Google report for keywords in an ad group can be configured to display the columns you prefer.

Courtesy of Courtesy of Google, Inc.

Bing/Yahoo! Search Marketing Specifics

If you decide to use Bing/Yahoo!, you might want to take advantage of several of the alternatives or complements to standard PPC that are described in this list:

- **Bing Business Portal** replaces the Bing Local Listing Service at `www.bing.com/businessportal`. Bing Business Portal is free, so this choice is another no-brainer.
- **Bing Shopping Search** at `http://advertising.microsoft.com/small-business/search-advertising/bing-shopping` was an excellent outlet for retailers; new merchant sign-ups have been halted temporarily.
- **Yahoo! Directory** still offers paid inclusion for directory placement, which is separate from Yahoo! search results. Yahoo! fans still like this yellow-pages-style directory. For $299 per year, Yahoo! quickly reviews and posts corporate sites. See `http://add.yahoo.com/fast/add?8101`.

- ✔ **Yahoo! Local** is an option for Yahoo! e-mail account holders, whether or not they advertise. It's especially valuable for companies seeking to drive traffic to a bricks-and-mortar store or an event. Yahoo! offers two different tiers for local advertising: basic (free) or enhanced ($9.95 per month) at `http://listings.local.yahoo.com`. Do it!

- ✔ **Yahoo! Sponsored Listings** offer paid appearance at the top of a specific search results page. Explore this option at `https://adcenter.microsoft.com`.

- ✔ **Yahoo! Travel Submit** is a fixed-rate CPC program rather than a bid program. It generally yields a higher conversion rate than regular PPC ads do. Travel-related clicks run 20 to 57 cents per click based on category. For more information, see `http://help.yahoo.com/l/us/yahoo/ysm/ts/index.html`.

You can find more helpful URLs for advertising at Bing/Yahoo! in Bonus Chapter 4 on the Downloads tab of the book's companion website.

Google AdWords Specifics

When you use Google AdWords, the minimum bid is not determined solely by what you're willing to pay. Instead, Google uses its Quality Score to measure the relevance of your keywords and establish a first-page bid estimate for every term.

As the Google AdWords Help page explains, your Quality Score is determined by your keyword's click-through rate on Google, the relevance of your ad text, the historical keyword performance on Google, the quality of your ad's landing page, and other relevancy factors. Your Quality Score is calculated anew at the time of each search query. From your perspective, deep-pocket competitors can't then "squat" at the top of a keyword list by placing a high bid to keep competitors out of contention.

A good ad with a good CTR and a good landing page can place your ad in one of the top four spots, even if you can't afford the highest bid. Of course, this strategy works for Google too, by maximizing its return on PPC ads. Google receives more revenue from an ad with a lower bid but a higher CTR than it receives from an ad with a higher bid that viewers don't click.

Google offers flexibility that Bing/Yahoo! has only recently duplicated. As part of your campaign setup process, you can select for such factors as time of day, delivery (evenly over time or accelerated), position preference, and geographical targets. Pages from the AdWords setup process are shown in Figures 11-8 and 11-9.

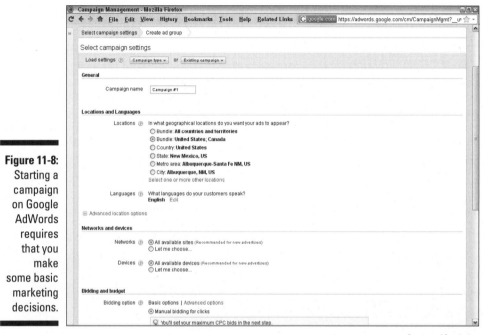

Figure 11-8:
Starting a campaign on Google AdWords requires that you make some basic marketing decisions.

Courtesy of Google, Inc.

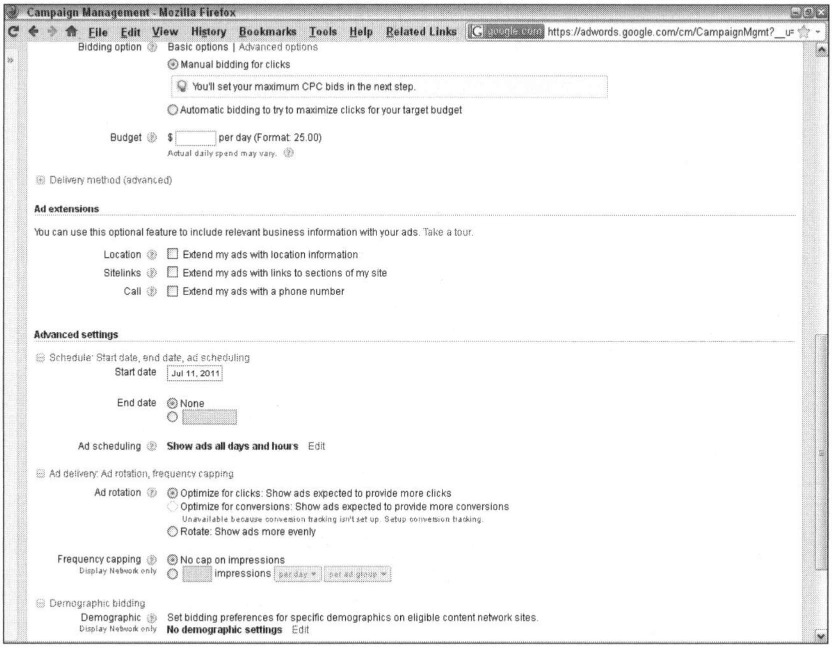

Figure 11-9:
You can use additional AdWords options to best serve your marketing needs.

Courtesy of Google, Inc.

Google now offers the option of integrating placement on specific content partner sites with regular keyword campaigns.

Here are some Google options to consider:

- ✔ **You can select which Google AdSense partner to use by topic, demographic, or name.** You can even exclude specific sites. Though these ads work well for branding, you're likely to experience a much lower CTR. Google allows both discounted CPC bids and a CPM option for content placement.

- ✔ **Google offers free local marketing for companies that sign up through Google Places.** Google has refined these free options to include a brief description, a logo, reviews, a map, and a coupon promotion. In May 2011, Google started offering free interior photos as a test to businesses in Orange County and the San Francisco Bay Area in California; St. Petersburg, Florida; San Antonio, Texas; and Phoenix, Arizona. Contact Google to see whether you can get in on this opportunity: `https://services.google.com/fb/forms/googlemapsbusinessphotos`.

- ✔ **Google AdWords can now incorporate a symbol that indicates acceptance via the integrated Google checkout system.** The tiered transaction fees based on volume are similar to those charged by PayPal.

- ✔ **You can select free ad extensions that differentiate your ads and attract attention.** They come in the following five flavors, some of which are shown in Figure 11-10:

  - *Location extensions* include your phone number and address for Google Places.

  - *Call extensions* use click-to-call on mobile results.

  - *Ad site links* are links to multiple pages on your site within a single ad.

  - *Product extensions* include images, titles, and prices of products in an expandable ad.

  - *Seller rating extensions* are user-submitted ratings for companies.

In the figure, note the Google +1 sharing icon on every result in the natural and paid search results, and note the magnifying glass, which pops open an image of the website landing page.

Look up details at `http://adwords.google.com` or view additional helpful URLs online in Bonus Chapter 4 on the Downloads tab of the companion website.

Ad site links   Product extension photos

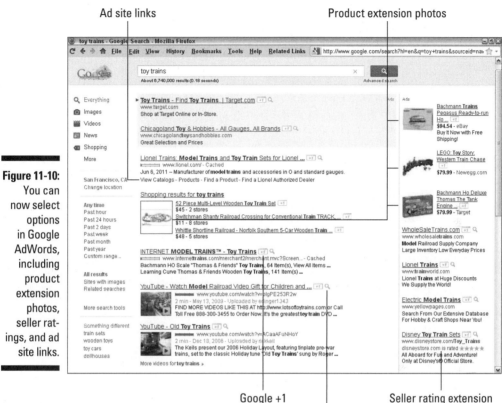

Figure 11-10:
You can
now select
options
in Google
AdWords,
including
product
extension
photos,
seller rat-
ings, and ad
site links.

Google +1   Open image of website   Seller rating extension

Courtesy of Google, Inc.

Assessing PPC on Social Media

In an effort to build brand loyalty among members of Generation Y (people born after 1979), who are the heaviest users of most social networks, some advertisers are turning to PPC models on Facebook, LinkedIn, and other social networking sites.

Reports to date on the results of PPC advertising on social networks are mixed. With a few exceptions, advertisers report plenty of impressions, especially on Facebook, but low CTRs and a low-to-negligible conversion rate.

If you aren't sure, test! Test identical ads, landing pages, and offers on sites such as Facebook versus those on search engines. Compare the results, and then make the decision that's right for you. What matters is what happens with your business, not with averages.

Consider your Facebook and other social networking PPC ads as part of a branding campaign for now. You're definitely getting your name in front of a lot of people. Instead of using sales-oriented PPC ads, place offers and advertising copy directly on your own wall or on fan pages where your followers will find them.

Twitter offers promoted products on a fixed-fee basis, not PPC; LinkedIn offers PPC ads directed at the B2B audience, which is somewhat different. I discuss the advertising models for the "big three" (Facebook, Twitter, and LinkedIn) in greater detail in their respective chapters in Part V.

Working with Shopping Search Engines

Shoppers often research product features, vendor history, and prices on the web before making purchases offline or online. Many product sellers should consider comparison shopping search engines such as NexTag, PriceGrabber, or Shopzilla. For an example, see Figure 11-11.

Figure 11-11: To appear in Google Product Search (called Shopping in the left navigation), merchants submit their products for free via a data feed.

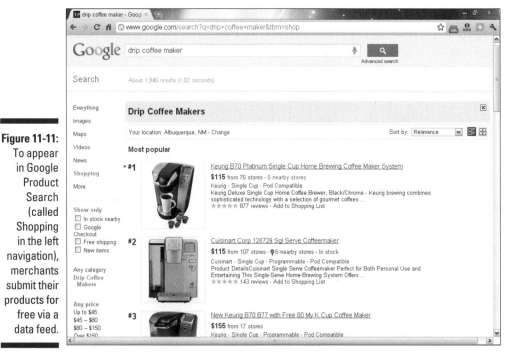

Courtesy of Google, Inc.

For more comparison shopping search engines, see Bonus Chapter 4 on the Downloads tab of the companion website.

Some shopping search engines operate primarily as directories of vendors; others offer sophisticated comparison features including shipping prices.

These comparison sites are especially favored for the purchase of small appliances, computers and accessories, electronics, auto parts, and brand-name items. They're less useful for jewelry, art, apparel, unique items, and high-priced luxury goods. If you're in the hospitality arena, consider listing on `http://travel.nextag.com`, `http://kayak.com`, or `http://travel.yahoo.com`.

The primary users of comparison shopping search engines used to be bargain hunters, shoppers comparing benefits and features, and buyers trying to find who sells a particular item. Now, according to statistics on the Ameromedia blog (`www.ameromedia.com`), it's just about everyone: 91 percent of U.S. Internet users compare product prices and features online, often on mobile devices.

If you spend the time, you can be as successful with your PPC campaign as Happy Hound Play & Daycare, whose website is shown in Figure 11-12 and whose PPC ad appears in Figure 11-13. Their PPC approach is described in the nearby sidebar, "Doggies win with Happy Hound's PPC ads."

Figure 11-12: The Happy Hound Play & Daycare in Oakland, California, has run a successful AdWords campaign since 2004.

Courtesy of Happy Hound Play & Daycare, Inc.

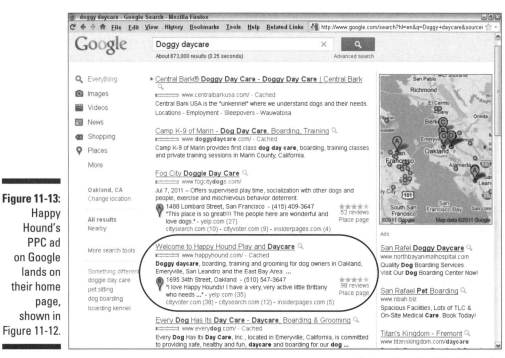

Courtesy of Happy Hound Play & Daycare, Inc.

Figure 11-13:
Happy
Hound's
PPC ad
on Google
lands on
their home
page,
shown in
Figure 11-12.

Doggies win with Happy Hound's PPC ads

Happy Hound Play & Daycare, Inc., provides dog day care, boarding, and training. This B2C company started online advertising within a few months of opening in March 2004.

Suzanne Golter, president of Happy Hound, has been running the campaigns nearly the entire time, primarily on Google AdWords but also, to a lesser extent, on Citysearch and Yelp. She focused on Google originally because "They have the greatest online presence with the most users, and therefore [were] the obvious target for my marketing dollars." Happy Hound also e-mails newsletters via Constant Contact and distributes brochures locally.

Rather than use performance metrics, Golter stresses the result of advertising — new client bookings. Whenever a new client fills out an application, Golter asks how the applicant heard about Happy Hound. "About 65 to 70 percent of the time, it's through Google. Some of that may be clients who get re ferrals at dog parks and then find me online, but what they remember is they found me — by searching the web."

Over time, Golter's AdWords presence has become more sophisticated. She runs only text ads, using geographic targeting to bring in clients who live nearby, and she keeps her monthly budget to less than $500. She now runs about five campaigns at a time, adding another whenever she rolls out a new service or when one isn't performing well. Overall, Golter finds that after the campaigns are set up, they're maintenance free.

"I am by no means a computer-savvy individual," she confesses. "I remember sitting at my desk, looking into an empty dog day care warehouse, wondering where I [was] going to get clients! I was messing around on the web and found Google AdWords. I was able to set up a few campaigns and start marketing my business. Within a few days, I started getting calls [and] booking appointments and assessments, and the clients kept flowing in!"

Setting up the campaigns took no time, she says — AdWords made it easy. However, as Golter's business grew, she had less time to manage the ads. In 2010, she hired an advertising agency to update her ads to promote new services. The agency now sends a monthly status report on AdWords performance. "Just last month they suggested I add more money because I could capture significantly more clients. So I did, and they were right."

"Do it!" she insists. "I don't know how a business in this economy can survive without marketing on the web. Figure out a budget that works for you, and do it!"

Chapter 12

Marketing with Paid Online Advertising

*L*inkable online display advertising, known broadly as *banner advertising,* is one of the more expensive methods of online promotion. From a strategic perspective, banner ads work well for *branding,* often pushing traffic to your site after running long enough for people to remember your brand.

Direct response banners with a clear call to action (intended to generate an immediate click to your site) generally have a significantly lower click-through rate (CTR) — 0.5 percent — than pay per click (PPC) search marketing — about 2 percent. (See Chapter 11 for more about PPC ads.) Like PPC ads, banner ads are now available on many social media channels and on websites, mobile media, and e-newsletters. In this chapter, in addition to describing banners, I address advertising with group coupons, site sponsorships, and online classifieds.

Depending on your budget, you might want to explore one or more of these paid advertising options. If so, check them off your Web Marketing Methods Checklist from Chapter 2, which you can download at full size from the Downloads tab at www.dummies.com/go/webmarketingfd3e.

Understanding Banner Advertising

Compared to the cost of print media, banner advertising — with the additional benefit of easy tracking — looks like a bargain. Indeed, some of the growth in Internet advertising historically has come at the expense of newspapers and magazines. Figure 12-1 shows the allocation of U.S. advertising dollars from 2009 projected through 2015; in 2010, online advertising reached a record amount of nearly $26 billion and is likely to reach $28.5 billion in 2011. Note that Internet advertising overtook newspapers by share in 2010.

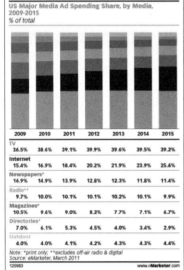

Figure 12-1: eMarketer displays the share of ad spending by medium for the United States from 2009 projected through 2015.

Source: eMarketer (www.emarketer.com)

The 2010 "Internet Advertising Revenue" report, from the Interactive Advertising Bureau (IAB) (available at www.clickz.com/clickz/news/2043354/online-industry-rebounded-2010) breaks down spending on online advertising by type. PPC search comprised 46 percent of online ad spending, compared to 24 percent for static banner ads. This report distinguishes additional types of banner ads, separately reporting *lead-generation* banners that offer webinar registrations or downloads of white papers to acquire prospects' contact information (5 percent), *video* banner ads (5 percent), and *rich media* banners that include animation, audio, or interactive elements other than video (6 percent).

One of the more complex aspects of online marketing, paid banner advertising is tantalizing and seductive but not always the most cost-effective use of your money. With a "good" return of CTR hitting only 0.5 percent, most banner ads produce only one-quarter to one-third as many clicks as the same amount of money spent on PPC search marketing.

If you decide to spend on banner ads, use clever planning to increase the click-through rate. In particular, you must target ads more carefully by audience, site choice, above-the-fold placement on the page, and context. Although rich media and video ads generally have higher click-through rates, they also cost more to produce.

Figure 12-2 is a graphical reminder that banner advertising is the most expensive of all forms of customer acquisition, exceeding even traditional media. By comparison, customer referrals (see the top line in the figure) are free. As always, word-of-mouth is the most cost-effective form of advertising.

Figure 12-2:
Banner ads have the lowest return on investment for all forms of Internet marketing.

Internet Marketing Tactics ROI Chart Courtesy of
Rapport Online Inc., roi-web.com

A developer generally handles no online advertising, although one with a strong background in marketing communications can produce banner and Flash ads. Because you need attractive, high-quality *creatives* (the files or artwork delivered to a publisher) to compete in the banner world, use professional services, especially for rich media ads using Flash, video, or sound. Some networks create ads for a price or offer banner-builders onsite.

You can place ads yourself by reviewing online media kits or calling a *publisher* — an individual website that posts ads. An online marketing company or ad agency can also help with your media buys. Table 12-1 lists some helpful resources.

Table 12-1	**Helpful Online Advertising Resources**	
Name	*URL*	*What You Can Find*
ADOTAS	`http://research.adotas.com`	Online advertising research and news
Advertising.com	`https://publisher.advertising.com/affiliate/glossary.jsp`	A glossary of interactive marketing terms
comScore Ad Focus Ranking	`http://ir.comscore.com/releasedetail.cfm?ReleaseID=586088`	The 20 largest online ad networks by number of visitors
DoubleClick	`www.doubleclick.com/insight/research/index.aspx`	Research reports
Google AdWords	`http://adwords.google.com/support/aw/bin/answer.py?hl=en&answer=97526&rd=1`	Popular ad sizes used on Google AdWords
iMedia Connection	`www.imediaconnection.com/Section.aspx?Section=Ad-Networks&Page=1`	Resources for online advertising
Interactive Advertising Bureau	`www.iab.net/iab_products_and_industry_services/1421/1443/1452`	A list of standard online ad sizes
Web Marketing Association	`www.advertisingcompetition.org/iac`	Internet ad competition
Webby Awards	`www.webbyawards.com/webbys/categories.php#interactive_advertising`	Internet ad competition
WebsiteTips.com	`http://websitetips.com/articles/marketing/banneradsctr`	Banner ad tips

Paid online advertising comes in a variety of forms:

- ✔ **Static banner:** Available in various sizes, as shown in Figure 12-3
- ✔ **Animated GIF or Flash:** Technical formats for displaying several images within one file
- ✔ **Digital video:** Kept very short (15 seconds or less) for online advertising purposes
- ✔ **Other types of rich media:** Often supplied with sound or interactive (engagement) elements
- ✔ **Pop-up:** Infamously appear over a page
- ✔ **Pop-under:** Visible after you close the browser window
- ✔ **Interstitial:** Appear before or between served pages
- ✔ **Expandable:** Grow to cover more of a page whenever a user hovers the mouse over the ad

An ad owes 20 percent of its success to the creative element, 40 percent to the offer, and 40 percent to the right audience. As with PPC ads, be sure to match your offer to your audience. Be careful also to link to the correct landing page on your site.

Get inspired to develop your banner ads by looking at award-winning ads at the Internet ad competition sites listed previously, in Table 12-1. (They're the eighth and ninth entries in the table.)

Performance varies among static ad sizes. The ad types known as large rectangle, leaderboard, and skyscraper generally perform better than overly familiar, 60-pixel-high banners (see Figure 12-3).

If you're willing to post ads on your site, you can test the waters with a banner exchange program such as the one at LinkBuddies (`http://linkbuddies.com`).

You can also use an exchange program to test one creative against another for efficacy before visiting an expensive publisher's site.

Keep in mind that the audience you gain by way of an exchange program probably isn't as targeted as the audience you gain by way of a paid network, and certainly not as targeted as individual sites that you identify yourself.

Figure 12-3:
Common
sizes of
static ban-
ner ads
are shown
on Google,
which
distributes
banners
only through
its content
partners
(see
Chapter 11).

Courtesy of Google, Inc.

Making Decisions about Banner Ads

When you decide to use banner ads in your campaign, you need to make six tactical decisions about them:

✔ What type and size of ads to run

✔ What amount you're willing to spend

✔ Whether to handle the campaign yourself or use a network or agency

✔ Where to advertise

✔ How to evaluate the return on investment (ROI) of your banner campaign

✔ Whether the use of paid advertising is appropriate in nontraditional venues such as blogs, social media outlets, or RSS feeds

Choosing a banner type, size, and position

Bigger is better! Choose medium in-line rectangle, leaderboard, and wide skyscraper ads (refer to Figure 12-3), in that order, if you can afford them. Advertisers favor larger options, with the single exception of medium rather than large rectangles.

The best positions for ads are on the right side by the scroll bar, as close as possible to the top of the page, and definitely above the fold. Rectangles integrated with page layout also work well. Avoid standard banner ads (468 x 60 pixels) at the top of a page — most viewers ignore them.

If you can't afford big ads, take small ones that are better positioned. Ask about supplying an animated (rather than static) .gif ad. If a publisher's ad server can handle small .gif or Flash ads, they attract more attention than large static ones. If an animated ad fits within the same file size as a static ad, you usually don't pay more for it.

If you want to create several alternative offers but can't afford to buy more than one position, ask whether you can supply several static ads to rotate in that position. Because you usually aren't charged for this strategy, you can compare CTRs to assess the effectiveness of your ads.

In Figure 12-4, you can see related static ads of different sizes that were created by designer Vance Bell (www.vancebell.com) for a summer campaign by the Philadelphia Center City District.

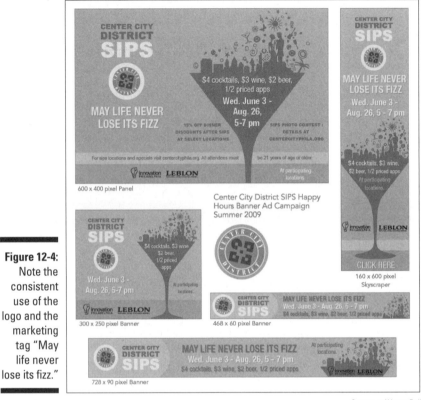

Figure 12-4:
Note the
consistent
use of the
logo and the
marketing
tag "May
life never
lose its fizz."

You can find free or low-cost software online for creating banners and animated ads. However, many of these ads look somewhat amateurish. If you're spending a significant amount of money on advertising, invest the $80 to $100 per ad that's necessary to hire a graphic designer.

Estimating costs

Unlike using pay per click ads, charges for most banner ads are either cost per thousand (CPM) impressions or a flat rate per month, quarter, or year. The more targeted the audience, the more you pay. Decide how much of your overall marketing budget to dedicate to paid banner advertising. Drive your spending from your budget, not from costs.

Most sites that accept advertising publish media kits online. The kit should include demographics, page views, banner size specifications, and rates. If you can't find the kit on the site, look for an Advertising link to locate contact information for a sales representative.

A broadly targeted, consumer audience might run less than one dollar per thousand impressions. A prequalified, narrowly targeted market, such as vice presidents of financial corporations, can have a CPM of $70 to $100 or more. Portal sites, which have a low CPM, generally have quite a high minimum CPM. Banners on highly trafficked sites — such as major news outlets, entertainment and sports sites, and other portals — generally have minimum CPM prices that are too expensive for small businesses.

Various factors affect the rate that's charged for an ad campaign:

- **Ad size and type:** A Flash ad that has only a few images can generally run for the same price as a static banner.

- **Location of an ad on the page:** An ad above the fold performs better because it's seen more often.

- **Number of ads sharing the same space in rotation:** The more ads that share a space, the less often yours is viewed.

- **Pages of the site on which the ad runs:** An ad that appears on every page is a *run-of-site* (ROS) ad.

- **The nature of the site:** An ad tends to fare better on content sites than on portals.

- **Contract length:** The ad contract specifies how long the ad runs.

Life is negotiable! A site that has just recently opened its ad program, or is trying to fill empty slots, might cut a deal with you. Watch for a *house* ad (an ad for the publisher itself) as a sign of unsold inventory. Sometimes, you can persuade a publisher to run an ad for several weeks as a free trial. Ask! What's to lose?

Doing it yourself versus using an agency or ad network

You might pay a premium of 10 to 15 percent over the cost of direct placement if you use an agency or a network to place ads. The CPM on some ad networks is fairly low, which indicates that their audiences are rather broad. If you plan to run ads on only a few sites, you can probably handle placement yourself.

If you intend to run an extensive branding campaign over dozens or hundreds of sites, you'll find it much easier to use a network, which automates placement and reporting. For an intermediate solution, try a self-service solution such as AdReady (www.adready.com), which automates the creation and purchase of ads.

Table 12-2 lists many online advertising networks and directories. Confirm that the network you select offers sites within your specific channel of interest or target demographics. Sometimes, a specialty network is a better solution, particularly for B2B advertisers.

Table 12-2   Online Advertising Networks & Resources

Name	*URL*
1800Banners.com (banner exchange)	www.1800banners.com
24/7 Real Media	www.247realmedia.com
About.com (network directory)	http://onlinebusiness.about.com/od/affiliatemarketing/tp/online-advertising-networks.htm
AdBalance (review of ad networks)	www.adbalance.com/ad-networks
AdDynamix (self-service network)	www.addynamix.com/selfserve/signup.html
AdReady (self-service ad network)	www.adready.com
AdRoll (retargeting company)	www.adroll.com
AOL Media Networks	http://advertising.aol.com
Blogads	www.blogads.com
Burst Media	http://burstmedia.com
LinkBuddies (banner exchange)	http://linkbuddies.com
New York Times (self-service banner ads)	http://nytmarketing.whsites.net/mediakit/index.php
PubAccess (self-service for site publishers)	https://pubaccess.advertising.com
Right Media from Yahoo!	http://rightmedia.com
Travel Ad Network	www.traveladnetwork.com
Tribal Fusion	http://tribalfusion.com
ValueClick Media	www.valueclickmedia.com

Retargeting ads

Have you ever wished you could trail those who visit your site, explore what you have to offer, and leave without making a purchase? Perhaps you simply want to remind them about your company as they conduct further research, or inform them about another product or service that might be more to their liking. Well, thanks to the wonders of *cookies* (little bits of code, placed on users' browsers or on your site, that identify the computer), you can now place just that kind of invisible cyberdye on their fingertips and follow them as they continue to explore the web. You not only follow them — you also present them with a display ad on other sites they visit. This entire process, brought to you through the wonders of the web, is known as *retargeting*.

Companies such as AdRoll place a bit of code on your site that creates a list of visitors. Your retargeting ads, which are distributed by way of various online advertising networks (refer to Table 12-2), are presented to those visitors by other sites that publish ads. By keeping your business "top of mind," retargeting brings window shoppers back to your site and enhances brand recognition.

Although retargeting campaigns may appear more expensive than traditional PPC or regular banner advertising on a CPC basis, they tend to have higher click-through and conversion rates. If you compare the cost of a retargeting campaign on the basis of conversion value, you may find them cost-effective compared to traditional banner advertising. If a broad branding campaign seems out of reach financially, consider retargeting as a way to achieve the best of both the natural search and banner worlds.

Considering multimedia and engagement banners

Rich media ads — animation, Flash, audio, interactive games, video, and other types of multimedia — attract more clicks than static ads, probably because movement catches a viewer's eye.

Ads that are integrated with a social activity, such as sending a virtual gift to a friend or replying to a one-question poll, tend to have a high rate of engagement and repeat usage.

Request the services of the same professionals who create audio and video materials for your site — most developers lack the skills to create ads with video, audio, or engagement features. Because these ads are more expensive to produce and may take longer to load, you might want to limit their use.

Deciding where to advertise

If you run an inbound link popularity report (www.linkpopularity.com) or view the clickstream report from Alexa (www.alexa.com) on your competitors, you might be able to identify where they're running ads. A banner ad is merely a link in drag, after all.

Gyrobike wheels its banners to success

Gyrobike's bicycle products deliver high stability at low speed to help keep riders upright. The most immediate application is an alternative way for children to learn to ride bikes: "Look, Mom — no training wheels." Founded in 2007 to commercialize patented technology developed at Dartmouth College, the company is headquartered in San Francisco.

Gyrobike sells directly to consumers through its own online store and also other retailers, both offline and online. Marketing director Ashleigh Harris says that as soon as the company launched its first product and website with an online store in December 2009, it also started running display ads. "As a start-up, we had very limited resources and a new product that no one had ever heard of, so we decided to augment our search campaigns with retargeted ads to build awareness and brand recognition."

By using AdRoll.com, Harris runs two display retargeting campaigns — one for general branding and the other for people who visit the shopping pages on the website. AdRoll helped with the initial setup of the ads, which took about a week. Since then, Harris has mostly managed the retargeting campaigns herself.

Harris, who spends less than $500 per month on the retargeting campaigns, changes the ads every couple of months. "I create some of [the ads] myself and I have a graphic designer do some. Initially, I probably wasted too much time creating ads myself using subpar tools, but our resources were tight and every penny counted. There are better do-it-yourself banner ad builders out there now."

Gyrobike also runs a PPC campaign on Google AdWords and is testing promotional videos on YouTube. "We tested some Facebook advertising, but it wasn't as cost-effective for us compared to our other campaigns," Harris explains. She relies heavily on traditional and social PR efforts, including media outreach and securing product reviews. Gyrobike also encourages its customers to spread the word and has begun to leverage Facebook with apps from North Social (http://northsocial.com).

Gyrobike monitors all its results by using Google Analytics at least monthly; tracking referral traffic, CTRs, site visits, bounce rates, and revenue generated; and focusing on CPC optimization. "You don't have to spend a lot of money to do [ads] well." It takes some experimentation," Harris acknowledges. "One ad campaign will not fit all of your needs. Segment, target, and test." She adds encouragement: "The bottom line is that you don't have to be an expert — most online advertising tools have excellent tutorials and resources to help guide you."

Look at other ads on a publication site as a clue to whether particular sites are appropriate for your business. Then check their online media kits. If you find no detailed information about demographics or page views or the number of ads sharing the same space in rotation, ask. Ask, too, about reporting options and how to track the results of your campaigns.

Rates are usually lowest for run of site (ROS) ads because they might appear on many pages that receive relatively few viewers. Rates are highest for the home page, which is usually the most highly trafficked page on the site. You might do well to select an inside page at the second or third level. Rates are lower, but visitors to the page might even be better qualified as prospects for your site.

Publishers generally don't divulge or predict CTR, which depends too much on the quality of the creative element and the value of the offer made in an ad.

Create a spreadsheet showing CPM, demographics, and banner options to compare alternatives more easily.

Many companies with new products find banner ads of great value in their branding campaigns. Figure 12-5 shows a sample of banner ads created for Gyrobike (www.thegyrobike.com), the maker of a self-stabilizing bicycle wheel; the nearby sidebar "Gyrobike wheels its banners to success" explains its advertising campaign.

Figure 12-5: Examples of the banner ads used in the online ad campaign for Gyrobike.

Courtesy of Gyrobike®

Benefitting from Display Advertising on Social Media

Advertising on social media channels, in spite of their promised demographic targeting, carries risk. Although Facebook and other channels deliver large numbers of impressions, the click-through rate (CTR) at 0.05 to 0.2 percent is significantly lower than search engine PPC campaigns. Search engine users are actively searching for what you have to offer — the people who read the ads are actively shopping. Therefore, they're more likely to become prospects or customers.

Ads on social media services vary widely. For example, an ad on Facebook is a cross between a text-only PPC ad and a small banner with an image, as shown in Figure 12-6. A paid ad on Twitter appears as a promoted tweet in boldface at the top of a page based on the search term that's used. Most social media channels use a bid-based PPC model, although some also offer an option for traditional CPM (cost per thousand) impressions. These and other social media advertising options are described in Table 12-3.

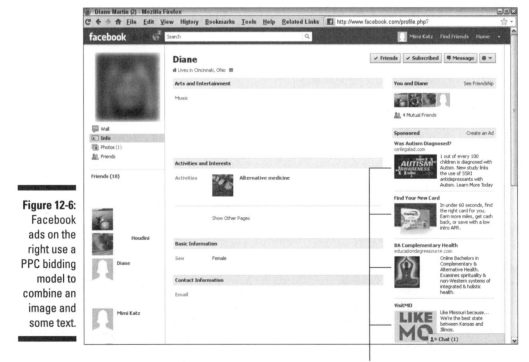

Figure 12-6: Facebook ads on the right use a PPC bidding model to combine an image and some text.

Sponsored ads

Courtesy of Diane Martin

Table 12-3   Advertising Options on Social Media Channels

Name	*URL*	*Typical Cost*	*Other Notes*
Digg	`http://about.` `digg.com/ads`	Cost per click bid auction	A social news site where ads that users don't like are voted on and forced to the bottom of a page.
Facebook	`www.facebook.` `com/advertising`	Minimum CPC $0.01; minimum CPM $0.02	Suggests bid ranges that are often much higher than the minimum; very low average CTR of 0.10 to 0.25 percent.

Flickr	`http://`
	`advertising.`
	`yahoo.com/`
	`products-`
	`solutions/`
	`flickr.html`
		Daily spend rate set by advertiser	Served by Yahoo! (`http://`
			`advertising.`
			`yahoo.com/`
			`products-`
			`solutions`).

LinkedIn	`http://linkedin.`
	`com/ads`
	
	`http://marketing.`
	`linkedin.com`
		Minimum CPC $2.00	Possible that suggested bid range may be higher.

MySpace	`www.myads.com/`
	`myspace/login.`
	`html`
		Monthly budget range between $5 and $25,000	Pay per click banner ads.

Reddit	`www.reddit.com/`
	`ad_inq`
	
	`www.reddit.com/`
	`selfservice`
	`oatmeal`
		Daily spend rate set by advertiser	Total number of daily bids is used to calculate every sponsor's portion of impressions; if you spend $100 per day and the total amount spent is $200, you get 50 percent of sponsored traffic that day.

(continued)

Table 12-3 *(continued)*

Name	URL	Typical Cost	Other Notes
Twitter	`http://business.twitter.com/advertise/start`	CPM only; monthly budget range between $5,000 and $9,999	No display ads but accepts promoted accounts, tweets, and trends.
YouTube	`www.youtube.com/t/advertising_overview`	Minimum $1 CPM for entire YouTube site; $2 CPM for specific content categories	Served by Google AdWords.

Even if social media ads may not be cost-effective for you, they're certainly working well for social media services. Facebook ad revenue is projected to jump from almost $2 billion in 2010 to $6 billion in 2012, according to the latest eMarketer projections. About 60 percent of the revenue derives from the self-service ads that appear on the right side of every page (refer to Figure 12-6), and the rest from home page banners. According to eMarketer, other big earners in social media advertising are MySpace, LinkedIn, Classmates.com, and Twitter — in that order. These high earnings are now driven by large corporate campaigns.

Compare bid rates carefully. Facebook and Twitter, in particular, attract large corporations with deep pockets, forcing up bid prices. Factor their lower CTR and higher costs into your budget to decide whether social media advertising is cost-effective for you.

Using Group Coupons and Daily Special Sites

A group of friends hitting the mall used to be the definition of *social shopping*. Now the term refers to a group of strangers saving money by collectively buying online. The *group coupon* has emerged as a new way to aggregate (collect as a whole) buyers — usually in specific cities — by offering a daily deal discount of 50 percent or more by way of a website or e-mail. The catch: A deal applies only if a minimum number of buyers sign up for it. A group coupon can help small businesses introduce new products or services, attract new customers, fill quiet periods or seasons, or build loyalty with current customers.

The best-known services of this type are Groupon (www.groupon.com), which filed an initial public offering in June 2011, and LivingSocial (www.livingsocial.com), though they have lots of deal-making competitors. You may find that your location and budget and the number of deals you can comfortably accommodate are better suited to a smaller deal provider.

Interested in investigating more group coupon options? Look at the list of group coupon and daily deal sites in Bonus Chapter 4 on the Downloads tab of the book's companion website.

As a merchant, you gain brand awareness, a direct appeal to locally targeted markets, word-of-mouth advertising, and high visibility to a new customer stream. The low-cost offer reduces, in theory, the risk of trying something new. It's your job to turn these one-time experimenters into loyal repeat customers.

Seller beware! Small businesses with shallow pockets sometimes can't handle the pressure of serving many customers at a price below cost. Many companies, especially restaurants, now report a loss in revenue whenever existing customers snap up their coupon deals. Rather than receive the full price for a meal or service, merchants see only 25 percent, turning coupons into an expensive loyalty program for existing clientele. Go to www.business insider.com/jesse-burke-groupon-nightmare to read a cautionary tale of Posies Café's experience with Groupon.

Everyone loves a deal

The users of these coupon sites have a coveted demographic profile: educated, young, single, working women who have a fair amount of discretionary income. And the numbers are stunning. Groupon claims to have sold, from its inception in November 2008 through January 2011, more than 22 million coupons to more than 50 million e-mail subscribers, and it contends that more than 97 percent of featured merchants want to make an offer again. LivingSocial claims 20 million subscribers.

This obvious business-to-consumer (B2C) technique can work well for both service and product companies, including bars and restaurants, tourist destinations, health-and-beauty salons, events, recreation, and personal services.

You can make this approach work for business-to-business (B2B) offers, though it's a little more complicated. A B2B offer would depend on the size and quality of the e-mail list that the service maintains, a product that applies to both individuals and companies (bookkeeping or office supplies, perhaps), or recommendations from employees to employers. Rapid Buyr (http://rapidbuyr.com) and Bizy Deals (www.bizydeals.com) are two of the companies focused on the B2B market.

These deals have become so popular for both consumers and merchants that many companies now offer additional side deals and advertising in their e-mail and on their sites. The new venue Groupon Now lets Groupon stores reach a wider audience in real-time, specifically when merchants have openings to fill. Groupon Getaways will be offered via a partnership with the Expedia travel site. LivingSocial, which already offers travel deals under LivingSocial Escapes, has created a category for family deals. The frenzy for deals may finally begin to slow as competitors saturate the coupon space; Google is still testing its entry, Google Offers, but Facebook has already pulled the plug on Facebook Deals.

Make them an offer they can't refuse

These basic principles govern most coupon deals:

- ✔ **The buyer receives 50 percent off the standard price.** The coupon service takes half of this amount, so you see only 25 percent of your list price. Thanks to the competition in this space, you may now be able to negotiate better terms.

- ✔ **As the merchant, you define the deal.** Be sure to set the minimum number of sales high enough to mitigate your risk and the maximum number of sales low enough to keep from going broke.

- ✔ **No one makes upfront payments, creating an attractive, low-risk form of advertising.** Your fees come from revenues only if the minimum number of sales occurs. The coupon firms collect payments from customers by credit card and send you a check for your half of the revenue, giving you a bit of a cash flow kick. Just remember that those deals may be redeemed eventually — and that the dealmakers may take longer to pay your share than you expect.

- ✔ **You specify the timeframe over which buyers can exercise a deal, usually several months to a year.** If you can't provide high-quality service to meet the demand with the staff or space you have, you may lose not only the customer but also your reputation, if poor reviews appear online. Protect yourself from unhappy customers by requiring appointments subject to availability and allowing adequate time to redeem the offer.

Set a maximum number of deals to limit both your financial and service exposure. A cap makes sense especially for event organizers and service providers. For example, your small theater company may have a fixed number of seats, you may have room for only a certain number of people in a dance class, or you may have enough stylists to handle only a certain number of haircuts per day.

✔ **You schedule the term of your offer so you don't have buyers showing up on your doorstep all at one time — unless the offer is for a scheduled event or if you set a short period for redemption.** Most merchants see a peak flow the first 30 days after an offer and the last 30 days before expiration.

✔ **Coupon deals often provide a stream of new customers in a relatively short length of time.** Compare the result to how long it takes other forms of advertising to produce new business.

✔ **You can turn prospects into satisfied new customers.** They may then proceed to spend more money using these avenues:

- *Impulse buys and add-ons:* Buyers receive 50 percent off on a specialty burrito and proceed to spend their "savings" on drinks and sides.

- *Take-home purchases:* "This slice of cake from the offer was so good that I'm buying a whole cake to take home."

- *Ongoing services:* One good massage and that client may be yours every two weeks for years.

✔ **Word-of-mouth works:** Buyers bring their friends to share the experience.

✔ **Factor estimated add-on purchases as well as lifetime customer value into your calculation.** Obviously, new customers who make multiple, repeat purchases are more valuable than customers who buy only once. Try to make your offer something worth a repeat buy.

✔ **Coupon companies select which businesses participate and set the schedule for featuring offers.** In preparation, you may want to create a separate landing page on your website for the offer; a link to your site appears in the offer.

✔ **Although some sites offer national deals, particularly for large, web-based retailers, they're primarily location-based social services.** For a national reach, you might target multiple, individual cities within your national audience with separate offers. This approach works for franchises or branches in several cities.

✔ **Local residents or tourists who are planning a trip to a specific destination comprise the primary audience.** Confirm that the service you select reaches your city! LivingSocial Escapes and Groupon are now offering separate, specific tourism-related deals.

✔ **Good coupon sites offer excellent analytics to track results.** Use them.

Even if you're offering a loss leader on one of these collective coupon sites, try not to sell too far below cost. Giving away hundreds of $4 ice cream cones for half-price is one thing; giving away hundreds of $40 haircuts at half-price may leave you short on the rent.

After the offer appears, you can promote the deal in your own newsletter and social media outlets and elsewhere, although you may not have much notice. This share-this-deal functionality encourages people who receive a daily coupon e-mail, or those who visit your site, to tell their friends about the deal via Facebook, Twitter, and e-mail.

Many companies offer extra incentives to their coupon buyers in the hope that deals will go viral:

✓ **Links to local activities and events:** Buyers have the opportunity to enter comments or otherwise participate in a social activity.

✓ **Easy-to-share links to send deals to friends:** If three or more friends share a deal, the referrer receives a freebie. Include this element as an allowance in your revenue calculations. If someone organizes a share campaign, total revenues may decline.

✓ **Affiliate options:** They generate internal "deal bucks" (not cash).

✓ **Easy integration with Facebook, Twitter, and e-mail to share deals:** Most services offer mobile apps for iPhone, iPad, Droid, and BlackBerry.

Speak with your accountant about how to handle revenue from Groupon, LivingSocial, and similar deals. Prepaid income is usually treated as a liability on your balance sheet until you fulfill the obligation or until the time expires to exercise the offer (gift cards, for example). You may also encounter state-by-state issues regarding sales tax.

Sponsoring Newsletters, Sites, Blogs, and Feeds

Sponsorships (a form of goodwill ads — think public broadcasting) garnered less than 3 percent of online ad spending in 2010, but you should not over-look them as a means of increasing your company's exposure on either for-profit or not-for-profit sites.

You can promote your products and services in only a subtle manner on not-for-profit sites, but you benefit from the goodwill of visitors who appreciate your support for something that matters to them, such as the environment or healthcare research.

This cost-effective advertising opportunity comes in three forms of sponsorship, generally requiring contributions at increasing levels:

- ✔ **Newsletter:** Offered by the issue or by the month. Advertising might consist of text or graphics, or both. This type of advertising gives you access to a targeted mailing list that may not be available any other way.

- ✔ **Site:** Usually button or text ads with different prices based on links and placement. Ethicurean is an example of a site that accepts paid sponsorships, as shown in Figure 12-7. Companies that sell through not-for-profit sites often contribute a portion of their profits to the organization. (See GreaterGood.com for many opportunities.)

- ✔ **Integrated:** Combines both site and newsletter sponsorships, with added visibility for the company name and logo in other offline media. This type works especially well if you adopt a particular not-for-profit related to your business mission as your company's focus for charitable giving.

Figure 12-7:
Ethicurean
solicits
sponsorships
for its site.

Courtesy of The Ethicurean, www.ethicurean.com

You can place banner ads or sponsorships in other places, including podcasts, RSS feeds, and blogs. Try Pheedo (http://pheedo.com/site/adv_overview.php) or Text Link Ads (www.text-link-ads.com/r/advertisers) for advertising options in RSS feeds.

Advertising with Online Classifieds

According to the Interactive Advertising Bureau, online classified ads collected 10 percent of online ad dollars in 2010.

Although individuals use classified sites as a grand electronic swap meet, your business can use them to sell merchandise, services, entertainment, or commercial rentals. Jean Antoine's Mobile Cafe, shown in Figure 12-8, advertises on Craigslist — one of the best-known classified-ad sites — to send a personal chef to your home.

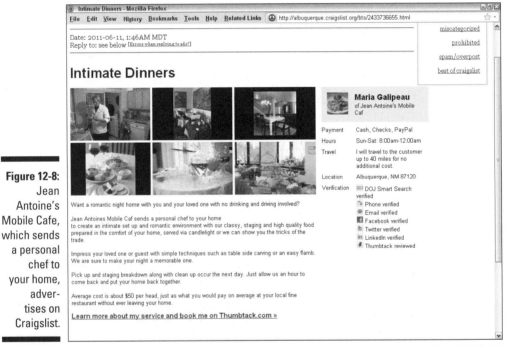

Figure 12-8: Jean Antoine's Mobile Cafe, which sends a personal chef to your home, advertises on Craigslist.

Courtesy of Jean Antoine's Mobile Cafe

Choose from either free or low-cost independent classified sites, classified sections of MySpace, Yahoo!, and other portals, or product-specific classified sites for cars, apartments, and pets.

A sampling of popular classified ad sites appears in Bonus Chapter 4 on the Downloads tab of the companion website.

Because classifieds are generally designed for local advertising, you must post them on multiple sites for broad coverage. To help you overcome this time-consuming hassle, services such as Postlets (`www.postlets.com`) and vFlyer (`www.vflyer.com`) offer easy, multiple postings to many classified sites at once.

Writing a good classified is an art. Keep these principles in mind:

- ✔ **Grab attention with the title.** Use strong, emotional words that pack a punch.

- ✔ **Repeat descriptive text from the title in the body of the ad.** This strategy creates maximum effect.

- ✔ **If you're offering a service, include its main benefit in the title.** Sales are always about "what's in it for me?"

- ✔ **Avoid the use of all caps.** They now often imply that you're shouting.

- ✔ **Avoid the excessive use of exclamation points.** Try to contain your excitement so that you don't wear anyone out.

- ✔ **Include a picture, if possible.** A picture is still worth a thousand words.

- ✔ **Give people explicit instructions.** Tell them how to find more information or make a purchase (call to action).

- ✔ **Include a link to your website.** Following this advice is good for search engine ranking, too.

- ✔ **Resist the temptation to post your primary e-mail address online.** Instead, create a free, temporary address at Gmail, Yahoo!, or Hotmail. You certainly don't want to receive more spam than you already do.

- ✔ **Test different titles and copy.** This way, you can find out what works best.

- ✔ **Write separate ads for different items.** It's easier to draw the right audience for one specific item than to attract multiple audiences to a smorgasbord of values.

- ✔ **Proofread your ad carefully.** Be sure that you use correct spelling and grammar.

These principles are a lot like the ones you use for writing pay per click text ads and web copy. Classified ads also perform better (draw a larger response) when you write them in active voice and second person (using the word *you*).

Evaluating Results

Publishers should provide *at least* the number of impressions and the CTR, by ad and by page. Small publishers might provide these only once a month; others might have an online dashboard for viewing results in near real-time.

Some publishers provide additional detail, including the performance of individual ads. Like Bing/Yahoo! or Google PPC programs, publishers might provide tracking code to place on landing or conversion pages. In other cases, a statistical program such as Google Analytics (see Chapter 6) supplies the number of visits from referring sources. If these options aren't available, you can still track specific ads placed with the same publisher by asking your programmer to follow the directions in the next paragraph.

Every linkable ad requires a URL for the *landing page,* the page on which a visitor arrives after clicking. Create different landing page URLs that designate the type and source, and perhaps even the date, in this format: `http://watermelonweb.com/?src=nmo0708leader2`. In this case, `/?src=` stands for source, and the information at the end identifies the publisher (`nmo`), date (`0708`), and ad style (`leader2` for leaderboard 2). Always test URLs, of course.

If you're selling online, your programmer can place a cookie for tracking a visitor from arrival to purchase.

If the functions of your banner and PPC ads are comparable, calculate your ROI for banner ads in the same way. However, you might need to measure by a different criterion. A banner ad designed for branding is not directly comparable to a PPC ad offering a special deal. You might want to calculate ROI by individual ad, ad type, publisher, offer, or period. Create columns on a spreadsheet to compare CPC, CPM, cost per conversion, and cost per conversion value.

The world of online advertising changes constantly, offering new publishing opportunities and new types of creatives. You can monitor these changes through your own exploration or by reading blogs and newsletters about online advertising. As always, pay attention to the changes that allow you to better target your market or increase the appeal of your ads.

Part V
Making the Most of Social Media Channels

In this part . . .

Social media channels are all the rage, but they can be difficult to use effectively for online marketing. Although these free services reach hundreds of millions of users, most of them aren't shopping. The challenges are twofold: Find your target market within this massive audience, and complete this task without becoming a sleepless zombie. Part V helps you identify which social media channels best fit your business and manage the social marketing process.

Chapter 13, which is a broad overview of social media categories, describes how to make a business case for social media and how to assess the value of integrating social media with other marketing efforts.

Chapter 14 reviews the marketing value of word-sharing on blogs, video-sharing on sites such as YouTube, photo-sharing on sites such as Flickr, and audio-sharing via podcasts.

Chapters 15, 16, and 17 are the "Big Three" chapters — covering, respectively, social networking on Facebook, microblogging on Twitter, and the use of LinkedIn for business-to-business and professional marketing. You can read about user demographics, marketing upsides and downsides, tips on optimizing for search, and the channel as a venue for paid advertising.

Chapter 18 addresses smaller, stratified social media options that may make it easier to reach your target market, such as geosocial media (such as Foursquare or Gowalla), meet-ups that use the web to bring people together, and social media sites segmented by vertical industry sector or demographics.

Chapter 19 provides an overview of tools that make it easier to manage your social marketing life, monitor your success, and extend your web presence via social sharing buttons, bookmarking, and social news services.

Chapter 13

Reaching Customers Using Social Media

Social media stories seem to monopolize the news, from revolutions in the Middle East to political scandals and from high-flying public stock offerings to high-risk invasions of personal privacy. From a business perspective, social media is also the latest trend in online marketing for acquiring new customers and providing customer support. The interactive, two-way communication component of social media channels sets them apart from websites, online advertising, and e-newsletters.

Hundreds of social media sites — far more than just Facebook and Twitter — enable users to share their content and views with one another. Are these sites merely parts of the latest craze in online connectivity? Do you have to participate in all of them to market effectively online? Or, can you escape with your sanity and your schedule intact by selecting only one or two?

Should you become a social media maven? For many businesses, the technological choices may seem overwhelming. However, the basic issues are the same as in any other marketing decision: Will social media help you make more money, by either gaining new customers or building loyalty with current ones? Is it a cost-effective allocation of your marketing time and dollars compared to alternatives?

If it doesn't make dollars, it doesn't make sense.

To help you answer these questions, this part of the book includes chapters on sharing multimedia content and on using the three social networking elephants: Facebook, Twitter, and LinkedIn. Part V concludes with chapters on smaller, targeted social media services and on using social media tools to make your efforts cost-effective.

Making the Business Case for Social Media

If you could fantasize the perfect marketing tools, you might come up with ones that

- ✔ Help you pinpoint prospective customers
- ✔ Provide opportunities to build your brand recognition
- ✔ Encourage customers to share your site, services, and products with their friends via online word-of-mouth
- ✔ Facilitate two-way communication so that you can eavesdrop on customers' concerns and respond quickly
- ✔ Involve no upfront marketing cost

Theoretically, I've just described social media as its committed proselytizers promote it. Given its rapid rise in popularity and its hundreds of millions of worldwide users, you'd think social media would flood your business with cyberbuyers and improve your profit margins at the same time.

On the face of it, this marketing miracle sounds too good to be true. No surprise: It is. You must consider the hidden costs of social media marketing:

- ✔ It can be quite time- and labor-intensive.
- ✔ It's better for branding than for sales.
- ✔ It can take a long time to see bottom-line results from social media efforts.
- ✔ Short-term profits are rare.

Although you never want to make a marketing decision just because everybody else is doing it, the experience of other small businesses may give you some comfort. By January 2011, almost one in three small businesses used some form of social media, according to the Network Solutions survey of small-business success in the "State of Small Business Report." Figure 13-1 offers details from the report, illustrating the growing use of social media by small businesses between 2010 and 2011.

Figure 13-1:
Small businesses are rapidly increasing their use of social media, especially social networking services such as Facebook and LinkedIn.

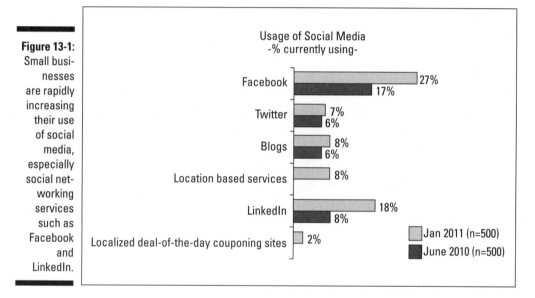

Courtesy of Network Solutions, LLC

You may want to research social media before you commit your resources. In particular, you might want to consult the *CMO's Guide to the Social Media Landscape,* at www.cmo.com/social-media/2011-cmos-guide-social-landscape, for suggestions on the best uses of social media by service, or consult the chart of social media demographics at www.flowtown.com/blog/social-media-demographics-whos-using-which-sites. Table 13-1 is loaded with additional helpful sites.

Table 13-1   **Social Media Marketing Resources**

Name	*URL*	*Description*
CMO.com	`www.cmo.com/social-media/2011-cmos-guide-social-landscape`	CMO's guide to the social media landscape
Flowtown	`www.flowtown.com/blog/social-media-demographics-whos-using-which-sites`	Excellent chart of demographic breakdown for social media

HubSpot	`http://blog.hubspot.com`
	
	`www.hubspot.com/state-of-inbound-marketing`
		Inbound marketing blog; 2011 report on state of inbound marketing

MarketingProfs	`www.marketingprofs.com/marketing/library/100/social-media`	Social media marketing tips, including B2B
MarketingSherpa	`www.marketingsherpa.com/social-networking-evangelism-community-category.html`	Social networking research with B2B focus
Mashable	`http://mashable.com`	Well-known social media guide
Network Solutions	`www.networksolutions.com/smallbusiness/wp-content/files/State_of_Small_Business_Report_Wave_5.pdf`	Report on small-business use of social media
Practical eCommerce	`www.practicalecommerce.com/blogs/5-The-Social-Retailer`	Blog about social marketing for retailers
Social Media Examiner	`www.socialmediaexaminer.com`	Humorous business guide to social media
Social Media Marketing Group on LinkedIn	`www.linkedin.com/groups/Social-Media-Marketing-66325?mostPopular=&gid=66325`	Professional, nonpromotional discussion group; approval required

Name	*URL*	*Description*
Social Media Today Blog	`www.socialmediatoday.com`	Social media blog
Social Networking Business Blog	`http://social-networking-business.blogspot.com`	Social networking blog for business
TechCrunch	`http://techcrunch.com`	Latest tech tips on social media and more
Top Ten Reviews	`http://social-networking-websites-review.toptenreviews.com`	Compares reviews of the top ten social networking sites for 2011
ZDNet	`www.zdnet.com/blog/feeds?tag=mantle_skin;content`	Social business news, trends, and strategies

After you decide to experiment with social media, you confront an overwhelming array of options. You can never use every technique and certainly can't do them all at once. Before you go further, let me categorize the choices.

Dividing Social Media into Channels

I try to constrain the phrase *social media marketing* to the use of two-way, online communication for relationship marketing — a topic you already know about. Social media channels, which are categories within social media, make innovative use of new online technologies to accomplish various familiar communication and marketing goals. Within a channel, you usually find several types of social media services. In this book, a social media site or provider refers to a specific, named online service or product.

The channels in the following list have fuzzy boundaries. They may overlap, and some sites can be classified in multiple channels (for example, some social networks and communities allow participants to share photos and may include blogs):

✔ **Social content sharing:** The services in this channel facilitate posting and commenting on text, video, photos, podcasts (audio), and other types of multimedia:

  • Blogs for letting readers easily post their own opinions or reactions to your content

    These services include freestanding blog sites such as WordPress, Typepad, Tumblr, and Blogger. Using blog software as part of one's own website and posting on someone else's blog are covered in Chapters 5 and 8, respectively.

  • YouTube, Vimeo, and Ustream for video sharing

  • Sites such as Flickr or Picasa for photo sharing

  • Audio sharing for lectures, music, plays, and interviews on sites such as Podcast Alley and BlogTalk Radio

  • Other media sharing sites, such as Slideshare (`www.slideshare.net`)

✔ **Social networking:** Originally developed to facilitate the exchange of personal information (messages, photos, video, and audio) to groups of friends and family, these full-featured services encourage participants to interact with others who share their interests or objectives. From a business point of view, many networks support internal groups with the potential for targeted marketing:

  • Full networks, such as Facebook, MySpace, or myYearbook, which facilitate communication between customers and companies. Squishable, a company that markets giant, plush stuffed animals, uses Facebook to interact with its customers (as shown in Figure 13-2). It holds caption contests on Facebook twice a week, plus weekly "Squish & Tell" sessions inviting people to share stories about their animals.

  • Microblogging (short message) networks such as Plurk or Twitter. Liberty Bay Books, an independent community bookstore shown in Figure 13-3, uses its Twitter account to provide information about its products and to promote events.

  • Professional networks such as LinkedIn and Plaxo. These B2B social networks are used primarily for establishing expertise, obtaining referrals to vendors and partners, making introductions to dealmakers, hiring, job searching, and acquiring sales leads, not for direct sales.

  • Other specialty networks within vertical industry sectors, demographic segments such as Bebo for college students, or activity clusters, such as Xfire for gaming.

Courtesy of Squishable.com, inc.

Figure 13-2: Companies such as Squishable often use Facebook to maintain an ongoing public dialogue with customers and prospects.

✔ **Social bookmarking:** Similar to private bookmarks for your favorite sites on your computer, social bookmark services are publicly viewable lists of sites that other people have recommended:

- StumbleUpon, Delicious

- Social shopping sites such as Kaboodle and ThisNext

- Other bookmarking sites organized by topic or application, such as book recommendation sites

✔ **Social news:** These peer-based services recommend articles from news sites, blogs, or web pages, and users often "vote" on the value of the postings:

- Digg, Reddit

- Other news sites

✔ **Social geolocation and meetups:** For a change, these services bring people together in real space instead of in cyberspace:

- Foursquare, Loopt, Gowalla

- Other GPS (global positioning system) applications, many of which operate on smartphones and tablets

- Meet-ups and tweet-ups

Courtesy of Liberty Bay Books

Figure 13-3:
Liberty Bay
Books takes
advan-
tage of
Twitter for
announce-
ments,
events,
news, sales
notices,
distribution
of promo-
tions, and
customer
alerts.

✔ **Community building:** Text-intensive, comment-sharing sites, usually devoted to a particular area of interest, have been around the online world for several decades. Sites offering forums, message boards, chat rooms, Yahoo! Groups, and Google Groups were social media long before the world made up a name for it. In the "olden days" of the web — say, ten years ago — sharing was generally limited to text with an occasional photo. The explosion of multimedia content, better production tools, faster transmission speeds, and greater bandwidth enabled the rapid proliferation of social media channels that I discuss in this part of the book. This channel also includes

- Ning, a community-building site with multiple sharing features

- Wikis, such as Wikipedia, for group-sourced content

- Review sites such as TripAdvisor, Yelp, and Epinions

Use Quantcast or Alexa to research the demographics of social media services, just as you do to profile your competitors.

I talk briefly in Chapter 18 about specialty networks and vertical market social media. In Chapter 19, you can find dozens of social tools, *apps* (free-standing online applications), and *widgets* (small functional program snippets placed on other sites or desktops) for monitoring, distributing, searching, analyzing, or ranking content. Many apps are specific to a particular social network. Others aggregate information across the social media landscape, including monitoring tools such as Google Alerts and Social Mention and distribution tools such as Ping.fm. Chapter 19 surveys some of these tools; service-specific tools are covered in their respective chapters.

Fish where your fish are. If your customers or prospects don't use a particular form of social media, don't bother.

Understanding the Benefits of Social Media

As you read the following list of the benefits of social media, decide whether the benefit applies to your needs. Ask yourself how important social media is to your business, how much time you would be willing to allocate to it, and what kind of payoff you would expect. In the Network Solutions 2011 Survey shown in Figure 13-4, you can see how small businesses rated the relative effectiveness of social media and the profitability of social media.

If you can't imagine your company gaining from one of the following benefits, perhaps social media is not the marketing answer for you:

- **Casting a wide net to catch your target market:** The audience for social media is huge. By mid-2011, Facebook claimed more than 800 million active users, more than half of which log on to Facebook on any given day. Twitter claims 175 million accounts with perhaps half of them actively following others. Surely, some of these people must be customers or prospects you can tempt to visit your site. The classic funnel model clearly implies that the more people who arrive at the top of the funnel, the more will make it through the end. Remember, though, that only 2 to 4 percent, on average, make it through a funnel regardless of what the funnel decision is.

- **Branding:** Basic marketing focuses on the need for branding, name recognition, visibility, presence, and top-of-mind awareness. Call it what you will — you want people to remember your company name when they need or want your product or service. Social media services, of almost every type, are excellent ways to build your brand.

Accomplishments Using Social Media
-Among business owners who use/may use social media-

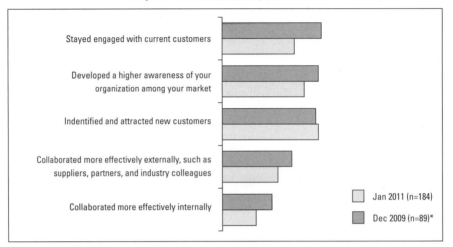

Business Use of Social Media Expectations
-Among business owners who use/may use social media-

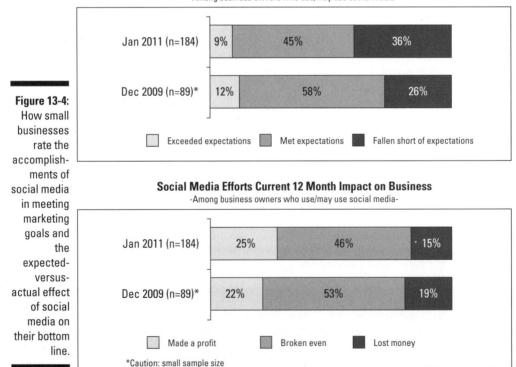

Figure 13-4:
How small businesses rate the accomplishments of social media in meeting marketing goals and the expected-versus-actual effect of social media on their bottom line.

Social Media Efforts Current 12 Month Impact on Business
-Among business owners who use/may use social media-

Courtesy of Network Solutions, LLC

Social media works for branding as long as you're putting your name in front of the right people. Plan to segment the audience on the large social media services. You can look for more targeted groups within them or search for specialty services that may reach fewer people overall but more of the specific people who are right for your business.

✔ **Building relationships:** To build effective relationships in social media, you must establish your expertise; participate regularly as a good "citizen" of whichever social media world you're inhabiting; avoid overt self-promotion; sell softly; and provide value with links, resources, and unbiased information. Watch for steady growth in the number of your followers on a particular service; the number of people who recommend your site to others; increased downloads of white papers; or repeat visits to your site. All these factors indicate that you're building relationships that may later lead to a direct sale or a word-of-web recommendation to someone who does buy.

✔ **Improving business processes:** Although individual applications depend on the nature of your business, consider leveraging social media to respond to customer problems; solicit feedback and input on new products; provide technical support; improve service delivery; locate qualified vendors; collect critical market intelligence; drive traffic during slow times; and acquire new customers.

Social media is a long-term commitment. Other than little experiments or pilot projects, don't start a social media commitment if you don't plan to keep it going. The initial time investment is too high.

✔ **Improving search engine rankings:** Just as you optimize your website, you should optimize your social media outlets for search engine ranking, as I discuss in Chapter 7. Now that search engines catalog Twitter, Facebook, and other appearances on social media, you can gain additional front-page real estate for your company on Google, Yahoo!, and Bing. Search engines recognize some, but not all, inbound links from social media to your site, which may also improve the page rank of your site. Optimization pays off in other ways: in results on real-time searches, which are now available on the primary search engines; on external search engines that focus on blogs or other social media services; and on internal, site-specific search engines.

Use a core set of search terms and keywords across as many sites as possible. In the following chapters, I explain how to optimize various services and sites for search purposes.

✔ **Selling when opportunity arises:** Conventional thinking says that social media is designed for long-term engagement, for marketing and branding rather than for sales. However, a few obvious selling opportunities exist, particularly for B2C companies, that won't offend followers:

- Sites such as MySpace, which caters to music and entertainment, are considered appropriate places to sell CDs and event tickets.

- Social shopping services such as Stylehive, which recommend products — particularly apparel, jewelry, beauty, and decor — generally include a link to your store.

- Many businesses offer promotion codes or special offers to their followers on particular networks to encourage them to visit a hub site to make a purchase. Others announce sales or events.

- Companies may place links to their online or third-party stores on their profile pages on various sites. Rarely can you sell directly from a social networking service, but some permit you to place a widget that visually showcases some of your products and links to your online store, PayPal, or the equivalent to conclude a transaction.

- Including a sign-up option for your e-newsletter can offer a bridge to sales.

- Scattering sales offers within a stream of information or news prevents your social media from becoming a series of never-ending advertisements. The chart shown in Figure 13-5 indicates that many businesses that make the effort succeed in acquiring customers by way of a social media channel.

✔ **Saving money on advertising:** For many small businesses, "free" social media services are the only advertising they can afford. If you decide to approach social media for this purpose, construct your master campaign just as carefully as you would approach a paid one. Outline target markets, ad offers, publishing venues, and scheduled "flights" for different ad campaigns. If necessary, conduct comparative testing of messages, graphics, and offers. Monitor results and focus on the outlets that work best at driving qualified visits that lead to conversions.

Should you join the crowd? If you want some reassurance, a 2011 CMO survey (http://cmosurvey.org/results) found that "businesses already spend 5.6 percent of their marketing budgets on social media marketing, with that figure predicted to grow to 9.8 percent by 2012 and 18.1 percent by 2016." In the end, however, only you can decide whether social media is a good investment for your business.

As you see traffic and conversions building from your social media marketing campaigns, you can reduce existing paid advertising campaigns. Just don't stop your paid advertising until you're confident that you have an equally profitable stream of customers from social media. Of course, there's no point continuing an ad campaign that isn't working.

Figure 13-5:
A 2011
HubSpot
survey
looked at
the per-
centage of
companies
that suc-
ceeded in
acquiring
customers
by way of
specific
social media
channels.

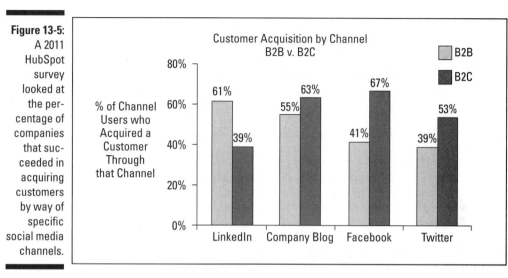

Customer Acquisition by Channel
B2B v. B2C

% of Channel Users who Acquired a Customer Through that Channel

Courtesy of Hubspot

Marketing is only part of your company, but all of your company is marketing. Social media is a ripe environment for this hypothesis, where every part of the company, from human resources to tech support and from engineering to sales, can be involved.

Understanding the Cons of Social Media

For all its upsides, social media has its downsides. As social media has gained in popularity, gaining visibility among its hundreds of millions of users has become increasingly difficult.

In fact, sometimes you have to craft a campaign just to build an audience on a particular social media site. The campaign is quite similar to conducting optimization and inbound link campaigns so that your site is found in natural search results.

The biggest downside in social media is by far the amount of time you need to invest to see results. Make an ongoing commitment to review and respond to comments and to provide an ongoing stream of new material. An initial commitment to set up a profile is just the tip of the iceberg.

Individually and collectively, social media is the biggest-ever time sink. Without self-discipline and a strong time schedule, you can easily become so socially overbooked that other tasks go undone. Scheduling time for social media and setting limits are both essential.

Remember what your mother told you: "You have two ears and one mouth so that you can listen twice as much as you talk." Mothers are always right, especially when it comes to social media. Spend about one-third of your budgeted time creating new posts; the rest is for reading and responding.

As you consider the social media options in this book, consider also the level of human resources that will be needed. Do you have the time and talents yourself? If not, do other people have the time and talent within your organization? What other efforts will you need to give up to make room for social media? Will you have to hire new employees or contract out services, leading to hard costs for this supposedly "free" media?

Integrating Social Media into Your Overall Marketing Effort

Don't mistake the part for the whole: Social media is only part of your online marketing effort, and online marketing is only part of your overall marketing effort.

Consider each foray into social marketing as a strategic choice to supplement your other online marketing activities, which may include a marketing-effective website, content updates, search engine optimization (SEO), inbound link campaigns, online press releases, event calendar postings, e-mail newsletters, testimonial and review collection, affiliate or loyalty program management, and online events or online promotions — not to mention pay per click ads, banners, or sponsorships.

Use social media strategically to

- ✔ Meet an otherwise-unmet marketing need
- ✔ Increase access to your target market
- ✔ Open the door to a new niche market
- ✔ Move prospects through the conversion funnel
- ✔ Encourage loyalty from existing customers

Social networking sites usually track the number of times your profile is viewed, the number of comments received, and the number of friends or followers acquired. Visits to your website originating from social media pages will show up in your referrer statistics if you use tools such as Google Analytics (see Chapter 6) and read about performance metrics for each of the specific social media discussed in Chapters 14–17.

You can use different e-mail addresses to track messages from prospects arising from social media (for example, `facebook@watermelonweb.com` or `twitter@watermelonweb.com`). Prospects may also choose to contact you privately by way of internal messages on many social media sites.

You must have a hub site to which web traffic is directed, whether it's a full-bore website or a blog. It doesn't matter where the site is hosted — only that you own its name, which appears as *yourcompany*.com or `blog.your company`.com. Although you can link to *yourcompany*.`wordpress.com`, you cannot effectively optimize or search for it. Besides, a domain name at a third-party site doesn't look professional. You can easily cross-promote between social media services and your website.

Developing a Strategic Social Marketing Plan

You can refine the marketing plan you created in Chapter 2 for social media marketing purposes. Like any other marketing plan, a strategic Social Media Marketing Plan (as shown in Figure 13-6) incorporates sections on goals, objectives, target markets, methods, costs, and return on investment. The most important function of the form is not that you follow it slavishly but, rather, that it forces you to consider the various facets of social media marketing before you invest too much effort or money.

To download a copy of the Social Media Marketing Plan, see the Downloads tab at `www.dummies.com/go/webmarketingfd3e`.

As you fill out the Social Media Marketing Plan, keep these points in mind:

✔ **Establish goals:** Prioritize your goals from the list of seven benefits of social media described in the section "Understanding the Benefits of Social Media" above, or add your own.

✔ **Set quantifiable objectives:** For every goal, set at least one quantifiable, measurable objective, such as *Increase number of visits to website by 10 percent or from X to Y.*

Social Media Marketing Plan

Overview

Company Name _____

Primary Domain Name _____

Date _____ Prepared By _____

Product or Service _____

Competitors _____

Strategy and Tactics

Target Market(s) – demographics and description _____

_____

Social Media Used by Target Market _____

Social Media Used by Competitors _____

What Sets Us Apart (Value) _____

Social Media Marketing Goal _____

Measurable Marketing Objectives and Meathods _____

_____

Social Media Marketing Budget for 1 Year $ _____

Costs (labor, service providers, equipment, etc.) $ _____

Estimated Revenue (Gain) from sales sourced to social media $ _____

Return on Investment = (Gain - Cost)/Cost = _____% over _____ (mos/yrs)

Available Resources and Skills

Staff _____

Social Media Skills _____

Outside Resources Needed _____

Time Allocation (Hr/Week) _____

Figure 13-6:
Download this Social Media Marketing Plan at the book's companion website.

✔ **Identify your target markets:** Specify one or more target markets by who they are. *Everyone who eats dinner out* isn't a submarket you can identify online. However, you can find *High-income couples within 20 miles of my destination who visit wine and classical music sites.*

✔ **Estimate costs:** Establish first how much money you're willing to invest in social media, including in-house labor, outside contractors, and miscellaneous hard costs such as purchasing software or equipment. Enter these amounts into the Cost section.

> ✔ **Determine your social media marketing mix:** Prioritize your social marketing efforts based on what you can afford, allocating or reallocating funds within your budget. This approach keeps your total social marketing costs under control.

Estimate two hours of work per week for every social media channel you select.

Figuring Social Media ROI

Return on investment (ROI) is the single most important measure of success for social media marketing. In simple terms, *ROI* is the ratio of revenue divided by costs for your business or, in this case, for your social media marketing effort.

Also set some realistic term in which you will recover your investment. Ask yourself whether you're willing to wait ten weeks, ten months, or ten years. Most forms of social media are unlikely to produce a fast fix for drooping sales, so consider what you're trying to accomplish.

Figure 13-7 presents a brief glimpse of how others assess the average cost of lead acquisition for B2B companies for social marketing compared to other forms of marketing. It's just a guide. Keep in mind that the only ROI or cost of acquisition that matters is your own.

Figure 13-7: Cost of B2B lead generation for social media and blogs compared to PPC, natural search, and other methods.

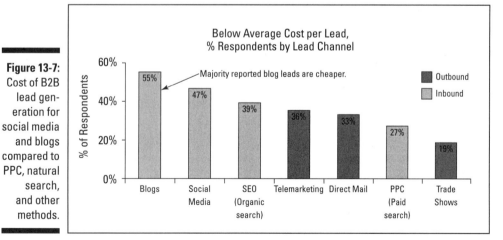

Courtesy of Hubspot

To make it easier to track costs, ask your bookkeeper or CPA to set up an activity or job within your accounting system for social media marketing. Then you can easily track and report all related costs and labor as well as revenues. Tracking costs is usually simpler than tracking revenues that can be traced back explicitly to social media. Chapter 19 lists tools for determining ROI.

Chapter 14

Capturing Customers with Content Sharing

Sharing information was encoded into the DNA of the Internet from its inception as ARPANET in 1969. Good content, whether it consists of text, video, audio, or images, attracts audiences, promotes your brand, and turns viewers into prospects. In this chapter, I talk about using all these techniques as a way to get your message out to your target audience.

If you decide to share some form of content to further your marketing goals, add your selected techniques to the Web Marketing Methods Checklist from Chapter 2 or to the Social Media Marketing Plan in Chapter 13. For your convenience, you can download the plans on the Downloads tab on this book's companion website, at www.dummies.com/go/webmarketingfd3e.

For more information on all these topics, buy a copy of *Social Media Marketing All-in-One For Dummies,* by Jan Zimmerman and Doug Sahlin.

Shooting the Breeze in the Blogosphere

In Chapter 5, I discuss incorporating a blog on your own website to build community. In this section, I look at how to use others' blogs, or a free-standing alternative, as a marketing technique.

You may recall that a *blog* (short for we*b log*) is an easy way to add content without having to know how to program and to encourage others to comment within an ongoing conversation. A blog acts almost like a two-way website. In June 2011, BlogPulse identified almost 165 million blogs!

The expansion of social media networks blurs the once-bright line around blogs. Within Facebook, Twitter, and many other social media channels, readers can comment on content just as they do on blogs. Furthermore, popular blog postings frequently cascade over social media by way of announcements, repostings, and links.

At the same time, many blogs accept uploads of photos and videos, making them more like networks. Blogs with videos and graphics are read and cited more often than text-only blogs. Full-featured blog components can be installed within networks such as Ning or by using a Facebook app. Watch for changes in the blogosphere over the next few years. Many blogs and their audiences may be absorbed by social media networks while the software platform itself continues to thrive as an easy way to build a web presence.

Blogging demographics and usage

Confirm that your target audience uses blogs before investing significant effort in this effort. Technorati (`www.technorati.com`), one of the largest blog directories, sheds additional light on the composition of members of the blogging community in 2010:

- ✔ Two-thirds of bloggers are male.

- ✔ Sixty-five percent are ages 18 to 44.

- ✔ Bloggers are more affluent and better educated than the general population.

- ✔ Seventy-nine percent have college degrees; 43 percent have graduate degrees.

- ✔ One-third have a household income great than $75,000; one-quarter have income greater than $100,000.

- ✔ Eighty-one percent have been blogging more than two years.

- ✔ Professionals have an average of 3.5 blogs and blog more than ten hours per week.

According to a 2010 study by the Pew Internet & American Life Project (`www.pewinternet.org/Reports/2010/Generations-2010/Overview.aspx`), only 32 percent of adult American Internet users across all age levels read blogs and only 10 to 19 percent write them. The percentage of use for either reading or writing declines with age.

Deciding what to blog about

Blogs written by professionals, whether self-employed or within the corporate setting, are popular for business and technology, whereas hobbyist bloggers, unsurprisingly, are more likely to blog about personal musings. A blog is a particularly appropriate platform for publishing quickly changing or controversial information in areas such as politics, news, environment, celebrity gossip, or entertainment.

Search `www.blogpulse.com/trend` to find current hot topics within your area and see where they're posted. Then you can add your two cents' worth. Select only among the top ten percent because there's not much point participating in a blog that is viewed by only its writer and a few friends. For your first filter, try `www.technorati.com`.

Whatever business topic you blog about, keep your posts short and end them with a question that invites others to comment. Blogs are meant to be a dialogue, not a monologue! IdeaPaint's self-hosted blog, at `www.ideapaint.com/blog`, is a good example of active conversations. By offering a valuable platform for customers to describe how they've used IdeaPaint or to ask questions, the blog becomes an excellent marketing tool, encouraging others to try their product (paint that turns almost any surface into an erasable white board).

For a handy list of blog resources and search engines, look at Bonus Chapter 5 on the Downloads tab of the book's companion website.

Optimizing blog postings for SEO

Whether you're writing your own blog or posting on someone else's, you can optimize individual posts to make them more likely to be found in search engines. Simply include keywords in the first sentence of your post.

If you need quick suggestions for good blog keywords, install the free tool at `http://labs.wordtracker.com/seo-blogger`. It sits next to a blog editor on the screen so that you can consider keyword suggestions as you write.

To view a well-optimized posting and its source code, take a look at the Changing Aging blog from Ecumen, a nonprofit organization specializing in senior housing and services. Note how the entry at `www.changingaging blog.org/posts/view/1371-ecumen-expanding-senior-living-options-with-ecumen-seasons-at-apple-valley` includes the phrases *senior living* or *senior housing* in its URL, post title, tags, categories, and text. The source code (right-click and select View Page Source to see the code) uses the same term in the title and keyword tags and indicates that the Ecumen Changing Aging blog has both an XML site map and an RSS feed.

Viewing Video As a Marketing Tool

The growth of broadband access, plus the advent of inexpensive video recording technology, has fueled a surge in video on the web, offering plenty of new opportunities to deliver content and place ads.

Creative examples abound. Although you experience a wonderful feeling when you grab the brass ring and create a funny viral video that millions of viewers pass around, video has plenty of other marketing uses:

- **Create your own videos to suit your needs.** Sample topics are product demonstrations, product updates, industry news, training, support, testimonials, and promotion. You can post them online in several places and cross-link to them from your own site, your blog, and all your social media pages.

- **Remember that certain subjects are natural candidates for video.** Cinema, sports, entertainment, and music cry out for video trailers, teasers, concert samples, or game excerpts.

- **Develop videos that enhance your brand image.** Document everything from community involvement to how-to programs in your industry area.

- **Tap into the creative potential of your target audience.** Encourage them to post videos related to your company or products (funny pet videos for pet stores, for example), perhaps as part of a contest. Here's a note of caution: When Chevrolet ran a contest soliciting Tahoe SUV commercials, it received many negative submissions complaining about poor gas mileage and environmental damage.

- **Advertise on video-sharing sites,** in which eMarketer expects to draw more than $2 billion in advertising dollars in 2011. To promote your company on YouTube, go to www.google.com/ads/video, or use a video advertising network, such as the ones at www.break.com, http://tubemogul.com, or http://blip.tv.

For a famous and funny example of successful video marketing, look at one of Blendtec's videos in Figure 14-1, their website in Figure 14-2, and their story in the nearby sidebar, "Blendtec becomes a video star." The video shows skis being fed into Blendtec's high-performance blender. You can view the entire ski video and link to other "Will It Blend?" hits at www.youtube.com/user/Blendtec.

Figure 14-1:
Blendtec
uses videos
on YouTube
and on its
own video
site to drive
traffic to its
site.

Courtesy of Blendtec for use of the Blendtec Trademark and www.youtube.com/user/Blendtec#p/u/26/4drHHSuDN38

Figure 14-2:
Blendtec
sells
high-end
blenders at
its primary
site.

Courtesy of Blendtec for use of the Blendtec Trademark and www.Blendtec.com

Blendtec becomes a video star

Blendtec, a manufacturer of commercial and consumer blenders and other small electrics, has been in business for nearly 30 years. Selling to both consumers and businesses, it was an early adopter of online videos, launching on YouTube in 2006.

The company uses videos to "show the crazy side of extreme testing." Featuring the Blendtec CEO, Tom Dickson, the videos demonstrate its blending insane products, from vuvuzelas to glowsticks, all with the disclaimer, "Don't try this at home."

"We were a hit!" exclaims Julie Owens, Blendtec's global marketing manager. "YouTube created brand awareness for us," which was their goal. They not only accomplished that in stars, but also drew large amounts of traffic to their website. Still, their number one aim is "to be real," she insists.

According to Owens, the audience on YouTube is typically male, ages 14–35, while target buyers of blenders are typically educated females from 30 to 65 years old. "The unique piece to this puzzle is that our YouTube views support or influence our buying demographic," she observes. When she analyzed how the viral fans influence buyers, she found that "We have kids point out our blenders to their parents. We have heard kids say, 'Mom, this is the one on Will It Blend?' The magic is when we hear the parent say, 'We love the blender that our kids told us we had to buy!'"

With more than 100 videos posted, Blendtec has made a serious commitment to video. It has a full-production facility onsite, with a full-time producer/director and a part-time assistant who plan and edit videos, though actual shooting time may be only one to two days a month.

Blendtec tracks its video results through analytics, watching both conversion rates and the size of its fan base. "Of course we love views," she says. "That lets us know we hit the mark." The number of visitors to the website indicates to her that the videos have successfully showcased the features of their blenders."

Although Owens is big on social media, she faces a marketing challenge. "We have [both] commercial and consumer products; we use all techniques because our markets are so different. We know we need to be in a trade show to share our wares with commercial accounts, and we know that raw foodies and vegans will be found on Twitter more often than Smoothie CEOs."

"Be real. Be you. Show what you do, don't tell," advises Owens. "Have fun and enjoy the journey so that your story is something others will share. . . . We like the house that Will It Blend built on our YouTube real estate. . . . We are happy . . . trying to make life smoother."

Video-sharing demographics and usage

Young adults (under 35) continue to comprise the primary audience for YouTube, which serves as a fairly accurate stand-in for video demographics overall when compared to the 2010 Pew Report "The State of Online Video" (www.pewinternet.org/Reports/2010/State-of-Online-Video/Part-1/Who-is-Watching-and-Downloading-Online-Video.aspx).

YouTube video users are also younger than the average Internet user, and minorities have a greater presence than they do overall, as shown in

Figure 14-3 (see `www.quantcast.com/youtube.com`). Note that Quantcast did not directly measure the data in Figure 14-3; these are estimates only. For additional YouTube statistics, see `www.youtube.com/t/press_statistics`.

The number of people sharing video is staggering. By 2012, Cisco expects video to account for more than 50 percent of online consumer traffic. ClickZ reports 172 million U.S. users of all ages — almost 82 percent of the country's Internet population — watched video online in April 2011. Even when only adult Internet users are counted, 69 percent have used the Internet to watch or download video — roughly half the *entire* U.S. adult population. If you want eyeballs, you want video.

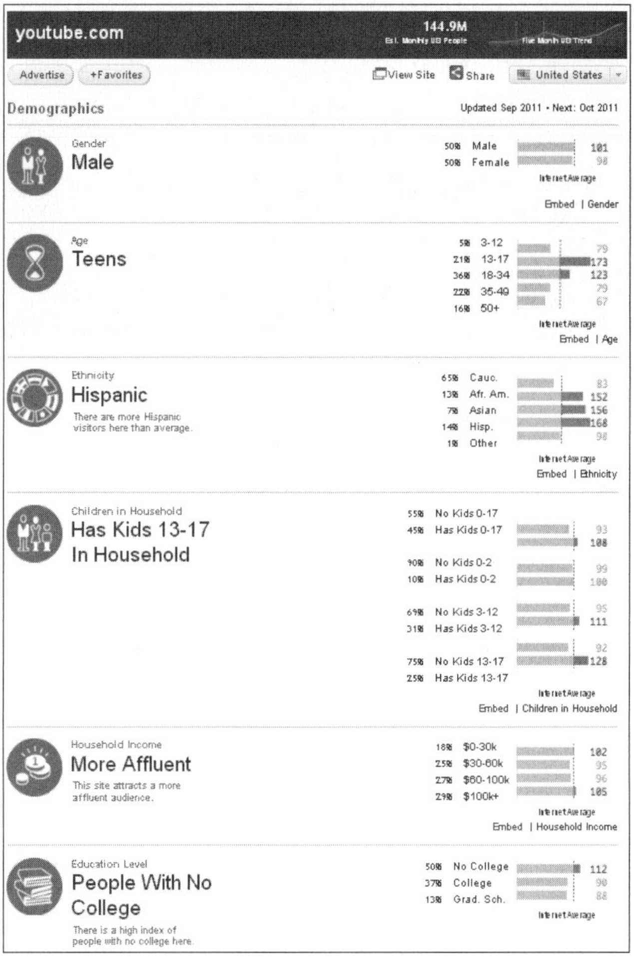

Figure 14-3: Estimated YouTube users as of September 2011.

Courtesy of Quantcast.com

The percentage of video watchers drops slowly with age: from more than 80 percent for users from 18 to 22 years old to 40 to 49 percent for people from 64 to 73 years old. Video watching drops below 30 percent only for users older than 75.

When non-YouTube sites such as Facebook are included in video usage surveys, women are shown to be as likely as men to upload and share videos.

In Bonus Chapter 5 on the Downloads tab of the companion website, you will find a list of video-sharing and vlog-sharing sites.

Optimizing video-sharing sites for SEO

Because search engines can't directly parse the contents of multimedia, you must take advantage of all opportunities to use your relevant search terms in every video title, description, and ALT tag or any other option you find.

You can often use existing keyword research, meta tags from your website or blog, or optimized text that you've already created. For more information on indexing multimedia, see `www.google.com/support/webmasters/bin/answer.py?hl=en&answer=114016`.

Take advantage of context and form fields, included on video-sharing sites, to make your videos easier to find. Here's a list:

- **Title and title meta tag:** Try to attract viewers by including relevant search terms in your title and meta tags.

- **Category or directory:** Select or name a category that draws your target audience. It never hurts if the label is a keyword.

- **Filename:** A name such as `video12` doesn't help with SEO as much as `tabby-cats-sing-jingle-bells` does.

- **Tag:** Use relevant keywords, just as you would with other social media.

- **ALT tag:** Use this type of tag for a short description with a search term — for example, *guided meditation mandala*.

- **Long description meta tag:** Try to incorporate four to six search terms, just as you would with the page description meta tag on your website.

- **Content:** Surround embedded multimedia elements on any web or social media page with keyword-rich, descriptive content.

- **Transcription:** Transcribe and post a short excerpt from a keyword-loaded portion of your video.

- **Anchor text:** Use keywords in the text link that opens your multimedia file.

- **RSS and XML:** Expand your reach with media RSS and site maps.

Marketing and measuring your video success

The steps for marketing are simple and consistent with other forms of social media and online promotion:

- ✔ **List all locations of your video clips in video directories and search engines.** Google and other search engines allow users to play videos directly from search results and to post thumbnails of video from other sites within a natural search.

- ✔ **Use cross-links efficiently.** Add them between your video-sharing sites, all other social media pages, and your website or blog.

- ✔ **Announce your new channel.** You can make a call to action to subscribe in your e-newsletter, blog, and social media pages. Do the same thing every time you post a new video.

- ✔ **Keep in mind that links to your website or other pages from any posted video will appear in the Referrer section of your analytics results (see Chapter 6).** On YouTube and certain other video-sharing sites, you can also monitor these internal performance metrics:

  - Number of views for every video

  - Number of subscribers to your channel and its rate of growth as different videos post

  - Number, tone, and quality of comments on every video

Featuring Photos and Slides

Photos and slide shows are excellent ways to showcase your products, services, activities, testimonials, and expertise. Although photos can always be posted on your own website or blog, photo- and slide-sharing sites allow other people to comment on them, forward them to others, and find out more about your company.

Although Flickr, Photobucket, and Slideshare are the best-known photo- and slide-sharing sites, many others work perfectly well. For a list of similar sharing sites, visit Bonus Chapter 5 on the Downloads tab of the companion website.

Use the search function on any of these image-sharing sites to see how many, if any, of your competitors use them. The presence of many competitors is a strong hint that your business needs to be there, too. The absence of competition is ambiguous: It can give you a temporary advantage or indicate that this effort isn't worth it. Being first isn't always the best idea.

You can achieve multiple marketing goals by following this advice for using image-sharing sites:

- **Cast a wider net for prospective customers.** Some prospects prefer looking at pictures to reading words! It's all part of finding new prospects where they are. Display images of your company, products, or services, accompanied by informative descriptions, to attract customers' attention.

- **Entice viewers with samples of your products.** For example, see Bleeding Heart Bakery at `www.flickr.com/people/thebleeding heartbakery`. Whether you're selling scarves or hookahs, candles or cupcakes, you can use image-sharing to lure visitors with representative products.

- **Display photos of completed projects.** Photos sites work exceedingly well for architects, builders, construction companies, and home painters as well as for interior, landscape, product, and packaging design companies and any other business with highly visual work results. This advice is excellent for service companies such as Wojcik Lawn Care & Landscaping at `http://s28.photobucket.com/home/sicnj` or McClain's Painting Service at `www.flickr.com/photos/mclainspainting`.

- **Build awareness of creative work.** In perhaps the most obvious application for photo-sharing, creative folks can display their portfolios to a broad audience. Because these sites make it easy to upload, catalog, and remove images, many artists use image-sharing sites as a free alternative to modifying websites. See ceramic artist Marylou Newdigate at `https://picasaweb.google.com/marylounewdigate` for an example.

- **Enhance branding and site traffic.** By using your logo, tags, web address, and links on profile pages on these services, you can build name recognition.

- **Improve search engine optimization.** Photo- and slide-sharing sites can be helpful to your search engine optimization strategy. Every site may be a bit different. I talk more about SEO in the later section "Optimizing images for SEO."

- **Supplement your website or social media pages with additional photos.** For example, you might display thumbnails on your website or one image from a set or a slide sequence of photos, with supplemental photos on a photo-sharing site.

- **Advertise to photographers.** Photo-sharing sites are a wonderful way to offer goods and services to photographers, such as cameras, lenses, photo-editing software, lighting equipment, workshops, studio space, or travel packages for photo safaris.

✔ **Improve customer service.** Upload images that are limited to use by specific customers or invitees, perhaps marking them private for limited visibility. You can post pictures of works in progress, images of prospective sites or buildings, or photographs of optional product features. This feature is particularly useful when photos interest a smaller audience than the one served by your website.

✔ **Collaborate on content.** Shutterfly has the special Share Sites feature (at www.shutterfly.com/sites/create/welcome.sfly) to help people easily collaborate on the creation of photo albums, whether private or public. For example, the American Youth Soccer Organization uses Shutterfly for online registration, to share pictures and videos, manage schedules, access volunteer assignments, and do even more at www.shutterfly.com/ayso.

✔ **Build community participation and buzz.** In a novel interactive application, Marvel Comics created a Flickr group for movie lovers to post photos of themselves with statues of the Incredible Hulk that had been placed in movie theater lobbies to promote the film. Selected photos from the group at www.flickr.com/groups/hulkstatues also appeared on the Marvel site (at http://marvel.com/news/movie stories.3421.Hulk_Crashes_Iron_Man~apos~s_Opening) as a way to increase its fan base and enhance word-of-mouth advertising.

✔ **Establish your expertise with presentations and slide shows.** Slide shows and PowerPoint presentations are extremely valuable tools in the B2B world. To increase your visibility and reputation as an expert, post your presentations from webinars, speeches, product demonstrations, and technical support directions on sites such as Slideshare (at www.slideshare.net). For instance, OTW Safety posted a presentation at www.slideshare.net/OTWSafety/final-longitudinal-channelizing-devices-7594672 (shown in Figure 14-4) to enhance their brand recognition. The company also posted great-looking images from a trade show exhibit at www.flickr.com/photos/44974791@N02.

Check the Terms and Conditions for every site. For example, you can't use Flickr simply to host images for products you're selling or to display a catalog, but you might want to maintain photos of a company event or conference or pictures of staff members or your storefront decor.

Continue to call images critical to your website from your web server, posting only copies on photo-sharing sites. In particular, avoid using these sites to host your website's logos, banners, icons, avatars, or other nonphotographic images.

Figure 14-4:
B2B companies such as OTW Safety take advantage of Slideshare.

Courtesy of OTW Safety, Innovators in safety and security.

Photo-sharing demographics and usage

The Pew Internet & American Life Project, in its 2011 report on Social Networking Sites and Our Lives Part 2 (www.pewinternet.org/Reports/2011/Technology-and-social-networks/Part-2.aspx?view=all), found that women constitute 58 percent of the users of photo-sharing sites. In other words, their participation now matches their level of participation on other social communication sites, from e-mail to instant messaging and blogging. The demographics of Flickr users are shown in Figure 14-5 (see www.quantcast.com/flickr.com). Note that Quantcast did not directly measure this data; these are estimates only.

Optimizing images for SEO

Because Google and Bing/Yahoo! crawl the metadata provided for public images, it pays to use good SEO practices. By aligning your image meta tags with your overall SEO strategy, you can improve the appearance of your business in relevant search results and indirectly increase traffic.

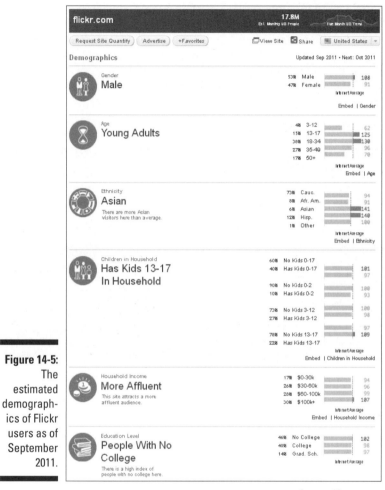

Courtesy of Quantcast.com

Figure 14-5: The estimated demographics of Flickr users as of September 2011.

Try to incorporate some of your preferred search terms in appropriate fields in the following list. Although the names or options may differ on different sites, you can usually find the equivalent. Make these fields as keyword- and content-rich as you can. As with video, you can take advantage of existing keyword research, meta tags from your website or blog, or optimized text that you've already created:

- ✔ **Filename:** If necessary, rename your files before uploading them. Be descriptive and include a search term such as *snowshoe-siamese-cat-plays-piano.jpg* instead of *image12345.jpg.*

- ✔ **Title field:** Like the filename, the title should be descriptive and include a search term.

- ✔ **Description field:** In addition to incorporating the search terms that appear in the title and filename, you might want to include your business name and address and your web address (without an active link), if appropriate. Don't use blatant calls to action or hard-sell language. From the point of view of an external search engine, the description is "surrounding content" and is essential to assessing the relevance of search terms.

- ✔ **Tag list:** Tags, which work like keywords, help users search for images internally as well as externally. You can include your business name, address, city, and sometimes your web address in your tags or profile.

- ✔ **ALT tags:** Originally meant to help people who are visually impaired, these hover tags can combine a description with a search term, for example, *large handcrafted cat tree for your Maine Coon.*

- ✔ **Caption:** As always, use keyword-rich, descriptive content.

- ✔ **Anchor text:** Use keywords in the text link that opens each photo.

- ✔ **Large images:** Upload large versions as well as the thumbnails that are visible on your blog or website.

Most of these sites make it easy to coordinate your social media efforts, saving time and helping you build your audience. In any case, always cross-link (with chicklets and Share buttons) between your image-sharing site, your website, and all other social media outlets you use. Cross-post images when segments of your market align in different channels.

Generating Leads with Podcasts

A *podcast,* coined as a term in 2004, is basically radio on demand over the Internet. The Pew Internet & American Life Project found that by September of 2010, 21 percent of adult Internet users in the United States had listened to a podcast in real-time or downloaded it to play later. That percentage now translates to close to 40 million U.S. listeners enjoying podcasts.

Podcast demographics and usage

RawVoice, a podcast advertising network, finds that the podcast audience is skewed toward young (67 percent ages 22 to 40), Caucasian, male (68 percent of listeners), educated (74 percent with at least some college completed), and relatively affluent (61 percent with household income over $60,000). The topic, more than anything else, determines the audience that a podcast will draw.

eMarketer forecasts that "as a percentage of Internet users, podcast down-loaders are expected to grow from 9 percent of Internet users in 2008 to 17 percent in 2013," with podcast advertising growing apace to more than $435 million.

Before you spend money producing audio programs, make sure your audience listens to podcasts.

Review the table of podcasting resources, from production tips to podcast directories and podcast advertising networks, in Bonus Chapter 5 on the Downloads tab of the companion website.

Getting the best results from podcasts

Before you decide to market with podcasts, listen to a few, such as the ones at www.blogtalkradio.com, shown in Figure 14-6. Or search podcast directories to hear how other businesses take advantage of this technique. To buy ads on existing podcasts, check out podcast advertising networks or find a podcast that you want to sponsor.

Figure 14-6: Blog Talk Radio is a popular online radio network for creating and listening to shows.

Courtesy of Cinchcast Inc.

If you want to create your own podcast, decide what you're trying to accomplish. Like webinars, described in Chapter 8, podcasts are best used for branding, lead generation, and content delivery — not sales. Also, take some time to think about your content. Unfortunately, just reading your newsletter aloud doesn't work. Audio is completely different from print; it definitely has a performance component. Will you riff on your own commentary? Interview someone? If so, whom — clients, colleagues, or decision-makers in your field?

Optimizing podcasts

Add meta data to your podcast when you upload it. Be sure to include your essential search terms in the title and description of every podcast. Make these fields as rich in keywords and content as you can.

As with other content-sharing services, use existing keyword research, meta tags from your website or blog, or optimized text that you've already created. Transcribe and post a short excerpt from a keyword-loaded portion of your podcast to help search engines find it easily.

Chapter 15

Facing the Future with Facebook

*F*acebook has become synonymous with social networking. By far the most popular of all the personal networking services — claiming 800 million active users worldwide in September 2011 — Facebook has now become a marketing channel for businesses as well. Keep an eye on sites such as Mashable and TechCrunch as Facebook positions itself for an initial public offering in 2012.

As these millions of people gravitated over the past several years toward a service that allows them to share news, text postings, videos, photos, blogs, and more with their friends and families, large companies followed them in a never-ending quest to attract new prospects, generate repeat visits from current customers, and multiply word-of-mouth referrals.

In theory, Facebook offers many companies a branding opportunity and a way to fill the top of their conversion funnels. In practice, marketing life isn't as simple. For many smaller companies, gaining traction on Facebook is as complicated as trying to gain visibility in search engines.

 If you decide to incorporate Facebook into your online marketing strategy, be sure to include it in your Social Media Marketing Plan. (See Chapter 13 or download the form from the Downloads tab at www.dummies.com/go/web marketingfd3e). Allow a minimum of two labor hours per week for your Facebook efforts.

Deciding Whether Facebook Fits Your Needs

For many small businesses with limited marketing budgets, time, and resources, Facebook represents a temptingly inexpensive way to advertise, with one study showing that 70 percent of companies that are at www.merchantcircle.com are already using Facebook. Given its high rate of adoption, ease of use, and relatively low barriers to entry, Facebook definitely has curb appeal. The problem isn't "doing" Facebook — it's doing it well enough to have a positive impact on your bottom line.

Audience adoption

Facebook's own statistics (www.facebook.com/press/info.php?statistics) contribute the following types of data to your assessment of its potential value:

- **Number of active users:** Fifty percent of active users log on to Facebook in any given day.

- **Number of minutes spent per month:** Users spend more than 700 billion minutes per month on Facebook.

- **Geographical location:** About 75 percent of Facebook users are outside the United States.

- **Number of connections:** The average user has 130 friends, connects to 80 community pages, groups, or events, and posts 90 pieces of content per month.

- **Site integration:** More than 7 million websites or apps have integrated with Facebook.

- **Mobile use:** More than 350 million active users access Facebook via their mobile devices.

Watch the numbers on Facebook. TechCrunch reported that for the first time Facebook lost users in the United States in May 2011, although its worldwide expansion more than made up for it. It remains to be seen whether this occurrence portends a true shift in usage, an inevitable slowdown in Facebook's rate of growth, or simply a blip in the numbers.

Be aware that averages can be misleading. Although the percentage of active Facebook participants is higher than on other social media, where a tiny percentage of users produce a high percentage of content, it can still be difficult to obtain active communication. The 2011 report "Social Networking and Our Lives," from the Pew Internet and American Life Project, found the following percentages for activities on an average day:

- ✔ **"Like" another user's content (the most popular activity):** 26 percent
- ✔ **Comment on another user's post or status:** 22 percent
- ✔ **Comment on another user's photos:** 20 percent
- ✔ **Update their own status:** 15 percent
- ✔ **Send another user a private message:** 10 percent

As a business seeking engagement from prospects or customers, you still face a steep challenge. Again according to the Pew Study, 56 percent of users update their statuses less than once per week, and 16 percent have never even updated them. In other words, more than half of Facebook's users are more or less missing in action. Half have fewer than ten friends, the minimum number that seems to produce involvement.

Facebook demographics

Quantcast demographics, shown in Figure 15-1, show that Facebook draws an audience that still skews young, in spite of the well-publicized rapid growth rate for older users (see www.quantcast.com/facebook.com#demo). Like many other forms of social media, the site draws a predominantly female user base. No surprise there — women are socialized to focus on communication and relationships.

Facebook etches detailed demographic portraits of its users based on the profiles they complete. In addition to filtering for age, gender, location, and language, Facebook advertisers can filter for likes and interests, connections, birthdays, relationships, education, or work.

To form a sense of the size of the Facebook population that meets your demographic profile, go to www.facebook.com/ads/create and pretend that you're creating an ad. As you select categories, Facebook displays the number of people in its database who meet your criteria. This activity helps you decide whether Facebook is worthy of your marketing efforts.

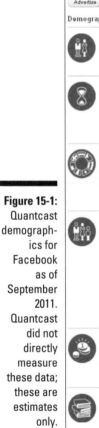

Courtesy of Quantcast.com

Figure 15-1:
Quantcast demographics for Facebook as of September 2011. Quantcast did not directly measure these data; these are estimates only.

Putting Facebook to Work

With the mammoth horde of users on Facebook, you might wonder what you can accomplish at the site. If you're clever, consistent, and attentive, you can accomplish quite a bit:

- **Brand, brand, brand.** Facebook is an inexpensive way to get your name out to the undifferentiated masses.

- **Drive traffic to your website.** Use links in your profile, wall postings, captions, and everywhere else you can in order to drive visitors to your website or other primary web presence.

✔ **Improve your appearance in search engine results.** Search engines find your company name, keywords, and inbound links from Facebook profiles and postings. All these elements may help improve your ranking on search engine results pages.

✔ **Support customers.** Many companies have started using Facebook as a way to address the specific needs of different users by setting up groups and responding quickly to any complaints that appear in postings. If prospects see that you treat customers with respect and honesty, your reputation will be enhanced. Of course, your reputation can be damaged as well.

✔ **Fill your conversion funnel, as discussed in Chapter 6.** Though Facebook isn't the best venue for driving sales, you can bring prospects to your website and start them down the path to purchase. Users are rarely thinking about buying when they're on Facebook. They certainly may follow someone else's recommendation to look at your page or at a product on your site, but unless they find a must-have item or an appealing impulse buy, converting them to buyers may be difficult.

✔ **Entice new customers with special offers.** Offer special deals to people who Like you or are members of a Facebook group. Run contests, polls, surveys, or games, or give virtual gifts — anything that will bring customers to your door.

✔ **Build your e-mail list.** Have people register on Facebook for a contest or give them something in return in exchange for their e-mail address and permission to send targeted messages.

✔ **Become an industry resource.** Although Facebook appears particularly well-suited for B2C purposes, B2B companies can use it to establish their expertise within their industry and provide technical support, especially by participating actively in groups.

✔ **Drive a viral campaign.** Encourage people to share your page and your website with others. This strategy works especially well with photos and videos.

✔ **Provide timely information.** If tweets are too short and blog posts are too long, Facebook entries may be "just right" for announcing new products, project status, appearances at trade shows, and current involvement in community activities.

For SEO and advertising reasons, do not make Facebook your primary web presence. Use a website or blog platform with a domain name that you own. At this time, websites support complex forms of database integration, transactions, and business transformation techniques that Facebook can't yet sustain.

Building a business page

Go to www.facebook.com/pages/create.php or click the link labeled Create a Page for Celebrity, Band, or Business at the bottom of the page at www.facebook.com. Select which of the six types of pages you want to create, choose the appropriate category from the drop-down lists, and fill out the remaining fields. After you agree to terms and click the Get Started link, you're asked to log in to an existing Facebook account or create a new one. After that, you can start working on the Business Page form, such as the one shown in Figure 15-2.

Click the Edit Info link at the top of the page to fill out details on your business page. This page, which is accessible to others by using the Info option in the left navigation area of your Facebook page, represents a key marketing opportunity. How you fill it out is not only an introduction to your company but also your best opportunity for search engine optimization, as I describe in the upcoming section "Optimizing Facebook for Search." The Scania Group has a well-written business page, at www.facebook.com/scaniagroup?sk=info, as shown in Figure 15-3. You might want to look at their wall as well by clicking that option in the left navigation pane.

Click to add details

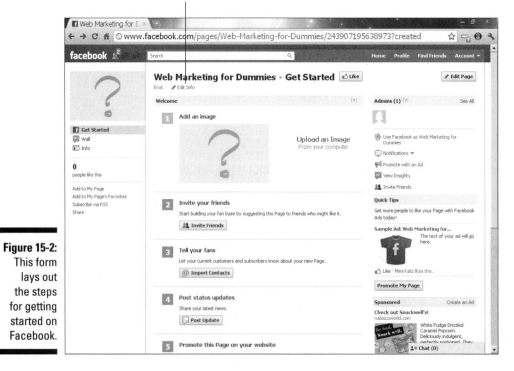

Figure 15-2:
This form lays out the steps for getting started on Facebook.

Courtesy of Scania Group

Figure 15-3:
Scania
Group has a
well-written
Facebook
business
page.

Creating a fan page

Every company seeks to create a unique graphical impression that grabs the viewer's attention. New third-party apps with templates for fan pages let you quickly create the kind of page that makes a statement. Many companies now use their fan pages as the landing page for any link to their Facebook presence. Some even require viewers to Like the company before they can access Facebook content for the business. Some fan page apps present a second page that rewards those who have Liked you with a special discount or coupon.

One of the easiest fan page apps to use is Wix (which is free) at `www.facebook.com/apps/application.php?id=129982580378550&sk=app_129982580378550`. Simply navigate to that page and follow your nose. You'll find more fan page apps reviewed at `www.socialmediaexaminer.com/top-10-facebook-apps-for-building-custom-pages-tab`.

For an example of what a custom fan page looks like, see Figure 15-4 from The Equine Practice. Their website is shown in Figure 15-5. To find out how this unusual company has been highly successful on Facebook, read their story in the nearby sidebar, "Facing customers with Facebook."

Figure 15-4: The Equine Practice created its Facebook fan page using the Wix app.

Figure 15-5: Website for The Equine Practice, Inc.

Facing customers with Facebook

Geoff Tucker, DVM and president of The Equine Practice, Inc., first started his website in 2007 as the hub for four other sites. Every site shares the overall goal of educating horse owners about veterinary care and horse husbandry. About two years ago, Tucker added Twitter and Facebook to his online corral. "I don't have a target market in the sense of demographics," says Tucker. "I just put out my message for those who are ready to listen." It turns out that mostly older women are listening because they just happen to own the most horses these days. Tucker primarily uses Facebook to drive people to his site by posting content. But he sees each of these social media services as a way of reaching different people. For Tucker, the more channels of communication he has, the better his chance of reaching his audience.

Tucker acknowledges several challenges with Facebook. "The biggest," he says "is just starting," especially with the confusing directions and frequent changes in user interface. He began before the days of business pages, when he had to create two profiles — one for personal use and one for business. He had to overcome the loss of thousands of Facebook friends when Facebook converted friends to fans. The time commitment is another challenge. Tucker spends about an hour a day responding to comments and posting pictures from the farms he visits; his wife spends time monitoring topical issues that need a comment, and his assistant spends another 20 minutes a day posting content from her archives. Tucker joined a few groups but finds them too time-consuming. "Don't let [Facebook] consume you," he warns.

Although Tucker watches for a constant growth in the number of fans, he finds that the number of monthly active users is more valuable as an accurate reflection of engagement. Tucker promotes his Facebook page with chicklets and a Like Me button on the top of every web page and in his weekly e-newsletter. He supplements his online marketing with word-of-mouth, signage, business cards, brochures, phone decals, and talks to small groups. He doesn't have much use for display ads or PPC, but SEO "is big" in his world.

Tucker advises starting with a Facebook fan page, not a profile page, for business use. Viewing Facebook as simply another communication tool offers some perspective. "In all my years working with horses, I have never, ever, not once, had a horse write me a check. Everything is a people business. Use Facebook as a way to meet new people, and your business will grow. "

See these URLs for The Equine Practice:

```
www.theequinepractice.com
www.equinedentistrywithout
    drama.com
www.horsesadvocate.com
www.irrefutablelawsof
    horsemanship.com
www.horsebarnpics.com
www.facebook.com/equinepractice
www.twitter.com/equinepractice
www.flickr.com/photos/
    theequinepractice
www.youtube.com/horzvet
www.linkedin.com/in/equine
    practice
```

Becoming well "Liked" on Facebook

It almost takes a special marketing campaign just to acquire a critical mass of Likes on Facebook. At the least, try to include a call to action, rather than a simple link to your Facebook page on your websites and other social media pages. Many companies have special offers for users who Like them, often a coupon code that can be redeemed for a discount.

You can also e-mail a brief message to appropriate contacts in your address book, by either sending invitations via Facebook or including the request in your e-mail newsletter. After contacts Like you, remind them to ask their friends to Like you, too.

To increase your company's overall presence on Facebook, ask all your employees to create their own Facebook accounts and Like your business page. Their own network of connections may help expand your reach.

After you have at least 25 people connected to your page, you can claim a username as your own at www.facebook.com/username rather than see a long string of numbers in your Facebook URL. After you select a name, you cannot change it.

For a list of helpful Facebook tools and URLs, please visit Bonus Chapter 5 on the Downloads tab of the companion website.

Advertising on Facebook

The self-service PPC ads on Facebook are structured similarly to PPC or CPM campaigns at Bing/Yahoo! and Google — with three major differences. First, all targeting is demographic or geographic rather than by context or search term. In other words, you can identify a target market by area of interest, location, or demographic feature, but not as a result of a search. (See the Tip paragraph in the preceding "Facebook demographics" section.) Second, the ads have quite a low CTR, less than that of banner ads (described in Chapter 12). Finally, you can incorporate an image into your ads.

You may want to think about using the ads for branding rather than for sales. Or, use the Facebook Ads for Pages feature (at www.facebook.com/pages/learn.php) to drive traffic to your Facebook fan page. (This is the one place where a Facebook URL is an acceptable landing page for a paid ad.) These engagement ads come with a built-in call to action to Like your page without the user ever leaving the ad.

For a shortcut to URLs for Facebook advertising, please visit Bonus Chapter 5 on the Downloads tab of the companion website.

Of course, you should cross-link Facebook with your website, blog, newsletter, and other social media pages. Use chicklets and Share buttons (see Chapter 19). Whenever possible, cross-post as well, especially between your blog, Twitter, and Facebook wall.

Optimizing Facebook for Search

Take advantage of myriad opportunities to gain traffic from your Facebook pages by applying optimization techniques. Next to blogs and LinkedIn, Facebook pages offer the largest number of opportunities to use SEO on social media to reach people who don't already know you.

The Search function on Facebook doesn't work particularly well, but you still have a better chance to be found in an internal search if you follow best practices for SEO. The techniques described in the following list provide opportunities for some of your Facebook pages to appear in search engine results:

- ✔ **Use, as your Facebook business page name, an easy-to-remember version of your business name, alone or combined with a search term.** Try to use the same username on both Twitter and Facebook, for branding reasons. Facebook doesn't like generic names.

- ✔ **In the Websites field on your business page (previously called a profile), list all relevant domain names, including your blog and other social media pages.** Later, you can place links to your website or blog or another type of social media within your posting stream.

- ✔ **Place keyword-loaded content in the first paragraph of every field, to help with onsite product searches.** *Note:* Contact and address information also help with local searches. Your page description meta tag may work well in the Mission field because it's already optimized for search terms. Include in the Products field all your brand names and all the products or services you offer.

- ✔ **As on Twitter, popularity matters.** The more Facebook Likes you have, the more internal links you have to your own page. Even better, when people comment on or recommend your content, Google sees reciprocal links between your page and your friends' pages, which may increase your PageRank.

- ✔ **More search term opportunities abound if you use HTML rather than iFrames or Fan graphics on a page.** You can create additional tabs to display text or images or links. Try to use a good search term in any tab name (limited to ten characters) and include text links in your content. It's a pain, but you can do this on your own.

You cannot "own" your Facebook URL, even after you claim your name. Your pages are still an extension of Facebook. This situation constrains your ability to advertise with it online, because you can't link from a paid ad to a page you don't own. You can't even submit the name `Facebook.com/`*`yourcompany`* to certain directories.

Search engines cannot "read" a graphical fan page or content within an iFrame. However, Google monitors wall postings in its real-time search, and all search engines can read your profile.

For an independent assessment of the quality of your business page (not fan page), try Facebook Grader from HubSpot: `http://facebook.grader.com`.

Links from Facebook to your website are visible under the Referrer section in Google Analytics.

Participating in Other Social Networks

Considering everything that Facebook offers, do you have any reason to select another social network instead of, or in addition to, Facebook? The answer is right out of Marketing 101: Absolutely, as long as your target audience uses that site.

Looking for a networking service other than Facebook? Review the broad-based alternative social networks in Bonus Chapter 5 on the Downloads tab of the companion website. For vertically segmented social networks, see Chapter 18.

The most notable recent entry in the social networking wars is Google+, which is growing exponentially. Hear all that noise in the background? That's the sound of two web elephants — Google and Facebook — crashing around in the cyberjungle.

Google+ is tightly integrated with Google's primary offerings (see Chapter 11). Users who search while signed in to their Google accounts can click the +1 button that appears in search and PPC ad results to recommend a site to their network of Google connections (`www.google.com/intl/en-US/+1/button`). Google is gambling that this feature will enable it to hold its advertisers in line. This fight will be one to watch — it's all about the money.

Chapter 16

Feathering Your Business Nest with Twitter

In This Chapter
▶ Deciding whether Twitter is right for your business
▶ Getting started with Twitter
▶ Optimizing Twitter for search
▶ Measuring your Twitter success

*W*hat is all that chirping about? When Twitter first cracked its shell in 2007, no one could figure out what to do with 140-character messages that appear either as text messages on cellphones (hence the character limit) or as part of an ongoing stream of chatter on computer screens.

Twitter is a *microblogging* service — as well as a social network — because its *tweets* (short messages sent by way of Twitter) started out as short journal entries about daily life to be shared with friends. Soon, however, tweets about what people were drinking during happy hour expanded to tweets about where to find low-price gas, commercial messages about special sales and discounts, breaking news about wildfires or traffic jams, and revolution in the streets of the Middle East.

In this chapter, I discuss ways that businesses use Twitter to share time-dependent information with customers and prospects, factors to help you decide whether this social media channel has potential for your company, and tips for getting started.

Understanding a Twitter Feed

Twitter is hard to imagine without seeing it. Take a look at the stream of tweets as seen on a computer screen for Olo Yogurt Studio in Figure 16-1. The left pane shows these elements.

✔ **Twitter handle:** Also called the username and designated as *@address* (in this case, @oloyogurt).

✔ **Stream of tweets:** Short posts displayed in reverse chronological order.

✔ **Shortened URLs:** Shortened links, which sometimes look like gibberish, are needed because of the limited number of characters in a tweet; Twitter and third-party sites, such as `http://bitly.com`, generate shortened URLs for you.

✔ **Hashtags:** Starting with a #, hashtags enable users to sort and find tweets on a specific topic.

In the upper-right corner of the right pane, you see

✔ **Profile:** A short description of the company, followed by the domain name for its website

✔ **Tweets:** Number of tweets sent by this account

✔ **Following**: Number of people this account receives tweets from

✔ **Followers:** Number of people receiving tweets from this account

✔ **Listed:** Number of lists on which this account appears

Twitter handle

Shortened URL   Stream of tweets

Figure 16-1:
Olo Yogurt's twitter feed displays a typical stream of tweets.

Deciding Whether Twitter Fits Your Needs

Now that you have seen what Twitter looks like, you may be as perplexed as many other business owners who ask, "What in the world would I tweet about?" The list of answers is limited only by your creativity. The best way to find out is to read other tweets, especially from your competitors and some of the leading tweeters, such as @GuyKawasaki.

Think about your marketing goals and objectives and the audience you want to reach. Then consider whether tweeting is appropriate for your business to achieve certain goals, such as

- ✔ **Improve customer relations.** Quickly identify and resolve problems.

- ✔ **Enhance brand image.** Tweet about community activities or charity participation, for example.

- ✔ **Announce special offers and discounts.** Distribute Twitter-specific rewards for followers or offers to the general public.

- ✔ **Promote events or services.** Promote webinars, trade shows, exhibits, training sessions, or tech-support hotlines.

- ✔ **Solicit customer input.** Ask about new features or product design, or conduct a poll or survey with a tool such as Twtpoll.

- ✔ **Publicize your schedule.** This task is a perfect use for Twitter if you have a business that moves around, such as a coffee cart.

- ✔ **Take orders.** The first tweet was a to-go order for a burrito.

- ✔ **Link to white papers, e-books, and industry blogs.** These links can be on your site or elsewhere.

- ✔ **Observe and comment.** Think about industry trends, the business climate, economic shifts, new technology, or whatever else interests the audience you're trying to attract. Consider retweeting other people's comments as casting bread upon the waters; they'll come back to you.

For a good example of how a tourism business takes advantage of Twitter to attract guests, see Figure 16-2 and read the nearby sidebar, "Tweets help Three Tree Inn take flight."

Whatever you do, don't create an endless list of tweets about your business. You don't want your Twitter stream to read like a list of advertisements. Aim for a ratio of no more than one promotional tweet to ten on other topics. Marketing is about your customers, not about you.

Twitter works best when it's used often. Plan to tweet at least three times per week — preferably, daily. A few times a day is okay, too! To reduce the hassle significantly, you can schedule tweets by using a dashboard tool such as TweetDeck or HootSuite (see Chapter 19).

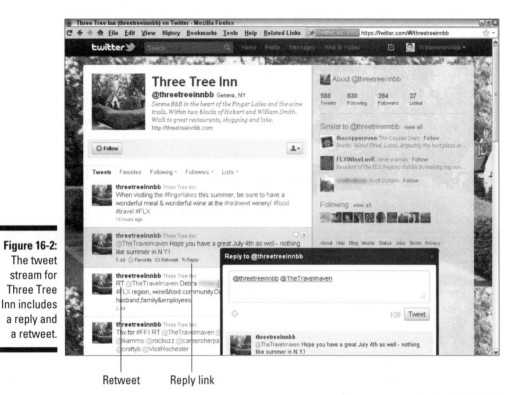

Figure 16-2:
The tweet stream for Three Tree Inn includes a reply and a retweet.

Retweet   Reply link

Courtesy of Three Tree Inn

Tweets help Three Tree Inn take flight

Three Tree Inn (www.threetreeinnbb.com) is a serene, three-bedroom bed and breakfast in Geneva, New York. When the inn opened in March 2010, the website went live simultaneously, says co-owner Marcia Swenson. "We immediately started receiving reservations." Now more than 90 percent of their guests find the inn online and make reservations.

About a year later, the inn went on Twitter (http://twitter.com/#!/threetreeinnbb) almost accidentally, when some of their best friends, Mike and Charneil Swenson (no relation), visited for New Year's. A conversation about Twitter turned into an account "and

the next thing we knew, Mike was making chili, and we were tweeting!" Mike helped the owners identify "the right people to follow," and sure enough people started following back. Visits to the website increased dramatically, from 149 in December 2010 to 517 in January 2011.

The inn tries to follow people on Twitter who like to travel, as well as people interested in wine, birding, biking, running, swimming, and nature. "The main marketing goal for our Twitter presence is to drive traffic to our website, but also to learn what it is that people are seeking," Swenson notes, giving credence to the need to listen, not just to talk, on Twitter.

"Because we are a very small business, our marketing budget is miniscule," explains Swenson. "Twitter interested us as a means of marketing, that would cost us time, but not money." She tries to avoid promoting the inn, focusing instead on up-to-date information and pictures about "things to do" in the Finger Lakes area, which would be cumbersome to update on the website.

Marcia and her co-owner Paul read and post on Twitter about three times a day between them. When Marcia had to take an unexpected leave of absence, visits to their website decreased. "All that aside, I miss following my favorite #'s, and especially the #'s for our area, that so many tourists follow."

"Retweets are nice," she says, "but what matters most . . . is the number of people that click through to our website, as well as the number of our followers." As of July 2011, the inn has amassed 394 followers, appears on 27 lists, follows 830 people, and has a retweet rank higher than 67 percent of all the other users on Twitter.

The inn also belongs to the Geneva Area Chamber of Commerce and the Finger Lakes Tourism Association, both of which have a strong Internet presence, and records excellent reviews on TripAdvisor. "Good, old-fashioned word-of-mouth has brought us guests, and we enjoy significant return visits, which we are the most proud of."

Swenson insists that Twitter is about relationships, not selling a product. "We have consciously chosen not to try to 'sell' our business, but rather offer people something of interest, something useful for them when they are traveling."

Even if you schedule tweets, you must still read, retweet, choose whom to follow, recruit followers, and monitor results. Allow at least two hours per week for all these Twitter activities.

To catch the attention of the largest number of prospects, schedule your tweets during the times of heaviest Twitter activity: 11 a.m. to 3 p.m. local time. Tuesday is the busiest day, followed by Wednesday and Friday. If you want less competition from other tweets, schedule other times.

Audience size

Twitter has not only found its voice but also given one to millions: Its 175 million registered account holders produce an estimated 200 million tweets a day. Some 13 percent of all U.S. adults online were using Twitter in 2011. Usage is projected to continue rising at double-digit rates. For more fascinating Twitter numerology, check http://thenextweb.com/twitter/files/2011/06/BuySellAds_TwitterUsers.png.

Twitter, in particular, is dominated by power users. The vast majority of users either read messages only or post only one or two messages per week. According to a 2011 study by Mashable, only .05 percent of Twitter users write 50 percent of the tweets read by everyone else. Many of those frequent tweeters are media companies that continually post news.

The true number of active users — even as readers — is much less than the number of accounts. In early 2011, Business Insider (www.businessinsider. com) found that only 68 percent of accounts followed at least one other user, and barely 50 percent had at least one follower. Figure 16-3 illustrates their findings.

Figure 16-3:
The number of accounts is much higher than the number of *active* users, defined as someone who follows at least ten others.

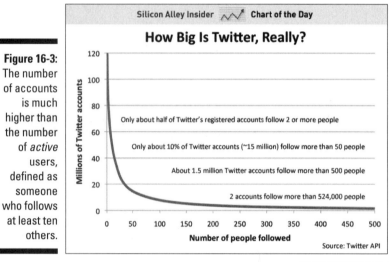

Silicon Alley Insider   Chart of the Day

How Big Is Twitter, Really?

Only about half of Twitter's registered accounts follow 2 or more people

Only about 10% of Twitter accounts (~15 million) follow more than 50 people

About 1.5 million Twitter accounts follow more than 500 people

2 accounts follow more than 524,000 people

Millions of Twitter accounts / Number of people followed

Source: Twitter API

Courtesy of Business Insider

Twitter demographics

Data shows that the highest rate of Twitter use occurs in the 18-to-34-year-old bracket, but it's growing quickly among older users. Figure 16-4 provides the Quantcast summary for Twitter demographics. Quantcast did not directly measure these data; these are estimates only.

If you plan to incorporate Twitter into your online marketing strategy, include it in your Social Media Marketing Plan. (See Chapter 13 or download the form from the Downloads tab at www.dummies.com/go/webmarketingfd3e.) For more information about Twitter, see *Social Media Marketing All-in-One For Dummies,* by Jan Zimmerman and Doug Sahlin; *Twitter For Dummies,* by Laura Fitton, Michael Gruen, and Leslie Poston; or *Twitter Marketing For Dummies,* by Kyle Lacy (all published by John Wiley & Sons, Inc.).

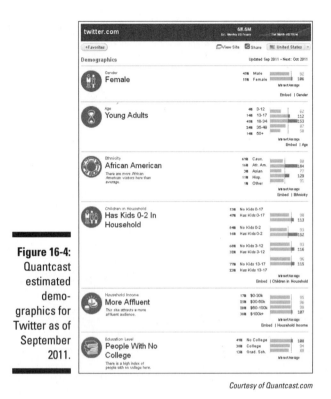

Figure 16-4:
Quantcast
estimated
demo-
graphics for
Twitter as of
September
2011.

Courtesy of Quantcast.com

Implementing Twitter

Creating a Twitter account and completing your profile are simple tasks. An account requires only your name, e-mail address, and password. Twitter verifies the information and suggests a username, which you can change. Leave your username in lowercase and try to keep it short!

Twitter walks you through interest areas to locate accounts you might want to follow and to offer a chance to add friends from your existing e-mail address books. You can skip these screens and return to them later.

Your last step is to write your *profile,* a short description of 160 or fewer characters. The profile appears on your public profile page and in search results and other locations. Be sure to include your geographical location and the URL for your primary web presence. Don't worry: All these entries can be changed later. Click Save and you're done.

Try shortening your 250-character page description meta tag (see Chapter 7) to use as your profile. Be sure the text includes at least one of your most important search terms. Note the search terms *frozen yogurt* in the profile for Olo Yogurt, shown previously in Figure 16-1.

Advertising on Twitter

Twitter's Promoted Products feature offers advertising options for folks with deep pockets. With a minimum monthly budget of $5,000, Twitter monetizes its site with ad revenues from major multinationals. Some reports show advertising running as much as $120,000 a day.

If you have ad dollars to spare, you can get started at `http://business.twitter.com/advertise/start`. Advertisers can obtain detailed analytics at `http://business.twitter.com/advertise/analytics`.

Promoted Tweets too rich for your blood? Try pay-to-play solutions from advertising services such as `http://sponsoredtweets.com` or `http://be-a-magpie.com/en`. These sites match your advertising, usually on a CPM basis, with influential tweeters who publish or retweet messages for a fee. Be careful: This approach can easily exude a whiff of spam.

For additional assistance with Twitter, check out two tables in Bonus Chapter 5 on the Downloads tab at the book's companion website. One table is a list of helpful Twitter URLs to access internal tools, and the other lists third-party Twitter apps.

Optimizing for search on Twitter

In addition to adhering to the standard admonishments about providing good content and using well-researched keywords (see Chapter 7), you can follow a few extra guidelines to improve your ranking in search results on both internal Twitter searches and external searches:

- ✔ **Your name on Twitter acts as a title tag.** To benefit from branding, use your company name as your @address.

- ✔ **Pack your one-line profile with keywords.** Your 160-character Twitter profile serves as the description meta tag on search engines.

- ✔ **On the same Profile page, use your business address as your location.** This helps your company appear on local searches.

✔ **Collect Twitter followers.** Followers are essentially internal links on Twitter. They carry special value if your followers themselves have a large number of followers.

✔ **Include keywords in your tweets and retweets whenever possible.** With its 140-character limit, Twitter is a good place to use single-word terms.

✔ **Stuff your hashtags.** Try to use keywords in Twitter #hashtags.

✔ **Remember the importance of the initial 42 characters in a tweet.** They serve as title tags in posts; your account name is part of the count.

✔ **Increase your visibility.** Link to your Twitter profile from other sites using your name, company name, or keyword (rather than your @ address) as the link anchor text.

Tweets used to be monitored by Google's real-time search. However, following the launch of its Google+ networking service and the expiration of its contract with Twitter, Google suspended its Realtime Search function temporarily in July 2011. Watch the presses on this one: It isn't clear when Google will relaunch Realtime Search or whether Twitter will be included.

Assessing Your Twitter Success

As with other forms of social media, a series of internal performance measures gauge how your Twitter campaign stacks up. Twitter provides only a handful of statistics: number of tweets you have posted, number of people following you, number of people you follow, number of lists you're on, and number of times a specific tweet has been retweeted.

Here are the most important internal performance metrics:

✔ **Number of qualified followers:** The more the merrier, but watch for spammy followers who hope that you'll mindlessly follow them back.

✔ **Ratio of followers to following:** Aim for at least twice as many followers as those you're following.

To help prevent spammers, Twitter may suspend your account if you follow many, many more accounts than those who follow you.

✔ **Number of retweets:** The more you retweet, the more your message spreads and the better you become at posting information that others find interesting; find this number by searching for RT@*yourusername*.

✔ **Number of searches:** Search for your topic #hashtag or #*yourusername;* searching for @*yourusername* tells you how many times other people mention you in their tweets.

✔ **Clicks tracked:** Use analytics from a third-party URL-shortening tool; Twitter's automatic link shortener doesn't include analytics.

Referral links from Twitter appear in Google Analytics. You can use a filter within Google Analytics to group all your social media into one category. For additional statistics, see Twitalyzer, TweetStats, or RetweetRank or other tools described in Chapter 19.

Chapter 17

Linking Up with LinkedIn

- -

In This Chapter

▶ Deciding whether LinkedIn is right for your business

▶ Putting the basics in place

▶ Making the most of LinkedIn

▶ Measuring your LinkedIn success

- -

Social media marketing is, first and foremost, a method of networking online. From your own experience, you already know the importance of offline networking to find vendors, employees, and prospects, to learn about industry trends, and to hear the latest insider gossip. From tip networks to trade associations and chambers of commerce, networking is a mantra for business owners. LinkedIn, at www.linkedin.com, turns that whispered mantra into a cybershout.

LinkedIn, whose initial public offering in May 2011 peaked at more than twice its initial valuation, has morphed into the primary professional networking site on the web. With 100 million members worldwide (44 million in the United States), LinkedIn claims that more than one user joins every *second:* http://blog.linkedin.com/100million.

More than 2 million businesses have created LinkedIn company pages; 1.3 million of those are small companies. In this chapter, I discuss why your business might want to be one of them, especially if you are a B2B firm. I also discuss ways to get the most out of your LinkedIn presence.

 If you decide to include LinkedIn as part of your social media activities, be sure to include it in the Social Media Marketing Plan, which you can download on the Downloads tab at www.dummies.com/go/webmarketingfd3e.

For more information about LinkedIn, see *Social Media Marketing All-in-One For Dummies,* by Jan Zimmerman and Doug Sahlin (John Wiley & Sons, Inc.).

Deciding Whether LinkedIn Is a Good Fit

Relying on the theory of *six degrees of separation* (everyone is connected by a chain of no more than five others), B2B (business-to-business) social networks such as LinkedIn are used primarily for finding prospective clients, introducing dealmakers, hiring people, searching for jobs, and finding *tips* (sales leads), not for direct sales. You can easily cross-promote between your website and LinkedIn.

You can receive 90 percent of the value of LinkedIn by using its free version, so joining is a no-brainer. When you join, your company profile will look similar to the one established by Red Frog Events, shown in Figure 17-1. Company profiles are visible to both members and nonmembers; LinkedIn members also see connections with staff and additional information.

More menu

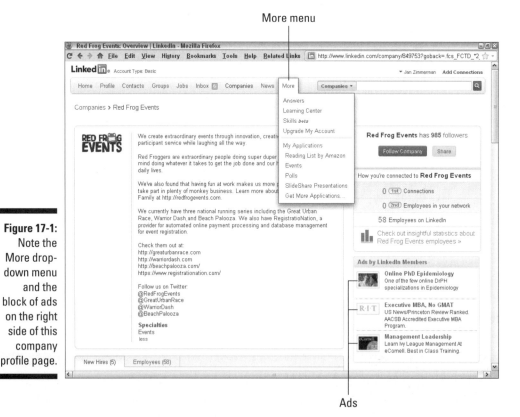

Figure 17-1:
Note the
More drop-
down menu
and the
block of ads
on the right
side of this
company
profile page.

Ads

Courtesy of Red Frog Events LLC, Warrior Dash, Great Urban Race, Beach Palooza

If you have a business of any kind, but especially if you sell to or buy from other companies (that's just about everyone), establish a LinkedIn profile for your company and have all your professional employees establish individual profiles.

LinkedIn users differ from the demographic profile on other networking sites, as shown in Figure 17-2. They're more likely to be male, older, Asian, and more affluent and better educated than Internet users in general; for an example, see www.quantcast.com/linkedin.com/demographics#demo. Note that the statistics in Figure 17-2 have been quantified with directly measured data.

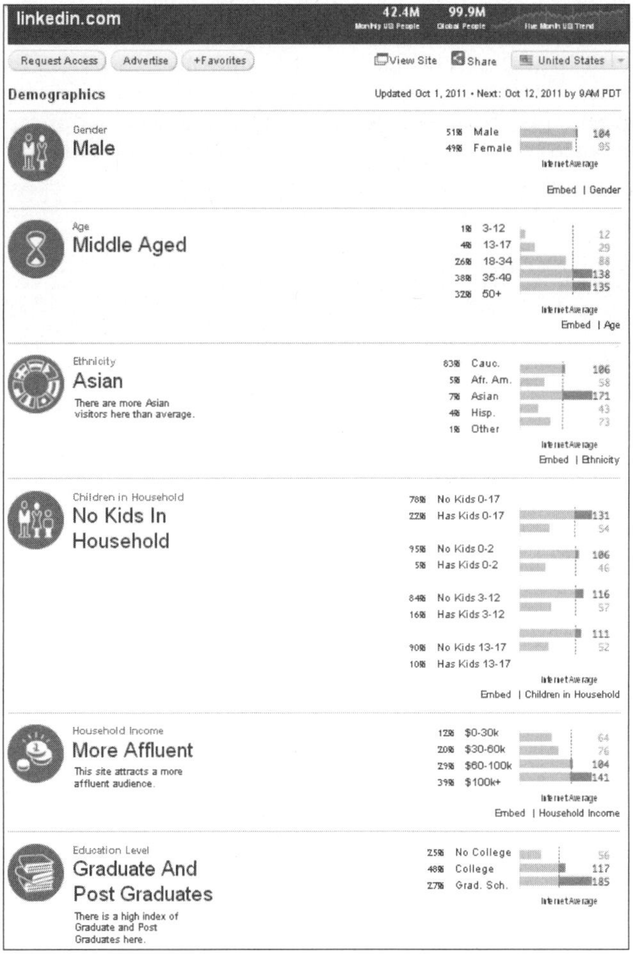

Figure 17-2:
The demographics of LinkedIn users in October 2011 differ from many other networking services.

Courtesy of Quantcast.com

Because LinkedIn is primarily a B2B network, sorting by vertical industry or job position can provide more valuable information than standard demographic profiles. You can search by people, jobs, companies, or groups under the drop-down menu. Take advantage of Advanced Search to filter results.

Implementing LinkedIn Basics

Joining LinkedIn is simple: You set up a simple account with an e-mail username and password. Then complete the profile, which is sort of an online resume for individuals (such as the one shown in Figure 17-3) or a corporate backgrounder for a company (refer to Figure 17-1).

LinkedIn is well designed, with obvious prompts and a straightforward, step-by-step structure. Click the See Examples link on various fields for additional explanation and tips. Because LinkedIn is always evolving, options and directions may change at any time. LinkedIn is good about notifying members of changes.

Figure 17-3:
A personal profile works well for freelancers and one-person professional companies, as well as for employees.

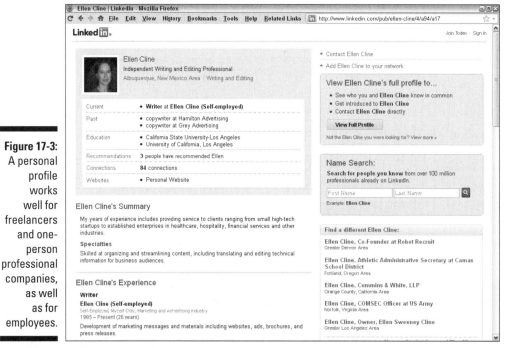

Courtesy of Ellen Cline, www.ellenwrites.com

Don't be boring! Use descriptive words that point out your achievements rather than just list employers' names and job titles. You can include a creative, short narrative or story in the summary and write a headline with a benefit, such as *creative problem solver* or *believer in zero defects*.

As always, cross-link between your website, other social media sites, and LinkedIn. Visit these links for buttons and widgets:

- ✔ **Custom Share button for web pages:** www.linkedin.com/publishers

- ✔ **Share button for browsers:** www.linkedin.com/static?key= browser_bookmarklet

- ✔ **Chicklets for members with and without calls to action:** http:// developer.linkedin.com/docs/DOC-1101#general-use

Getting the Most Out of LinkedIn

Because you're competing for visibility against millions of other individuals and companies, you need to undertake some targeted activities to reach the people you want to reach. LinkedIn gives you five primary methods: Groups, Answers, Recommendations, Advertising, and using *LinkedIn Today*.

Visit Bonus Chapter 5 on the Downloads tab of the book's companion website to find a convenient list of helpful LinkedIn URLs.

Participating in LinkedIn groups

LinkedIn groups, like Facebook groups (see Chapter 15) and Twitter hashtags (see Chapter 16), give you the chance to identify users who share your interests and who might become potential clients, vendors, or helpful connections. The key, as always, is first to monitor potential groups and then to offer helpful suggestions and comments, without overtly selling your products or services. Standard forum etiquette applies! To view potential groups, use the drop-down menu under the Groups tab in the top navigation pane.

Providing answers on LinkedIn

One of the best ways to develop visibility on LinkedIn is to become an "expert" in the Answers section. To see the Answers section, go to the More tab in the top navigation pane (refer to Figure 17-1) and choose Answers from the drop-down menu.

Collecting recommendations

LinkedIn claims that "users with recommendations are three times as likely to get inquiries through LinkedIn searches." Use the Advanced Search feature to sort results by *relationship + recommendations,* so that profiles with the highest number of recommendations appear higher in search results.

Now is the time to call in cards from your friends, colleagues, satisfied clients, and compatriots. You can review any recommendations you receive, so you can always decide whether or not to publish them. To request or receive recommendations, simply choose Recommendations from the drop-down menu on the Profile tab in the top navigation area.

Advertising on LinkedIn

With its capability to segment a hard-to-reach B2B audience by industry, job title, and other categories, LinkedIn can deliver "eyeballs" that may be more difficult or expensive to achieve by using other paid advertising. For more information on LinkedIn advertising, see www.linkedin.com/advertising or http://partner.linkedin.com/ads/faqs.

LinkedIn members can select text-only ads in a single line across the top of various pages, or they can select a combination of small image and text ads in the rectangular ad unit in the right column of a page. These self-service ads offer a choice between a standard PPC (pay per click, as discussed in Chapter 11) with a $2-per-click minimum and a CPM (cost per thousand impressions) option. The campaign structure is comparable to that of Google AdWords or Bing/Yahoo! To see examples of the right-side ad block, refer to Figure 17-1; the top ad appears in Figure 17-3.

LinkedIn also offers *display* (banner) ads on specific pages. You must negotiate display ad costs separately with LinkedIn. (See Chapter 12 for more information on banner ads.)

Reading LinkedIn Today

Found on the drop-down menu under the News tab, *LinkedIn Today* aggregates business news from dozens of prime sources. You can customize your news selection by publication or industry, or both, by electing to follow various options in the Browse All section on the top menu.

Early anecdotal evidence from LinkedIn members indicates that both profile views and referral links have increased since LinkedIn Today was introduced.

Assessing Your LinkedIn Success

LinkedIn offers two levels of statistical reports:

- ✔ **Profile Stats:** For free accountholders
- ✔ **Profile Stats Pro:** For Premium members

For more information, see `https://help.linkedin.com/app/answers/detail/a_id/4508/~/profile-stats-and-profile-stats-pro` or `http://learn.linkedin.com/the-homepage/profilestats`. According to LinkedIn, the standard option provides this information:

- ✔ The number of connections and recommendations you have
- ✔ As many as five results of who's viewed your profile
- ✔ The number of visits to your profile
- ✔ The number of times you've appeared in search results

The Premium version adds a full list of who's viewed your profile, trends, and breakdowns of profile views by keyword, industry, and geography.

If you remain anonymous, which is the default setting for a free member, you see no statistics. You must select the option to display your name and head-line on the pop-up screen labeled What Others See When You've Viewed Their Profile. This screen pops up on login or whenever you edit your profile (`www.linkedin.com/profile/public-profile-settings`). You can change your settings back to Anonymous at any time.

To view your stats, log in to your LinkedIn account and enter `www.linkedin.com/wvmx/profile` into your browser's Address field. Additional statistics are available with paid memberships. (Alternatively, enter `http://learn.linkedin.com/the-homepage/profilestats` and click the button labeled View Your Profile Stats on the right side.) See a typical statistical screen in Figure 17-4. Note the toggle between Views and Appearances in Search on the chart as well as the paid text ad at the top of the page.

LinkedIn is fully compatible with Google Analytics. Visits to your website from LinkedIn appear in your referrer statistics. To track e-mails from LinkedIn, specify a different e-mail address for contact purposes in your profile. (For example, mine might be `linkedin@watermelonweb.com`.)

Toggle between these two options

Paid text ad

Figure 17-4:
A LinkedIn
results page
from Profile
Stats.

The element that truly counts is the return on your investment of time, not intermediate performance criteria: Having 12 connections that bring you business is better than having 112 that don't. This philosophy had a major effect on Barrett Foundation (an organization that helps homeless women and children in New Mexico), whose mention in a LinkedIn group (see Figure 17-5) brought it an ongoing donor relationship with a wine company, as described in the nearby sidebar, "Barrett House builds a foundation with LinkedIn."

LinkedIn isn't the only business social network. For the names of others that reach a more specific market, review the list of other business networks in Bonus Chapter 5 on the Downloads tab of the companion website.

Barrett House builds a foundation with LinkedIn

While Barbara Lemaire, PhD, was the director of development at Barrett Foundation (`http://barrettfoundation.org`), a nonprofit organization that helps homeless women and children in Albuquerque, New Mexico, rebuild their lives, she started the LinkedIn group Non-Profit Organizations of New Mexico.

The group helped Barrett Foundation get noticed by Billington Wines, the maker of Big Tattoo Wines, which donates 50 cents of every local sale to a local charity. When the company entered the New Mexico market in 2008, it chose the Barrett Foundation as its beneficiary. The demographic profiles of LinkedIn members are quite close to the demographics of the Barrett Foundation's typical donor.

Founded in 1985 by Brother Mathias Barrett, the Barrett Foundation provides emergency shelter, food, clothing, case management, critical skills training, and support for women to establish a more stable future for themselves and their children. Although Barrett Foundation has no LinkedIn profile itself, it uses its website and newsletters, direct mail, Facebook, print ads, and social networking offline.

LeMaire created her own LinkedIn profile and then the group's profile, after participating in a webinar and reading many articles. Now the chief strategist and CEO of Social Media Made Simple, LeMaire recommends that small businesses contribute to groups, participate in LinkedIn Answers, reach out to connections, and offer excellent content in their updates. "I measure my success by the number of discussions I can contribute to," and of course, by new clients. "Recommendations are an important part of my profile."

Figure 17-5: A mention in the LinkedIn group Non-Profit Organizations in New Mexico led to donations for Barrett Foundation.

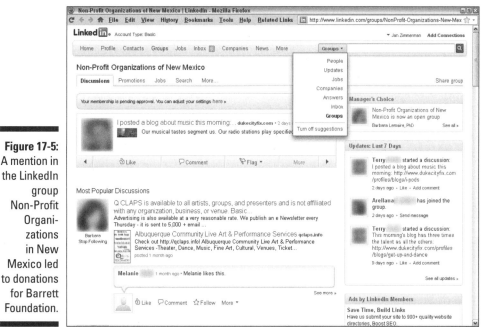

Courtesy of Social Media Made Simple

Chapter 18

Reaching Customers with Other Social Media Services

Without a doubt, Facebook, Twitter, and LinkedIn are the elephants in the social marketing zoo, at least in terms of the largest number of visits per month. But this is one big zoo! In this chapter, I look at several medium-size members of the zoo: geolocation services, meetups, and your own custom community. Then I point you in the direction of many other social channels.

If you decide to include one or more of the social media channels in this chapter as part of your social media activities, be sure to include them in your Social Media Marketing Plan, which you can find on the Downloads tab at www.dummies.com/go/webmarketingfd3e.

Comparing the Benefits of Other Social Media

With the exception of Ning (which can become your primary web presence if you use your own domain name), the more targeted social media sites I discuss in this chapter are best used to supplement your other online marketing efforts. A quick look at the chart in Figure 18-1 from the StatCounter Global Stats site shows you why.

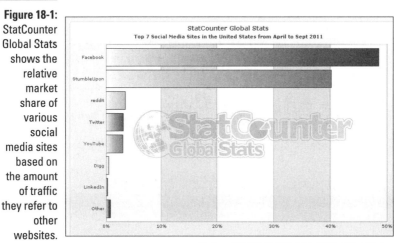

Courtesy of Stat Counter Global Stats http://gs.statcounter.com

As the StatCounter graph at `http://gs.statcounter.com/#social_media-US-monthly-201104-201109-bar` clearly indicates, other services don't offer the reach of Facebook. Market share on this site is ranked not by traffic to the sites themselves but, rather, by "the amount of traffic they refer to other sites." This approach may be especially valuable for business analysis because it discounts personal users who stay on social media sites solely to communicate with their friends. If you don't see your pet social media channel on this chart, it ranked too low to be visible.

Neither overall traffic on a social media site nor its number of referrals truly reflects its potential value to your business. As you consider the sites in this chapter and the next, ask yourself whether the site reaches the prospective target market you seek. If so, the value of that site may be beyond rubies. I now look specifically at geosocial and custom meeting services.

Going Geosocial or Staying Put

Location. Location. Location. It works in real estate. Now it's another key to successful social media marketing. Several applications of location-based services, including social mapping (identifying where people are) and location-based games, now exist. They're evolving quickly into loyalty programs that reward consumers for patronizing particular retailers.

The convergence of GPS, mobile phones, and social media offers the holy grail of opportunity for marketers. Theoretically, you can inform potential customers that you offer exactly what they're looking for, when they're look-ing for it, and within just a few miles of their locations.

For most businesses, geolocation marketing involves a teaser deal that attracts nearby residents or out-of-town visitors who "check in" online when they arrive at the establishment. This concept is particularly attractive for events, tourist sites, restaurants, and entertainment venues. Almost all these services, such as Foursquare, Gowalla, and Loopt, notify subscribers by text message or on their mobile sites whenever an offer is available nearby.

For additional geolocation services, look in Bonus Chapter 5 on the Downloads tab of the book's companion website.

Each service operates a little differently, with some offering virtual badges or special offers to repeat customers (those who check in most often) or first-timers. Unlike group coupons (see Chapter 12), these offers are generally inexpensive, so merchants face no significant losses.

In March 2010, Foursquare, one of the most prominent geolocation services, added a tool that lets businesses monitor — by number, gender, day of week, or time of day — visitors who check in to Foursquare. Retailers won't see a better breakdown until cyberpsychics start offering marketing services.

Promote your geosocial participation in as many ways as possible: on your other social media accounts and websites, on signs at cash registers, and even on sandwich boards on sidewalks.

Because most individual users select only one service, it doesn't hurt to sign up for several of them to increase your coverage. To make your life easier, try a tool such as PlacePunch (at `http://placepunch.com`) to coordinate multiple location check-in services.

Considering your decision

Whether you should use these social mapping services depends on the nature of your business, whether your customer base is using them, and which location-based activities consume your prospective customers' time. Most of these services work on multiple smartphone, tablet, and desktop platforms, so the choice of device isn't a concern. Consider these issues:

- ✔ **Many cellphone apps already offer a service (for example, weather reports, road conditions, and lists of gas prices at various stations around town) and then add a sponsor.** If all you're trying to do is reach the consumer-on-the-go who is ready to buy, ask yourself whether you need more than that. Maybe a pay per click (PPC) ad on a mobile search engine is enough.

✓ **Enough people living near or visiting your location have to use a particular geolocation application to make it worth the effort.** This issue is nontrivial because most services don't publicize this data. Research the number of users in your area with both the service provider and a third-party source, such as Alexa. The numbers can fluctuate widely.

After you estimate the size of the potential audience (the *reach*), remember that only a small percentage of the audience is likely to become customers. Your best bet: Ask existing customers which location-based services they use.

Like politics, geomarketing is local. No matter the size of the total user base for a specific location tool in your area, you may draw a large audience of geosocial users if you happen to own the pizza place across the street from the computer science department at the community college.

✓ **Your prospective customers have to be willing to participate.** A TechCrunch report (at `http://techcrunch.com/2011/06/20/foursquare-now-officially-at-10-million-users`) found that the Foursquare user base shifted from two-thirds male and one-third female in 2010 to a gender-balanced audience in 2011. However, other surveys show that three-fourths of women avoid location-based services, partly out of fear of stalking and partly from lack of interest. You must take privacy issues into account.

✓ **Demographics characteristics matter.** Be cautious: The demographics and statistics on these sites change quickly as they become more popular and move out of the early adopter stage. ComScore found that location services in 2011 drew a predominantly young audience — more than half under 35 — and a disproportionate number of full-time students (23 percent).

✓ **The temptation is great to "go geo."** Current estimates show that locally targeted ads may produce results as much as ten times better than untargeted advertising.

To get an idea of the number of members on one of these sites, try creating a user account or look at their profile on Quantcast. Then scan the list of places in your area (sometimes called *venues* or *spots*) for the inclusion of neighbors and competitors, and look at the maximum number of check-ins at those locations. Of course, a high-tech conference that draws a huge number of users may be a one-time opportunity worth taking advantage of.

Qdoba Mexican Grill counted on the Foursquare demographic profile of young males with its funny Foursquare promotion shown in Figure 18-2. The restaurant chain awards a free lunch to the best shout (comment) on Foursquare about how to beat "burrito boredom." To further extend the effect of its Foursquare campaign, the restaurant randomly gives gift certificates to people who also tweet their Foursquare check-ins.

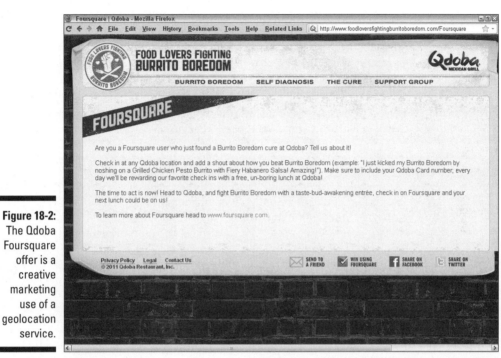

Figure 18-2:
The Qdoba Foursquare offer is a creative marketing use of a geolocation service.

Courtesy of Qdoba®; Qdoba Mexican Grill®; Qdoba Restaurant Corp®

Having geosocial fun

Each of the services described in the following list offers somewhat different rewards and options, so explore to find the ones that best serve your needs:

- ✔ **Foursquare** lets business owners manage a variety of rewards based on frequency of use, new use, or other factors; users earn virtual badges.

- ✔ **Gowalla** combines business offers with game-style activities, such as picking up or leaving articles in a location (as in geocaching), and rewards users with virtual "stamps." For every location displayed on the screen, viewers can see how many other Gowalla Passport holders visited and how many times they checked in.

- ✔ **Loopt** enables users to share comments, photos, and personal recommendations with friends for a particular location in real-time; friends can compete to win rewards for merchants.

✔ **Twitter** lets users opt in to include geotags with their tweets. Some third-party developers use this feature already: Some examples are Twellowhood (`www.twellow.com/twellowhood`), `http://TwitterLocal.net`, Twitter Nano (`www.twitternano.com`), and NearbyTweets (`www.nearbytweets.com`). Twitter is now using geotagging within its Promoted Products to expand advertising opportunities.

✔ **Yelp**, a well-known restaurant review site, has added a location-based, check-in feature to its smartphone version.

For a creative use of Foursquare, see how Earthjustice integrated Foursquare with billboards in a fundraising campaign, as shown in Figure 18-3. The campaign drove traffic from mobile devices to the Earthjustice website. Read more about Earthjustice, a nonprofit environmental law firm in San Francisco, in the nearby sidebar, "Earthjustice locates donations with Foursquare."

Figure 18-3: To raise funds, Earthjustice used a Foursquare call to action on billboards.

Courtesy of Earthjustice/earthjustice.org

Earthjustice locates donations with Foursquare

Earthjustice, headquartered in San Francisco, is the nation's leading nonprofit environmental law firm. Because all its work is done pro bono (free!), Earthjustice relies on marketing and fundraising. Ray Wan, manager of marketing and design, notes that the firm's interactive website remains the central hub for public communications and interaction.

Earthjustice rolled out its innovative Foursquare ad campaign (refer to Figure 18-3), in San Francisco in the summer of 2010 for three to four months. Wan says, "We know that the average Foursquare user is much younger than our traditional donor base, but we wanted to broaden our appeal to a younger audience — [they] will be our future supporters!" The campaign had two other explicit goals: raise money for legal work and raise brand awareness through media exposure from publicity about the campaign itself.

"Checking in on Foursquare is fast and simple — something you can do in minutes while you're waiting for the train," explains Wan, "whereas providing a regular web URL requires the user to complete a lot more online steps before they can take the desired action. The longer the process, the more people you lose at every step."

The most important metric was the number of check-ins at each ad. The more check-ins received, the more money their major donor would give. Earthjustice used Foursquare itself to track campaign performance because that data is built in.

To promote the campaign, Wan included the Foursquare chicklet to convey immediately which social media tool to use. He points to the catchy headlines and visuals used to attract people's attention. "It's not every day that you see a giant hamster-like animal (the endangered pika) staring at you during your morning commute." Earthjustice also had a minimal presence for the campaign on Facebook and Twitter.

"Aside from the prominent ad placements in some of San Francisco's heaviest trafficked Metro stations, and the press release that we pitched to reporters and social media blogs, we did not advertise the ads in any other way. We knew that the concept's novelty (the first creative use of Foursquare for nonprofit fundraising) would attract some media attention, so we just let the ads speak for themselves."

"Outdoor advertising is not cheap!" Wan cautions. "From the cost of the advertising space to the production of the actual physical ads, the costs can be prohibitive for small or medium-size businesses. Luckily, Earthjustice was able to get many of the services donated or at reduced rates." He suggests that other nonprofits consider partnering with socially responsible businesses that already have physical storefronts to eliminate the cost of having to buy physical advertising space. Wan is forthright about the benefits and limitations of Foursquare. "For example, there is no way for a person who checks in to leave an e-mail address. "You can individually message them on Foursquare, but if you get thousands of check-ins, it's very labor intensive. Since this was a stand-alone, experimental campaign, we decided it was worth it. But if a future campaign required . . . e-mail [captures], we would consider a different . . . platform."

Look for Earthjustice at `www.earth justice.org`, `www.facebook.com/ earthjustice`, or `www.twitter.com/ earthjustice`.

Organizing Social Meetups

A *meetup* bridges the gap between the cyberworld and the one we live in. A meetup lets people with similar interests easily organize meetings for fun, advocacy, or learning — or simply to meet one another.

Meetup (at www.meetup.com), which has been around since 2002, bills itself as "the world's largest network of local groups," claiming that more than 7.2 million members have attended some 250,000 meetings held by 79,000 local groups located in 45,000 cities. Meetup charges organizers a fee ranging from $12 to $19 per month for using its platform.

Meetup technology lets people find or start a group located near them. The system includes an easy-to-use interface to identify meetings within a certain distance and to reply by RSVP, find directions, and check out the history of a Meetup group. Meetup integrates nicely with Facebook events and RSVPs; it has an application for integrating with other services. In an inevitable mash-up, Meetup now allows Groupon fans to hook up at official and self-organized events via www.meetup.com/Groupon.

What an easy way to find your target market in a location close to you! Figure 18-4 shows a typical meetup screen for a salsa dance group in San Diego.

Figure 18-4:
A Meetup search for salsa dance groups near San Diego produces several results, including this one.

Courtesy of SalsaCrazy (Evan Margolin)

Building a Community of Your Own

Ning, which bills itself as "the social platform for the world's interests and passions online," is an easy-to-use platform for creating a web presence with built-in social networking capabilities. In addition to text pages, Ning (at www.ning.com) offers customizable options for member profiles, blogs, forums, photo and video uploads, and other social marketing tools. For more in-depth information, check out *Ning For Dummies,* by Manny Hernandez (John Wiley & Sons, Inc.).

The power of Ning rests on the idea that real communities of shared interest will hold people's attention and participation over time. For businesses, this concept translates into building a community that addresses the content area in which customers operate, what they do, and what they care about. In turn, communities build customer loyalty, which translates into word-of-mouth advertising and increased sales.

Figure 18-5 shows a typical Ning community site from the tool manufacturer Kreg Jig (at www.kregtool.com), which cross-links between its Ning community and its website, YouTube, and Facebook pages.

Figure 18-5: A typical Ning community site from Kreg Jig, a manufacturer of woodworking tools.

Courtesy of Kreg Tool Company

Slicing and Dicing Social Media

Social networking communities can be sorted vertically by industry or horizontally by demographics (age, gender, ethnicity, education, or income). After doing a little research, you can stratify communities according to other, commonly used marketing segmentation parameters, such as geographical location, life stage (student, young married, family with kids, empty nester, retired), or psychographics (beliefs or behaviors).

Stratified sites have a much smaller audience than the major social networks do. However, if you choose correctly, the users of these sites will closely resemble the profile of your typical client or customer, making them better prospects. Consider the difference between advertising at the Super Bowl versus distributing a flyer at a local high school football game. It all depends on where your audience is.

Your business can make a much bigger splash on smaller sites. Frankly, gaining visibility and traction on a large social networking site is so difficult that you need a marketing campaign specifically for that purpose (for example, to acquire 2,000 followers on Twitter). On a smaller site, your business becomes a big fish in a small pond, quickly establishing itself as an expert resource or a source of useful products or services.

To pursue stratified sites in greater depth, look in Bonus Chapter 5 on the Downloads tab of the companion website for the sections about selecting social networks by vertical industry sector and selecting social networks by demographics. See also in Bonus Chapter 5 the list of social network research URLs in Table BC5-13.

To find out even more about some of these other social media channels, see *Social Media Marketing All-in-One For Dummies,* which I wrote with Doug Sahlin (John Wiley & Sons, Inc.).

Chapter 19

Using Social Media Tools

*P*articipating in several social media channels could quickly become overwhelming if services and tool sites didn't help business owners keep everything under control. In this chapter, you find out how to spread your company name around the web with social news and social bookmarking services and then track your cyberfame by using social monitoring tools.

Practical tools such as Follow Us and Social Sharing buttons help you cross-link all the rapidly proliferating components of your web presence, and new tools for content distribution and dashboard management save time and increase efficiency.

Getting Famous with Social News Services

Rather than rank news stories by having editors determine what's important, *social news services* such as Reddit, Digg, or Sphinn post stories recommended by their readers. Many services rank stories within a topic on the basis of popular vote.

These services have a voracious and never-ending appetite for new content. If your business generates frequent, time-dependent news within an industry or a geographical area, posting links to your stories on social news services is almost mandatory.

Try going to Digg.com, just one of many social news sites, and search for a topic such as *iPad apps.* You'll quickly find that users must log in to vote on story quality, but anyone can read the postings. As with other types of social media, using keywords within headlines helps with search engine optimization.

Social news services complement traditional press release and public relations efforts by providing *additional* outlets for news; they don't replace a regular online and offline press release campaign.

Post links to your online press releases on as many appropriate social news services as you can. Be sure that the service carries stories about your industry and is visited by the population you're trying to reach.

For a list of popular social news services, look at Table BC5-16, in Bonus Chapter 5 on the Downloads tab at `www.dummies.com/go/webmarketing fd3e`. The table shows whether you can submit your own site or press releases and whether the news service uses popularity voting. It also indicates whether the site passes *link juice,* indicating whether search engines will recognize a transfer page rank from the source page along with the link. Focus on sites that pass link juice.

Bookmarking Your Way to Fame

Perhaps you're familiar with bookmarking favorite websites on your own computer. Web-based social bookmarking services like StumbleUpon, Faves, or Google Bookmarks not only let you access your bookmarks from anywhere but also permit you to share your favorites with others.

Unlike social news services, which focus on time-dependent articles, bookmarking sites are useful for longer-lived content, including specific content pages on your website and product detail pages from your online store. Like social news, many bookmarking sites rely on user popularity to rank bookmarks within topic areas.

For a table of popular social bookmarking services, see Bonus Chapter 5 on the Downloads tab of the book's companion website. The table shows whether you can submit your own site and whether the site passes link juice. Again, focus on sites that pass link juice.

Because you cannot submit your own URL to certain bookmarking sites, ask a friend, customer, or colleague to submit a bookmark for you.

If you do nothing else with social media channels, create social bookmarks for several pages or products. It can't hurt, and it might help.

As always, try to use search terms from your standard set somewhere in category names, tags, text, or titles for search engine purposes.

Bookmarking services for specific applications provide a much more targeted audience by subject area. Shopping sites such as Kaboodle, ThisNext, and Stylehive are terrific places for fashion product mentions. You can rarely recommend your own URLs on these outlets, but a coordinated campaign from friends, colleagues, or customers can help drive traffic to your site and vote it up.

See Bonus Chapter 5 on the Downloads tab of the book's companion website for a table of bookmark sites for specific applications. The table shows the names and topics for many such sites.

Just as you use calls to action for visitors to Like you on Facebook, you can use calls to action to ask visitors to vote for your products on shopping bookmark sites.

Social bookmarking services now attract automated spammers who promise to submit your website to hundreds of bookmarking sites for a fee. Google and other search engines watch for these spammers, and you can be blackballed from their natural search. Avoid these sites.

Keeping Up Appearances with Social Monitoring

The buzzword of the social media whirl is *engagement.* The only problem is that no one truly knows what it means! The broadest definition is how often a visitor to any of your social media pages takes an action of some sort that benefits your business.

Every form of social media has its own internal performance measurements, which I discuss in their respective chapters. Other social media tools try to measure the value of social media across multiple services, making up their own parameters as they go. For instance, Social Mention (`http://socialmention.com`), shown in Figure 19-1, uses the concepts described in this list:

- **Strength:** The likelihood that your brand is discussed in social media expressed as a ratio of mentions in 24 hours divided by total mentions.
- **Reach:** The range of influence defined as the number of individuals referencing your brand divided by the total number of mentions.
- **Sentiment:** The ratio of positive to negative mentions. (Be aware that linguistic analysis is often inaccurate.)
- **Passion:** The likelihood of repeat mentions of your brand by the same person.

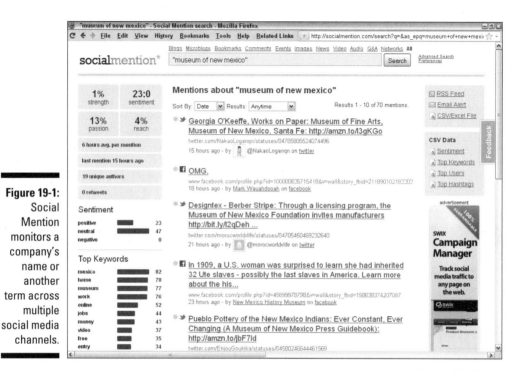

Figure 19-1:
Social
Mention
monitors a
company's
name or
another
term across
multiple
social media
channels.

To see a list of social monitoring and reputation-checking tools, look at Table BC5-19, in Bonus Chapter 5 on the Downloads tab of the companion website. No one truly knows what these internal performance metrics mean for business success. Is someone who tweets twice about your company a better qualified prospect than someone who never does? Do mentions in multiple blogs truly increase your business's brand recognition? How many times must someone post to your Facebook wall before they purchase something?

Because different companies may calculate self-referential parameters differently, you can't draw meaningful comparisons between different tools; you can only watch for trends.

Although computers are good at counting (they'll count whatever you ask them to), keep your eye on the bottom line. It's the only number that truly counts.

Going Viral with Follow Us and Social Sharing Buttons

Social media buttons fall into two categories:

- ✔ **Follow Us:** This button, sometimes called a *chicklet,* encourages visitors to any component of your online presence to visit your other components. *Badges* are giant-size Follow Us buttons; they often include a social component such as followers or live tweets in a larger display. Every component of your online presence should link to every other one.

- ✔ **Social Sharing:** This button lets visitors easily post links to your content on any of *their own* social media accounts, expanding the former idea of tell-a-friend e-mails into a whole new dimension of word-of-web marketing. Put these reminder buttons on every page of your online presence, and even on individual posts within a blog.

Use *calls to action* to remind people what you want them to do with these buttons, such as Like on Facebook and Follow Us on Twitter.

The companion website offers a handy list of sources for Follow Us chicklets (Bonus Chapter 5) and another list of sources for social sharing buttons (Bonus Chapter 2). Whenever possible, choose a tool service that offers analytics so that you can see how well the buttons are working. Look on the Downloads tab for this information.

Unless you're comfortable posting snippets of HTML into your source code, have your web developer or programmer place these icons for you. Some sites, such as Constant Contact e-newsletters, now insert Social Sharing and Follow Us buttons for you.

Managing Your Social Life with Online Tools

If keeping track of all your social media channels isn't daunting, I don't know what is. Fortunately, you can find tools to help you distribute your content simultaneously to more than one location; schedule your posts in advance, manage your overall task schedule, and collect all your tasks and feeds into one convenient online dashboard.

Distributing your content

You have two basic options for distributing *(syndicating)* your content. One is to use the familiar RSS format (Real Simple Syndication); the other is to select one of the proprietary sharing options provided by various social media services or third-party tool providers.

See the companion website for sources for social syndication and content distribution. Look in Bonus Chapter 5 on the Downloads tab for this information.

RSS (real simple syndication) is definitely right up Geek Alley. Depending on your skill set and the services you're trying to match up as content sources and destinations, you may need a developer's assistance in setting up some of the other social syndication tools.

Many other syndication tools, such as Ping.fm by Seesmic, Postling, and Hootsuite, are much easier to use. For instance, Butter Lane Cupcakes, (whose site at `http://butterlane.com` is shown in Figure 19-2) quickly found that it needed to take advantage of social tools to manage a complex campaign and to support the part-time community manager it hired to tame the time-consuming content demands of the social media beast. Butter Lane chose Postling, which is shown in Figure 19-3, as a management tool. The company tells its story in the nearby sidebar "Social media ices the marketing cake for Butter Lane."

Figure 19-2:
Butter Lane Cupcakes found social media to be a great way to grow its business.

Courtesy of Butter Lane Cupcakes

Figure 19-3:
Butter Lane
Cupcakes
manages
its multi-
pronged
social
media cam-
paign with
Postling.

Scheduling with a social calendar

If you aren't already using a calendar to manage your marketing campaign, let social media become your excuse to establish one. You don't need anything fancy — the free calendars from Google, Mozilla, or Yahoo! work fine, unless you want the elaborate features that are available with more expensive options.

For a list of calendaring software, see Table BC5-22, in Bonus Chapter 5 on the Downloads tab of the companion website.

For every posting, be sure to list dates, the specific site, and who's responsible. If you sync your calendar with the Social Media Marketing Plan (discussed in Chapter 13), you have the basic management tools to integrate social media with all your other marketing efforts. You can also download the Social Media Marketing Plan from the Downloads tab on the book's companion website.

Plan your work; work your plan.

Social media ices the marketing cake for Butter Lane

Since its opening in the East Village in New York City in November 2008, Butter Lane Cupcakes has expanded from selling cupcakes to selling cake pops and Blue Bell ice cream, as well as teaching cupcake baking classes. Just a few months after opening, it added online ordering and opened a second store in Brooklyn. It draws customers to its stores and website with social media.

"There's a pretty broad target market for cupcakes," laughs co-owner Maria Baugh, who owns Butter Lane with Pam Nelson and Linda Lea. "We sell to hipster foodies, kids, 20-something single women who come in packs, gay tastemakers, soccer moms, the old, the middle aged, the young, and everyone else."

Butter Lane invests a lot of time, energy, and money in Facebook, Foursquare, Groupon, Twitter, and Yelp, in addition to Constant Contact e-mail newsletters, Google SEO, Google PPC, Tumblr, and more. With all these channels, social media management became critical, so the company signed up for Postling.com in August 2009.

Baugh quickly set up the Postling account herself, to track what's being said on Facebook, Twitter, and Yelp. Postling sends an automatic update whenever anyone refers to Butter Lane online and a daily digest of all mentions; she can respond to a mention with one click.

Though their company's social media presence definitely helps drive people to their website, Baugh cites many other benefits: getting out the Butter Lane name in a relatively inexpensively manner; building customer loyalty; engaging with customers in real-time; and managing customer service quickly and easily.

Baugh says, "It's so easy to use social media to really engage our customers and fans," noting that she can add or modify specials, promos, or contests any time from any location. "To change something on our website, I have to e-mail our website administrator, have several e-mails back and forth, then go through a few rounds of edits and tests. Then it can finally go live. I can post a contest on our Facebook page in about 30 seconds with the potential to reach thousands."

Baugh was spending 20 hours per week or more on social media until she hired a community manager in spring 2011. Sharing the responsibility has allowed the company to expand its efforts and presence significantly. "We've seen a huge increase in all our analytics. It's an investment I wish we'd made a lot earlier . . ., even when I thought we had no budget to do it," Baugh says ruefully. "It's hard to imagine spending money on something like that — isn't part of the beauty of social media is that it's 'free?' But in the long run, it's worth it."

Butter Lane uses Google Analytics, SEOmoz, and occasionally Alexa to track its marketing results. Facebook is its number one referring site, followed by Mobile Meteor, Yelp, Groupon, and Twitter. Improved conversion rates are quite important to Baugh, but she also loves the raw numbers (performance metrics), such as Facebook Likes, Twitter followers, and Foursquare check-ins. "Basically, I'm willing to try anything to get out the Butter Lane name."

"We engage with bloggers who have an interest in food. And we look for other unique and cost-effective ways to advertise, for example by sponsoring an RSS feed on the Swiss Miss (cocoa company) blog, targeting specific groups on Meetup or LinkedIn . . . and making videos for a YouTube channel." Butter Lane also plans to try out Roost, a platform that automates posting on Facebook and Twitter and helps create content. Baugh is also interested in augmented reality (computer plus real imagery) and the new Square card device, which lets people pay by using their smartphones. "I'm constantly reading Mashable.com, looking for the next thing for Butter Lane to try."

To drive people to their social media network, Butter Lane uses more than chicklets and share buttons. "We have an iPad mounted in the shop and offer a free icing shot if you Like or Follow Us while you're there. We occasionally send blasts to our e-mail list and encourage people to Like or Follow Us. We also use PlacePunch, a digital loyalty program that automatically tracks check-ins at the shop, on Foursquare, Facebook, Twitter, Yelp, and other sites."

Baugh offers nothing but enthusiasm for social media. "Do it! Use anything and everything you can. Stay current. Social media is changing by the hour, and there's a lot of opportunity. And whatever you do, read Mashable.com and *Web Marketing For Dummies,* of course!"

Here's a list of URLs for ButterLane:

```
www.butterlane.com

www.facebook.com/butterlane

https://foursquare.com/venue/
    44933

www.linkedin.com/company/
    2238041

http://butterlane.tumblr.com

www.twitter.com/#/butterlane

www.yelp.com/biz/butter-lane-
    new-york

www.youtube.com/user/Butter
    LaneCupcakes
```

Setting up a dashboard

If social media seems like a marathon, not a sprint, you have the right idea.

Consider implementing one other tool that will at least give you the illusion of control. A social media dashboard lets you collect all your various posting, reviewing, monitoring, and analyzing activities into one convenient screen. Instead of recalling umpteen different logins, you can log in once to your dashboard and take care of everything you need.

In Figure 19-4, Chris Dodson customized his NetVibes dashboard to display, on one easy-to-access screen, multiple social media channels: Digg, GoogleMail, LinkedIn, Twitter, and stories from three blogs.

Depending on your skills, you may find setting up a dashboard to be somewhere between tedious and terrible. If the experience tends toward the latter, ask your web developer for help.

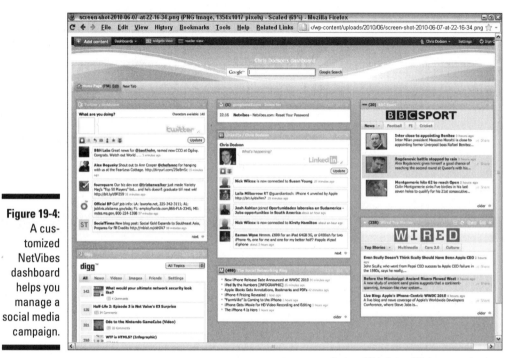

Courtesy of Chris Dodson, MD of conceptcupboard.com

Figure 19-4: A customized NetVibes dashboard helps you manage a social media campaign.

For a list of social media dashboard resources, see Table BC5-23, in Bonus Chapter 5 on the Downloads tab of the companion website. Find one that has a user-friendly display and interface and that covers all the services you use or intend to use and provides the functions you desire (such as scheduling tweets and other posts).

To explore ROI calculator tools, see Table BC5-24, in Bonus Chapter 5 on the Downloads tab at www.dummies.com/go/webmarketingfd3e.

Part VI
The Part of Tens

"It's web-based, on-demand, and customizable. Still, I think I'm going to miss our old sales incentive methods."

In this part . . .

Y ou'll find two quick wrap-ups of the principles in this book. Whether you're only initiating your website, redesigning an existing one, or maneuvering somewhere in between, it's always entertaining and educational to consider a list of things that can go wrong.

Free works when you market to others, and *free* can work for your marketing. Chapter 20 runs down ten free techniques to bootstrap your web marketing effort, with particular attention to social media.

If your tired website has dried up as a source of leads or sales, try the ten methods listed in Chapter 21 to figure out the problem and solve it. It's a must-read chapter for anyone planning to redesign and relaunch a site.

Chapter 20

Ten Free Ways to Market Your Website

In This Chapter

▶ Kicking off your web marketing strategy with free techniques

▶ Using simple, free methods in e-mail and on your site

▶ Taking advantage of social media

▶ Conducting a free link campaign

*F*ree. There's nothing like it. *Free* works when you market to others, and *free* can work for your marketing. Use the ten free techniques in this chapter to bootstrap your web marketing effort. As you make money from your web investment, you'll have the funds for paid advertising.

Even if you're one of those lucky ducks with money, you still need to start in this chapter. The first six techniques apply to every website. The only difference is whether you hire help or do it yourself.

Put Your Domain Name on All Stationery and Packaging

There's no added cost to include *YourDomain.com* (substitute your own domain name) on every public piece of paper that leaves your office: business cards, letterhead, invoices, packing slips, presentation folders, marketing collateral, spec sheets, and press releases.

Don't forget to include your domain name on PowerPoint presentations and in the footer of white papers and proposals. Be sure that your URL appears in all forms of advertising, whether you use promotional items, print, radio, billboard, or TV. And of course, include your URL on all forms of packaging: cartons, labels, lids, bags, wrapping paper, ribbon, and boxes.

Include Your URL in Your E-Mail Signature Block

E-mail programs allow you to create a signature block that appears on every e-mail you send. In addition to your name, title, company name, address, phone number, and fax number, include your five- to seven-word marketing tag, a link to your website or primary blog, and Follow Us On links to all your social media pages. If you use the format `http://www.`*`YourDomain.com`*, the text automatically becomes a link in outgoing mail.

Use Calls to Action in Your Text

Calls to action are imperative verbs (such as *buy now, save, register to win*) that encourage your site visitors to take a specific action on your website. The word *free,* as a textual link, is an implicit call to action. Use links and calls to action to help visitors navigate your site and to let them know what you'd like them to do. If you don't tell visitors, they won't know. They aren't mind readers.

Collect Customer Testimonials

Recommendations from customers are golden! Whenever customers spontaneously offer praise, ask for permission to include their recommendations on your site. You don't have to identify the individuals in detail, but you need something more than "anonymous" as a source. You can collect testimonials from letters you receive, notes in a guestbook, or comments on a blog or social media page.

Scatter the testimonials throughout your site on pages with related content rather than place them all on one page.

Submit to Three Main Search Engines

Submit your website to the three main search engines. It doesn't cost you a penny, and not even much time. Submit to

- **Bing** at `www.bing.com/webmaster/SubmitSitePage.aspx`
- **Google** at `www.google.com/addurl/?continue=/addurl`
- **Yahoo!** at `http://search.yahoo.com/info/submit.html`

Conduct a Link Campaign

Inbound links from other websites not only bring you targeted traffic from other sites but also can improve your ranking in Google's search results. This time-consuming but free method brings high-quality visitors to your site.

Start by running a report at Google to find your own, existing inbound links. After verifying your site (see `www.google.com/support/webmasters/bin/topic.py?hl=en&topic=8469`, as discussed in Chapter 7), you can review all inbound links to your site that Google sees. For a short list, type **link:** ***www.yourdomain.com*** in the Search box, where *yourdomain.com* is the URL for the website for which you want to obtain a list of inbound links. Your goal is to acquire about 30 inbound links from sites with a Google page rank of 5 or higher to improve your Google search ranking.

For links on Bing or Yahoo!, go to `www.linkpopularity.com` and enter the domain name you want to check. To identify your competitors' links, first search for one of your keywords at Google and review the inbound links of the top three or four sites that appear. For other potential links, look for directories related to your industry, professional associations, and vendors. You may also get ideas by looking at the Related Links or Clickstream categories for a competitor at Alexa (`www.alexa.com`) or the Audience Also Likes category at Quantcast (`www.quantcast.com`). If you make a practice of looking for ten links every week, this task doesn't seem as difficult.

Use Social Sharing and Follow Us Buttons

The simplest of all viral marketing techniques is word-of-mouth. A social media sharing button on your website or blog encourages web visitors to e-mail their friends a link to your site or share the link on *their own* social media pages, such as their Facebook walls. Your developer can quickly install free code from AddThis (`www.addthis.com`) or ShareThis (`http://sharethis.com`) or another social sharing service (see Chapters 3 and 19). In addition, make it easy for visitors to follow you on Facebook, Twitter, YouTube, and many other social marketing services by placing chicklets icons that link directly to your pages on these services. You can obtain these logo icons from individual services or from `www.evohosting.co.uk/blog/web-development/design/more-free-social-media-icons`. Include a call to action as well, such as Like Us on Facebook.

Exploit Google Places and Yahoo! Local

Both Google (`www.google.com/places`) and Yahoo! (`http://listings.local.yahoo.com`) offer free local listings tied to their map sites, allowing users to search for businesses within a specific geographical area. Although hospitality, tourism, and entertainment sites are obvious beneficiaries of local search, local listings are valuable for every company. Many consumers like to buy locally so that they can easily obtain post-purchase service or support local businesses. Local search is also critical when people seek a nearby vendor using smartphones or tablets.

In addition to the listing (which is essentially a free ad), Google lets you offer a coupon (`www.google.com/support/places/bin/answer.py?hl=en&answer=142916&ctx=checklist#coupons`) and include your logo. Free is a great price for advertising, even if it brings in only a few customers.

Submit Your Shopping Site to Google Product Search

Most shopping sites are either pay per click or pay per listing specialty search engines. The Google shopping search engine, at `www.google.com/intl/en/products/submit.html`, is free to merchants. You can upload your inventory monthly (which is the minimum required frequency) or establish an RSS feed to update your online feed whenever your inventory changes.

List Your Site on Social Bookmarking Services

You may already be familiar with how to bookmark favorite sites in your own browser. Social bookmarking services perform the same function online, but settings allow your recommendations to be publicly available. Simply create an account, insert your favorite URLs, and add a brief description. Some bookmarking sites don't let you submit your own site, so you may need to recruit staff, friends, or family to recommend your site. Include both general social bookmarking services such as `http://delicious.com`, `http://faves.com`, and `www.stumbleupon.com` and specialty sites such as `www.kaboodle.com` and `www.stylehive.com` if you sell retail fashion. Check the Mashable list at `http://mashable.com/2007/08/8/social-shopping-2` for more specialty bookmarking sites for shopping.

Chapter 21

Ten Tips for Tired Sites

*W*oe is you! All of a sudden (*was* it sudden?), your website or blog has dried up as a source of leads or sales. The number of buyers flowing through the conversion funnel is trickling. What to do? Run around in circles and shriek to the skies? Blame your employees? Point a finger at your developer? Take down your site? Ignore the whole mess until a temporary lack of sales turns into a real loss of money?

Instead, try these ten ways to figure out the problem and solve it. If you plan to redesign and relaunch your site or blog, read this section first. It's a must-read diagnostic list of problems to fix the next time around.

Diagnose the Problem Correctly

Before you begin solving any problem, determine when the problem started and how long it has lasted. If the problem occurred suddenly, be sure that your site has been running with no problems. Check your daily site statistics. If you notice hours or days with no traffic, contact your developer or host right away — your server might have a serious issue.

If you just launched your site, your expectations might be unrealistic or your fears might be well founded. If your site has been up for more than three years, it's probably due for a tune-up, if not a complete redesign. If you haven't tended your site or blog with loving care, your competition might have outdistanced you online.

Review your web results to identify the starting point of the problem. Check Alexa (at `www.alexa.com`) or Quantcast (at `www.quantcast.com`) to compare your traffic to your competitors'. Search for your current competitors online and review their sites. Are you competitive with products, prices, website sophistication, value, and use of social media? If you think you should still be near the top of the heap, sort your problems into one (or more) of these categories: user appeal, site traffic, sales results and conversion rate, and the bottom line.

Check Traffic Statistics for User Appeal

After you check for external problems, your web analytics (see Chapter 6) come into play. To check whether your site or blog has lost its appeal, look at the following values in your traffic statistics:

- ✔ Number of unique users (a decline in this category alone is probably due to traffic)
- ✔ Number of repeat visitors
- ✔ Number of sessions or visits
- ✔ Number of pages viewed per visit
- ✔ Average time per page
- ✔ Average time per session

Go back at least three months before your site became anemic. A pattern of decline in any category means that your site can use a makeover.

Review Your Design for User Appeal

Whether your site or blog is old or new, take time to review it with new eyes. Use the Website Assessment Form in Chapter 3 to rank your site for concept, content, navigation, decoration, and marketing efficacy. Have several people you don't know, but who fit the demographics of your target market, do the same.

Finally, ask several customers who have never used your site to accomplish a task or purchase an item and give you feedback. Usually, five people provide enough feedback to develop an accurate assessment of what's going on.

 Every site must grab new viewers in the first few seconds after they arrive, keep users on the site to see two or more pages, and entice them to make repeat visits. Where does your site fall down? If you're seeing a slow, downward drift in time spent onsite, maybe your site is growing old. If you haven't updated in more than two weeks, try posting new content.

Make Site Operation Easy for Users

Check all links, including to and from social media, to make sure they're working properly. Ask your developer to run a link verification program such as Xenu's Link Sleuth (at `http://home.snafu.de/tilman/xenulink.html`) to ensure that all the internal and external (outbound) links on your site are working. You have to confirm by hand that those links are truly going where you want them to and that all external links open in a new window. Make sure that all e-mail links function. If you ask users to download PDF files, make sure they open properly and that users can download the current version of Adobe Reader. If you have forms, ensure that they work, too. Does the site have gracious error handling for phone numbers, e-mail addresses, or required fields that have been left blank? Is there a Thank You page to confirm that a request has been submitted? That's not only a matter of courtesy and usability but also an essential strategy for tracking lead conversions.

Review the following statistical categories for hints on identifying specific pages for repair:

- Most and least viewed pages
- Path through site
- Entry and exit pages
- Browsers and operating systems
- Countries and languages
- Download time for key pages
- Page status reports, particularly *Not Found* and orphan pages

Most of all, make sure that essential calls to action are easy to follow. Make it simple to book a room, reserve a table, place tickets on will-call, or buy online.

Check Page Statistics

People find your site in one of three ways: They either type your URL, link from somewhere else, or use a search engine. Look at your traffic statistics for the past few months. If possible, compare them to usage in comparable months from the preceding year. Cyclical variations in traffic are normal for every site.

Cross-check your search engine position ranking at a site such as the Digital Point search engine position tool at `http://tools.digitalpoint.com/tracker.php`. If you find a rapid loss in search engine ranking, check search engine forums such as `www.searchengineguide.com` or `http://searchenginewatch.com` to see whether Google or Yahoo!/Bing has changed its algorithms. If so, you may need to reoptimize your site.

Search engines look for recent updates, depth of information, and links from social media; if you see a slow, downward drift in search engine position, try improving those attributes.

Look at the following data to detect changes from earlier months that might indicate a problem:

✔ Comparable month usage trends

✔ Unexpected variations in use by hour of day or day of the week

✔ Entry pages coded to ads

✔ Referrer URLs

✔ Search engines used

✔ Keywords used

✔ Search engine ranking (from Web Position or DigitalPoint or another tool)

Use Multiple Techniques to Build Traffic

Don't put all your marketing eggs in one basket. If overall traffic is down, you aren't getting people into the top of the conversion funnel. Check the Web Marketing Methods Checklist in Chapter 2. Make two copies: On one, check off all techniques you're now using, and on the other, check off new ones to try instead of, or in addition to, existing methods.

Use a combination of onsite, online, social media, and offline marketing techniques to ensure that you have many ways to reach your audience. Choose from

✔ **Free tools:** Signature blocks, links in entries on your own or other people's blogs, Google Groups or Yahoo! Groups, linking from all your social media pages to your website

✔ **Onsite techniques:** Product reviews, message boards, wikis, event announcements, content updates, games, coupons, surveys, free samples, social media sharing icons such as AddThis, and online communities

✔ **Word-of-web online techniques:** Blogs, social networks, social media sharing sites, social bookmarks, online press releases, search engine optimization, and inbound link campaigns

✔ **Paid online advertising:** Pay per click campaigns, e-newsletters, newsletter sponsorships, and banner ads

✔ **Offline advertising:** Literature, stationery, packaging, promotional items, community events, direct mail, telemarketing, and coordinated ads in other media

Check Statistics for Leads, Sales, and Conversions

Your *conversion rate* — the percentage of visitors who take a desired action, such as requesting a quote or making a purchase — is your single most important statistic. Sales are easy to measure with store statistics. To track leads, you usually need to decide in advance what you'll measure and set up a method for counting, such as a different phone extension for calls generated from your website.

For store statistics, analyze which products move. Are you losing people at checkout when they discover shipping costs? (Consider hiding certain shipping-and-handling costs in a higher item price or offering free shipping for orders over a certain amount.) Check out these categories:

- Sales breakdown by product
- Shopping cart abandonment rate
- Shopping cart drop-off point (usually shipping!)
- Upsales rate
- Repeat sales

Optimize Your Site for Sales

Assuming that your site fits the criteria for sales, review it to be sure you're doing everything necessary to convert browsers to buyers. Here are some techniques you might use:

- Provide product search capability on the site.
- Update merchandise regularly.
- Sell benefits, not features.
- Use marketing's three-letter word: *you!*
- Require only two clicks to order.
- Make the shopping process easy — offer options to continue shopping, change an order, view a total, or estimate shipping.
- Offer reasonably priced shipping.
- State customer policies clearly.
- Include detailed, keyword-loaded, product information.

✔ Use marketing's four-letter word: *free!*

✔ Increase the conversion rate with calls to action — you might offer options labeled Add to Cart, Reserve Now, and Register to Save.

Embrace the Worms

When you turn over the web rock, the business worms crawl out. If you have *any* problem with your business, from short staffing to vendor behavior to poor recordkeeping, going online makes it worse. Solve your problems first.

If you can't find the reason your website is losing money, the problem might originate outside the site itself. Refocus on your target markets and business essentials. The following options might help you turn your website into a profit center:

✔ Improve the bottom line with back-office efficiency.

✔ Integrate your website with your real-world storefront and other marketing efforts.

✔ Remember the 4 *P*s of marketing: product, price, placement, and promotion.

✔ Set a realistic budget.

✔ Set realistic expectations.

Never Stop Working on Your Site

Like your children, your website will be with you for the length of your (business) life. If you ignore your site, it will flag, sag, drag, and ultimately collapse from neglect. Before you start, recognize the commitment that's required.

Index

Apple & Macs

iPad For Dummies
978-0-470-58027-1

iPhone For Dummies,
4th Edition
978-0-470-87870-5

MacBook For Dummies, 3rd
Edition
978-0-470-76918-8

Mac OS X Snow Leopard For
Dummies
978-0-470-43543-4

Business

Bookkeeping For Dummies
978-0-7645-9848-7

Job Interviews
For Dummies,
3rd Edition
978-0-470-17748-8

Resumes For Dummies,
5th Edition
978-0-470-08037-5

Starting an
Online Business
For Dummies,
6th Edition
978-0-470-60210-2

Stock Investing
For Dummies,
3rd Edition
978-0-470-40114-9

Successful
Time Management
For Dummies
978-0-470-29034-7

Computer Hardware

BlackBerry
For Dummies,
4th Edition
978-0-470-60700-8

Computers For Seniors
For Dummies,
2nd Edition
978-0-470-53483-0

PCs For Dummies,
Windows
7 Edition
978-0-470-46542-4

Laptops For Dummies,
4th Edition
978-0-470-57829-2

Cooking & Entertaining

Cooking Basics
For Dummies,
3rd Edition
978-0-7645-7206-7

Wine For Dummies,
4th Edition
978-0-470-04579-4

Diet & Nutrition

Dieting For Dummies,
2nd Edition
978-0-7645-4149-0

Nutrition For Dummies,
4th Edition
978-0-471-79868-2

Weight Training
For Dummies,
3rd Edition
978-0-471-76845-6

Digital Photography

Digital SLR Cameras &
Photography For Dummies,
3rd Edition
978-0-470-46606-3

Photoshop Elements 8
For Dummies
978-0-470-52967-6

Gardening

Gardening Basics
For Dummies
978-0-470-03749-2

Organic Gardening
For Dummies,
2nd Edition
978-0-470-43067-5

Green/Sustainable

Raising Chickens
For Dummies
978-0-470-46544-8

Green Cleaning
For Dummies
978-0-470-39106-8

Health

Diabetes For Dummies,
3rd Edition
978-0-470-27086-8

Food Allergies
For Dummies
978-0-470-09584-3

Living Gluten-Free
For Dummies,
2nd Edition
978-0-470-58589-4

Hobbies/General

Chess For Dummies,
2nd Edition
978-0-7645-8404-6

Drawing
Cartoons & Comics
For Dummies
978-0-470-42683-8

Knitting For Dummies,
2nd Edition
978-0-470-28747-7

Organizing
For Dummies
978-0-7645-5300-4

Su Doku For Dummies
978-0-470-01892-7

Home Improvement

Home Maintenance
For Dummies,
2nd Edition
978-0-470-43063-7

Home Theater
For Dummies,
3rd Edition
978-0-470-41189-6

Living the
Country Lifestyle
All-in-One
For Dummies
978-0-470-43061-3

Solar Power Your Home
For Dummies,
2nd Edition
978-0-470-59678-4

Internet

Blogging For Dummies,
3rd Edition
978-0-470-61996-4

eBay For Dummies,
6th Edition
978-0-470-49741-8

Facebook For Dummies,
3rd Edition
978-0-470-87804-0

Web Marketing
For Dummies,
2nd Edition
978-0-470-37181-7

WordPress
For Dummies,
3rd Edition
978-0-470-59274-8

Language & Foreign Language

French For Dummies
978-0-7645-5193-2

Italian Phrases
For Dummies
978-0-7645-7203-6

Spanish For Dummies,
2nd Edition
978-0-470-87855-2

Spanish
For Dummies,
Audio Set
978-0-470-09585-0

Math & Science

Algebra I
For Dummies,
2nd Edition
978-0-470-55964-2

Biology For Dummies,
2nd Edition
978-0-470-59875-7

Calculus For Dummies
978-0-7645-2498-1

Chemistry For Dummies
978-0-7645-5430-8

Microsoft Office

Excel 2010 For Dummies
978-0-470-48953-6

Office 2010 All-in-One
For Dummies
978-0-470-49748-7

Office 2010 For Dummies,
Book + DVD Bundle
978-0-470-62698-6

Word 2010 For Dummies
978-0-470-48772-3

Music

Guitar For Dummies,
2nd Edition
978-0-7645-9904-0

iPod & iTunes For
Dummies, 8th Edition
978-0-470-87871-2

Piano Exercises
For Dummies
978-0-470-38765-8

Parenting & Education

Parenting For Dummies,
2nd Edition
978-0-7645-5418-6

Type 1 Diabetes
For Dummies
978-0-470-17811-9

Pets

Cats For Dummies,
2nd Edition
978-0-7645-5275-5

Dog Training For Dummies,
3rd Edition
978-0-470-60029-0

Puppies For Dummies,
2nd Edition
978-0-470-03717-1

Religion & Inspiration

The Bible For Dummies
978-0-7645-5296-0

Catholicism For Dummies
978-0-7645-5391-2

Women in the Bible
For Dummies
978-0-7645-8475-6

Self-Help & Relationship

Anger Management
For Dummies
978-0-470-03715-7

Overcoming Anxiety
For Dummies,
2nd Edition
978-0-470-57441-6

Sports

Baseball
For Dummies,
3rd Edition
978-0-7645-7537-2

Basketball
For Dummies,
2nd Edition
978-0-7645-5248-9

Golf For Dummies,
3rd Edition
978-0-471-76871-5

Web Development

Web Design
All-in-One
For Dummies
978-0-470-41796-6

Web Sites
Do-It-Yourself
For Dummies,
2nd Edition
978-0-470-56520-9

Windows 7

Windows 7
For Dummies
978-0-470-49743-2

Windows 7
For Dummies,
Book + DVD Bundle
978-0-470-52398-8

Windows 7 All-in-One
For Dummies
978-0-470-48763-1

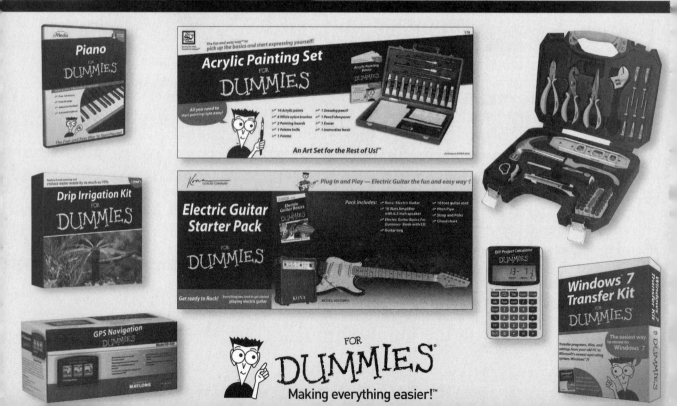